Alberto Kalach
Taller de Arquitectura X

Anybody can become angry — that is easy; but to be angry with the right person, and to the right degree, and at the right time, and for the right purpose, and in the right way — that is not within everybody's power and is not easy.
—Aristotle

Alberto is an angry architect, but not because he is angry with the world. He is angry because he wants to do things, to challenge the *status quo*, because he is not satisfied with the limits and confines that the profession sometimes tries to impose on us. He is, in that sense, a very rebellious figure: someone who is never entirely at ease in any context.
—Hernán Díaz Alonso

In the course of the forty years I have been learning the craft of the architect, many young friends and architects have spent time in our little workshop, sharing labor, knowledge, dreams, and many late nights.

The work presented here is the product of all their efforts, and especially those of Adriana León, with whom I set out on this journey.

—Alberto Kalach

Poetics and Politics in the Architecture of Alberto Kalach — Eduardo Vázquez Martín

According to the Catalan physicist and philosopher Jorge Wagensberg (1948-2018), creator of CosmoCaixa Barcelona and a promoter of the dialogue between scientists and artists, architects, and musicologists, the ability to appreciate beauty was part of the groundwork of human evolution.

> Natural selection was to favor those hominids that took pleasure in beauty. Why? Beauty has to do with symmetry and symmetry has to do with a certain degree of repetition in space and time. Repetition in space produces harmony; repetition in time, rhythm. So whoever takes pleasure in beauty takes pleasure in the harmony and rhythm perceived by the five senses... This is doubtless someone better prepared to realize that spring, that winter returns..., better prepared to make predictions, to deal with uncertainty, to share in abstract knowledge. Put very simply: beauty is a concept prior to intelligibility. Moreover, a predisposition to beauty predisposes to abstract knowledge, to symbols. First there was beauty and then there was intelligence. Beauty and intelligence: the two keys common to art and science.[1]

Those ancient beings to whom Wagensberg refers sheltered themselves in caves, but later, when their instinctive inclination towards beauty allowed them to develop agriculture and become sedentary, they needed to create habitable spaces near the lands they were cultivating that would protect them from the elements and from predators. And so they developed, with the very tools their sensibility had provided – a sense of harmony, rhythm, and abstraction –, the art of designing and constructing: they created architecture.

Alberto Kalach shares the spirit of those founders of human civilization for whom beauty and abstraction are at the origin of knowledge, a knowledge that can be transformed into art and technique, design and creation, abstract imagination and constructive action. Hence the fact that, in his work, functionality is beauty itself. I do not mean simply that beauty favors function or stands at its service, but rather that the function itself is interpreted as beauty, so that the design and the finished work are born free of all unnecessary decorative gestures, as the purest expression of materials and volumes, to which it is impossible to deny the agency they manifest, the spirit they possess. That is why Kalach makes use of both traditional and contemporary constructive processes without compunction or affectation, in which, as the poet Jorge Guillén has put it, "this is lime, this is wicker," and where steel is steel and concrete is concrete; where there is no pretending or simulating that anything is other than what it really is, and where the space created to receive and to shelter, to be lived in, reveals its nature as drawn beforehand with pencil or

[1] Jorge Wagensberg, Robert Terradas, and Esteve Terradas, *Cosmocaixa, el museo total por conversación entre arquitectos y museólogos* (Madrid: Terradas arquitectos / Actar / Sacyr-Sau, 2006).

ink, with a steady hand and a lively sense of time, freely, fluently, without encumbrances, fully aware of the discipline that geometry requires but allowing chance and the unexpected to operate as partners in the design.

Our architect carries his stripped-down conception of beauty into the realm of fabrication. His attitude to the work is far removed from the aristocratic imposture of those willing to delegate to others their dealings with engineers, foremen, and construction workers, for Kalach considers these his peers: creators like himself. Like the architects of the Renaissance and the old mural painters, he is fond of putting on his overalls, rolling up his sleeves, and getting his hands dirty, especially when a garden is involved. There is a great deal of the simple builder in Alberto Kalach, albeit a learned and inspired one, who maintains his individual stance and thinks critically about his time and about tradition, while always remaining a mason, carpenter, painter, and gardener in the end. "One cannot live as though beauty did not exist," Alejandro Aura used to tell me, quoting another poet: Luis Rius. What Alberto Kalach proposes is not only to contemplate beauty, but to inhabit it, to live in accordance with its presence, to participate, as Wagensberg would say, in its symmetries, its rhythms and harmony. In this way, each one of us seeks to discover an echo of beauty in ourselves, so that all architecture becomes a temple of art, from where reality demands our attention and we are called on to renew, as Octavio Paz expressed it in "Sunstone," the "forgotten astonishment of being alive."

Thus far I have been trying to understand Kalach's poetics, but I would also like to reflect on his *politics*. At once art, science, and technique, architecture has always been experienced collectively. It is the common space of living and working, at once marketplace and place of worship, house of studies and refuge of leisure and pleasure: Teotihuacan, the Mexico City cathedral, the house of Luis Barragán and Ciudad Universitaria, the gardens of the Alhambra and prisons. That is why architecture always involves a decisive participation in the *polis*, an act of belonging to the city. In this sense, I have pointed out more than once that Alberto Kalach is a committed champion of the *common good*, as Thomas Aquinas conceived it: as care for the community. For Kalach, every project in which he participates must involve a public benefit, even if it happens also to be a private one. He does not believe there is an unbridgeable gap between private interests and those of the community, and although he is aware of the asymmetries imposed by inequalities, his interventions aspire, in one way or another, to socialize benefits more generally. His architecture expresses the possibility of understanding the common good as an action, a creative act, in which private interests benefit in turn from the general welfare. For Kalach, architecture should not be a tool of extractive depredation that despoils the community and the environment, imposing itself upon nature and society. In the politics of Alberto Kalach, architectural work is not understood as just another mechanism by which to perpetuate privileges and accentuate hierarchies, but rather a creative exercise capable of widening collective access to beauty and wellbeing.

The political action of the architect also has to do with the act of sharing knowledge. I know architecture firms with the pyramidal atmosphere of political power or the business world, in which the staff is clearly seen as subordinate, as an element alienated from the creative process, serving only to develop the ideas of others. But in the various ateliers of the architect Kalach that I have had the opportunity to get to know in the course of more than twenty years, there is an almost academic atmosphere, with something of the classroom but also a touch of a carpentry workshop: spaces radically different from those self-satisfied firms in which the architects display the trophies, diplomas, and other images – including family photographs – that attest to profitable services rendered to the power of money and the state. In the case of Kalach, it is not uncommon for certain potential clients, whether private or institutional, to feel uncomfortable, or even intimidated, by this architect incapable of fawning or flattering, whose proposals always demand an intelligent, intuitive, and imaginative response. Nor is it uncommon for these potential clients to leave the workshop disconcerted, turning to "firms" they consider more trustworthy, and feeling that so much freedom must involve acknowledging a certain degree of uncertainty.

Kalach's vocation as a teacher has been developed not only in his workshops, a breeding ground for further professional vocations, which often develop independently into fruitful projects; it has also been exercised, intermittently, in universities – in the Universidad Nacional Autónoma de México (UNAM) and the Universidad Iberoamericana, for example – and in lectures and seminars, delivered with the generosity of a respected doyen and the energy of a young rebel. During his time as a professor at the architecture school of the UNAM in the mid-1990s, he set up, at the invitation of Felipe Leal, the director of the school, an interdisciplinary space called Taller Ciudad de México, aimed at developing new urban planning proposals for the capital city. The starting point of this academic initiative was to revive the Texcoco Plan, a hydrological recovery project proposed in 1965 by Mexican engineers Nabor Carrillo and Gerardo Cruickshank.

> The Texcoco Plan – wrote Cruickshank in the mid-1960s – was devised to address two serious problems of concern to the federal government: the tremendous need to supply the growing population with a larger volume of water and to reduce the depletion of the water table, as well as to combat the pollution caused by the storms of dust and detritus that lash the metropolitan area during the first months of every year.[2]

[2] Gerardo Cruickshank García, *Proyecto Lago de Texcoco / Rescate hidrológico* (Mexico City: Gobierno del Distrito Federal, 1995).

In 1998, inspired by the positive results of the Texcoco Plan and the urban planning imagination of Teodoro González de León (1926-2016), who, at a time when Ciudad Nezahualcóyotl and Ciudad Azteca were emerging and existing bodies of water were drying up, had understood the need for new housing developments alongside salvaged and rehabilitated bodies of water ("a possible new city, which would restore the original lacustrine city"), Alberto Kalach, originally in collaboration with Cruickshank and González de León himself, proposed expanding the lacustrine system of the Nabor Carrillo lake and undertaking the comprehensive hydrological recovery of the Anáhuac basin. This project was published under the title *Vuelta a la ciudad lacustre* [Return to the Lacustrine City]:

> The fundamental thesis of this project – wrote Kalach – is based on the idea that Mexico City was not only once a great lake but that it potentially remains so, and that the future urban development of the city should be governed by an environmental hydrological recovery plan.... The comprehensive planning of a regional urban project would definitively foster the rescue of Lake Texcoco, transforming it into the most important axis of development in the Valley of Mexico. In just three years, by treating 15% of the city's residual water, we could re-flood 12,000 hectares of highly saline, mostly desert lands still available on the former Texcoco lakebed, with a view to expanding public spaces and green areas, thereby transforming the driest and most depressed zones of the city into a model of development for the new lacustrine city. A new urban growth with public and private investment projects aimed at harmonious development and the possibility of full coexistence among the city's constituent parts and with its natural surroundings.
>
> The recovery of this great lake, equivalent to nine percent of the total urban surface area, will bring ecological, economic, and social benefits.[3]

[3] *Vuelta a la ciudad lacustre / Memorias del Congreso,* Mexico City, Instituto de Cultura de la Ciudad de México (October 1998).

Twenty years have passed since *Vuelta a la ciudad lacustre* appeared. During this lapse of time, Teodoro González de León and Alberto Kalach, in collaboration with a large team

Alberto Kalach's workshops in México City

of architects, engineers, and professionals from other disciplines, worked on the idea of salvaging the rivers and lakes with a scientific and technical rigor absent in any other urban project since. In the face of the need for a new airport for Mexico and its capital city, the team of specialists conceived the possibility of rendering the rehabilitation of the lake compatible with the new airport infrastructure, which Kalach's atelier proposed enriching with the development of public spaces, green areas, university campuses, cultural and recreational spaces, and new housing developments, in short, a great stretch of waterfront – longer than that of Acapulco – that would serve as the axis of a radical renovation undertaken for the benefit of all of the city's inhabitants and visitors, but above all for the least privileged residents of the eastern part of the capital. This project was called Ciudad Futura.[4] Unfortunately, no one with any political clout in the city has so far given due attention to this project. The authorities in turn have either approved the airport but disdained the urban planning, environmental, and social proposals made by Kalach and González de León, or have directly opposed the project and simply ignored the proposal for the recovery of the former lake. And not only that: when Norman Foster and Fernando Romero designed their airport, which entailed the destruction of the Nabor Carrillo lake, they effectively put an end to the Texcoco Plan and to the lacustrine and hydrological recovery of eastern Mexico City, in fact facilitating its increasingly rapid environmental and climatic decline.

Underneath a pictogram of Tláloc, the god of rain, Cruickshank placed the following verses by the poet-king Nezahualcóyotl as an epigraph to his book *Proyecto Lago de Texcoco*: "Seek in the rhythm of nature / the harmony of your spirit." Once more rhythm and harmony as the foundation of knowledge, once more nature and beauty as the guiding threads of design and planning, and again, the spirit of the common good informing creative action. The "future city," conceived as part of the Texcoco Plan and the "return to the lacustrine city," is a great exercise in urban planning, of architecture and engineering, but above all an expression of love of the city, of love in the Thomist sense, as that form of desiring what is best for the object of one's love: in this case, Mexico City and its inhabitants. It is true that these proposals have a certain utopian air, but it is no less true that the architect always starts from a wide-ranging and well-documented diagnosis, a rigorous cost-benefit analysis that takes into account their economic and technical viability. Above all, he starts with a social awareness that draws on rational lucidity, historical memory, and poetic creativity to propose possible solutions to complex problems.

It was precisely the symbolic force of Tláloc, the god of water and rain, depicted by Diego Rivera in the second section of Chapultepec Park, along with the visual and didactic riches of the painter's mural *Water, Origin of Life on Earth* – based on the scientific theories of Alexander Oparin –, that led us in 2007 to undertake a project to salvage the artistic and architectural elements of the hydraulic infrastructure that has connected, since the mid-1950s, the Lerma-Cutzmala system with the engineering work that preceded it, made up of a great aqueduct, four storage tanks, and a lower chamber, fed by the waters of Xochimilco, Tláhuac, and Milpa Alta, which began to be constructed in the late nineteenth century and was inaugurated in the early twentieth. Rivera's Tláloc consists of a mural and bas-relief sculpture submerged in a pool of water, with the image of the Mexica god accompanied by various iconographic elements, including a *milpa*, or small plot of cultivated land, a corncob, some grains of corn, and an image of the plumed serpent, Quetzalcóatl. Tláloc lies stretched out, with his arms extended, exposed to a sky crisscrossed by airplanes arriving in the city. Diego Rivera wanted whoever arrived in the valley by air to be welcomed by the tutelary god of Great Tenochtitlan, but this makes the work difficult to appreciate from ground level. Kalach, in an act of poetic justice, has proposed restoring and completing the entire group of the pool, the mural, and the building housing the mural – the work

[4] The idea of this new city, Ciudad Futura [Future City], was formulated in a book with texts by Teodoro González de León, Alberto Kalach, Gonzalo Celorio, Gustavo Lipkau, Humberto Ricalde, and Juan Palomar, among others. See Alberto Kalach and Gustavo Lipkau (eds.), *México. Ciudad Futura* (Mexico City: RM Verlag, 2010).

of architect Ricardo Rivas, in a "Toltec-classical" style, according to Rivera himself – by means of a piece of similar inspiration, which responds to the original esthetic by means of a "pyramidal agora" that makes it possible to appreciate the complex as a whole and which, by embracing it, creates a public plaza and open-air auditorium. Kalach's renovation project salvages this work of hydraulic engineering that is also an important piece of artistic and architectural heritage, a space which, before its renovation – executed by the Instituto Nacional de Bellas Artes (INBA) at the urging of the Museo de Historia Natural –, was in a state of neglect.

Kalach's interest in the lacustrine nature of the city goes far beyond the rational use of the resource as considered from the vantage points of engineering and ecology, although of course it includes, and indeed prioritizes, these perspectives. But Kalach has an urban vision that is both political and historical, and which implies a thorough transformation of the prevailing model of urban development, based on the desiccation of the lakes, the exploitation of the aquifer, and financial speculation with the territory and its potential uses. A descendant of peoples who (originally from Syria) migrated from North Africa into Spain, Alberto Kalach shares the poetical fascination with water of the Nasrid architects who erected the Alhambra. As Gaston Bachelard has explained in *Water and Dreams*, this substance constituted by hydrogen and oxygen, which makes possible the existence of the primordial "paste" (*pâte*) from which life emerged on our planet, has a female dimension in our human imaginary, in which woman is source and origin.[5] The idea of water also invites a spiritual reading: one of purification and redemption, of baptism and rebirth. In this sense, all of Kalach's works possess this double character of being celebrations of the female world (through their recovery of rivers and lakes, of woodlands and gardens, and through urban greenery and the capture of rainwater) and of the historical world (as a reconciliation with nature and the lacustrine nature of the city, but also as a sustainable model for our survival, as a viable project for the future).

In 1998 I saw Alberto Kalach standing in front an immense tract of land, surrounded by clouds of dust and saltpeter, in Iztapalapa (a zone where the city has deposited its garbage for decades, where it has locked up its delinquents and housed its workers and migrants), and refer to the place as a lakebed, watching him build there what Homer would have called a "hollow ship": a building which, by design and vocation, should have been inaugurated with a bottle of champagne broken against its walls, as if it were a seagoing vessel. It was there, in the year 2000, that the first Fábrica de Artes y Oficios was built in Mexico City: the FARO de Oriente. In the middle of a 2.5-hectare lot, crossed by a fault line, the architect constructed a building in the form of a merchant vessel, capable of capturing and storing water, with a great quarterdeck and a body pointing its bow to the east, toward Ciudad Nezahualcóyotl. The structure is embraced by a mound that shelters it as if it were in a shipyard. The deck is connected to the ground by a hanging bridge and, on one side, a vertical structure evokes the lighthouse of a port (indeed, *faro* means 'lighthouse' in Spanish). Originally conceived as public offices, the project was abandoned in the early 1990s. Almost ten years later, under the first democratically elected government of the capital city, the recently created Instituto de Cultura de la Ciudad de México, headed by the poet Alejandro Aura, transformed the structure into an exemplary decentralized, communitarian, self-governing cultural intervention, designed to provide informal training in the arts and to serve as a focus of social cohesion in the zone. The FARO de Oriente was born in principle out of a dialogue between architecture and the context, between architecture and politics, in which the interlocutors are the cultural community, the local residents, and the cultural promoters: a dialogue that includes, to be sure, a utopian dimension, envisioning as it does the possibility of overcoming neglect, marginalization, and violence through the intervention of the creative and productive processes of art and poetry.

[5] Gaston Bachelard, *Water and Dreams: An Essay on the Imagination of Matter*, trans. Edith R. Farrell (Dallas, TX: Dallas Institute of Humanities and Culture, 1999).

Renovation of Water Garden Museum in
Chapultepec Park, Mexico City

In his reformulation of the project, which assumed its new vocation of educational and cultural center, Kalach was able to express what the Instituto de Cultura of the administration of Cuauhtémoc Cárdenas (1997-1999) was promoting in terms of public policy: the decentralization of cultural infrastructure, increased access to cultural goods and services as an exercise of social justice, and both artistic and job training as a foundation for human development and wellbeing, in which the design and creation of quality public spaces for city neighborhoods, the free expression of cultural identities, and the promotion of books and reading were motivated by an acknowledgment of culture as a basic human right. Moreover, the architect enriched this vision with rainwater collection, the creation of green spaces, and the environmental and social recovery of eastern Mexico City. From then until the present day, the experiment has stimulated the development of an entire network of new "lighthouses" in different parts of the city and has inspired similar projects all across Mexico and Latin America, as for example the library-parks promoted by then mayor of Medellín, Sergio Fajardo. Already present in the FARO de Oriente, which in fact contains a library —named by the local community after the poet Alejandro Aura shortly before he died, it occupies the "bridge" of the vessel—, is the seed of what is thus far the architect's most noteworthy public project: the Vasconcelos Library, inaugurated in the spring of 2006.

Alberto Kalach invited architects Gustavo Lipkau and Juan Palomar and landscape designer Tonatiuh Martínez to collaborate with him on this library project. It was the largest public cultural infrastructure project of the first administration that followed the seventy-year hegemony of the Partido Revolucionario Institutional, or PRI. The design was chosen by means of a public tender organized by the Consejo Nacional para la Cultura y las Artes and, as the major undertaking of the six-year administration, was the focus of a fierce political debate. In their winning proposal, the team of architects outlined the following principles:

01: Mexico City is one of largest, most polluted, and most aggressive urban environments in the world. We believe that the design of public buildings must always foster the expansion of open spaces and green areas free of vehicles.
02: The specific area where the project is located was an unused lot.
03: The building and the grounds create a new pole of urban ecological regeneration that spreads out into a densely populated area.
04: The library is in itself an attempt at reorganizing human knowledge.
05: The botanical garden contains a comprehensible arrangement of endemic Mexican flora. Culture and nature, often considered opposing poles, form a unity in which visitors can be reconciled to their coexistence. The reading areas offer users the opportunity to experience a direct contact with nature. All the areas enjoy natural light and ventilation.[6]

[6] Alberto Kalach, *Biblioteca José Vasconcelos* (Mexico City: ArchDaily 2011). Available online at https://www.archdaily.mx/mx/02-67254/bibliotecajose-vasconcelos-alberto-kalach.

The guiding principles of the project have to do with the environment and the city, but also with its cultural vocation. Nevertheless, it was in the design of the library itself, rather than in the gardens and the environmental value of the building, that the architectural imagination proved itself most daring and innovative. First of all, it changed the point of support of the central element of a library: the book stacks. Ever since the library of Alexandria, stacks have rested on the ground, with shelves going from top to bottom, but the stacks of the Vasconcelos Library hang down from an aerial structure like bunches of grapes. Inside, everything seems to float suspended in the air: books and users, tables and desks... Everything is air, as if the hand of the architect had wished not to design the structural framework of the body of a library, but rather to build with air and transparency as his principal constructive elements. The visual depth of the spaces frees the minds of those

FARO de Oriente, Mexico City

Vasconcelos Library, Mexico City

[7] Gaston Bachelard, *Air and Dreams*, pp. 47 and 25.

entering the building. Even before taking up a book, the visitor has entered the realm of fiction, in which the dominant poetics is the lightness of air: "Through it all [air], life and movement are possible," writes Gaston Bachelard, for whom air has more to do with the subjective dimension than with reason itself. In any case, air, like literature, is "a way of tying together the private dream and the objective experiment."[7]

This vessel inhabited by books and air, by rivers of words, by seas of human dreams, is surrounded by a network of gardens. Going against the current of architectural tradition, which has tended to surround libraries with blank walls to protect collections from sunlight and from the exterior – in the aim, to be sure, of creating a silent space for concentration, but also one in which a certain ideology prevails, that of the book as sacralized object, of difficult access – , the Vasconcelos Library places the book within arm's reach, its "leaves" in dialogue with those of the surrounding trees. In this way it has established, on a symbolic level, the possibility of unlimited access to books, even as it proposes an interplay of mirrors between two spaces that share the same characteristic: both are gardens of "leaves." The reading rooms of "the Vasconcelos" – as young people call it, with easy familiarity, when they plan to meet there – float in the air, surrounded by a musical hum: the sound of the enormous crew of hundreds of souls come together in that immense vessel to look for books and to plunge into their pages, or to converse in hushed tones, but without inhibition, for the generosity of the space makes room for words that do not interrupt the reading of others, even when boisterous groups of children or students are visiting the library. The inside of the library offers moments when a musical hum predominates, but also great reservoirs of silence: long days of reading amidst the muffled footsteps of users walking the aisles or descending the hanging bridges, as if the words themselves were flying through the minds of the readers.

Like the FARO de Oriente, the Vasconcelos Library is a vessel, but of much greater dimensions: an ocean liner. In contrast with the Biblical story of the disobedient Jonah, whom God put into the belly of a great fish to persuade him to perform his will, the great library holds in its belly the skeleton of a whale, a structure of bones into which the artist Gabriel Orozco has intervened, drawing in pencil on each bone a sequence of patterns that refer to the movement of the waves or the transmission of sounds in both water and air.

In addition to the gardens surrounding the library, which can be glimpsed through every window, and a small lake hidden behind a bamboo curtain, one of the most striking elements is the recycling of a former electrical substation as a botanical garden. Scattered about the exterior gardens, like paleontological remains, are large pieces of obsolete machinery from the former substation, while the interior garden has been invaded by vegetation. A worthy representative of the industrial revolution, the old machinery enters into a dialogue with the plants, an interchange that evokes the end of modernity but also the persistence of humanism, for when decrepit and obsolete machines are overwhelmed on all sides by plants and fungi, penetrated by twisting roots, rusted and corroded by dampness, words are reborn, proliferate, and remain.

The Vasconcelos Library has suffered the storms and shipwrecks of its time, but it remains afloat thanks to the thousands who visit its spaces every year for an encounter with books. The large number of users, which exceeds that of many other libraries in Mexico, must be taken into account: it likely has a great deal to do with Kalach's unique vision of its architecture, conceived as a dynamic public space, far removed from the solemnities of so much of cultural life. Thriving in this lively and hospitable space is an interdisciplinary spirit which, starting from the knowledge contained in and communicated by books, fosters the pleasures of the senses, the playful and creative use of free time, and opportunities for encounter, dialogue, and harmonious coexistence.

I have dealt with only four works by Alberto Kalach: the "Return to the Lacustrine City" project, the Water Garden Museum, the FARO de Oriente, and the Vasconcelos Library. Of course the present volume covers the full range of his production in all its richness and diversity, from private residences to airport infrastructure, from small gardens to large apartment buildings, from educational centers to museum designs still awaiting the political will and resources that will make them possible, as for example the great Mexican biodiversity museum in Chapultepec Park or the museum of the whale in Guerrero Negro, Baja California. I have attempted to reflect, on the basis of the four projects dealt with here, on Kalach's poetics, ethics, and politics, but I have to conclude by sharing the expression by which the architect often defines himself: "I am a gardener."

In the face of the malformations suffered by Mexico City – a "disproportion... that provokes an intense crisis" and "dizzying growth" that becomes a source of "unease," in the words of Le Corbusier[8] – Kalach proposes the vigorous intervention of nature. Instead of decaying façades, palm trees; on busy thoroughfares, jacaranda trees; more and better parks; less cement and more greenery. Kalach finds in gardening and landscaping the sole architectural element capable of imposing beauty on chaos, trash, visual noise, the unremitting ugliness of an immense territory in a state of constant growth. It is not that he renounces the possibility of planning or the intervention of architecture and urbanism in improving the contemporary city. Quite the contrary: he wishes to call on the residents of the city, on its architects and administrators, to reconsider the healing power of gardens, to make the most of the environmental characteristics of a specific urban context – the plentiful rainfall during the rainy season, which provides treatable water, and the temperate climate of the Mexican highlands – to transform the city by means of the very vegetation that thrives there. The architect Alberto Kalach is fully aware of what Borges wrote about the garden in one of his poems: "it is like a feast day / in the poverty of the earth."

[8] Le Corbusier, *Puerta de hielo: L'esprit nouveau 1920-1925* (Castellón, Spain: Ellago Ediciones, 2005), p. 87.

Botanical garden in the industrial building
adjacent to the Vasconcelos Library

The Convex Garden: Some Remarks on Three Works by Alberto Kalach
— Carlos Jiménez

Between seeing and making,
contemplation or action,
I chose the act of words:
to make them, to inhabit them,
to give eyes to the language.
Poetry is not truth:
it is the resurrection of presences,
history
transfigured in the truth of undated time.
Poetry,
like history, is made;
poetry,
like truth, is seen.

— Octavio Paz, "Nocturno de San Ildefonso"

Vasconcelos Library

Mexico City has enthralled me since my first visit in 1972. It was my first exposure to a world city and sparked my appetite for travel. I had visited Panama City and Guatemala City, but nothing prepared me for the scale, sights, and sounds of Mexico City's multifarious culture, an unrivaled confluence of images and experiences. I was captivated by the endless textures of the millennial city, from the striking narrative of its history to its unforgettable ballads, from the Zocalo's charismatic expansiveness to the warmth and nobility of its people.

I have returned countless times, always longing to experience, as if for the first time, the city's vivid, complex, and mesmerizing energy. Fifteen years ago, during one such visit, I left Mexico City transfixed by an indelible image: a cross-section drawing of an ark-like structure glowing with internal luminescence. Flanked on both sides by a primeval forest, the long, multi-level building depicted in architectural drawings was bracketed by interminable but matching layers of suspended bookshelves. The design struck me with its urgent yet immemorial desire: a willed effort to store and display all knowledge known and all knowledge yet to be within the glowing ark. That was my first impression of Alberto

Kalach's competition entry for the Vasconcelos Library. Perhaps it was the project's clarity and vision that evoked such legible intimations, or perhaps it was the way Kalach's design synthesized past and future types in a conceptual instant.

Kalach's entry was one of seven finalists chosen during the first phase of an international competition to design the Library of Mexico – as the Vasconcelos Library was called at the time –, held in June 2003. I was a member of the competition jury. Once our selection of finalists for the second stage was complete there would be a few months' wait for the seven second-stage entries to be developed further and for another jury to select the winning scheme. I recall that during and after our jury deliberations, there was a presumption that the commission would go to one of the foreign architects – perhaps to counter local sentiments that such an important commission ought to be awarded to an established Mexican architect. This was, after all, a new era, heralded by the post-PRI government of president Vicente Fox, an era of transparency, inclusivity, and optimism. To the surprise of many, from government officials to architects alike, Alberto Kalach's scheme was selected as the winning design. This was a daring choice, buttressed by a bold proposal that highlighted the singularity of Kalach's design and confirmed his stature as one of the most gifted architects of his generation. In Kalach the client found an architect inspired by universal themes nurtured by the roots of his native city.

Soon after its May 2006 dedication, the Vasconcelos Library was closed following a mixture of local politics and construction irregularities, circumstances that ultimately did not diminish the building's dazzling power. Since reopening in 2008, the Vasconcelos Library has astonished visitors. I have seen the wonder that the building elicits in the expressions of students I bring to the library as they experience, all at once, this formidable gathering of books, seemingly endless in their suspended totality. This feeling is experienced on entering the library's central shaft. It reverberates when crossing from one aisle to another, looking down from the top catwalk, or standing at either end of the building. The sensation of astonishment grows ever more intense as one slowly traverses the entire library at ground level. It is then that the building reveals its startling choreography: an unfolding play of suspended trays with book-filled shelves, neatly ordered yet multiplying in all directions, producing Piranesian perspectives. The structural properties of suspension are framed with experiential tension, making one question just how this can be possible. The feeling of awe echoes that experienced in the circular reading room of Erik G. Asplund's Stockholm Library, where bookshelves spin in their circular dance as tall upper windows march to a more measured rhythm, and in the marvelous weight of time one feels inside Gordon Bunshaft's Beinecke Rare Book and Manuscript Library at Yale University. The Vasconcelos Library is a worthy addition to the lineage of wondrous libraries that inspire visitors with their structural and spatial legibility, transcending the limits of time to invite readers to linger, read, discover, learn, and remember; libraries that bring to mind Jorge Luis Borges's axiom: "I have always imagined that Paradise will be a kind of library."

The Vasconcelos Library demonstrates Alberto Kalach's mastery of structure and modularity in constructing a new type of library that accommodates analogue and digital media and ignites the imagination just as it starts to dream.

Reforma 27

Reforma 27, an innovative residential slab completed in 2010, displays Kalach's structural assurance. What impress about this 25-story building is the rigor, clarity, and versatility of its modular framework and the tension between its assured anonymity along the Paseo de la Reforma and the brilliant terracotta pigment of its reinforced concrete exterior. The building is almost unnoticeable at times, especially at ground level, where an elegant array of trees signals the crossing of a shaded threshold, a pedestrian pause before entering the discreet building. Constructed of reinforced concrete, Reforma 27 surprises with its unexpected lightness, which is perceptible at the intermediate lobby spaces between the building's two halves. This critical space splits as well as joins the armature of the building's floor plate, admitting light and views and allowing the mirrored fire stairs free flight to project into the near or far cityscape as one descends or ascends. As with other residential works by Kalach, Reforma 27 abounds in a modest yet rich materiality, an earthy composition of finishes whose luxury resides in their tactility, rawness, and durability. Another parallel to the architect's residential works is in his desire to create gardens of all types. Kalach has often stated that "paradise is a garden." At Reforma 27 gardens find their way to unusual locations throughout the building, from the marvelous sloping garden that culminates the entry axis from the Paseo de la Reforma to the exuberant double-height garden on the building's top floor. There, the gardens interweave native flora with terrace and pool to deliver as close a sensation of paradise as can be experienced twenty-five stories above Mexico City.

Reforma 27, Mexico City

Constituyentes 41, Mexico City

Constituyentes 41

The mixed-use building Constituyentes 41, completed in 2014, is a construction of complex yet elemental efficiency. Kalach built the nine-story tower to house his architecture studio and to offer tenants loft-like spaces atop a geometrically challenging site. Maximizing the limits of the site with lyrical acuity, the architect constructed a svelte tower across Avenida Constituyentes from Chapultepec Park. Nothing could be diagrammatically simpler than this elegant tower bracketed by two lateral reinforced concrete walls, between which uninterrupted, diagonally arrayed, steel-framed floor plates span, matched by floor-to-ceiling planes of operable and fixed glass facing north and south. The column-free trapezoidal floors provide as much flexibility as possible on the seven tall office floors, which span above the triple-height, open-air lobby-*huerta*. The lobby is an antidote to noisy Constituyentes, ascending to the insulated interior of the building. The soothing effect of the profuse garden is immediately felt the moment one walks through the high wall separating number 41 from the street. Another garden waits on the top floor terrace, crowning the roof platform with varied native plants and incomparable views of Chapultepec Park. The views to the park increase in prominence from floor to floor. At the terrace level they achieve a panoramic reach. Suddenly the vast park in front is drawn into an intimate conversation with the gardens of 41, and their different scales and distances dissolve.

These reflections on three buildings by Alberto Kalach highlight not only his probing, evolving sensibility but also his mastery of craft. It is not often that one comes across an architect who, in a few works, manages to reveal architecture's practical yet magical framework, which contains the possibilities of past, present, and future lives. It is inspiring to occupy buildings that defy the limited view of a future that never seems to arrive, or one manipulated by suspect interests. The future is the least predictable of all time tenses, the easiest to sell, and the one that ages the most rapidly. In these works by Kalach and his studio TAX, architecture exists in the urgency of the local and the present, yet also in the confidence with which it faces the uncertainty of the future, absorbing the wisdom of the past by filtering the joy of the moment. Quietly these architectures reach out to the world, forgetful of the forces that incessantly sell futures as shiny objects to behold, as if they could make us forget that architecture is a garden of daily delights.

Readings of Alberto Kalach

— Fernando Fernández

I think it must have been sometime in 1987 that Alberto Kalach read in the newspaper that Octavio Paz had just refused a proposal by the authorities in Mexico City to have his name given in tribute to a park that was being refurbished in the old Mixcoac neighborhood, between the Revolución and Patriotismo thoroughfares, near the house where the poet had spent his early years. Paz argued that the growth of the city had disfigured that now inhospitable space and he referred to the "hammering" –or perhaps even the "shelling": I no longer remember exactly– produced by the passage of all kinds of vehicles, whose speed and noise had annihilated the tranquility of the old village in which he lived as a child. I remember the incident because Kalach, to whom Paz's views seemed to betray a certain ignorance of the deeper nature of cities, or unwittingly to embody a hypocrisy common to those of us who live in them, asked me to help him write a letter to the editor of the newspaper. We wrote it –or rather I did, following his indications– and we put it in the mail.

That reaction to the views of Octavio Paz characterizes Kalach perfectly: it sums up the stances he has taken on various issues, both in public and in private. Anyone who knows him, who has conversed at length or walked along the street with him, who has lived in the spaces he has imagined and constructed, knows that he is a sort of enthusiastic fatalist, who willingly accepts the facts on the ground. The fact that he may try to transform what is put in front of him does not mean that he refuses to accept –albeit never without some degree of irony– whatever has resulted from several centuries of urban inanities, or that he fails to respond optimistically to the contrarieties and absurdities of a city almost entirely made up of them. If, on the one hand, he has promoted an admirable plan to address the most serious problems of the Valley of Mexico (those having to do with the air we breathe and the water we drink), a project to restore a part of the ancient lakes to their former lakebeds, he has also, on the other hand, created dwellings on the all but impossible remnants of land left over by the high-speed thoroughfares crisscrossing the city, inventing habitable spaces within just a handful of square meters.

One would think that the battle to restore to the Valley of Mexico some of the splendor of its ancient lakes –an ambition with an undeniably utopian air– might distract his attention from the pragmatic actions expected of an architect with his feet placed firmly on ground and a desire to continue working. But this is not the case: in Kalach there is none of that arrogance accompanied by elegant paralysis that is conferred by the prestige of the utopias. There are those who preach about the city, but prefer to avoid all its sound and fury –with complete justification, of course–, and therefore build spaces in which the circumambient silence and serenity allow one to think, to work, even to breathe. Kalach will have none of this. Witness, for example, the place where he himself lives: the house

Adolf building, Mexico City

Green House, Mexico City

he bought and renovated at one end of the San Miguel Chapultepec neighborhood, along Avenida Constituyentes, one of the busiest thoroughfares in the city, which veers off from the Circuito Interior and runs many kilometers further on into the highway to Toluca. It is true that on the other side of this raucous avenue is Chapultepec Park, and that is the reason Kalach decided to make his home on the site, accepting the high cost in terms of tranquility involved in living along such an intensely busy thoroughfare. Indeed, the woodland across the street does not prevent the house from being shaken, at all hours of the day and night, by the passing freight trucks, many of them with twin trailers, and all the noise and rumble following in their wake, which would be prohibited in any less corrupt and chaotic city. When the noise became unbearable – that "hammering" that so offended Octavio Paz, which he refused to have associated with his happy childhood in the neighborhood –, Kalach lined the little room in which he sleeps with wine bottle corks to insulate it from the noise. The cars still go roaring by, the twin-trailer trucks shake the buildings to their foundations... but he refuses to reject it all. Which does not mean that he does not use all his ingenuity to adapt and protect himself, always in the aim of interconnecting with a tone-deaf city, uninterested in dialogue.

One day I was walking with Kalach along Constituyentes in the direction of the Circuito Interior, heading for a restaurant where we had a rendezvous with a friend. We were on the Chapultepec side, with just a grille separating us from the trees of the park. Along the way, he pointed out, to our right, on the other side of the street, the gap between two buildings. He told me he was planning to visit the owners of those building to propose to them how to fill in that intermediate space, that void: a proposal to insert the missing piece, which would serve as an element of continuity between them. What Kalach is doing is nothing less than a reading of that fragment of the street, to which he would like to add what he feels it needs. As if it were a uncompleted phrase, and one therefore lacking its full meaning: the architect proposes the words required to compete the message, so that that portion of the street may better express itself. My attention was drawn to a singular phenomenon, which had to do with Kalach's reading: at first both buildings seemed to me rather unfortunate and mediocre, but when I looked at them more carefully, after my friend had helped me to appreciate *not what they are in themselves, but what they could be as part of a complete solution*, I found them more appealing. What is more, the one on the right, a cube that seemed to have been resolved incorrectly, even became a beautiful and successful achievement.

Since we are on Constituyentes, it may be worthwhile to go back a few steps and take a brief look at the building where Kalach and I met a few minutes before, in order to walk to together to the restaurant. This is Constituyentes 41, one of his more recent works (2014). The building's silhouette rises with striking lightness: from a certain vantage point, as slender as a blade, yet revealing, from another, an arrangement of volumes oriented so as to make the most of the climatic conditions and sunlight. Unlike any other architect who might have also been the owner of the building, and who would have preferred to reserve for himself one of the upper levels, with the best vistas of Chapultepec, Kalach installed his Taller de Arquitectura X on the ground floor, where the park across the avenue can be viewed as if it were an extension of the horizon. Seated at his desk, he can almost feel himself beneath the foliage of the trees, while the clouds are in the place they belong. Both clouds and trees are subject to their natural metamorphoses, according to the season of the year and the hour of the day. All of this becomes part of the direct experience of those working in the atelier, and helps them to forget that down below, just a few meters away, Constituyentes is rushing by with a roar...

Something different happens on the top floor, a great rooftop terrace on which the visitor finds a slice of an *almost rural* landscape... Although there are precise calculations and intentions behind Kalach's gardens, they tend to have something of the unconstrained ease of natural surroundings, even when they are required to flourish, as we have just seen, on a rooftop. My visit to this one reminded me of the time I asked Kalach to give me some advice about transforming a roof garden, or what often receives that name (in fact, it was just a small, rectangular, open-air space, with clay tiles), into a studio with terrace. He took a look at the site and said the best thing would be to cover it with soil and a few plants, so that *they* could make sense of that little corner: a sort of naturalization of the space, as I understood it, entrusted to the earth and the plants, even if the miracle was to take place on a fifth-floor urban rooftop.

Before leaving Constituyentes 41, I would like to mention a detail that would be without importance, if it did not reveal, in its apparently insignificant way, the kind of fatalism and adaptability concealed behind some of Kalach's decisions. I am referring to the sliding bolt on the door of the single, very compact bathroom in his workshop. The bolt is not where it is usually placed, on the side of the door that swings open, but rather on the other side, near the hinges. The bathroom is so small that there is not enough room to turn around and slide the bolt where it would normally be. It has been placed where it is because it is *on that side* that it is easier to manipulate. To be sure, when I asked Kalach about it, he replied that it was all a mistake... a mistake which, in any case, he did nothing to correct.

I have pointed out above, making use of a ready metaphor, that our architect can read a stretch of the street as if it were a phrase that is missing the few words needed to express its full meaning. Kalach is a voracious reader and his conversation reflects the fact. It is no surprise, therefore, that one of his most important works is an extraordinary repository of books (the Vasconcelos Library, 2004). I think of what comes to mind after having heard him talk of books for more than thirty years, always in a delightful and amusing way, without a hint of pedantry or solemnity. When he had some difficulties with his talented teenaged son, for example, he looked for explanations by reading one of Dostoyevsky's novels. Once, when I told him the school I taught at was on Calle Pitágoras, he told me that Diogenes Laertius, in his brief life of the great mathematician, recounts how students in the Pythagorean school were not even allowed to open their mouths for the first year. On another occasion I heard him praise a book by Tanizaki, because of the Japanese writer's explanation of the treatment of light and shadow in his country's traditional culture. From time to time I hear him mention books that one would never expect to be among the reading matter of an architect, except one, of course, who understands his discipline as part of a social contract of a wider scope, and who therefore feels the need to read Rousseau. On yet another occasion he expressed doubts about the quality of a certain novel by Paul Auster, leaving it in my hands shortly after reading it himself. And on that very afternoon I have mentioned, when we both had lunch with a mutual friend, being charmed, as he told me, by the acute observations and even the philosophy of a certain bestselling author, he did not hesitate to recommend him.

One of the most striking characteristics of the house he designed for himself in Valle de Bravo, toward the beginning of his career as an architect (1996), is that the staircase leading up through the bedroom tower is also a library. It may be worthwhile to take the opportunity of this mention of his house to leave the city for a moment, for it is far from the city that Kalach has attempted several readings – if I may continue so to call them – which reveal a great deal about his way of thinking and working, as for example the house in Valle. Whenever I stay there I am overcome by a feeling that I am camping out in the midst of nature, at a prudent distance, if you will, but in direct contact with it, enveloped by the greenery, or the intense sunlight, or the heavy rains, depending on the season. I even get the impression that certain details have remained deliberately unresolved, provoking a certain unease in those of us who prefer the wall-to-wall comforts of city life: the fact, for

Valle House

example, that there is a scarcity of electric light at night, or that the water in the swimming pool remains unperturbably chilly, or even that the living room has been designed almost to interpenetrate with the garden, allowing us to experience, in surprise and bewilderment, as night falls, the most unfamiliar entreaties from the insect world, strange sounds that bring us closer, in a way, to a less artificial life than the one we are accustomed to. Perhaps that is why they clearly appeal to Kalach.

The house in Valle de Bravo is configured in terms of two simple lines, one horizontal and the other vertical. In the words of Juan Palomar, it is the result of a combination of the tower and the simple shed, a recurrent phenomenon in Kalach's work. In the many years since my last visit, those two lines, conceived with economical concision in the aim of freeing up space for the garden, have doubtless ended up surrounded by exuberant vegetation. On the horizontal plane –that of the shed– are the living room (mentioned above), the dining room, and the kitchen, all on the ground floor, as well as, on the upper level, a swimming pool surrounded by hammocks and with the finest views of the lake. These are spaces for family and friends, for eating and drinking, for talking or playing. On the vertical plane –that of the tower– is a little building of exposed brick, three storeys high, which contains the bedrooms (all three of the same size), one per floor, one on top of another, each with its corresponding bathroom. These are the spaces reserved for privacy, study, and rest.

At the heart of the vertical plane is that striking idea that perfects the definition of the tower and enhances its practical function: a library embedded in the walls, which accompanies anyone going up or down the stairs. Indeed, in a book that describes the house there is a deliberately provocative and amusing reference to "a vertical library that *also* functions as a stairway" (*Kalach+Álvarez,* Rockport, 1998). How many times, on the way to my bedroom, have I taken one of the volumes offered to me on the shelves of that library ascending to the realm of sleep, as I also was doing? A sleep of emotion and depth, guaranteed by the angel's trumpets flourishing in the garden below, whose dreamlike fragrance is wafted straight up the outer walls of the tower.

A shipment of books was among the first things that went into the cabins Alberto Kalach built on a stretch of beach in Oaxaca in 2014. We have finally been led to them by the notion of reading, and by the books we began to talk about when we set out to show how the architect interprets the street. It is interesting to contrast the house in Valle de Bravo, located on a slope in front of a lake, some 1,850 meters above sea level, in the chilly highlands of Estado de México, with the cabins built a quarter of a century later on the torrid sands of the Oaxacan coastline, facing the impetuous Pacific Ocean.

In early 2018, when I went to see them, I had just suffered a painful loss, and during the four days and three nights I spent on the beach I performed a deep immersion into myself, accompanied by the sun, the sea, and the mobile, flexible spaces of the cabins. It was a healing process, in a way: although my tribulations did not abandon me, my stay by the seaside and the stimulus of the work of my architect friend served to put me back on track, wounded but still whole.

The site is an enormous stretch of beach, extending from east to west and facing the open sea. It is an almost empty expanse of sand and scattered vegetation, which at present contains only two landmarks, distant one from the other: the Casa Wabi of Japanese architect Tadao Ando and the Hotel Escondido. At the western end of the stretch of beach, Kalach built two cabins, which have turned out to constitute a genuine declaration of principles. His aim was to establish a real dialogue between the climatic conditions and the local construction materials and processes. In this sense, it is an attempt to understand the best and most lasting way to occupy the place harmoniously. Thus, in addition to designing the cabins, Kalach also sketched out the garden that would surround them, as he had done twenty-five years before in Valle de Bravo, producing a spontaneous composition, full of intuitions, aimed at maintaining the wildness of the surroundings and even the natural acrimony of the species of the zone. And not only that: he also used as a reference, or even a counterpart, the creation of the celebrated Japanese architect, who has erected in the blazing Mexican tropics, literally embedding it in the sand, a sumptuous concrete palace.

Each of Kalach's cabins is a wooden box with a rectangular floor plan measuring seven meters by fourteen, mounted on a platform slightly separated from the sand by eight concrete bases. It is raised almost a meter above the ground, like the traditional *hórreo*, or granary, of northern Spain, and open to the four winds, with sliding wood-and-palm-leaf doors on the long sides of the rectangle (facing east and west) and folding doors of the same materials on the short sides (facing north and south). The resulting combination of separation from the ground and openness to the elements lends the cabin a sense of lightness such as that of a vessel. Moreover, since the platform is larger than the habitable box, a corridor runs around the outer perimeter on all four sides, like the deck of a ship.

The most charming aspect of the cabins is the way Kalach has dealt with the roof. The obvious need to slant it, so that rainwater will run off, led him to propose a solution which, seen from the outside, is the very epitome of grace. The two double beams that sustain the cabin longitudinally from below, resting on the eight small piles embedded in the sand, correspond to the two double beams that sustain the roof. But the latter are arranged with contrary inclinations, so that the roof receives a sort of twist that puts a very graceful, even beautiful, stamp on the design. The result evokes a Basque *txapela* on the head of a country person looking at the sea: a little more open on the side on which the sun rises, where nature herself, even on the coast of Oaxaca, calls at times for the heat of the sun, as the entire cabin begs to be bathed in light, and slightly closed on the side on which the sun sets, where the blazing tropics cast their most inhospitable flames.

One of the most admirable things about the "huts" (*chozas*), as Kalach likes to call them, is that, observed from afar, they barely peek out from above the vegetation, thereby fulfilling the principle implicit in the philosophy on which they are based: to be as unobtrusive as possible within the natural surroundings. What is more, seen from the side of the beach, with the sea at one's back, the twist in the roof of the cabin closer to the ocean is the only thing, though almost imperceptible, that interrupts the continuous line of the horizon.

Each cabin is equipped with a water tank, which doubles as a sink. The first cabin was constructed in a sort of experimental spirit: something went wrong and what was going to be the water cistern was turned into a frog pond. Kalach allowed it to happen, acting in accord with the empathetic resignation he tends to feel about the results of his work. And speaking, by the way, of unpredictability, it is still not certain how the cabins will fare during the rainy season, which at the time of this writing has not yet taken place, and then later, when this fragment of coastline fills up with other constructions, with other identical pieces the architect has already been commissioned to build, as well as several projects already in progress, which will necessarily answer to different aims and visions.

Opening up a path through the vegetation, Kalach has created a sort of vestibule on the sand between the first cabin and the sea, occupied by the trunk of an *ahuehuete* tree, which traces an elegant curve about six meters long. Hence the name given to the space (*La Media Luna*, 'The Crescent Moon'), a veiled allusion to the name of the hacienda in Juan Rulfo's novel *Pedro Páramo*. (By the way, another section of the trunk of the same *ahuehuete* is on the rooftop of Constituyentes 41, where it serves as an enormous bench.) Moreover, the architect has traced the first section of a road that will run parallel to the seafront, linking up the rest of the constructions toward the east, i.e., the Hotel Escondido and, beyond it, the Casa Wabi. In addition to guaranteeing an appropriate framework for his own work, he has provided the beginnings of an organization of what is bound to come later.

It is obvious that Kalach's cabins are a response to the Casa Wabi, so it is legitimate and even necessary to take a brief look at that work. The Japanese architect's building is a splendidly ambitious construction that contains several of the principal recurring elements in the work of the winner of the 1995 Pritzker Prize: the characteristic display of concrete, the daring geometric lines, even the discreet presence of water.... I must confess that, for me personally, it is a cold building on the one hand, and on the other a scorching one. Let us start with this latter aspect: on the beachfront side, one is welcomed by a thin sheet of concrete that serves as a vestibule, running toward the great *palapa* that is at the heart of the project. During sunlight hours, it is impossible to cross it without burning the soles of one's feet, since there is no protection at all from the rays of the sun, except for a swimming pool and a reflecting pool, placed there more perhaps for esthetic reasons than for practical ones. Once inside, I was given a guided visit by a member of the domestic staff, a woman who was not familiar with the house, as she admitted to me, since she had only been employed there for a few days. I also felt the brunt of the sun as we walked down the long corridor that generates, on the seafront side, the wall running parallel to the coastline, no less than three hundred meters long, which, along with the *palapa*, is the most emblematic characteristic of the design.

Yet at the same time, the Casa Wabi felt cold to me. The reader already knows that I was going through a period of emotional turmoil: I had sunk into an intense interior monologue and my whole being was bubbling with materials that could be transformed into some kind of sensitive matter, which took the form of writing in my case. Of course I blame Tadao Ando less for the feeling of coldness that his spaces produced in me than what was actually taking place in my inner being, but it is true nevertheless that the architecture, designed to provide an ambience suited to working out one's emotions and turning them into art, did not seem precisely stimulating to me.

Of course, what architects call the "program" could not be more different in the case of the Casa Wabi and that of Kalach's cabins, but no there is no less a contrast between the general principles that govern each of the two designs. If it is climate that should determine style, as Vitruvius declares (and as Kalach recalls at every step), the Japanese

Casitas by the Sea, Puerto Escondido

architect, apart from incorporating the traditional palm leaf roof of the zone, has maintained his own, in spite of the singularities of the surroundings in which the Casa Wabi was built. In terms at least of reading the climate and the materials, one is tempted to say that the splendid Oaxacan villa of Tadao Ando (who has never actually visited the site) is the result of a translation.

Was it the inflexibility of the concrete that denied me the conditions to acclimatize myself immediately, immersed as I was in the heat of the Oaxacan coast? Experiencing those contradictory sensations, I recalled how the cabins at the other end of the beach, with their folding or sliding doors, always allowed me to modulate the temperature in keeping with the time of day. In the morning, I would keep the sliding doors on the eastern side just half-closed, so that the sun would provide some light and warm up the living area in which I was reading, but without bothering me with its direct rays. Meanwhile, the doors facing west would be completely open. In the afternoon, on the other hand, I would perform the opposite operation: I would open the doors facing east completely and close those facing the afternoon sun, to protect myself from its powerful rays and thus keep the living room cool. Of course, at any moment I could open the doors facing north, in order to cool down the cabin from the side opposite to the ocean. Thanks to the freedom offered by all these movements, the cabin seemed to me an admirable mobile instrument, always flexible in responding to variations in light and heat.

With their wooden materials and the vegetation surrounding them, with their proportions and the possibility of opening up to the four winds, above all with their lightness and flexibility, Kalach's Oaxacan cabins prove that it is possible to make things in more imaginative ways and more in keeping with their environment. Will they continue to function in the long run? Will the exacting marine conditions respect their fragility, with the salt air, the long rainy season, the tornados and sudden violent downpours? All those things, including the result, whatever it may be, are part of the risks assumed by the architect. In this respect, I am amused by what he himself said to Juan Palomar, with an exquisite sense of humor: as a response to the brutal excavation in the sand that had to be made to support Ando's ostentatious concrete objects, he wanted to dig as little as possible. As a result, the foundation of the eight small piles under each one of his cabins performs the function, not so much of sustaining their weight, which is minimal, as of making them more heavy, to prevent them from *blowing away in the wind*...

Is it possible to reconstruct the contents of the letter addressed by Albert Kalach to the editor of *Excélsior*, in which he reproached Octavio Paz for his refusal to allow a city park, overexposed to the onslaughts of an aggressive and chaotic city such as ours, to bear his name? The letter was never published, but not, I suspect, because it was lacking in well-grounded arguments, or even because of its vein of healthy insolence, but rather because Kalach preferred to sign it with a pseudonym, so that we were unable to submit verifiable sender information with it. Neither Kalach nor I knew anyone in Paz's circle at the time, so delivering it in person was out of the question as well. The letter never reached its intended recipient.

Even so, I would like to think that, over the last thirty years, spurred on by the views of the poet, the architect has managed to respond through his own work. Cities grow, change, become more complicated or more ugly, deteriorate, and even despair: sometimes they are used as political booty or fall victim to petty tyrants who manage them according to their own whims, with a view to personal enrichment, or to gaining power, or to serving the interests of private capital. The case of Mexico City is exemplary in this respect, owing to the way in which hasty, interested, and erroneous decisions have done away with urban spaces or transformed them for the worse, at times as if they had really been the consequence of some catastrophe.

The name of Octavio Paz is not connected with that space in Mixcoac, which I have visited now for the first time in the more than thirty years since his refusal. It is true that it is a place without much charm, that the palm trees (of two species at least) have grown with a certain awkwardness, unable to offer the serenity necessary to confront the frenzied activity of the two violent avenues that run by on either side. It is obvious that the miracle Kalach seemed to refer to, when I asked him how to transform a little rooftop, has not taken place here. And it certainly remains true that vehicles of all kinds and sizes go by hammering, or shelling, or even producing a noise similar to the "rattling" of a machine gun. (Was that perhaps, now that I think of it, the word the poet used?) None of all that matters: this little corner of the city provides a place to breathe to the unfortunate pair of urban palm trees and is by no means unworthy of honoring the memory of a great man, even in the cacophonous vortex of a degraded city. (Is that not the role played by the work of Octavio Paz himself, amidst the confused hammering and obstreperous rattling of our present time?) That is the city and, in more general terms, those are the spaces bequeathed to the architect, who attempts to intervene in them, seeking harmony and order in circumstances that must be confronted without hypocrisy, doing everything in his power to understand them and make them better.

All of which reminds me of the frogs that accompanied me during those difficult nights of self-absorption in Kalach's oceanfront cabins. My friend told me they had arrived in the wake of some water lilies sent to him from a beach in Jalisco. The first night I spent in one of the cabins, although I was almost unable to sleep, I hardly noticed them. The next two nights I had to listen to their monotonous and obsessive croaking, which did not stop until just before dawn, long after the rest of the nocturnal life of the area had settled down. In the course of those solitary seaside nights. I felt there was something in their calls that could be interpreted as gratitude: the gratitude of whatever is understood, at times even beyond what is possible or reasonable to expect, and which has allowed itself to be acclimatized, in order to fulfil the noble aim of simply enduring.

Reflection, Invention: In the Steps of Vitruvius — Juan Palomar

Warning: The Insolence of the Evidence

Why would one architect attempt to draw an architectural —and therefore, a human— portrait of another architect? Perhaps because the starting point, however much it may be argued, is not really debatable: he is the most important architect practicing in Mexico in recent years. Expressed in broader and —I fear— more bombastic terms: he is one of the most significant architects on the entire contemporary panorama. But there is another reason, inextricably intertwined with the foregoing and no less relevant: because of the *person* Alberto Kalach happens to be. I would argue that there is no valid division between the work of an artist and his or her human manifestation. It is a longstanding question, which has been much debated over the years. The present writer has no hesitation in taking sides: Kalach's architecture is Kalach. Not a single wall he has ever erected can be fully understood unless the personality of the architect is taken into account. An arduous endeavor: the product of chance, of the privilege of friendship and proximity, of the experience of being comrades-in-arms for many years, of having so often repeated, with Rudyard Kipling: "triumph and disaster... those two imposters."

In order to situate the architect's character, failing which it would be impossible to understand the purpose of this book, we might begin by remarking on the ironical and even cheerful skepticism with which Kalach has been able to confront competition losses, predestined defeats, all the various reverses of an architect's unpredictable existence, as well as the serenity, the responsibility, the contained and private satisfaction he shows in reaction to his still more frequent triumphs. This is no small matter in an attempt, such as this one, to produce a living portrait, inseparable from any theorization about the intellectual and artistic development of a creator. There is in principle an impetus, an enthusiasm for life and its wonders, for the splendor of a landscape or a garden, of a few lines encountered by chance, of a certain piece of music, among so many others. All of this is at the root of Alberto's vital and architectural energy.

There is an idea undergirding this essay: that Alberto Kalach is utterly insolent. The word comes from the Latin *insolēnt- em*, the present participle of *solēre*, 'to be accustomed,' preceded by a negative prefix: unaccustomed, unusual, excessive, immoderate... His insolence is reflected in the audacity of his behavior and, in particular, of his speech: what is not usually said or done, the unusual. Any possible usefulness these pages may have is derived from this essential characteristic of Kalach's personality and work. From the already extensive career of an artist —and I have chosen the word carefully— who insists on revealing the world, the possibilities of the world, by means of a central operation:

the discovery, with rigorous and smiling insolence, of the evidence. There is always an ironical component, a deliberate distance, and, at the same time, a ferocious mockery in what Kalach thinks, says, and does; indeed, perhaps even in what he is. Using these tools, and endowed with exceptional lucidity, Kalach generates evidence, tangible and conclusive proofs of how architecture can be, of how one way –or another way– of inhabiting the world is manifested. By naming it, by making it better.

From Arthur Rimbaud's *Lettre du voyant*, the poetics of the reticent *rock star*:

> This is obvious to me: I am present at this birth of my thought: I watch it and listen to it: I draw a stroke of the bow: the symphony makes its stir in the depths, or comes on to the stage in a leap. / I say one must be a *seer*, make oneself a *seer*. The Poet makes himself a *seer* by a long, gigantic, and rational *derangement of all the senses*. All forms of love, suffering, and madness. He searches himself. He exhausts all poisons in himself and keeps only their quintessences. / I continue: Therefore the poet is truly the thief of fire. He is responsible for humanity, even for the animals; he will have to have his inventions smelt, felt, and heard; if what he brings back from down there has form, he gives form; if it is formless, he gives formlessness. A language must be found. / Meanwhile, let us ask the *poets* for the *new* –ideas and forms.

The utility of the effort: by following the line of visions and proofs, to create from these reflections a tool for the young –both the biologically young and the others. A tool whereby, in the best scenario, each reader may discover affinities and differences, seeing in them the elements with which the artist, the architect, or the poet contributes to improving the world.

A word of warning: in order to understand an architect's efforts it would seem to be necessary to view them from a particular standpoint, whereby the character and mood of the architect can be explored. Hence the attempt made in these pages, in this book: to propose a vision which, however limited, seeks to approach what is already an extensive body of work in an all-embracing way, though it may still fall short of Alberto Kalach's own efforts and vital commitment to architecture. It should be noted that this sketch has been drawn from an experience of several decades of close friendship, of extensive collaborations, and of a shared spirit, one which could be described, for want of a better term, as "socio-Jesuitical," far removed, as it happens, from strictly commercial modes of operation. What is written here has been filtered, therefore, through an irremediable closeness (for which the author is grateful). It is an attempt to read the position staked out by Kalach in his life and his architectural career.

There has been no shortage, of course, of both agreements and disagreements in this long professional and human relationship. Long dialogues punctuated by cigarettes and glasses of tequila, travel and urban explorations, arguments and divergences, occasionally opposing architectural viewpoints, different stances assumed in the face of the same problem, but always in a spirit of cordiality, with the fierce defense of certain alternatives and a dialectical –the term is inevitable– reconciliation of differences.

Three or four studios ago, Kalach traced an inscription, with a vigorous hand, on the edge of a tabletop in his workshop: *Vive o/culto*.[1] A whole program in itself: the option of surrendering to life and assuming it in all its breadth, or of reducing it to submission to a dogma, and perhaps to the complacence and self-satisfaction of pride. To take the phrase on the fly: the desire to hold oneself apart, far from the fatuous spotlights of the moment, the ideal of cultivating, with humility and determination, as Voltaire would have it, *one's own garden*. Perhaps, from the other side of friendship, there might be another inscription informing these pages: *Con/vida*.[2] To have the privilege and the responsibility, so often assumed, to share, with all its rough patches, the passage through life, the *invitation au voyage*...

[1] 'Live concealed,' with a play on the element *culto* ['cultured'] in the Spanish word for 'concealed.' (Translator's note)

[2] The point of the untranslatable wordplay here is the amalgam of *convida*, 'offer in friendship,' and *con vida*, 'with life.' (Translator's note)

The Place and the Site

As a member of a generation that began to do architecture in the 1980s, one of Kalach's outstanding references was doubtless the work of Christian Norberg-Schulz: *genius loci*. The spirit and expression of the space in which the architectures would be constructed, but also the spirit –primordial for an architect– of the emplacement, in the sense of occupying a space from which the work can be done. Thus, it is possible to list his studios and environments, out of which a continual creative ebullition generated designs, initiatives, reflections.

If memory serves, the cortège began on the Calle Atlanta, not far from the bullring. Soon afterward the energetic arterial thoroughfares would make their appearance, with the consequent chopping up of various urban contexts. There would follow the discovery of certain residual lands and their possibilities, an effort to insert housing with unusual typologies into them: the beginning of a long series of residences whose constant has been the attempt to draw new resonances out of the universal fact of inhabiting. Then came the period on the rooftop of the pavilion located at the back of the garden created by Luis Barragán in Tacubaya, at Francisco Ramírez 17. Emerging from there were the first speculations on a grand urban scale, the efforts on behalf of the hydrological recovery of the Valley of Mexico and the outlines of a new airport alongside Lake Texcoco, which may have been the motor that set the process off.

Then came the move to the experience of the metropolitan center, the storming of the downtown stronghold: the workshop at Filomeno Mata and Cinco de Mayo. The appearance of an enormous map –a large-scale aerial photograph– on which Kalach would patiently draw a succession of ideas about the city, in varying doses. Networks, programs, general criteria, specific actions. The wide single bay of the old building provided plenty of air later on to the competition –successful this time– for the Vasconcelos Library. A large model of the bookshelf-labyrinth, suspended from the structure of the enormous vessel, hung from a beam. Those years also produced the direct experience and the radical criticism of methods of salvaging heritage environments. A hand-to-hand combat with the intense density of the urban core. One of the obsessions worked out on the mural map doubtless generated the later magnetic attraction exercised by the surroundings of Chapultepec Park.

Thus, in a ramshackle workshop on Avenida Constituyentes, which had served for the filming, as legend would have it, of some hardcore porn movies, the explorations were to continue. The projects multiplied, as did the competitions –one of them for the Library of Jalisco was unfortunately lost–, while the studies to recover the former lacustrine city, the territorial essence of ancient Tenochtitlan, were broadened and deepened. A new airport was the propellant of these possibilities of a future. In the center of the workshop, on a pronounced incline, Alberto tried out and explored one of his most pronounced theoretical concerns: the creation of gardens, by means of a very careful and deliberate vegetal palette, demonstrating the principle that it is possible to invent new kinds of gardens on rooftops, unexpected planters full of hanging blossoms, wild corners of paved areas...

Constituyentes 41 now rises over the site of that old workshop. It is difficult to reconcile the memory of the flimsy shed that housed that workshop with the towering lookout now erected in its place. A building which, for the first time perhaps from this particular angle, embraces with its gesture and pose, the whole splendor of Chapultepec Park. On top, there is a common garden, designed for the benefit of all the users of the tower, which offers a full view of the urban horizon, of the distant volcanoes, and the airplanes passing incessantly overhead. There is another garden down below, at the entrance, disconcerting and profuse: a metaphor, perhaps, of the prodigious nature we abandon in order to

Renovation of Jardín 17,
Mexico City

install ourselves in the aridity of daily office work or the noisy bustle of the roaring street. But gardens know how to wait: the one that welcomes and bids an affable farewell to visitors; the one that flourishes atop the building, offering repose to the exhausted; and the one which, in all its vastness, can be jealously watched over and cherished from the tower itself, Chapultepec Park.

The workshop as an inexhaustible quarry. It is worth mentioning how the form – and the spirit – in which Kalach's architecture studio has functioned over the years, in its various settings and locations. Everyone works with full concentration, with intensity. There is no time to lose: everything is urgent. From the architect's notebooks, from his almost always accurate parties, from quick sketches or carefully prepared drawings emerge the initial lines in which the ideas are geometrized and proportioned. Plans are laid out and corrected with more sketches, with continual adjustments. Three-dimensional models are also always used to give shape to alternatives, to try out solutions, fostering a forest of figured architectures which, over the years, have filled up the workshop. Presences that are now realities, sketches that remain as the testimony of a will, of a hypothesis: on the chessboard of chance these pieces remain immobile beneath the changing light of day. There is almost always music, and at times the pounding of the notes deepens the tension that the severity of the workshop demands.

Several generations of young architects have passed through the studio by now. The Taller de Arquitectura X. Perhaps a trace of humor and distance, an elementary equation with its unsolved unknown. Any studio, studio X: and yet it is this one. From this school of doing things, of interpreting spatial needs and resolving them, down to the last detail, have emerged quantities of knowledge and skill, always produced as a team, the offspring of multiple initiatives encouraged by Kalach's close and implacable direction. The young members of the team later follow their own careers, try out their own practices, forming their own teams in turn. It is certain that a stint at TAX means a lot: an educational effort, constant attention, a careful expectation of other possibilities. A long discipline in work well done, in rigor, in imagination, which renders concrete what began as one of Alberto's conjectural intuitions, built up from an uncertain beginning.

Two Houses

It is necessary to speak, not without risk, of two of the houses the architect has lived in. One is on a slope that dominates the village and reservoir of Valle de Bravo. The beginning of a tower and the lean-to as guiding elements. Plus a pool that in some way encloses and conceals the composition: water as the soul of the place, liquidity as an interpretation of the *locus*, the ever-present garden, fashioned with care, yet also left to its own devices. The frequent interplay of penumbras, characteristic of Kalach's work, encounters an inflexion here, almost a metaphysics of light. In the late afternoon, there is no recourse to electric switches; the dominion of the space is turned over, rather, to wax, to the changing and tremulous light of candles. A restricted dominion, of spaces transfigured by shadows and sheens. There seems to be a marked asceticism, an instinctive quest for timelessness in these endeavors. Characteristics which, to a greater or lesser degree, have constituted constants in Kalach's work, and which in this house in particular, designed and built by him, find a fertile terrain, free of restrictions. The tension between verticality and horizontality in the design is resolved in a difficult balance that the pool, with a succession of screens, synthesizes. The lessons of Japanese architecture, of Barragán's influence in its purest form, are clearly there. There is still another protagonist, as there had to be: the garden, in which all the blues of the reservoir, the surrounding hills, the clarity of the sheltering sky, are assumed. The other house is a consummate essay in revitalizing an old property from the 1930s, once more with a foreshortened view of Chapultepec Park. A single-family residence has thus been renovated to create three dwellings. The third is a new rooftop space. It is at once an evocation of the venerable abbé Laugier's primitive hut, the refuge of some urban Crusoe, and an Oriental pavilion floating amidst the treetops. For all its precariousness, it is refuge and shelter, intimately connected by a garden suspended miraculously in the air itself. There is a patient attempt to make the garden levitate, to join its greenery with that of the surrounding woods, and so acquire, for the house, together with the lofty quality of an ivory tower, the right to the city shared by all. Late at night, the air horns of the passing transport trucks resonate in the air stilled by the woodland frontier. The ground of the modest dwelling vibrates like a seismograph, confusing the shaking of the trucks with that of the frequent earthquakes of the region. Perhaps this sober house is the one that best and most purely expresses the architect's domestic ideal: the strict essentiality, the austere, stripped-down elegance and constructive exactitude, the sense of privacy, suited to contemplation and the rituals of daily life, the celebration of the beauty of the world in the shoots of the young plants, the beauty of the stars that the uncertain air of the immense city still allows a glimpse of.

Generational Signs: Some Memorable Conversations

It was the year 1986. Alberto Kalach was working late. He recounts how he would spent the better part of a night preparing a poster to announce some architecture days at the architecture school of the Universidad Iberoamericana. The old Letraset technique was arduous and slow, but little by little he progressed in his task. The illustration, which looked like a drawing by Aldo Rossi, reflected the temper and spirit of the times. The list of participants was almost done. It was a sort of X-ray, however incomplete, of the architectural voices that Kalach and his companions in the organization of the symposium were listening to, of the presences – of different generations, fully consolidated or still in process of formation – that at that moment formed an active, multiple, and cogent group. The invocation of a zeitgeist, of an atmosphere propitious to learning, and even to the confrontation of opposing stances. There was the old teacher Ignacio Díaz Morales, along with Teodoro González de León and José María Buendía: three definite and enduring influences on Alberto Kalach. There were Ricardo Legorreta, Francisco Serrano, and Alberto Yarza; Creixell, Ballina, and Robalo. Then a younger generation, just starting out on their careers: Agustín Landa; Albin, Elizondo, and Vasconcelos; Enrique Norten; Barquet, Chávez, and Vigil; Kalach himself, along with Daniel Álvarez and Adriana León; and even Bricio Fernández, Kuni Hartung, and the present writer participated in that conversation of multiple voices.

That attention to other voices, to other architectural ambits, has been a constant in Kalach's career. Ambits that, over the years, have progressively widened, making him a frequent – though somewhat reticent – interlocutor in the contemporary architecture debate, both in Mexico and internationally. A revealing sign: his founding participation in the magazine *Arquitectura*, which in the 1980s attempted to introduce a new platform for professional exchanges and the expression of a range of different visions of building in the city.

There are still other testimonies of Kalach's way of conferring a public dimension on his practice. Among them are the volumes *Vuelta a la ciudad lacustre* [Return to the Lacustrine City], *México. Ciudad Futura* [Mexico: City of the Future], and *Atlas de proyectos para la Ciudad de México* [Atlas of Projects for Mexico City], all written, revealingly, in collaboration with other authors, as well as other books about his own work and numerous contributions to Mexican and international publications.

The *Atlas* turned out to be a project of particular interest. It is a compendium of reflections and architectural exercises on every scale, all with a view to creating a more beautiful and functional city, as well as a more generous and just one. Each one of these initiatives was produced in complete independence, with no expectation of financial gain, in order to participate with responsibility and coherence in solving various urban problems: from the apparently simple act of planting trees on sidewalks or in parking areas to the salvaging of the Texcoco lake system, and including the creation of limits to urban sprawl, the transformation of degraded neighborhoods, the generation of extensive green areas, and the definitive rehabilitation and establishment of Greater Chapultepec Park.

Coming at the beginning of Kalach's mature production, the *Atlas* is a civic contribution, an educational effort, an architectural *communiqué*. It is a pedagogy of air: the city seen as a unity whose components it is possible to analyze and understand, in which it is feasible to take measures, whether subtle or radical, to transform it. It is an invitation to the younger generations to get involved in their habitat, to use the newest technological tools, together with traditional graphic representations, with a view to grasping urban realities, assuming them, acting on them. In all of these undertakings there is a vocation of contributing to the population's living conditions, an activism, exemplary in terms of its constancy, with the sustained goal of creating, through the architecture, a more decent, worthwhile city.

From a Dissatisfied Architect: A Galeana for the City

Kalach is a Mexican architect and he lives on a permanent war footing against the injustice, ugliness, unhealthiness, and madness of the capital city. He took possession of an old house in a certain neighborhood and decided to live there, densifying the construction, with mixed uses, in a reasonable way. On the rooftop he installed a garden that pours down over the edges to ground level, spreading out on the sidewalks. Everything is very green. He fixed up the pavement of the sidewalks and noticeably increased the mass of plants and trees in the planters lining them.

It was not long before a respectable lady, head of a neighbors' association, demanded (in shouts) that he get rid of all the plants: all this greenery was ugly and just got in the way. The authorities were called in to restore "order." Fortunately, the lady and the authorities both failed miserably. The corner is now a shady grove. Of course there were reprisals and acts of vandalism against the anomalous process of thus rescuing the lot from greyness and mediocrity, which seems to have been the neighbor lady's ideal. The architect, with kindly insolence, would just keep laughing and put in more plants.

A little later, having calmly considered the place for the umpteenth time, the architect analyzed the use of the roadbeds of three streets coming together at his house. He concluded that there was far too much asphalt and that a key piece, the corner itself, served no purpose but to increase the city's carbon footprint. He decided to plant a tree. But not just any tree: he managed to find a *galeana*, or fountain tree, more than thirty feet high. Some workmen brought it and built a large round concrete planter on the unused part of the roadbed. He wreathed it with little reflecting lights, so that it would look good at night. He completed the arrangement with some shrubs in the ample circle around the trunk of the tree. And he added a provident image of Our Lady of Guadalupe.

The lady who headed the neighbors' association made another appearance. Scandalized, she expressed her indignation, her objection... and spoke to the authorities. Why was the sacred space reserved for automobiles allowed to be soiled by a tree and some shrubs? Where was the uniformity, the order, the delightful mediocrity that, among other things, had made her the head of the residents' association and a force in the neighborhood? The authorities arrived once more and tore their hair out: the tree was an intolerable act of rebellion. Worse: it was something unthinkable. Trees instead of automobiles? For decades now the opposite had been the rule. But once more, the lady and the authorities came up against a wall, against impeccable and friendly reasoning, against common sense. They failed again. The architect still laughs about it.

Today, the *galeana* is flourishing and happily greets neighborhood residents: it is a banner. It will be blossoming soon. The subversive tree sets an invaluable example. It shows that the streets are public space, a space for all. That, for the benefit of the community, these spaces can be appropriated, upgraded, improved. The architect knows that very well, and he has also known for a long time that what he did then with his corner is necessary all over the city, and in all cities. For too long now, we inhabitants of the city have been held in thrall to alien interests, to inept urban management by all manner of authorities, to injustice and ugliness. The *galeana* growing on what used to be car pavement is a small victory over the genuine barbarity of a system which, in its urban manifestation, makes so many millions of city-dwellers unhappy. It is a sign and a symbol, and remember: these can be invincible. For the time being, let's plant more *galeanas*. And we will see what else occurs to us.

More news of Our Lady of Guadalupe. One never knows who will be the symbolic bearer of the miraculous *tilma*, or cloak. A massive new threat to the image of Our Lady of Tepeyac, on her lowly altar, made of shrubs in a planter, against the young *galeana* crowning the group. Two backhoe diggers, of the kind used for demolitions, and as many dump trucks ready to carry away the hypothetical debris, some police cars, and thirty construction workers were preparing to destroy the transgressive little garden. The city district and the neighborhood residents were the protagonists of a renewed assault on the anomaly that attempted –wonder of wonders– to make the street more livable, occupying a piece of pavement unused by the all-powerful automobiles. The unexpected bearer of the imaginary rose-lined *tilma* managed to strike a hasty truce and appeared before the authorities –the new Zumárragas– to argue, to allege, to demonstrate the goodness of the apparition. He will never be sure, but perhaps the ineffable irradiation of a silhouette on stone, the recent pieties that presence provokes on any street corner, his dry eloquence, dictated by something greater than him, ended up convincing the powers that be. The demolition force withdrew, the heavy machinery left a trail of smoke behind it, and a murmur of astonishment was heard from the workers as they abandoned the site in amazement: the *galeana* finally had room to breathe, Our Lady was smiling again. And the word continues to get around...

The foregoing description summarizes, perhaps, in the form of an isolated, apparently minimal intervention, Alberto Kalach's essential attitude toward the city, toward architecture. There have been examples of music that, for the blaze of an instant, have seemed to sum the deeper meaning of an ethical stance, of a quest, of a collaboration: definitely *Combat Rock* by The Clash, as well as, typically enough, the battle-hardened beat of Rage Against the Machine, at some key moment when the compasses of certain designs were turning. Or perhaps the most ethereal moments of Brian Eno, the unmatched immediacy of a flamenco cadence, or the vertigoes of Brahms...

The scale varies, but the focus does not change. More than a quarter of a century ago, the architect decided to understand his city, to know what would make it better and more just, more polished and more beautiful. He challenged its immense territory to a hand-to-hand combat, patiently examining it in explorations, cartographies, maps, plans, and chronicles. He assembled a team that has accompanied him over the years. With the same fervor as when he planted the *galeana* on a neighborhood corner, he has proposed changing the lives of more than twenty million inhabitants of Mexico City: bringing the water back to the valley as a whole, salvaging the legendary Lake Texcoco, sowing on its shores the possibility and the hope of a better life for so many.

Only the characters change, the plot is the same: imagining a chair, fixing up a commercial space, building a house, erecting a building or a handful of them, designing a tall tower, arranging a small garden or a large park, organizing a neighborhood, conceiving a city, planning an entire region. This ability to assume the heroic dimension of his discipline comes, curiously enough, from a modest yet audacious absence of preconceptions in the face of each problem that arises, of an approach both playful and lucid, informed by the scientific rigor of the difficult indifference with which Alberto Kalach –as in Kipling's poem, already quoted above– is accustomed to deal with "triumph and disaster... those two imposters." But it comes above all from an intense concentration, exercised without concessions, in the face of tried and true conventions and methods, from an untamable passion for risk and speculation, for architecture, for life.

Piti/less, im/patient, self/referential, in/trospective, de/fiant: these are some of the architect's characteristic features. No pity for mediocrity and foolishness. He will skewer with a sarcastic phrase, spoken as if in passing, the nonsense he seems to encounter on his path: in architecture and in life. An urgency about doing things: the urgency of one who knows that our days are numbered and that it is essential to change –insofar as we are able to– our battered and unjust circumstances. He lost long ago his patience for waiting to begin; he resigned himself long ago to losing fat commissions because of his convictions. Rapid, decisive judgements, without fear of lurking error or potential enmity: incisive, summary. The calculation of the factors considered is done quickly... then on to the next thing. References, almost always, to a philosophy developed over the years, through long reflection: an appeal to experience, an insistence on method, an accumulation of failures, of unbuilt architectures that are still there and –who knows?– may still see the light of day. Right or wrong, he energetically defies conventions and conveniences: the tightrope on which he walks brings him both fervor and rejection. Nevertheless, few figures in Mexican contemporary art dare to risk such direct architectural hypotheses and urban proposals, to defend them tooth and nail, to persist, at times, in errors and blunders, and to insist so strongly on certain –laborious– illuminations. This brief compendium of biographical, personal traits, is not gratuitous. It may be part of the reason Kalach is Mexico's central architect: no one else bids so high.

The Virgin and the Menorah

Perhaps one of the most revealing works in Kalach's career, in strictly personal terms, is an intervention into the Menorah of his ancestors. An image of Our Lady of Guadalupe, with a veil over her face, was grafted onto the seven-branched candelabrum. A declaration. An acceptance of roots and affinities. Many years ago, at a book fair, Alberto came across a stand at which the notorious artist Alejandro Jodorowsky was offering public consultations with his well-known psychomagic technique. Without hesitation, Alberto got in line. When his turn came, he explained to the self-styled wonder-worker his concerns about his so far unsuccessful efforts to convince the authorities –and the public– of the urgent need to fill up Lake Texcoco again. Jodorowsky supplied the prescription without a moment's hesitation: "Go to the Villa de Guadalupe, you and your friends, fill up a flask with holy water, each one of you, and walk in procession to the dry lakebed. Pour the holy water onto it and pray. The lake will return." The pilgrimage has not yet been made. Nevertheless, Kalach has the necessary recipient ready: a plastic bottle in the form of the dark-skinned Virgen of Guadalupe, whose crown is the cap that turns the image into a flask. One day the

The Virgin and the Menorah

architect and his band will doubtless proceed down the Calzada de los Misterios, in silence, each one with his or her portion of purifying water, on the way to Texcoco.

Alberto Kalach Draws a Planet

01: It might be said that he is indifferent to the esthetic aspect of the matter. His way of tracing lines on the pages of notebooks, on plans, is always the same: urgent, concise. He doesn't seem to think while he draws: he seems rather to be following a dictation that is always too fast. Lines. Outlines that sometimes deserve to be revisited and given another layer of shade, or a sudden gilding, or a note. Then on to the next one.

02: The lessons of a tree. He learns them as he draws or transcribes, in simple lines, what he sees from the rooftop of his office. At any hour of the day or night, he will climb the precipitous stairway that emerges onto an unexpected slanting garden and spend hours tending his plants. From there, a vigilant guardian, he zealously inspects Chapultepec Park. And he draws. It may the union of a leaf and branch, the secret of an articulation, that intrigues him. Or the results of a cactus's turn to blossom. Or it may also be the full outline of the lost lake, besieged by stupidity and neglect, whose shores he fills with architectures: trees, or unknown plants, or nothing but air.

03: With several pencils. A signal privilege, and a pure and essential pleasure: drawing in tandem with Kalach, as the design slowly emerges, like a boat out of the mist. Tequila, to be sure. The dance of curling cigarette smoke. More lines. Thousands of drawings, one after another: visions, heartbeats, intuitions turned into space. From a certain line may come the solution of a hinge, or a building with hundreds of apartments, or a city with millions of lives. One never knows what will follow: a final crossing out and another drawing, or a move to construction plans. Again. The years go by and the notebooks accumulate, the record of a quest: a world seeks to take form in their wandering pages. A planet, perhaps, on which architecture can change and improve lives. Alberto Kalach's drawing exercises are an indispensable journal, a tool of humor and learning, a strictly necessary activity. A way of laying permanent siege to the Muse, who is always distant and evasive. But at times, a flame burns at the tip of the pencil.

Constellations

For some time now, Alberto Kalach has been engaged in a singular exercise. It consists of something apparently simple: namely, of drawing, on the same scale and with an identical northern orientation, all of his projects. There are no indications of date and each endeavor is identified only by a tiny caption. Executed with white lines on a dark background, the group of designs resembles a series of constellations in an endless firmament. Contributing to this impression is the vague grouping of geometrical typologies, which generate a certain tension among the different series of plans, in patterns that seem to evoke ancient representations of the heavenly bodies.

This compendium of architectures, represented solely by their earthly traces, by their floor plans, constitutes an instrument of deep reflections, a recapitulation of strategies, an account of achievements, failed attempts, and unexecuted designs, a general examination of an architectural –and a personal– career. As in the case of the constellations, it falls to the observer, with his or her telescope, to discern the particularities of each visible body and of their relation to other nearby bodies, to an entire universe of possibilities and absences. Or indeed to discover an association, a name, a figuration that renders them recognizable, even familiar, as they once were – for long, endless nights – to the ancients. One intention deserves to be emphasized: the absence of any difference in the expression of those designs that took full bodily form and those that never went beyond the stage of drafting paper and cardboard model. This simple fact underlines the ideal character of a continuous spatial production, the identical intensity with which, in the initial impulse of any creative process, it is necessary to approach an architectural problem. The constellations unify the existential discourse, giving it its comprehensive meaning. In this way they propose to the viewer the possibility and value of formulating one's own creative universe.

Carefully considered, Kalach's constellations are a rigorous autobiography. It is impossible to separate from each line the circumstances of those days, the mood changes, the influences of other architectures, the travels and encounters, the simple twists of fate. The medieval copyist, and the renaissance engraver also left, in their meticulous workmanship, the unmistakable traces of their own souls. This personal portrait, much more potent and self-referential in these circumstances, is able to provide an account of the architect and his creed, his conception of building, his obsessions and explorations.

What is striking from the very beginning is the twofold impression: that of the diversity of the traces of each architecture and that of an almost inexplicable unity, a profound affinity among all the different forms expressed. One might speculate that this is the result of a sort of constant emotional frequency informing each line and accumulating in the notebooks from the very first sketches, as the years go by. More obviously, it reveals a desire to find the purest and most concise geometry for the solution of each problem. The *measurement of the earth*, to use the word's etymological meaning, is the genetic code shared by all of Kalach's spatial formulations. And perhaps not only in terms of dimensions, but in the total measurement of a given geographical site: its altitude and temperature, the quality of its surroundings, its inner nature, the soul of the place, the *genius loci*. And also in terms of the human need to be sheltered and resolved. Because this last condition is the one that validates any transcendent architectural endeavor, far beyond the virtuosic display of one's skill and the more or less forceful formal results one achieves.

The collection formed by the constellations is like the display on a vast canvas of the specimens captured by a lepidopterist, like a cabinet of minerals laboriously assembled by a geologist. Both of these two facets are there: the delicate and essential zoological morphology, and the timeless and inflexible materiality of stone. From each of these a principle can be derived: that it is structure that gives them form and meaning. Even if it be a flat, two-dimensional representation which is observed here, the carefully arranged structural elements, with their precise lines, offer a hint of the third dimension of its development, the quest for a complete space, with its functional and expressive qualities. It the representation, finally, of a desire and a will.

There is something archaic in this contemplation, as of glyphs carved on stone plaques of unknown origin. Nevertheless, an unmistakable trace of something unparalleled is involved in the examination of each work, and above all in its grouping within this virtual and impossible firmament. Each work, in itself, constitutes a specific stance, a message to the future, an account of the battle to be waged – so long as there is a will to fight – for a better world. The general endeavor, with its wide variations in scale and typology, involves a sustained attempt to explore the limits of architecture and even a sort of revolt that takes convention and fashions by storm, constituting in itself the pronouncement of an original avant-garde in the field of contemporary architecture.

This review of an entire body of work —including of course constructed buildings— denotes a remarkable variety and even, in certain cases, an apparent arbitrariness in the face of the dictates of logic. We find ourselves with the Platonic volume, the precise pavilion, the pattern articulated with a rigor that is suddenly interrupted, in order for a different order to be established. There is a tessellated reiteration of elements, a membrane of tensions and accents, a reminiscence of bird nest construction, the subtle music of chance.

Within this invariable geometry, exercised as both strict discipline and playful *ars combinatoria*, one encounters a dogged quest for the crystallization of a spatial envelope capable of containing the vastness and indeterminacy of existence. Hence the frequency of accident, of controlled distortion, of rupture: a way of assuming, more or less conscientiously, the zeitgeist of our era; of expressing the fragility and finitude of all human endeavor, the vertigo and disorientation against which all architectures have arisen in order to give meaning to the practice of providing a habitat for humankind. In the end, any human construction is destined to be a ruin: all that remains, perhaps, under several geological layers, will be the vaguely recognizable traces of the foundations of these very architectures now before our eyes.

Perhaps the constellations of Alberto Kalach are a variant of the experience potentially to be had, in different times and spaces, in real —or simply constructed?— works, in those the architect has actually seen materialized, at the end of a difficult process. His efforts, after all, are inseparable from this exercise so often undertaken. The importance, therefore, of this interpretation derived from a multitude of signs is the unitary possibility of reading his poetics. As any etymological dictionary will tell us, the word 'poetry' (and thus 'poet,' 'poem,' and 'epopee') is derived from the Greek word ποίησις, through Latin *poesis*. Now ποίησις is related to the verb ποιεῖν [*poiein*], meaning 'to make, construct, create,' derived in turn from the Indo-European root *k^{w}ei* of the same meaning.

Poiesis, power... A quest for the appropriate, for arduous simplicity, for the timeless triad whose enduring validity Kalach professes: *firmitas*, *utilitas*, *venustas*. Explorations of new ways of living on this earth. Because there also exists, within this region of the new, the unseen, a possibly deliberate archaism, always rendered valid by any gesture that invokes the indeterminacy, the fleetingness, the distortions or ruptures of these turbulent times. It is in these territories that the work of Alberto Kalach continues to be done. A body of work with affinities to the protean and the unexpected, demanding evocation and, at times, homage. A body of work akin also to evanescence and smoke, to the ephemeral and definitive joy of humankind's —and of one architect's— passage on this earth. Akin perhaps to the inexhaustible desire that underlies all the architect's endeavors: the quest for a fleeting beauty, capable of giving joy and meaning to a life.

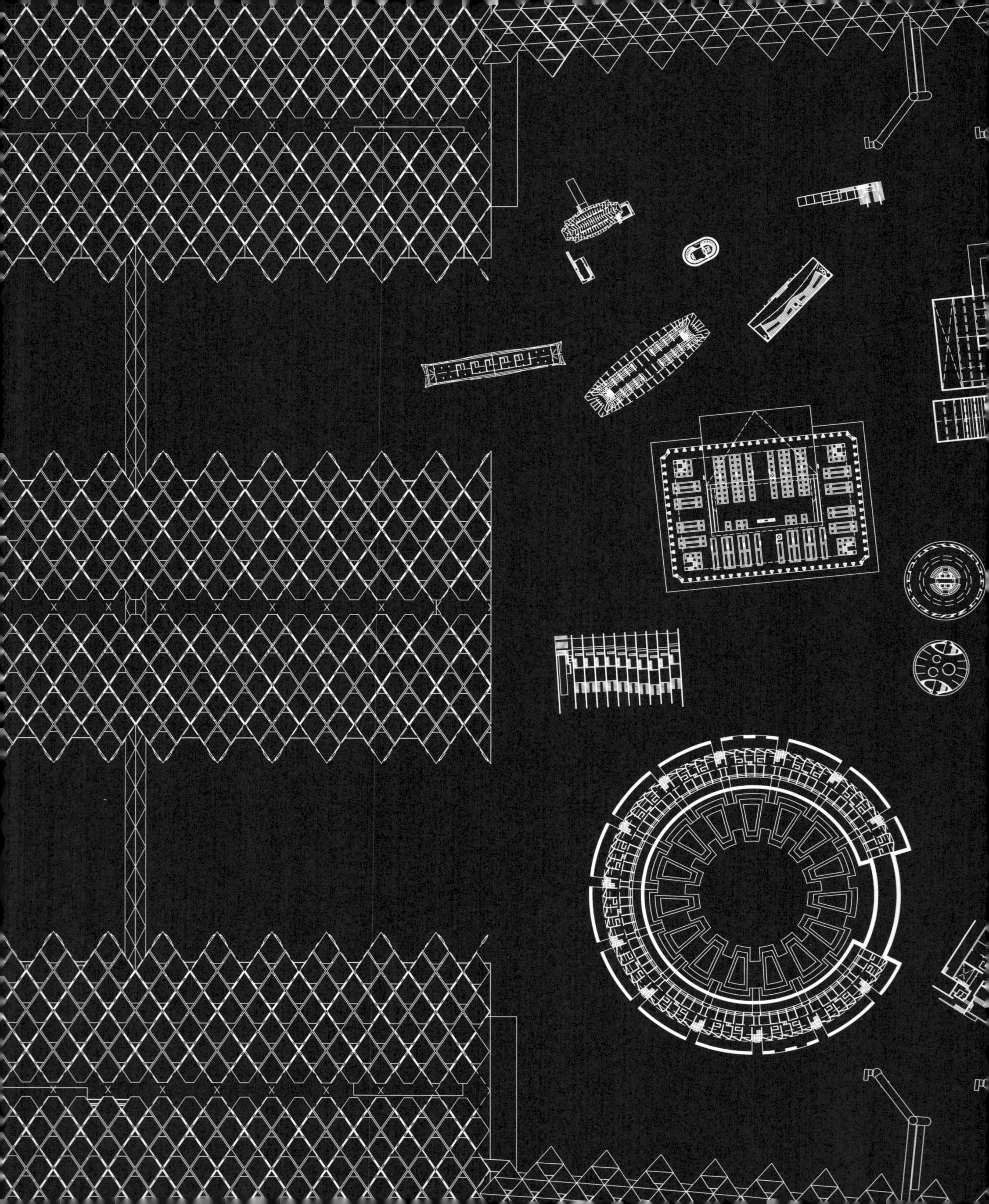

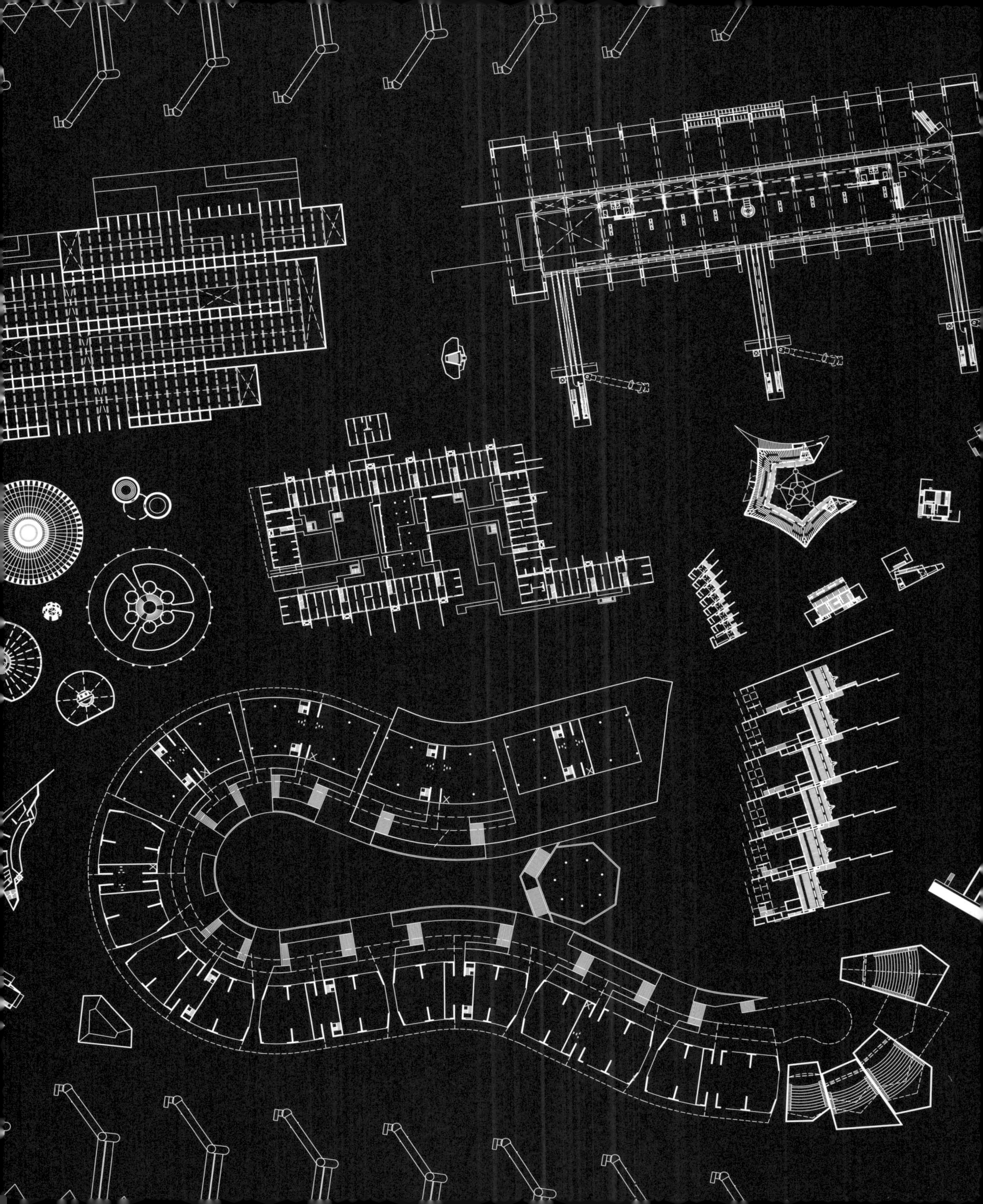

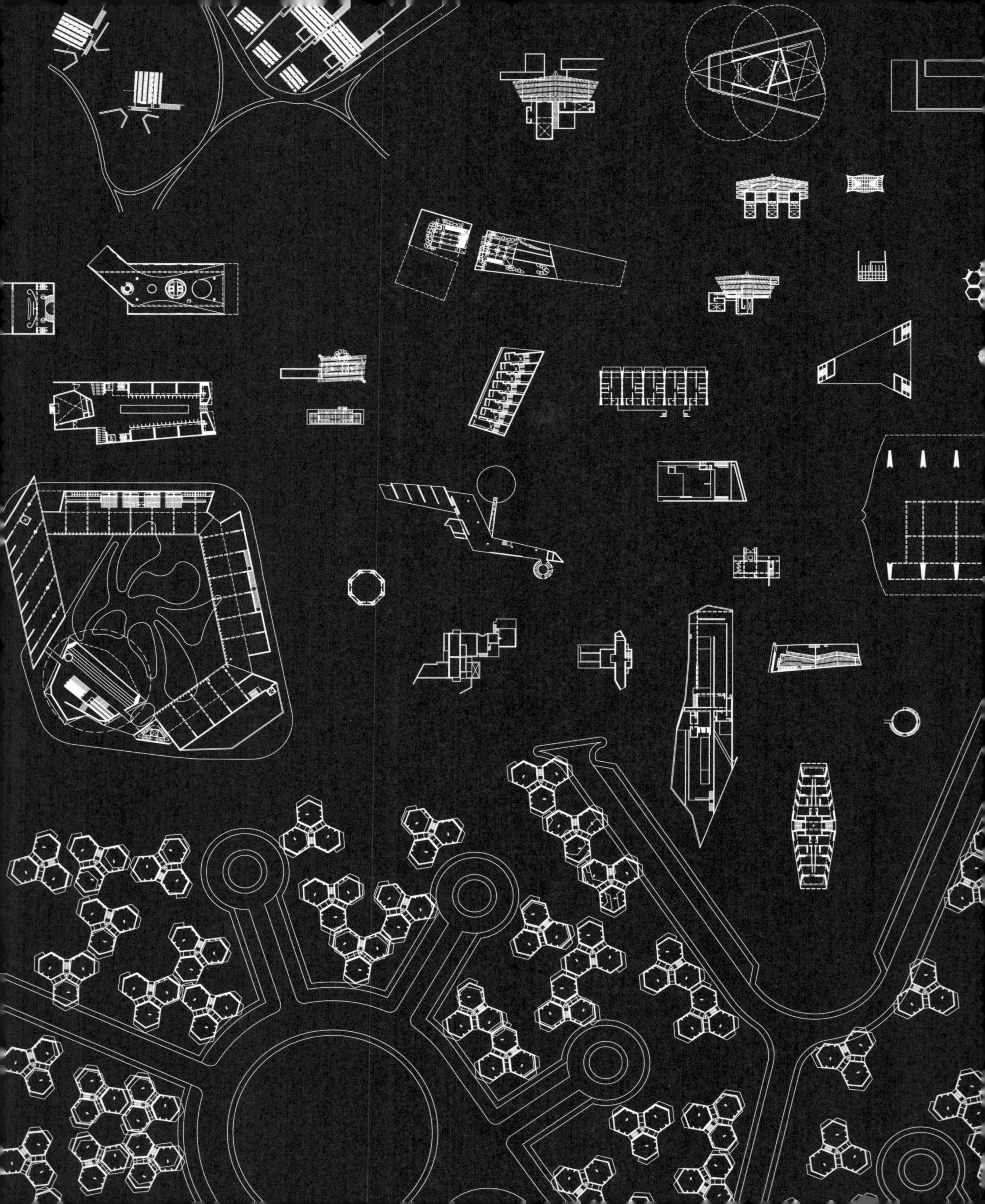

Essential Lines

— Miquel Adrià

In the six chapters devoted to different typologies, the texts printed in the sans serif font (Aa) are by Miquel Adrià, while those printed in the serif font (Aa) are by Alberto Kalach.

Alberto Kalach is an audacious architect. His architecture is at once landscape and city, now evoking a ruin or emerging as a tower, now concealing itself beneath a palm leaf roof or sculpting concrete volumes to be bathed in light. Three decades of tenacity overflow with recurring forms and materials that explore the creative limits of an architecture that requires no adjectives, but rather walls, floors, water, vegetation, shadows, and light. The formal audacity is not limited to any personal, national, or generational style: it never stops risking and exploring.

Alberto Kalach (b. 1960 in Mexico City) is also an original architect. His buildings are radical responses that emerge from the origins of architecture by way of the lines of his sketches and the geometry of his plans. Kalach proposes works as points of reference in the framework that articulates the urban landscape. Thus, each building is a piece, a brick, in the great collective project of architecture created over the course of time.[1] His constructions elude the obvious, the predictable. Creative, visionary, and a fine draftsman, Alberto Kalach is an architect of pencil and paper. His designs come directly from his left hand, not as the result of any methodological inertia: they emerge from the repetition of lines that help him imagine a course, a space, the intersecting light. His designs emerge from the grooves traced on the table and into his subconscious, where his own reiterated gestures gradually acquire different attributes: recurrent, automatic doodles, which come and go, derived from past and future projects, filling up with notes from both memory and fleeing reality, to give birth to another form, another place.

I can still stand by what I wrote fifteen years ago about the architect: "Alberto Kalach tackles varying scales of design with the ingenuous, insolent attitude of someone forever starting from scratch: from the domestic object, the house which stretches forth, to the garden, typological exercises about communal housing or major urban issues. At the small scale, he resolves any needs that arise, designing screens or lamps according to the logic of his own common sense, but never as a 'designer.' It's around the residential issue that he's made inroads with greatest freedom, confronting, as per the happenstance of spatial sequences, the domestic labyrinth and the interior-exterior relationship, in order to extend the inorganic design of the house to the organic one of the garden by means of lattices, pergolas and freestanding walls. Passing time modifies and completes the inhabited space with clumps of bamboo and lichens that blend in with the concrete walls... Alberto Kalach constructs with time.... A builder of minimal elements that are everything, he catalyzes architecture by assembling walls and roofs. He is not satisfied with possible designs –with client included– but rather questions all scales, in order to transform reality creatively.... Provocative, proud and personable, Kalach explains his work in an apathetic way, as if it were all the obvious outcome of a few needs he had merely to attend to."[2]

His work is nourished indiscriminately by those absolute architectures that have marked his memory: from pre-Hispanic ruins to the mosques of Istanbul, where Mimar Sinan[3] fused the architectures of the Ottoman empire and the Italian renaissance; from Roman baths to the Kimbell Art Museum of Louis Kahn; from the expressionist domes of Hans Poelzig or Bruno Taut to the catenary arches of Gaudí; from the intimate, organic gardens of Luis Barragán to the mounds and concrete brise-soleils of Teodoro González de León. As with all the greats, it is easy to associate him –however little he may like it– with other great architects who have constantly returned to the cave, the hut, or the primitive temple. He worked briefly with González de León in 1989. He made two admirable perspective drawings for the competition to design the International Tribunal for the Law of the Sea in Hamburg. Since then, a friendship forged in a mutual passion for the city has united them. Teodoro González saw in Kalach someone "rebellious, provocative and profoundly creative... [with] a distinct and personal touch that enriches fin-de-siècle architecture... [and] speak[s] the revitalized abstract language of the modern movement."[4] And to quote myself again: "Kalach designs timeless, robust spaces in which light is filtered through cracks in

[1] "A building is a brick in the great collective project that is the city" (Teodoro González de León)

[2] Miquel Adrià, "The Architect's Garden," in *Alberto Kalach,* edited by Miquel Adrià (Barcelona: Gustavo Gili, 2004), pp. 7 and 13.

[3] Mimar Koca Sinan ibn Abd al-Mannan, Sinaneddin Yusuf, or Abdulmennan oglu Sinan, known as Koca Mi'mâr Sinân Âgâ or Mimar Sinan, was a prolific Ottoman architect, a contemporary of Andrea Palladio, Michelangelo, and Juan de Herrera.

[4] "Foreword" (by Teodoro González de León), in Aaron Betsky, *Kalach + Álvarez* (Gloucester, MA: Rockport Publishers, 1998), p. 6.

the solid walls.... He is able to grasp the essence of architecture and to construct extended roofs of shingles or palm leaves, grasping the prototypical virtues of *palapa* (reed thatch) or of structures in wood..., to trap the changing shadows of the trees, provoking an ambivalence of sorts between interior and exterior.... His architect-cum-gardener's constructions blend in with the landscape, and the living rooms are flooded with views and gardens.... Like Barragán he avoids obviousness and plays with the subtle qualities of light, semi-darkness and surprise. At each step, with each line, he gradually transgresses the geometric rigor with which he defines the strategy of the design, attending to the particularities of the space or the specific views in order to allow the garden to blur the rigidity of his volumes, in the same way that matter ends up malleablizing their forms."[5] Albert Kalach's sketches, some of them done with a thick pencil or a black marker, others with ink and gouache, in blotches of red and gold, bring us closer to the notion of a certain artistic autonomy in the architectural design. They are a first distillation of the creative process, giving shape to ideas informed by the architect's reactions to the site and the program. They are the initial, imprecise intuitions that capture some certainty, now typological, now formal, resting on those two bases of beauty proposed by Manfredo Tafuri – the natural and the geometrical –, as the redundant lines give time for form and then matter to emerge. Drawing is discovering, allowing oneself to be led toward the design. As with Alvar Aalto and also with RCR, out of the radical quality of the line there appears the diagram that will be its essence. There is no architectural proposal that cannot be expressed in a few essential lines that synthesize resonances and forces. Drawing – for Kalach as for Aldo Rossi – is never an end in itself: it is always architecture, because it reflects a condition, a moment of his own life, of reality.[6]

[5] Adrià, "The Architect's Garden," in Adrià (ed.), *Alberto Kalach*, p. 11.

[6] See Gianni Braghieri, *Aldo Rossi* (Barcelona: Gustavo Gili, 1981), p. 13.

Finally the architectural design appears, subject to geometry, and so the ideogram implicit in the pencil strokes of the first sketches acquires its autonomy. If concepts, forms, and spaces are suggested by the personal sketch, it will be the working model, of cardboard or wood, that corroborates these haptic and optical intuitions. As Kalach's mentor Humberto Ricalde has written: "In the workshop of Alberto Kalach ... the models of pending projects stacked up like unfinished ziggurats and the photographs of buildings under construction bring to mind piles of planks, props, and logs, their rough textures exuding warmth, of big pieces of porphyry still with the mark of the force that ripped them from the bosom of the earth, or the forceful presence of steel girders of a workmanlike structural geometry, impressive in their high technology.... The processes of ideation are clear for all to see, spread around in an aleatory, creative order: maquettes undergoing changes, expectant plans in random layers, pads with sketches, diagrams and notes on them, green, blue and gold drawings alongside their inks and colored pencils; an odd mix of books, all having something to do with each other: 22,135 industrial regulations, manuals on gardening and maritime engineering, ironwork, grasses, steel crafts, Teotihuacan, *Design with Nature*, etc."[7]

[7] Humberto Ricalde, "A.K. 43", in Adrià (ed.), *Alberto Kalach,* pp. 15 and 17.

Paradoxically, although Alberto Kalach is one of the most outstanding contemporary Mexican architects – if not *the* most –, he flees all rhetoric of "Mexicanness" as "a designation of origin." I was present at an initial interview between the architect and some prominent potential clients for an important restricted competition, who insisted on guarantees and unmistakable signs of his Aztec pedigree, to whom Kalach simply replied that if he was commissioned to undertake the project and if it was built in Mexico, it would not only necessarily be Mexican but would also be the best. To be sure, the essence of Mexican architecture – exemplified in the Avenue of the Dead at Teotihuacan, in colonial Mexico City, in the Colegio de México by Teodoro González de León and Abraham Zabludovsky, in the gardens of Luis Barragán –, which favors voids on a monumental scale, more formal than functional, and explores the ambivalence between interior and exterior space and the solar condition of its elements (patios, pergolas, brise-soleils), is inherent in the work of

Alberto Kalach, without any loss of universality. His architecture breaks barriers between different disciplines (urbanism, landscaping, architecture, industrial design) and different scales (territory, landscape, city, building, residence) and different meanings.

It is difficult, in the face of so complete and so singular a universe, to structure a reading of his oeuvre that embraces in two-dimensional fashion the finest examples of his work over the course of thirty years, without neglecting those projects that perhaps catalyzed germinal and inconclusive ideas and without confining his creative freedom in a canonical classification –chronological, typological– that would betray its spirit. This book is intended to be a safe conduct to the world of Alberto Kalach, in which one project leads to another and the ideas and forms jump from one space and time to other spaces and times. This printed container must be multisensorial, appealing to touch, hearing, and smell, just as Kalach's work does. We have therefore created constellations of works with certain affinities, whether it be the shape of their plans (circular, hexagonal, parallel) or their uses and functions (libraries, residences, collective housing) or the architectural elements that define the design (*palapa*, tower, or shed). In each constellation there is one work –the most brilliant stars– that stands out, but the lesser stars that trace the pattern are not neglected.

Thus, the building at Reforma 27 sums up a long exploration of typologies of collective housing, especially in the form of high-rises. The relation of the elevators and stairs to the habitable cells was approached through a wide range of solutions: unconstructed designs that ended up as svelte maquettes crowding the walls of the architect's studio. The office building at Constituyentes 41 concludes a series of projects located on almost residual spaces in the city, small triangles on the borders of the urban fabric, across from Chapultepec Park. The Vasconcelos Library also condenses the rigor of previous work –including the FARO de Oriente, the San Juan de Letrán subway station, the hospitals of the Instituto Mexicano del Seguro Social (IMSS), and in part even the Kurimanzutto gallery–, while the GGG house draws on the morphological and spatial experiences and experiments of many other houses. The isolated single-family dwelling provides an opportunity to explore the domestic potential and its interrelationship with the landscape as no other typology. The Mayan houses and the Mestiza House, all in the Hacienda Tzalancab, as well as La Platanera, where the lush surrounding vegetation invades walls and columns, show another facet of these isolated dwellings that give a privileged place to landscape.

The Metropolis

Alberto Kalach is constantly thinking about the city and about the transforming power of architecture in it. His metropolitan atlases are part of an endless stream of topographical sketches and photos of the city that help him to imagine other urban plans superposed on Mexico City. This visionary architect, who likes to swim against the current, has championed for decades the salvaging of the lacustrine city that lies sleeping beneath the concrete metropolis. Always radical, but with an empathy for nature, Kalach questions the form of the city. With the same unprejudiced freedom with which he approaches any design, on any scale, he has been sowing buildings for decades into a new metropolitan landscape, on the undeniable premise that the Valley of Mexico continues to be, potentially at least, the lake it once was. The atlas he proposes is a collection of wishes and desires. Rather than a mapping of the city, intended to record what is there, it is a catalogue of potential futures, of multiple realities imagined in the architect's fresh, bold, and forceful lines. If the transformation of the city is a complex process, which involves a large cast of actors and forces, the metropolis sketched out by Kalach would seem to suggest that the opportunities are so manifest that the construction of the future should simply follow the lines

Urban planning proposals published in the *Atlas de proyectos para la Ciudad de México*

of his marker, brush, or pencil. Like Rem Koolhas, Kalach knows that an architect has to be an optimist and that, however much he may require the collaboration of other agents and stakeholders, he should start with visionary intuitions. Bruno Taut sought a fusion of subject, nature, and culture with which to give birth to a new architecture identified with the landscape as a single whole. Le Corbusier needed only a few sketches to present his idea of the ideal modern city, to convey the essential concepts of his *Ville radieuse*. Pedro Ramírez Vázquez started from a holistic vision of the metropolitan sprawl understood as a living organism in order to rearrange essential pieces on a new urban chessboard. And Teodoro González de León salvaged the skyline of Le Corbusier's city to illustrate the new lacustrine landscape of Texcoco. It was precisely in Texcoco that González de León and Kalach proposed a site for the new Mexico City airport, in the aim of recovering the lake and generating an economic stimulus for the impoverished eastern neighborhoods of the capital city.

Alberto Kalach's proposal is a master plan that offers concrete solutions to the problem of integrating Chapultepec Park with the rest of the city. There are currently some 800,000 people living within a kilometer of the park, 560,000 of whom are behind traffic barriers that impede access to it. The aim of the proposal is to create the necessary conditions through the rehabilitation of spaces, generating points of encounter and interchange within an organic whole that embraces social, cultural, natural, and urban aspects. *Gran Chapultepec 2019* is the result of an interdisciplinary collaboration that remains open to new ideas and contributions from landscapers, botanists, engineers, artists, and other architects, as well as joggers and athletes, small businesspeople, and citizens in general. It is also an invitation to both specialists and the general population to establish a dialogue in which the participation of local communities and of ordinary citizens is essential, since the issues are of common interest and benefit. Kalach's master plan generates the ideas and the aims, made up of two types of projects: those ready for execution and those with their place assigned in one of the four sections, which will require public competitions in order to be developed.[8]

The aim of the urban utopias is to transform an invisible reality into a visible one. And the immediate images sketched out by Kalach give an appeal to the opulence of development from a certain post-Le Corbusier polarization that combines greater density and height with more natural greenery, more trees and parks: a sort of oxymoron formulated by Le Corbusier in his *Ville radieuse* that was echoed by Mario Pani in Mexico with both Ciudad Universitaria and the Nonoalco-Tlatelolco housing project. In a way, it is a question of the esthetic fusion of nature and artifice – as Iñaki Ábalos has formulated it – in which the place itself plays an active role, with the incorporation of time as a factor in the esthetic experience and the primacy of the visual.

According to Aaron Betsky, the city is a collage of structures, colors, and forms,[9] and Mexico City is one of the most spectacular examples of this, owing to its size, its many different layers, and its complexity. Similarly, Kalach sees the city as an enormous laboratory, as a spontaneous force of nature, on which to project urban imaginaries – to paraphrase Manuel Delgado – that are not representations but rather patterns of representation. Kalach sees the great Mexican metropolis as a grand opportunity or, indeed, as a collection of opportunities for work to be done.[10]

[8] See the précis of the master plan for *Gran Chapultepec 2019* by Alberto Kalach and an interview with the architect conducted by Miquel Adrià at https://www.arquine.com/conversacion-y-propuesta-de-alberto-kalach-para-el-bosque-de-chapultepec/.

[9] Betsky, *Kalach+Álvarez*, p. 8.

[10] Miquel Adrià, *Atlas de proyectos para la Ciudad de México* (Mexico City: Conaculta / Contornos / Arquine, 2012), vol. 1, p. 6.

Urban planning proposals published in the *Atlas de proyectos para la Ciudad de México*

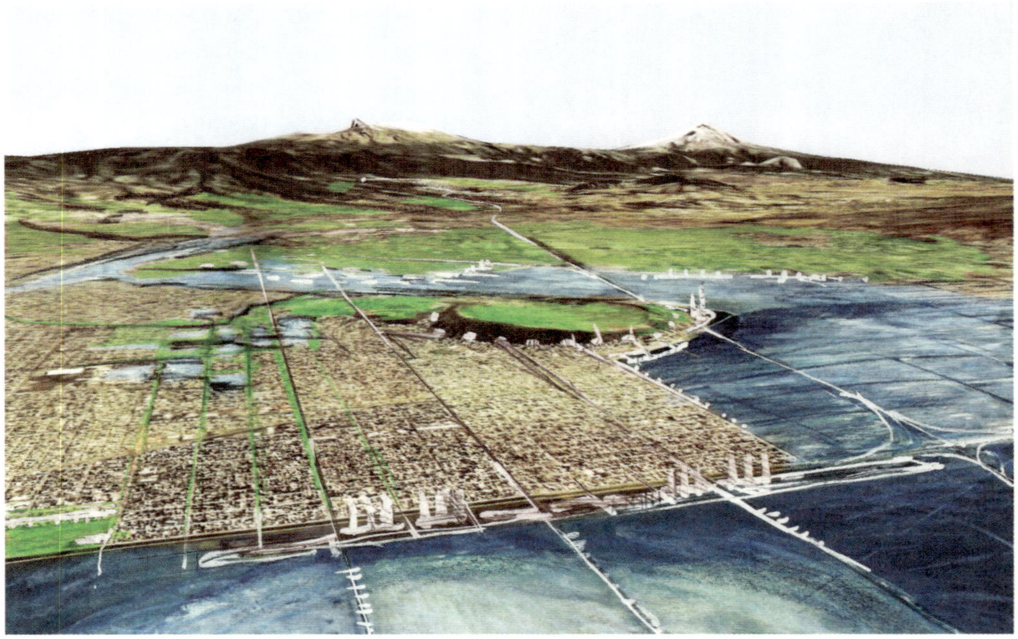

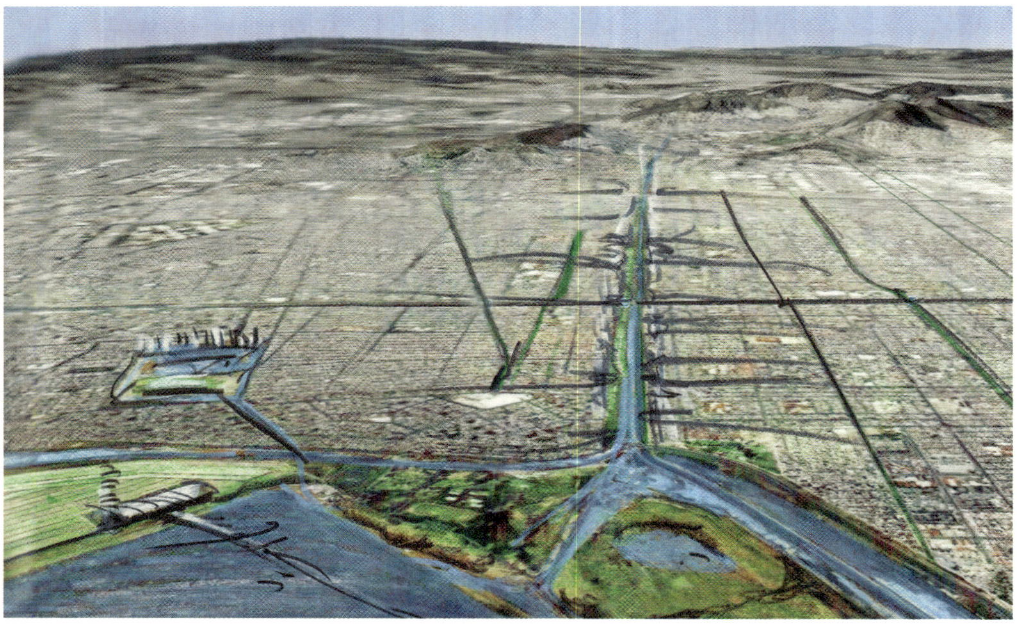

Urban planning proposals published in the master plan *Gran Chapultepec 2019*

Bays

The definition of a space designed to contain activities is the very essence of architecture. Alberto Kalach has undertaken numerous projects starting from the autonomy of the place, defining unitary spaces, containers, large halls, or bays capable of housing complex programs within the striking simplicity of a single wrapper. Like the Biblical ark, they are buildings that go beyond the expression of a program, housing indifferently a range of contents that could potentially vary over time. It is not a matter simply of form over function, but rather of a timeless spatial concept that embraces different programs at different conjunctures.

Kalach's first ark was the FARO de Oriente in Iztapalapa. Other vessels have followed: large, bright unitary spaces housing markets and airports, where the essence of the design is the extruded section.

Kalach's most spectacular work in this typology is the Vasconcelos Library. An archaic structure, like that of a mastaba, it contains the library even as it incorporates time as a factor in the design, with plants growing on the raw surfaces, unfinished and exposed, so that the vegetation fills up the space with time. The idea – described in the architect's précis – consists of the creation of an ark, a bearer of human knowledge, immersed within a lush botanical garden. Thus, the 35-meter-wide bay extends for a length of three modules and sustains an independent structure, an enormous bookcase capable of holding more than a million and a half books, as required by the program. The reading rooms are laid out along the sides of this central spine.

Alberto Kalach— The Spanish word for a 'bay' in architecture is *nave*, which also means 'vessel' or 'ship,' and as such goes back to the ark, voyaging in our imaginations. Archaic ages, remote in time. Vessel and nave, *navis* in Latin, and *naos*, 'temple' in Greek. Vessels that voyage with Homer in the *Iliad* and with Phidias in the Parthenon. Some vessels travel in space and others, the static ones, in time. Vessel, nave, or bay: an inescapable theme of architecture.

BIBLIOTECA UNIVERSITARIA 20 JULIO 2003

FARO de Oriente

With— Axel Arañó, Julio González, Walter Lingard, and Rosa López

Mexico City / 2005

— There is a painting by Massimo Scolari that has captivated me ever since I first saw it, of Noah's ark run aground. The image has haunted several of my designs since then. This vessel, run aground on the former Texcoco lakebed, is perpetually awaiting better times.

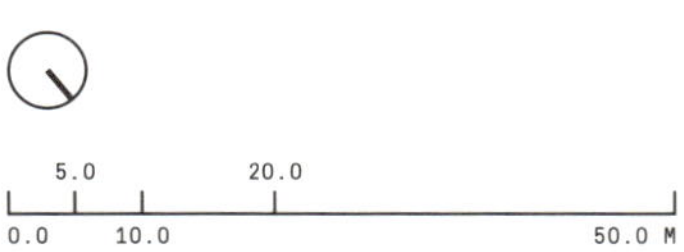

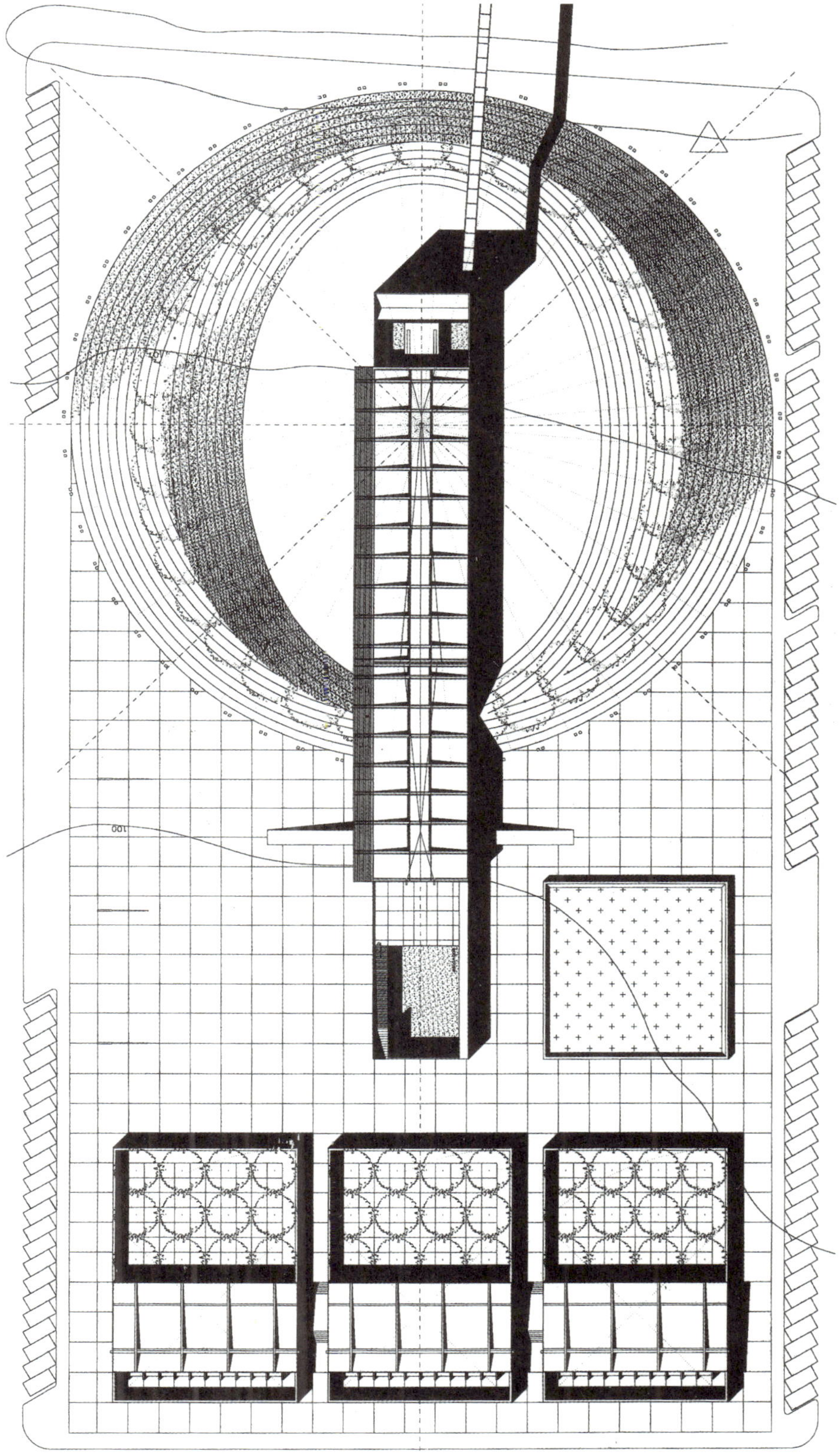

The FARO de Oriente [Eastern Arts and Crafts Workshop] is a building that recalls a boat floating virtually on the space formerly occupied by Lake Texcoco. The program is devoted to the practice and promotion of different artistic disciplines among the inhabitants of a troubled and violent part of the city.

Kurimanzutto Gallery

With— Héctor Módica

Mexico City / 2007

The Kurimanzutto Gallery addresses the theme of the void. This renovation of an industrial bay generates an ample museum space based on the subtle austerity of the preexisting structure. The design overturns the canonic idea of the museum as a white cube by integrating apertures for natural light, materials such as concrete and wood, stone paving, a central skylight in a pitched roof, and a garden space that follows the central axis of a second patio.

— The wooden bay is concealed behind the austere and inexpressive street-level building. The whole project is a retransformation of constructions that existed previously on the site. In collaboration with Mónica Manzutto and José Kuri, we restructured them. We gave them light, meaning, life.

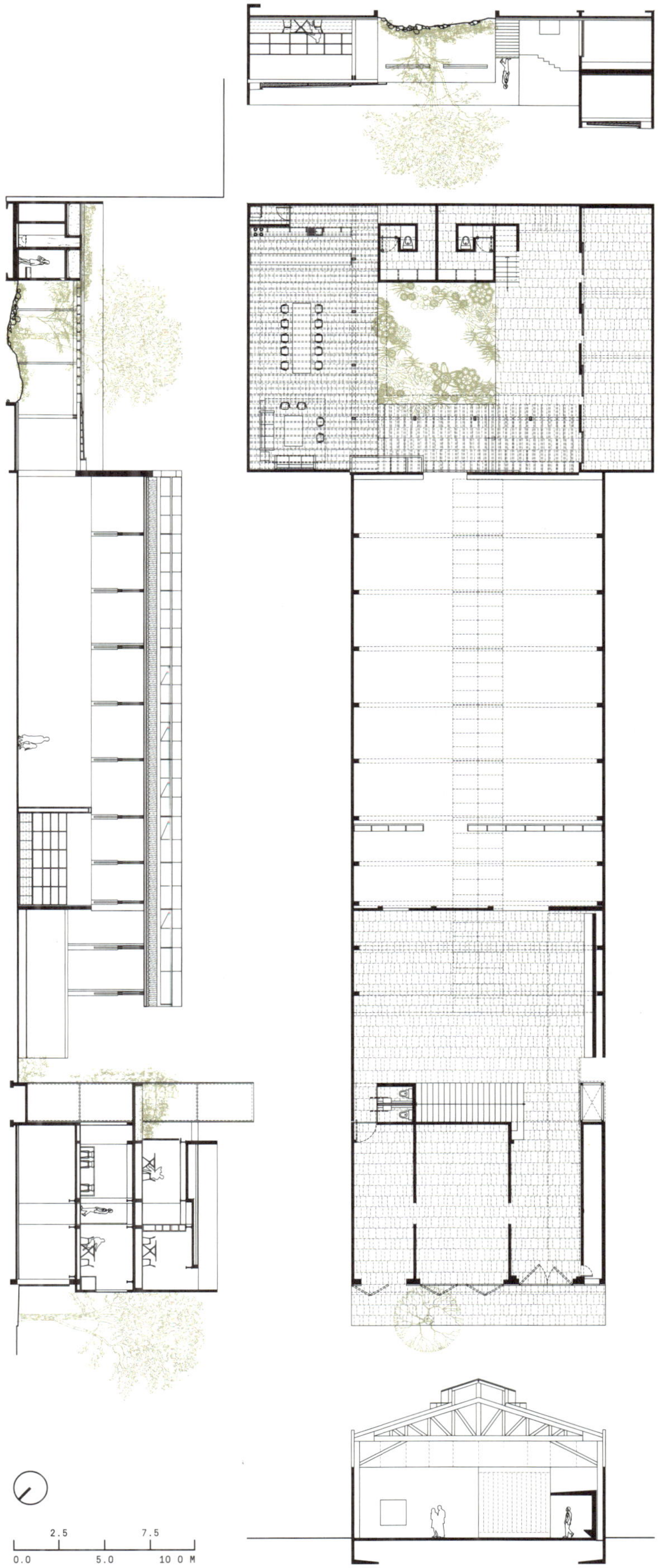
2.5 7.5
0.0 5.0 10 0 M

Corona Market

With— Juan Palomar and David Martínez

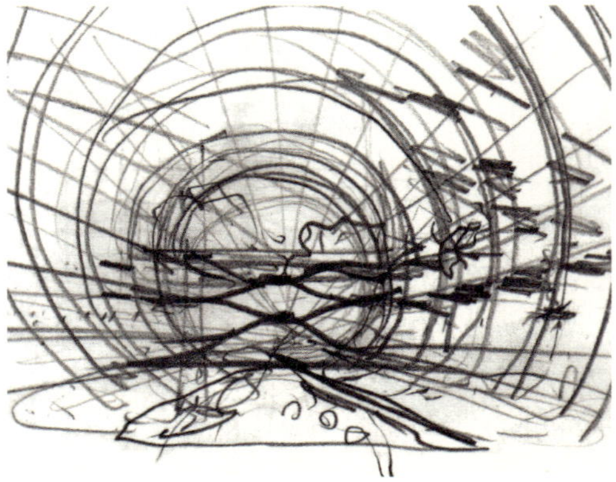

Vitruvius. Basilica at Fano

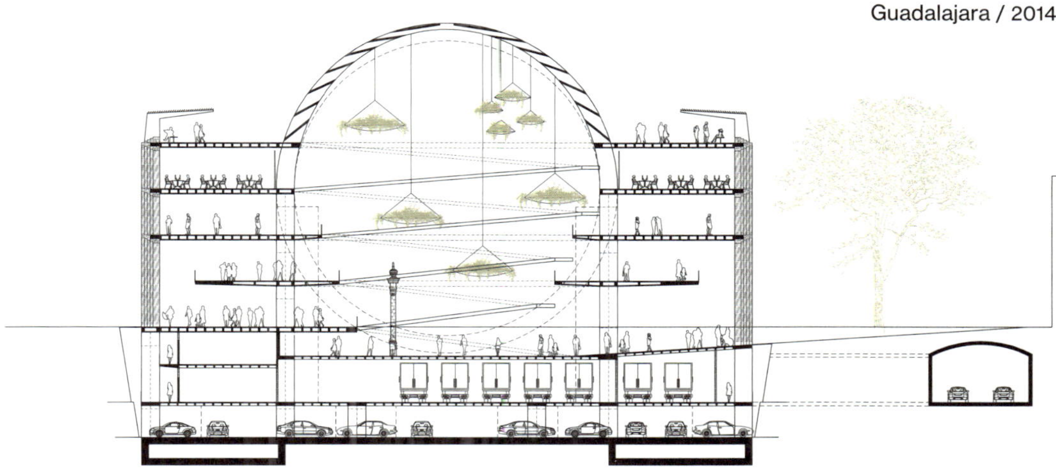

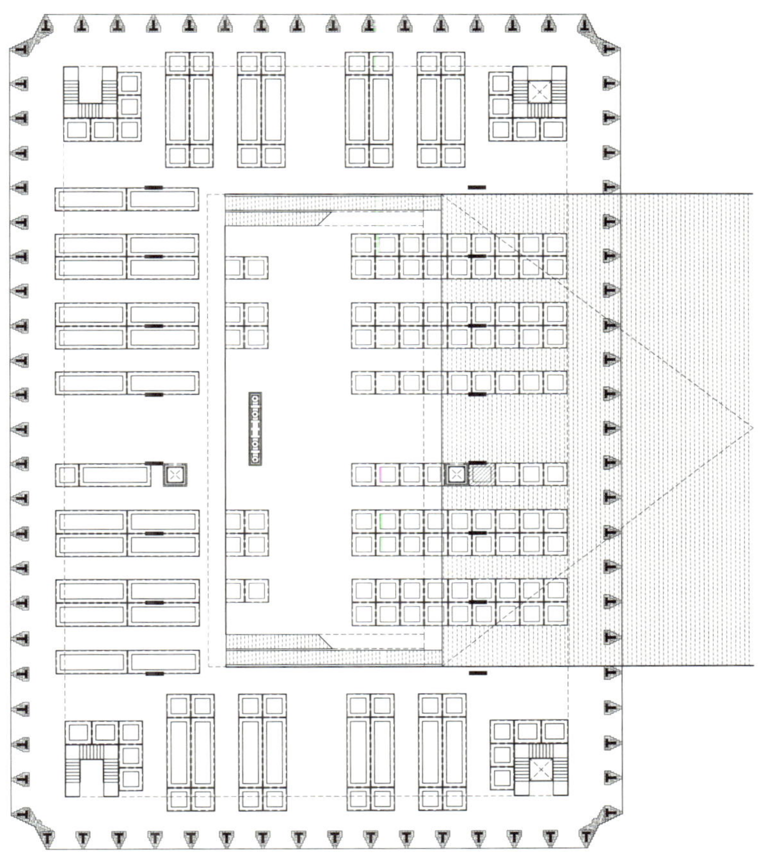

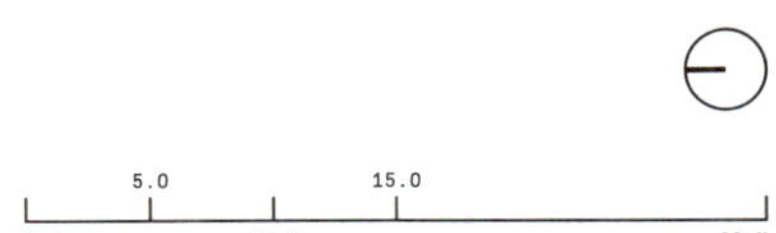
5.0
15.0
0.0
10.0
30 M

Vasconcelos Library

With— Juan Palomar, Adriana León, Gustavo Lipkau, Emmanuel Ramírez, Tami Tamashiro, Ignacio del Río, Enrique Rosas, and Jose Luis Reyes

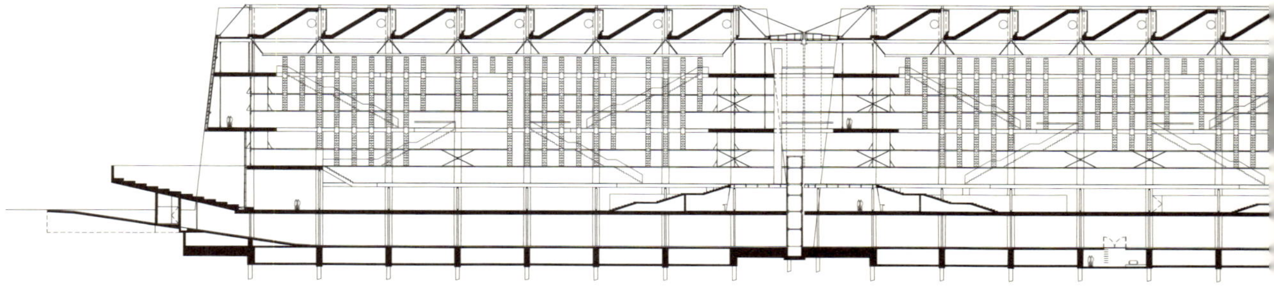

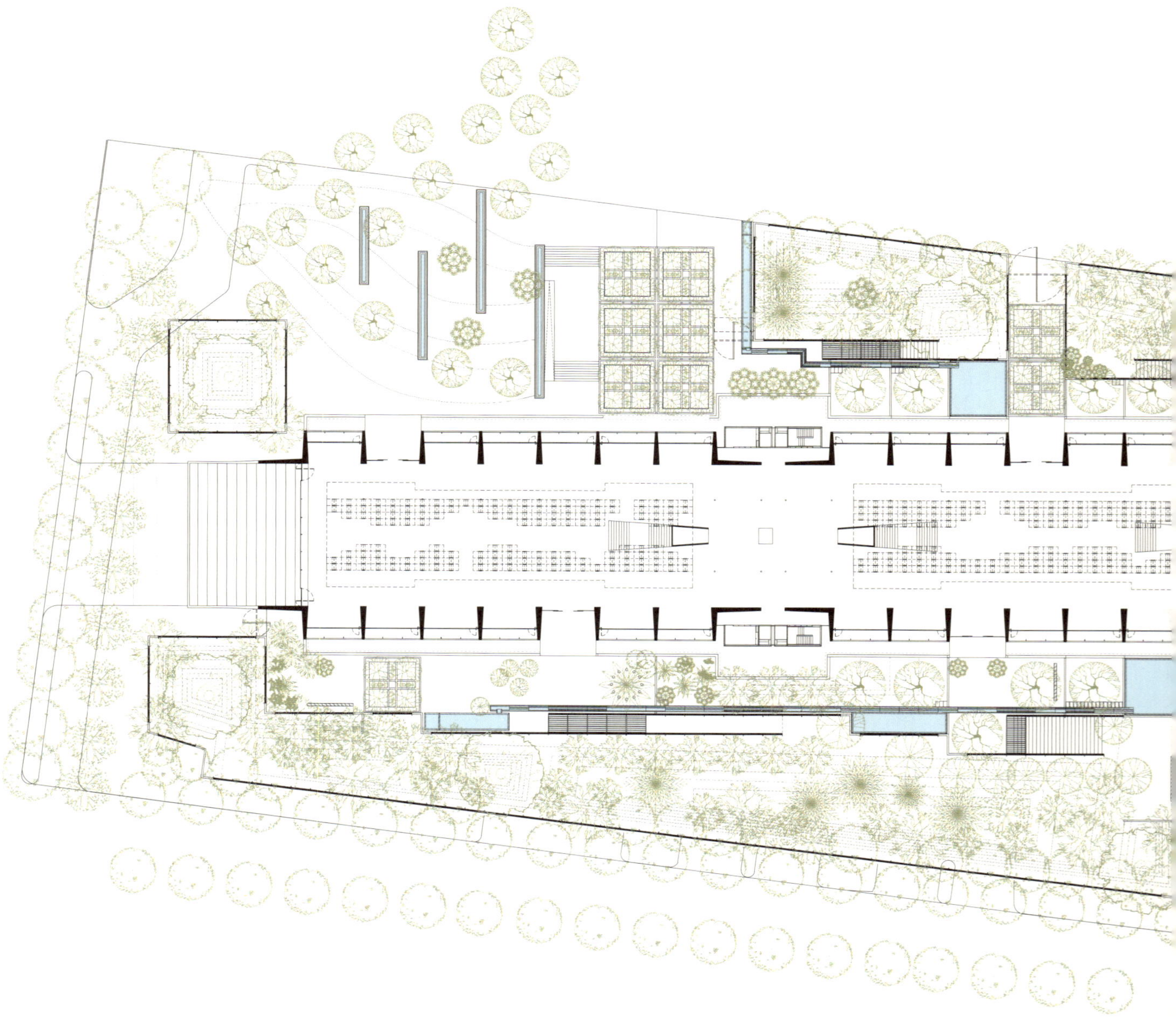

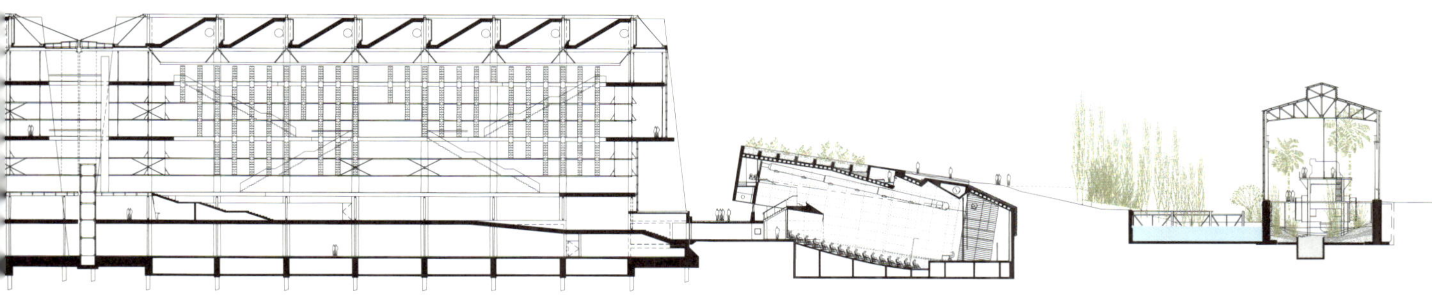

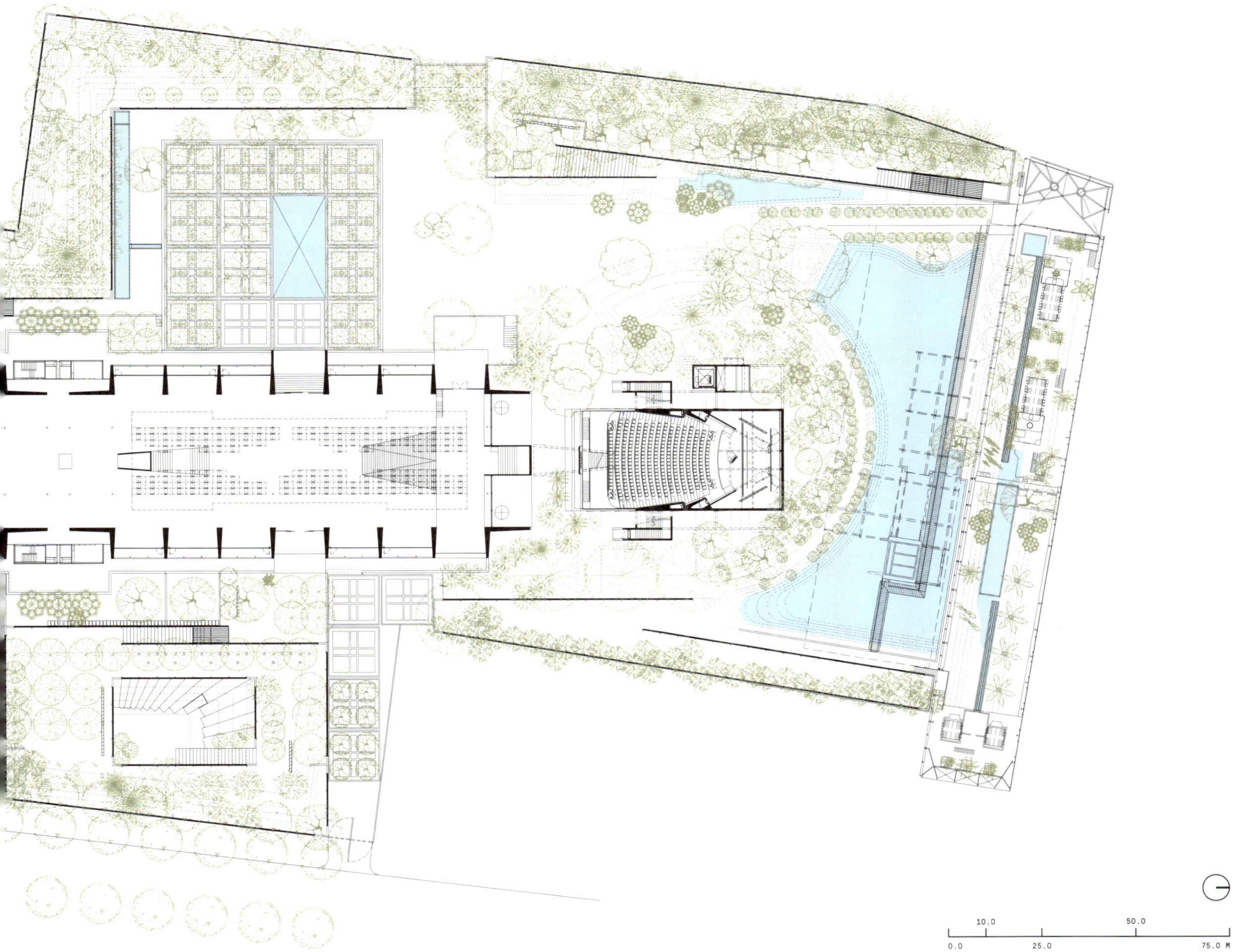
10.0
50.0
0.0
25.0
75.0 M

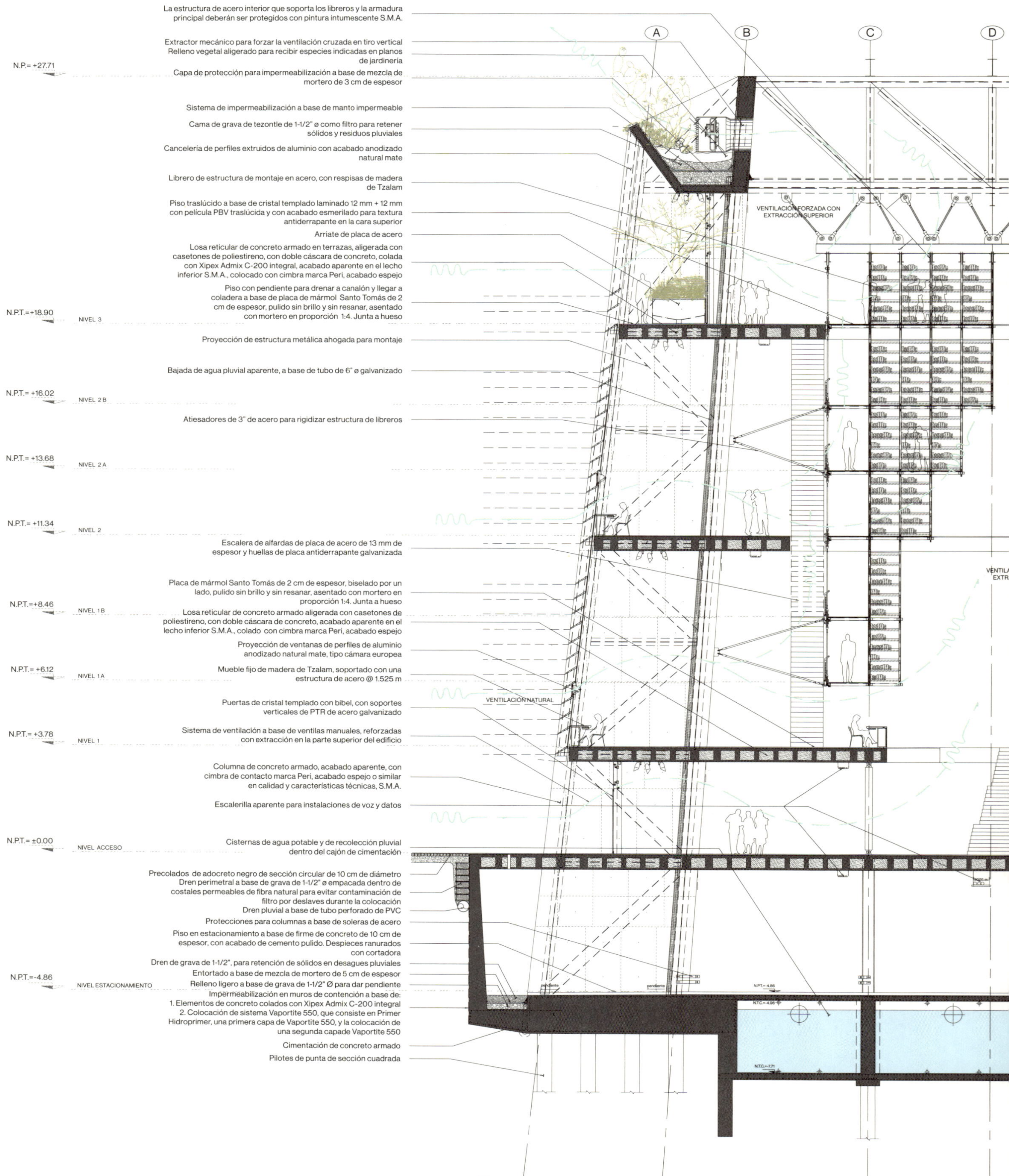

La estructura de acero interior que soporta los libreros y la armadura principal deberán ser protegidos con pintura intumescente S.M.A.
Extractor mecánico para forzar la ventilación cruzada en tiro vertical
Relleno vegetal aligerado para recibir especies indicadas en planos de jardinería
Capa de protección para impermeabilización a base de mezcla de mortero de 3 cm de espesor
Sistema de impermeabilización a base de manto impermeable
Cama de grava de tezontle de 1-1/2" ø como filtro para retener sólidos y residuos pluviales
Cancelería de perfiles extruidos de aluminio con acabado anodizado natural mate
Librero de estructura de montaje en acero, con respisas de madera de Tzalam
Piso traslúcido a base de cristal templado laminado 12 mm + 12 mm con película PBV traslúcida y con acabado esmerilado para textura antiderrapante en la cara superior
Arriate de placa de acero
Losa reticular de concreto armado en terrazas, aligerada con casetones de poliestireno, con doble cáscara de concreto, colada con Xipex Admix C-200 integral, acabado aparente en el lecho inferior S.M.A., colocado con cimbra marca Peri, acabado espejo
Piso con pendiente para drenar a canalón y llegar a coladera a base de placa de mármol Santo Tomás de 2 cm de espesor, pulido sin brillo y sin resanar, asentado con mortero en proporción 1:4. Junta a hueso
Proyección de estructura metálica ahogada para montaje
Bajada de agua pluvial aparente, a base de tubo de 6" ø galvanizado
Atiesadores de 3" de acero para rigidizar estructura de libreros
Escalera de alfardas de placa de acero de 13 mm de espesor y huellas de placa antiderrapante galvanizada
Placa de mármol Santo Tomás de 2 cm de espesor, biselado por un lado, pulido sin brillo y sin resanar, asentado con mortero en proporción 1:4. Junta a hueso
Losa reticular de concreto armado aligerada con casetones de poliestireno, con doble cáscara de concreto, acabado aparente en el lecho inferior S.M.A., colado con cimbra marca Peri, acabado espejo
Proyección de ventanas de perfiles de aluminio anodizado natural mate, tipo cámara europea
Mueble fijo de madera de Tzalam, soportado con una estructura de acero @ 1.525 m
Puertas de cristal templado con bibel, con soportes verticales de PTR de acero galvanizado
Sistema de ventilación a base de ventilas manuales, reforzadas con extracción en la parte superior del edificio
Columna de concreto armado, acabado aparente, con cimbra de contacto marca Peri, acabado espejo o similar en calidad y características técnicas, S.M.A.
Escalerilla aparente para instalaciones de voz y datos
Cisternas de agua potable y de recolección pluvial dentro del cajón de cimentación
Precolados de adocreto negro de sección circular de 10 cm de diámetro
Dren perimetral a base de grava de 1-1/2" ø empacada dentro de costales permeables de fibra natural para evitar contaminación de filtro por deslaves durante la colocación
Dren pluvial a base de tubo perforado de PVC
Protecciones para columnas a base de soleras de acero
Piso en estacionamiento a base de firme de concreto de 10 cm de espesor, con acabado de cemento pulido. Despieces ranurados con cortadora
Dren de grava de 1-1/2", para retención de sólidos en desagues pluviales
Entortado a base de mezcla de mortero de 5 cm de espesor
Relleno ligero a base de grava de 1-1/2" Ø para dar pendiente
Impermeabilización en muros de contención a base de:
1. Elementos de concreto colados con Xipex Admix C-200 integral
2. Colocación de sistema Vaportite 550, que consiste en Primer Hidroprimer, una primera capa de Vaportite 550, y la colocación de una segunda capade Vaportite 550
Cimentación de concreto armado
Pilotes de punta de sección cuadrada
N.P.= +27.71
N.P.T.=+18.90
NIVEL 3
N.P.T.= +16.02
NIVEL 2B
N.P.T.= +13.68
NIVEL 2A
N.P.T.= +11.34
NIVEL 2
N.P.T.= +8.46
NIVEL 1B
N.P.T.= +6.12
NIVEL 1A
N.P.T.= +3.78
NIVEL 1
N.P.T.= ±0.00
NIVEL ACCESO
N.P.T.= -4.86
NIVEL ESTACIONAMIENTO
A
B
C
D
VENTILACIÓN FORZADA CON EXTRACCIÓN SUPERIOR
VENTILACIÓN NATURAL

Bays

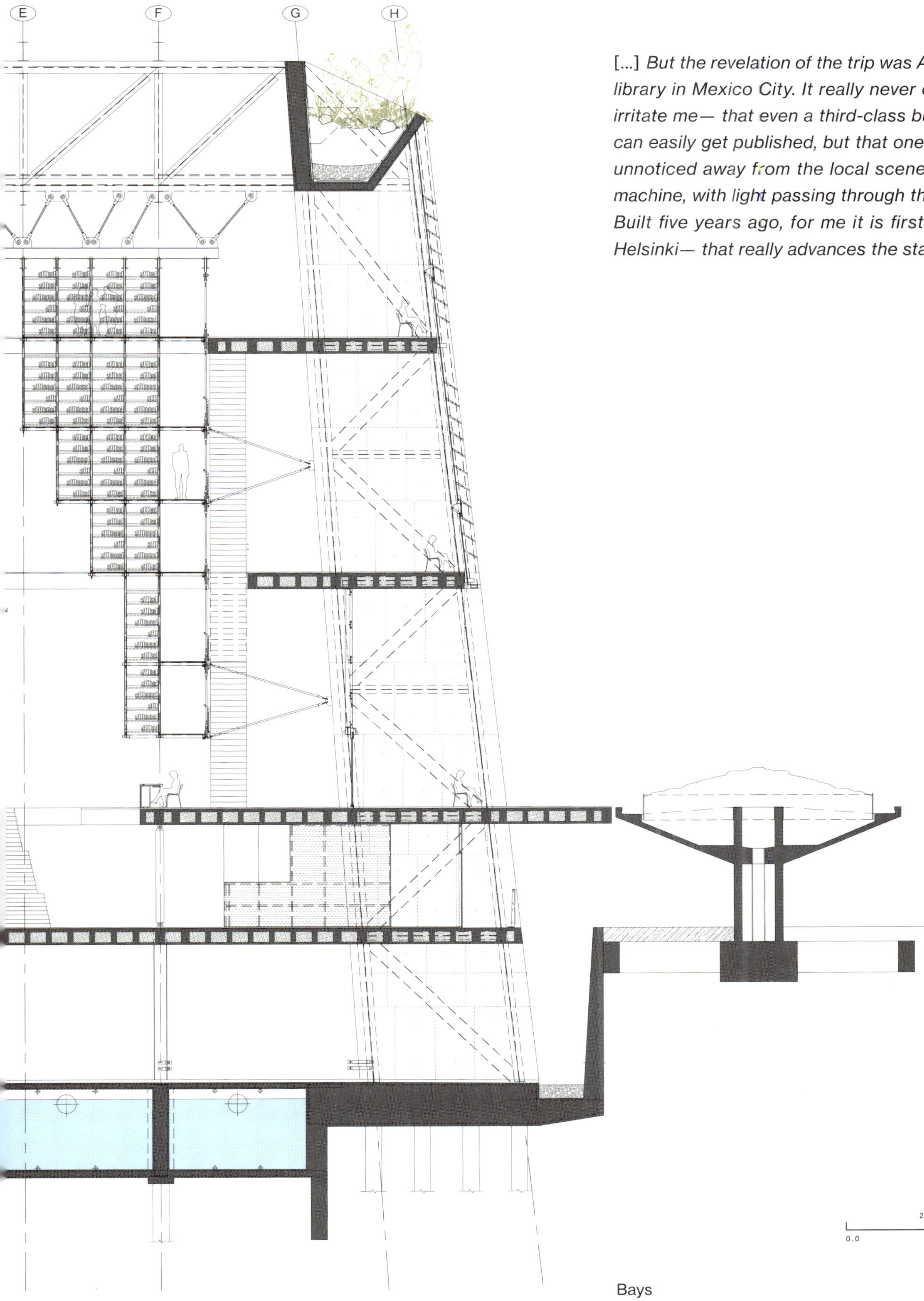

[...] *But the revelation of the trip was Alberto Kalach's extraordinary library in Mexico City. It really never ceases to surprise me —and irritate me— that even a third-class building in a European country can easily get published, but that one as impressive as this can go unnoticed away from the local scene. It is an enormous, dynamic machine, with light passing through the hanging, adjustable stacks. Built five years ago, for me it is first library —since Asplund's in Helsinki— that really advances the state of the art.* —Peter Cook

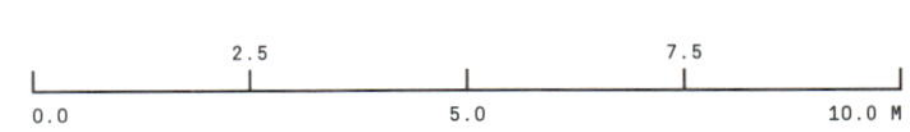

The Vasconcelos Library was the winning design of an international competition, conceived as both building and botanical garden. The large scale of the project makes it a striking and decisive presence in the urban context. The horizontal scale-like elements on the exterior and the slanting of the saw-tooth roof protect the reading rooms from direct sunlight, while still flooding the interior with light. The plan of the building is the map of the library, the support for a cartography of knowledge that reflects an encyclopedic desire to understand and to order both container and contents.

Bays

An extensive concavity, 250 meters long and thirty meters deep, allows light to penetrate the slanted walls and the roof, from which the stacks hang, loaded with books. As timeless and schematic as a ruin, the structure projects the weightiness of its blank walls and the taut force of the tensors holding up the stacks.

Bays

The auditorium, with seating for five hundred people, and the informal reading area are at the end of the central bay. The administrative offices and other complementary areas are located in two modules: one is accessed from off the central spine, while the other is an independent structure, an old industrial building located toward the back of the lot.

Bays

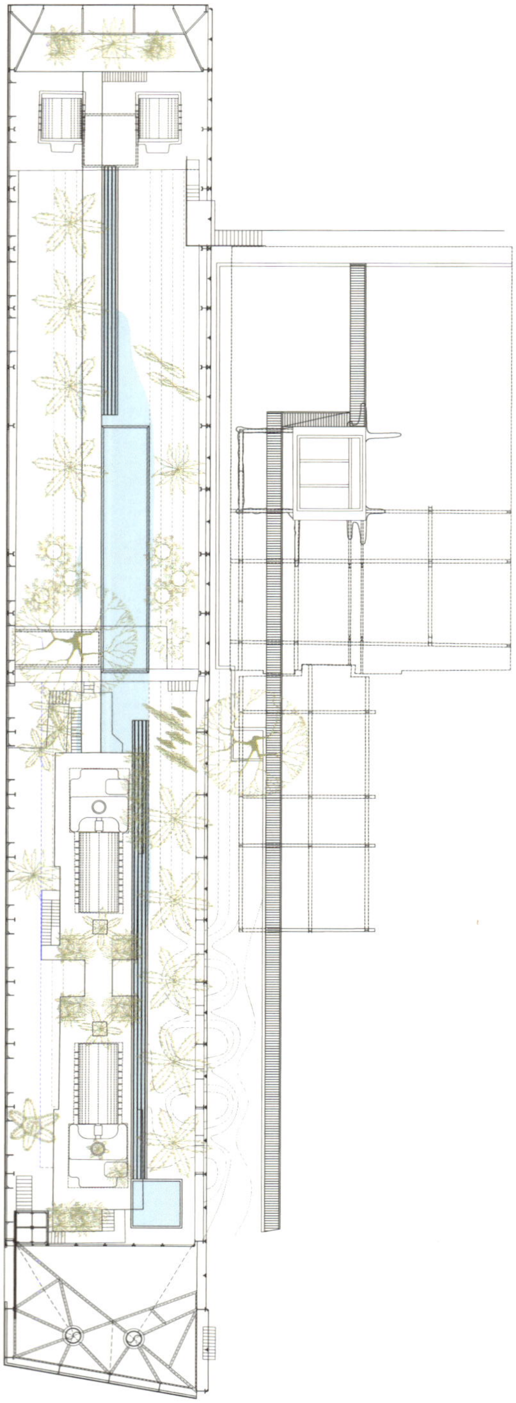

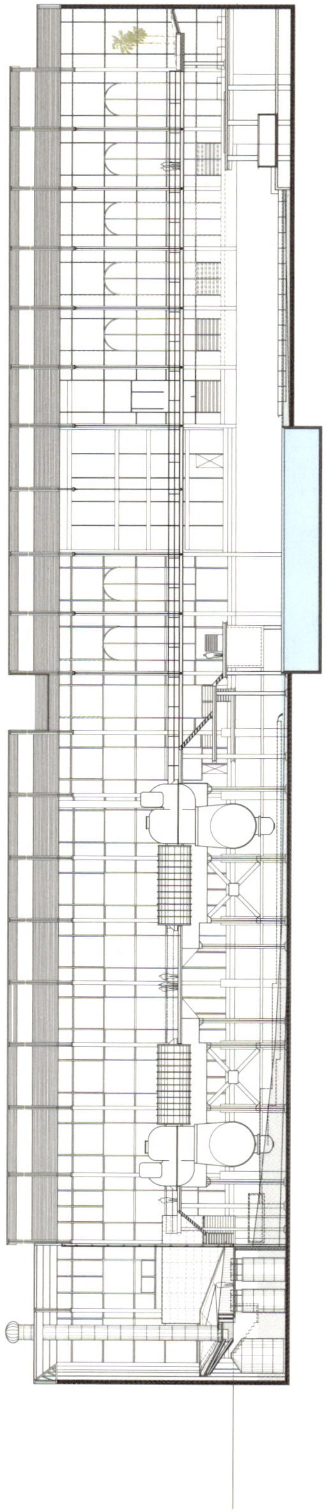

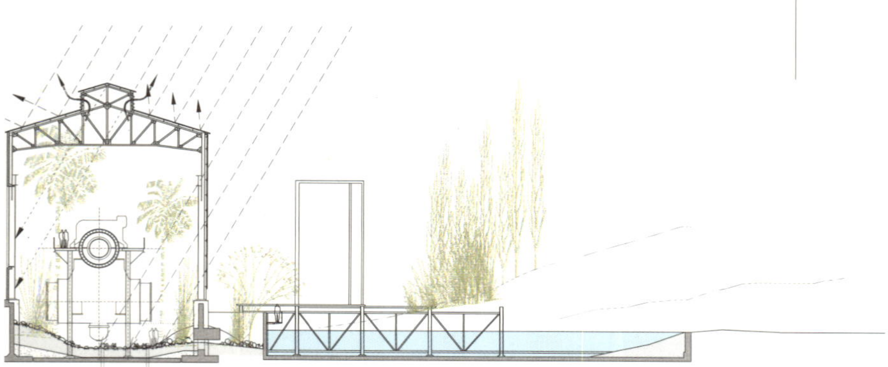

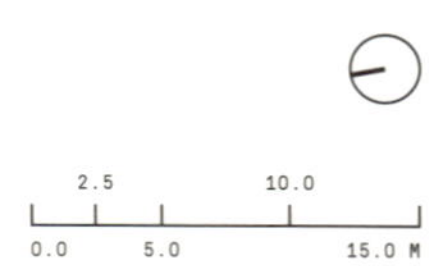
2.5
10.0
0.0
5.0
15.0 M

A greenhouse is housed in this reused construction. The turbines of the subway system's emergency generator were wrapped in a structure that buffers the noise and is integrated harmoniously with the green areas and the new building.

Buenavista Train Station

With— Enrique Rosas

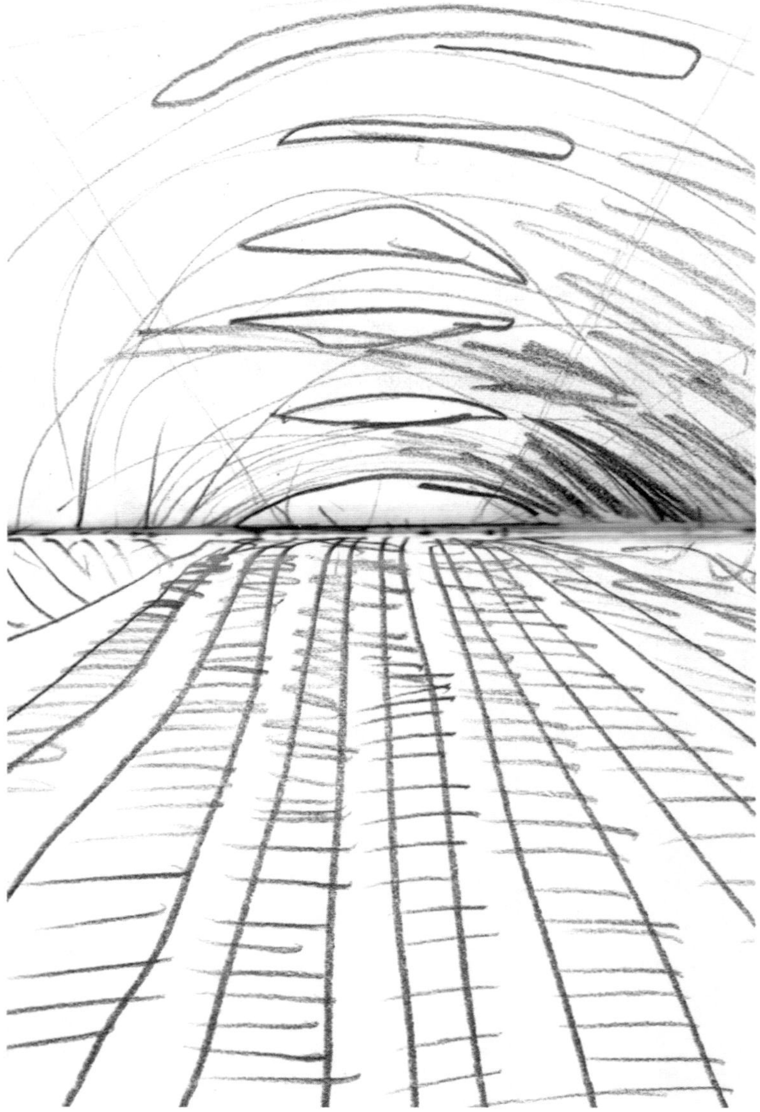

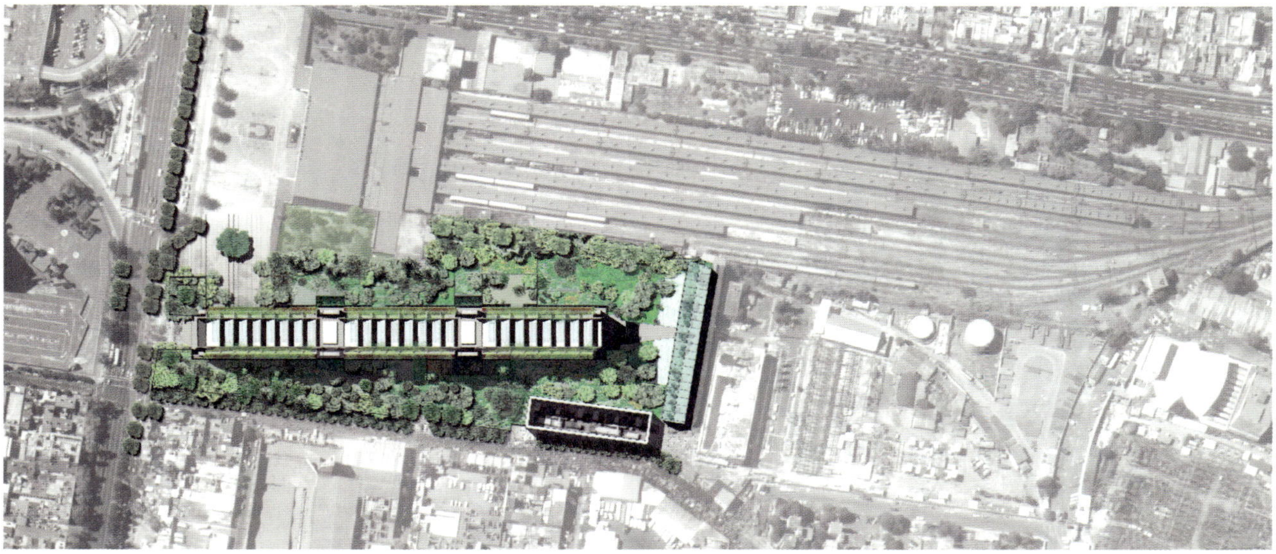

— At one point, full of optimism, we once thought of expanding the gardens of the library over the tracks and plaza of the Buenavista train station, of creating a public park along Avenida Insurgentes: a structure curved like one of Pier Luigi Nervi's roofs to form the outer shell of the bay for the trains, with the park climbing up its back.

ICA Office Building

With— Héctor Módica and Takemune Takuma

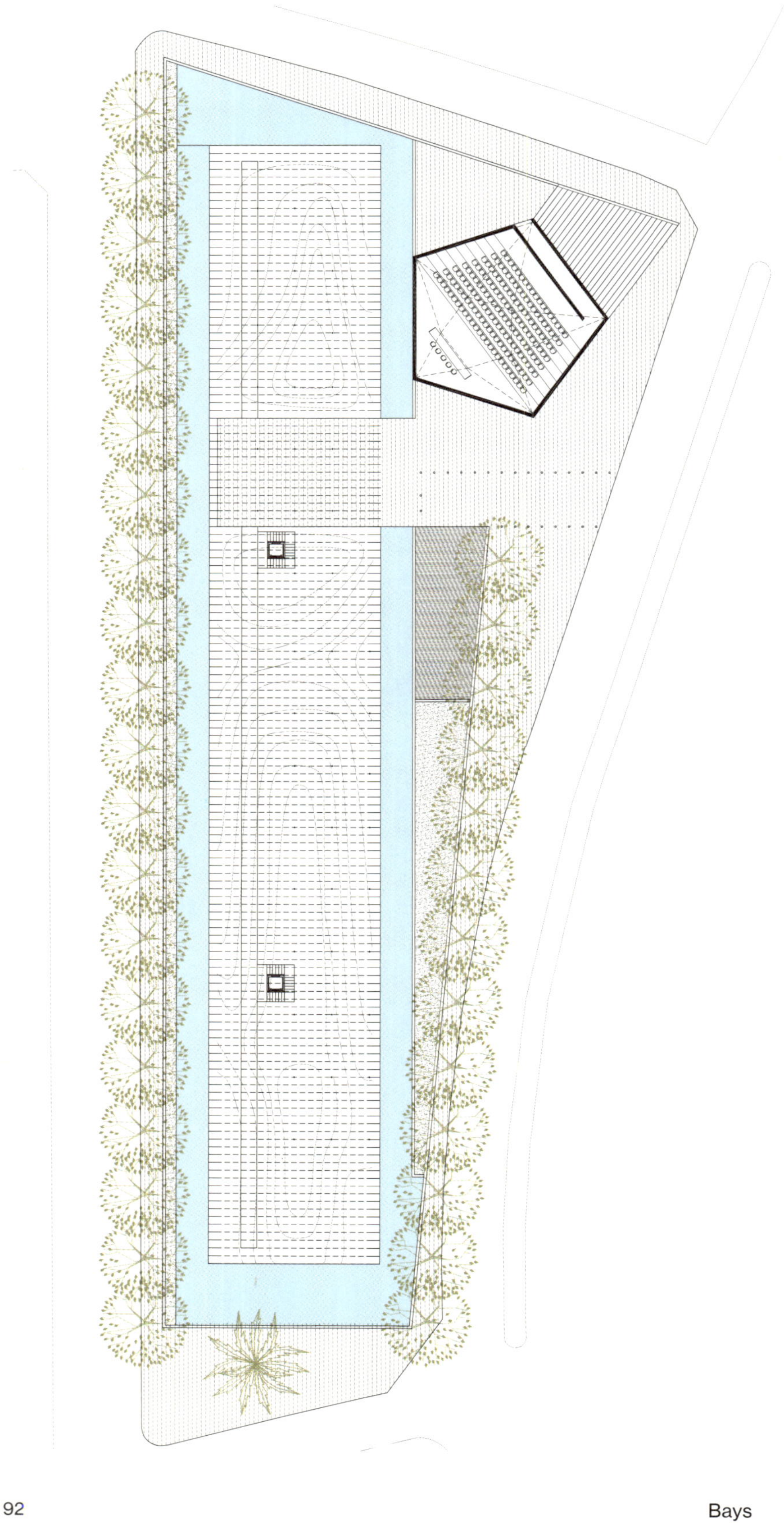

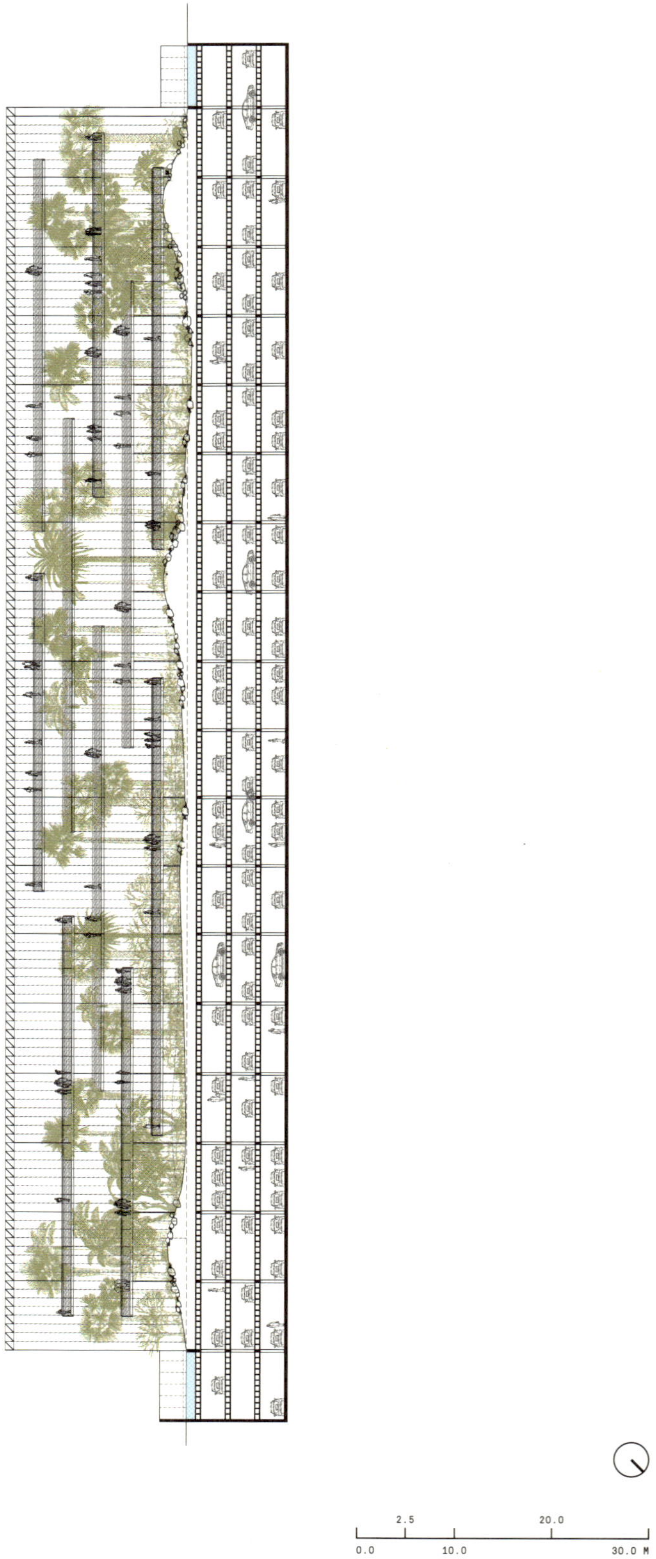

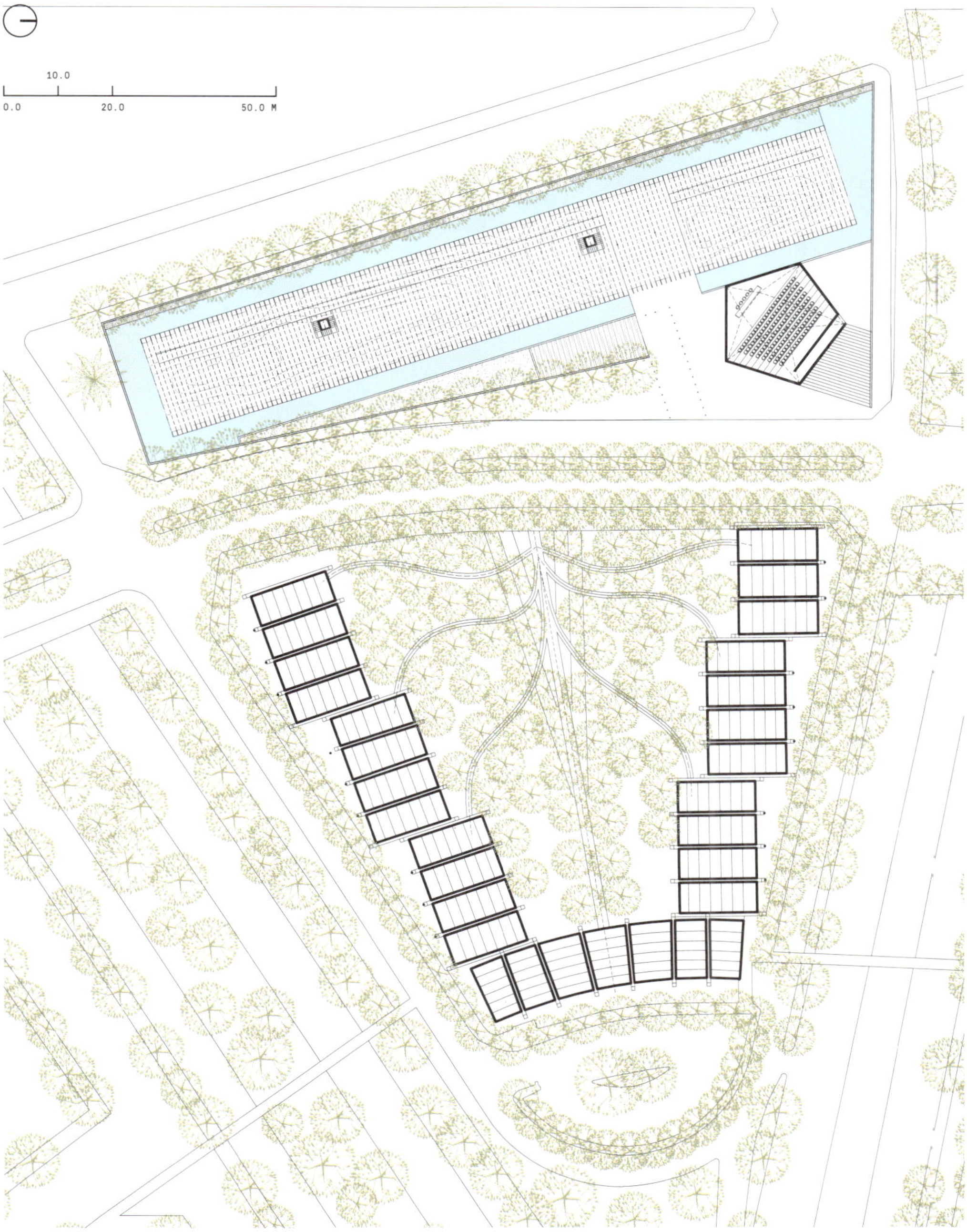

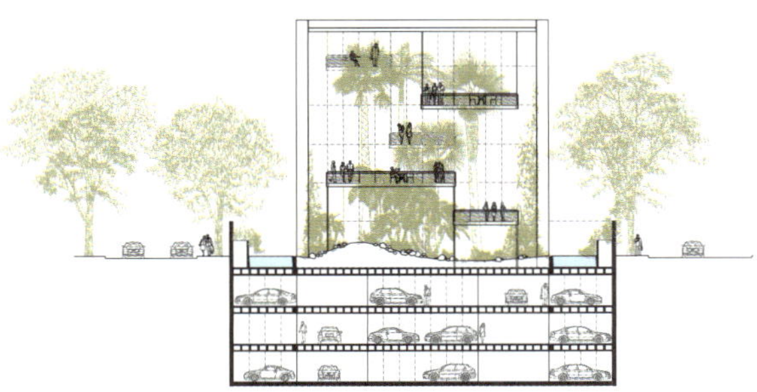

— A complement to the ICA office building constructed by José Villagrán in 1970, this container of open office spaces is designed as a greenhouse.

Texcoco Air Terminal
first version

With— Juan Cordero and Gustavo Lipkau

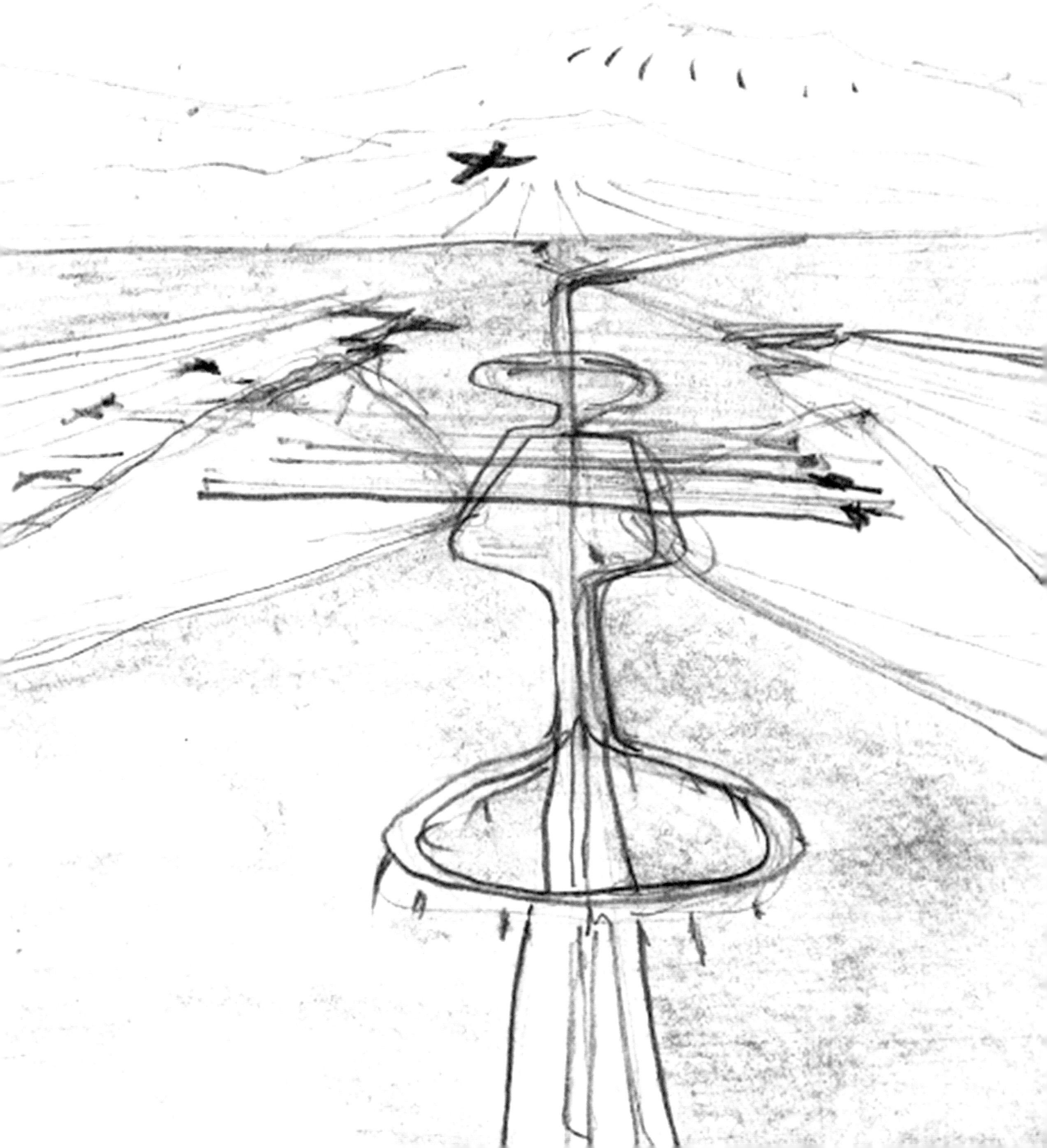

Texcoco Air Terminal. First version

Texcoco Air Terminal
second version

With— Emmanuel Ramírez
and Ignacio del Río

On an Islet / 2010

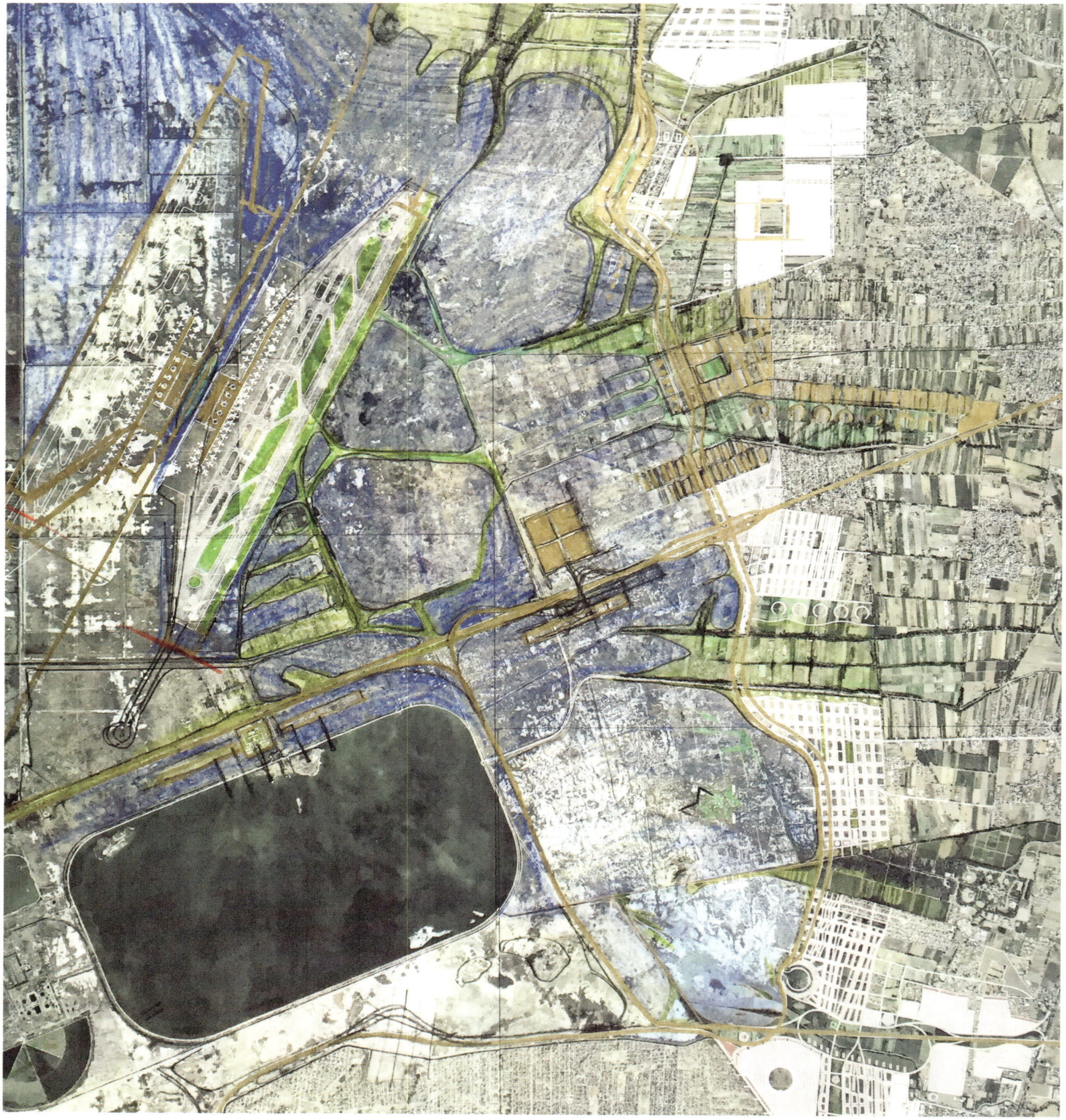

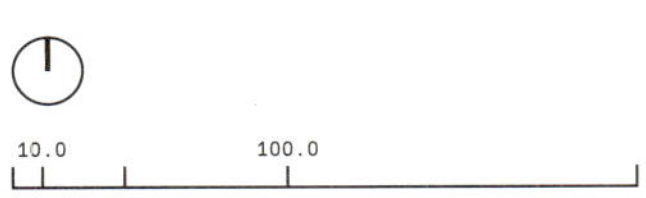

— After twenty-three years of governmental mismanagement in carrying out this project, I continue to believe that an airport combined with the environmental rehabilitation of the Texcoco zone is both feasible and desirable.

Texcoco Air Terminal
third version

With— Teodoro González de León
and David Martínez

On an Islet / 2014

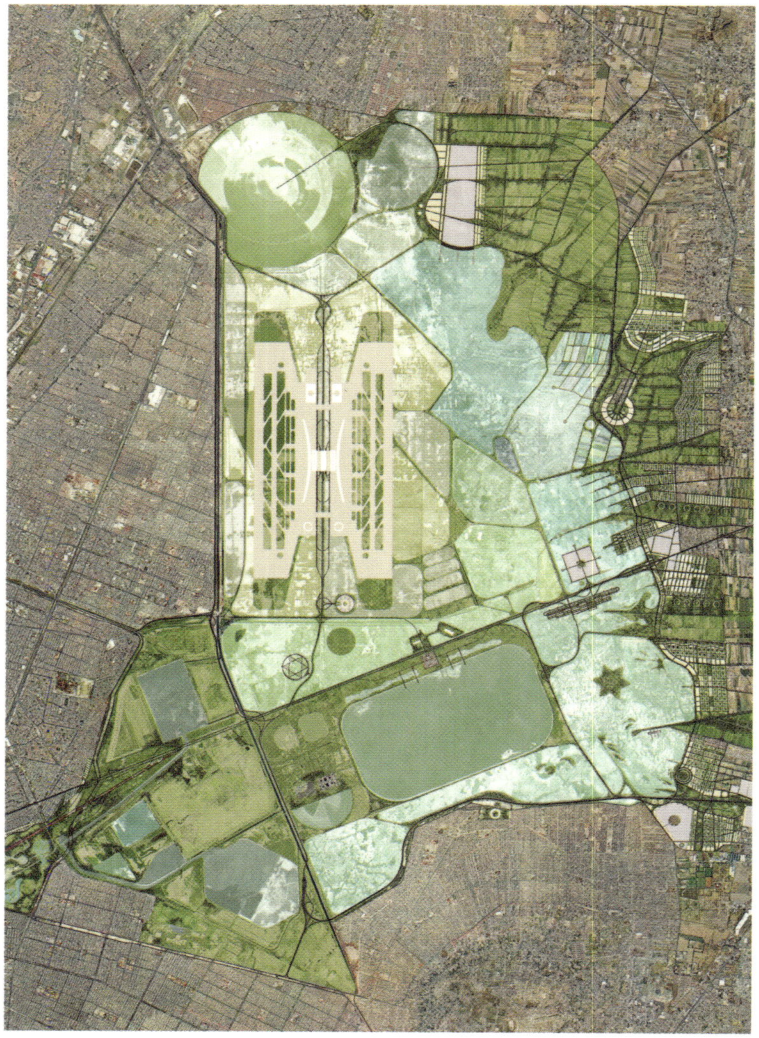

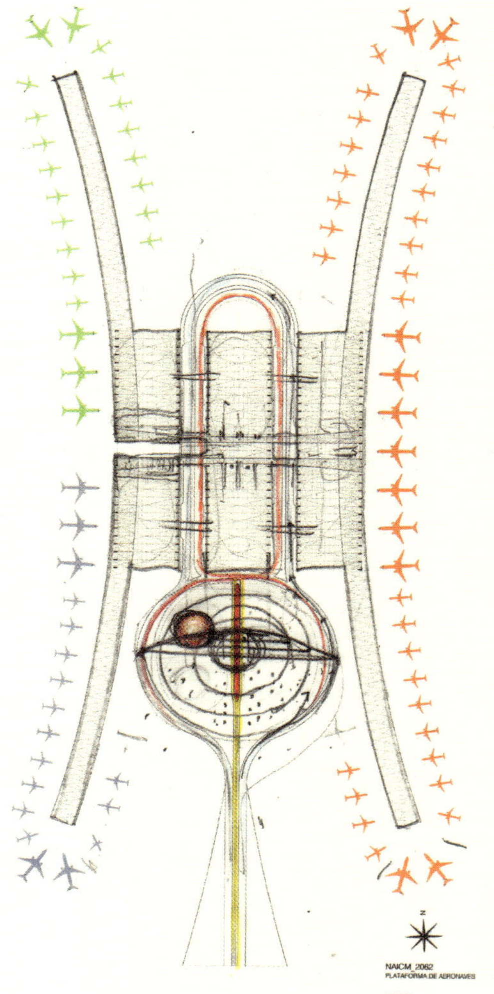

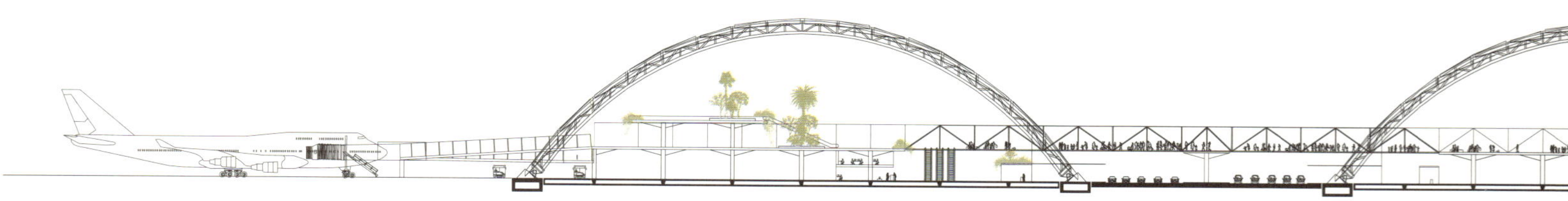

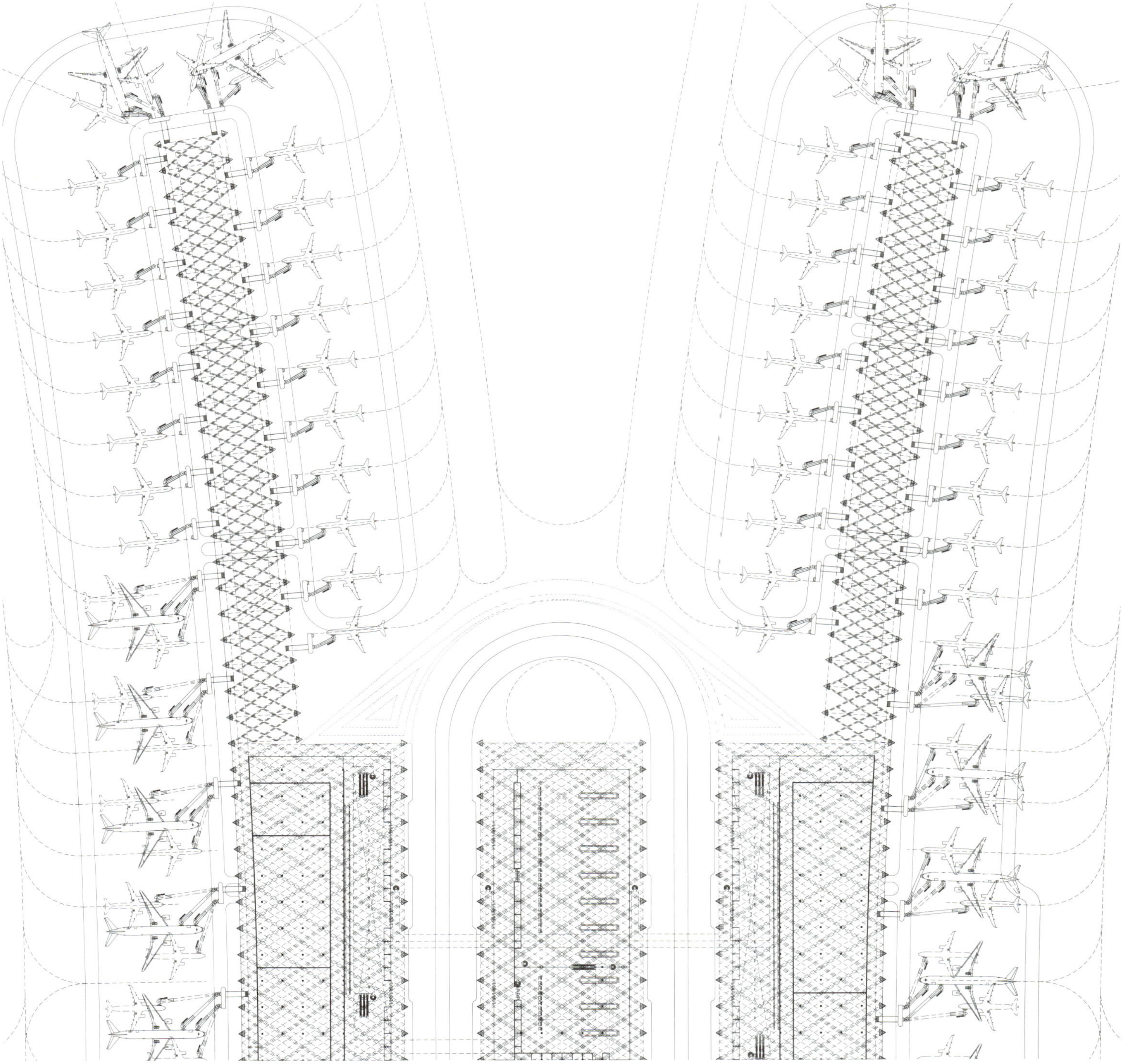

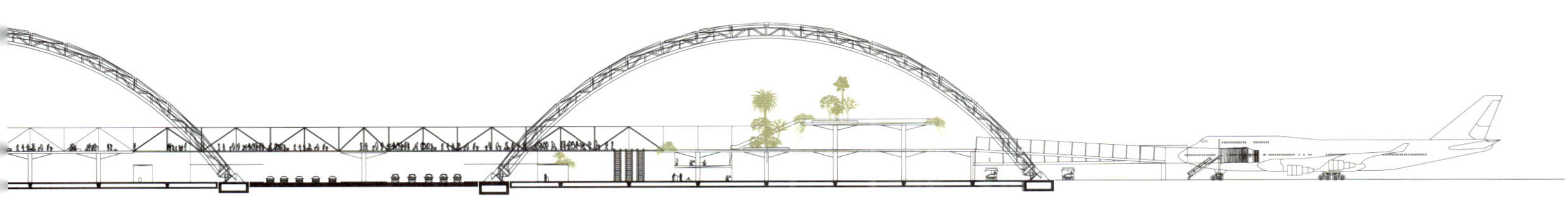

Texcoco Air Terminal. Third version

— Working together, the great Teodoro González de León and I designed this final version of an airport terminal that is unique of its kind, streaming arrivals along a central bay, with two important advantages. First of all, the ultra-light vaulted bays are on a single level, floating atop the former lakebed and rendering the construction economical, environmentally-friendly, and easy to erect. But more importantly, arrivals (and their circulation routes) are not relegated to a level below departures, as is usual in airports nowadays. As a result, absolutely all of the spaces have plenty of natural light and ventilation, with views of the sky and the surrounding landscape.

Salvaging Lake Texcoco

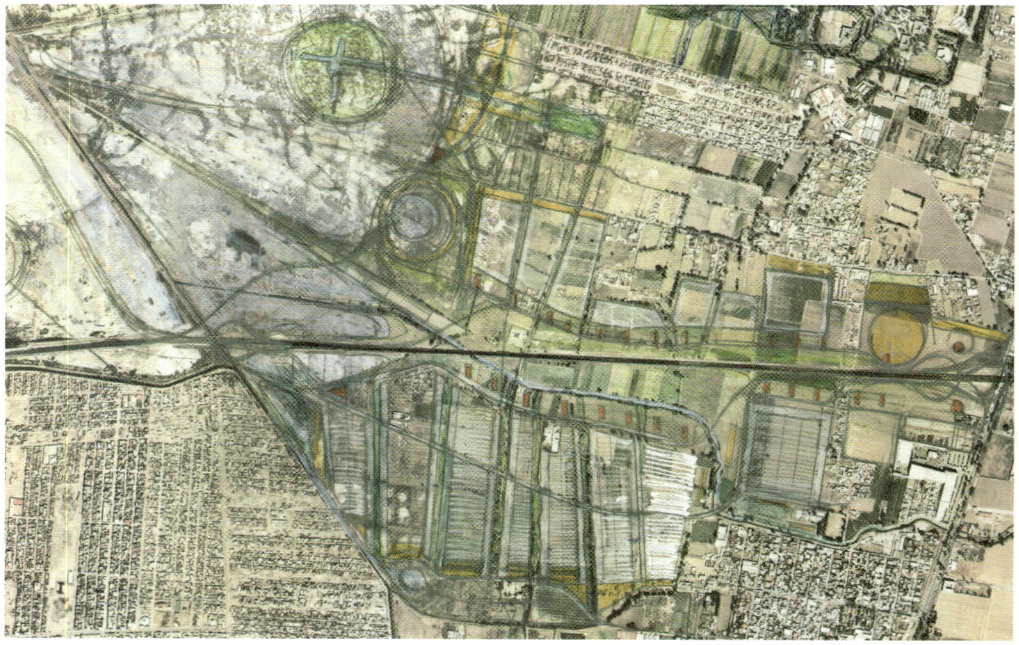

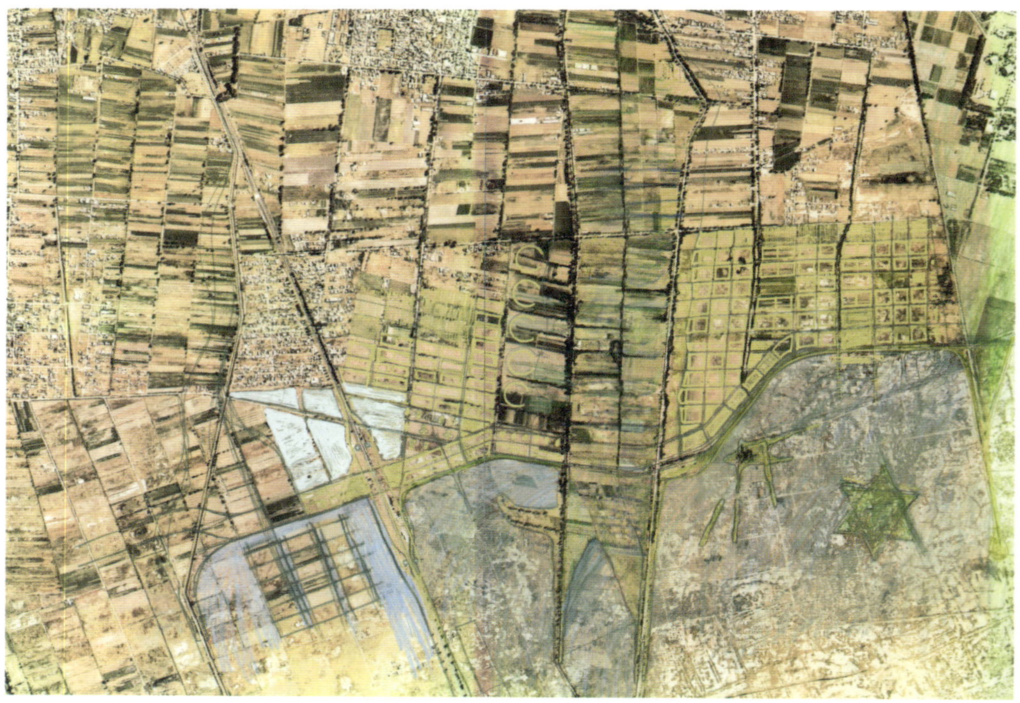

Environmental Benefits

- Rehydration of the subsoil.
- Increase in ambient humidity.
- Natural oxygenation produced by the lake.
- Creation of a natural barrier to the uncontrolled growth of the metropolis.
- Recovery of regional flora and fauna.
- Dissipation of atmospheric pollution.

Economic Benefits

- 12 million square meters available for urban development between the reserve zone and the lake.
- The possibility of "orchestrating" the growth of the city for the next twenty-five years.
- Development of approximately 80 square kilometers.
- Reactivation of the construction industry.

Social Benefits

- Positive impact on the economy and ecology of the valley.
- Improved infrastructure and services.
- Greater balance between the east and west of the city.
- Creation of a large public space.
- Increase in green areas.

Acapulco Airport
second version

With— Héctor Módica

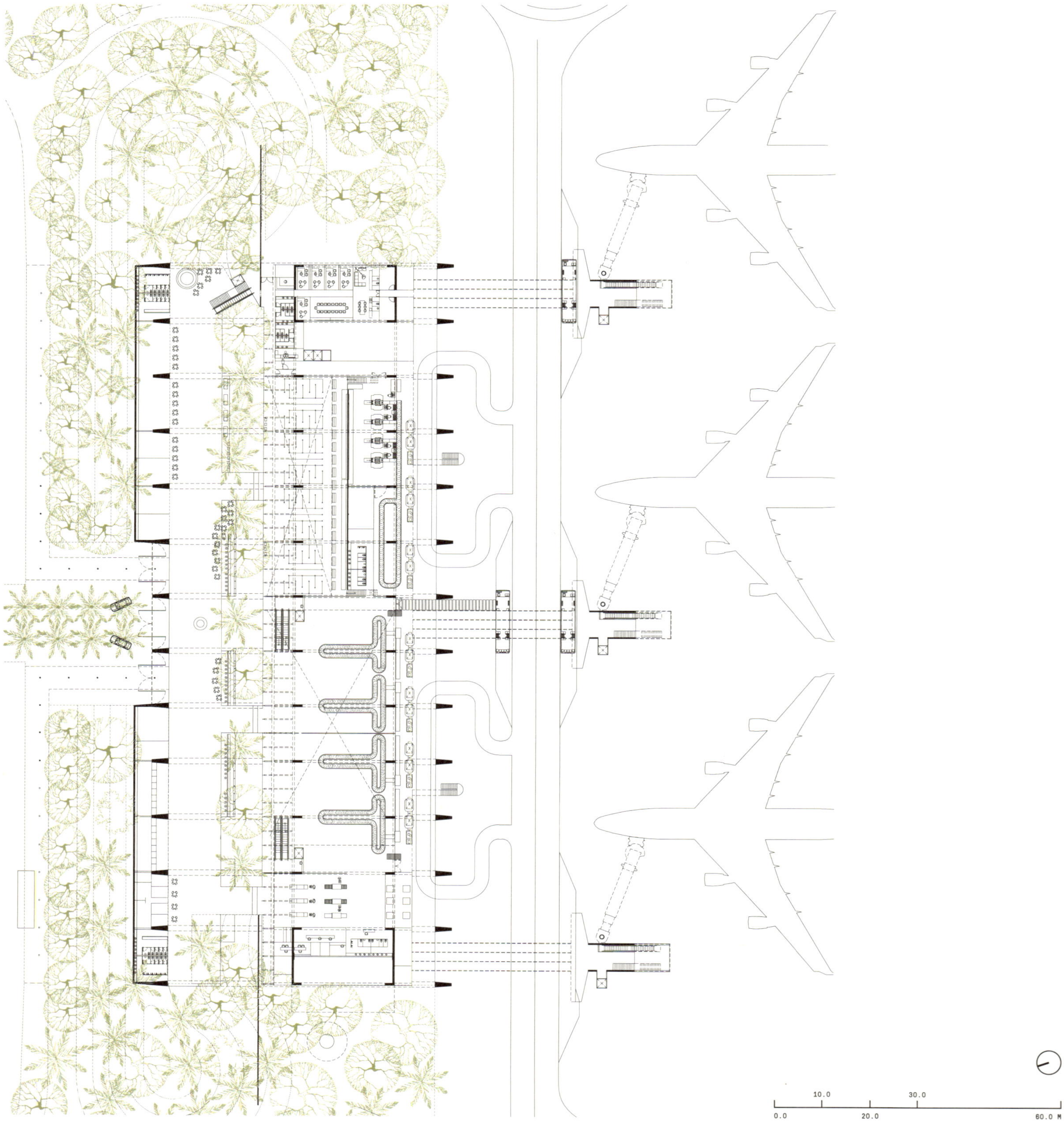

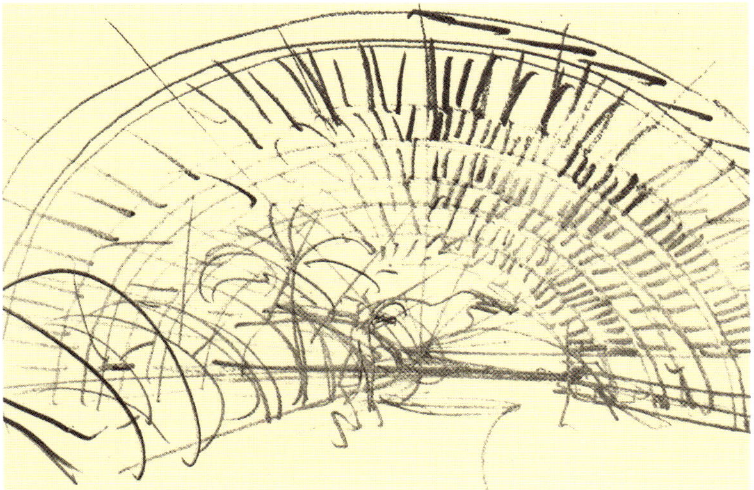

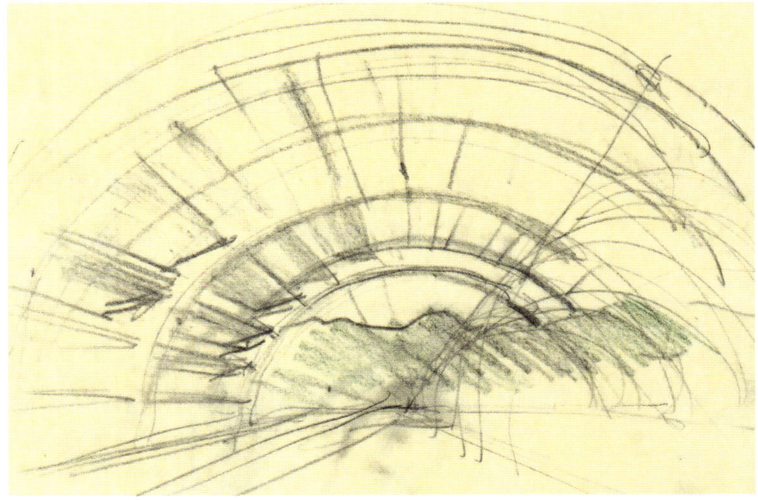

espejo
talud

Puerto Vallarta Airport

With— David Garza, Raquel Font, and Lucas Elizondo

— The Romans knew it: the most efficient form for covering a large space is a vault. In the nineteenth and twentieth centuries, we saw some astonishing examples in steel and concrete. Its efficacy is unquestionable. And the rotundity of the form elicits admiration.

Two versions of vaulted naves for two airport terminals on the Pacific coast —in Acapulco and in Puerto Vallarta— illustrate the extraordinary unity of the space, its structural logic, and its linear layout, ideal for marshaling and "filtering" passengers.

Making for maximum energy efficiency, the vault within a vault creates a shaded, ventilated transition space with no need for air conditioning, to be used exclusively for the documentation, baggage pickup, and final boarding areas.

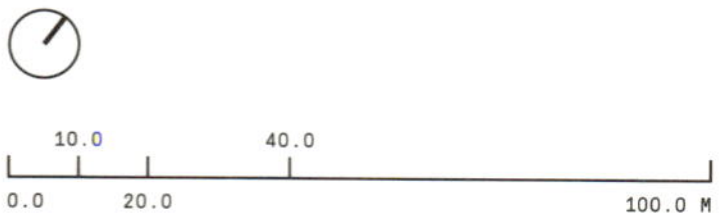

Total Space

All through the history of architecture, the quest for total space has been a constant, from the legendary temple of Solomon to the Pantheon in Rome, from Étienne-Louis Boullée's cenotaph for Newton to the gardener's house and cemetery designed by Claude-Nicolas Ledoux for the Ideal City of Chaux, not to mention the total theater of Walter Gropius, Hans Poelzig's great playhouse in Berlin, Louis Kahn's library for the Phillips Exeter Academy in New Hampshire, or his National Parliament House in Dhaka, Bangladesh. Alberto Kalach started from these expressions of total, self-absorbed spaces to create his own proposal for the library in Guadalajara, consisting of a sphere-shaped void within a cube, or his series of experiments in the emotional handling of light in churches, synagogues, and other spaces for withdrawal and reflection.

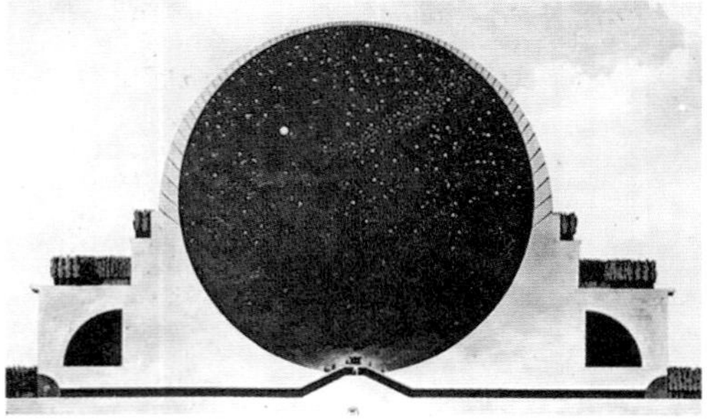

Étienne-Louis Boullée.
Cenotaph for Newton (1784)

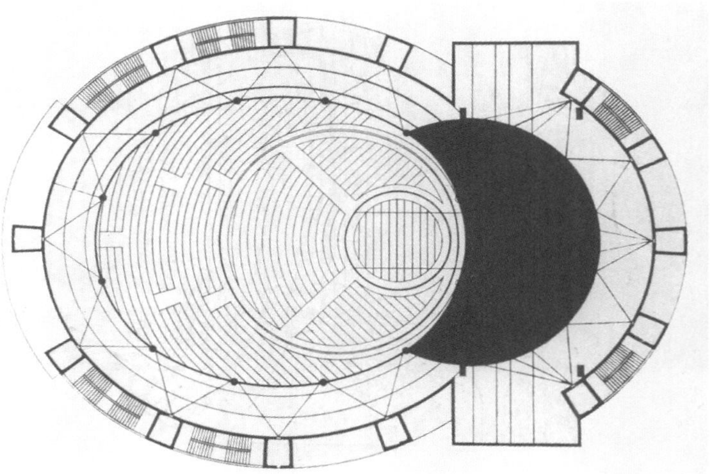

Walter Gropius. Total Theater (1927)

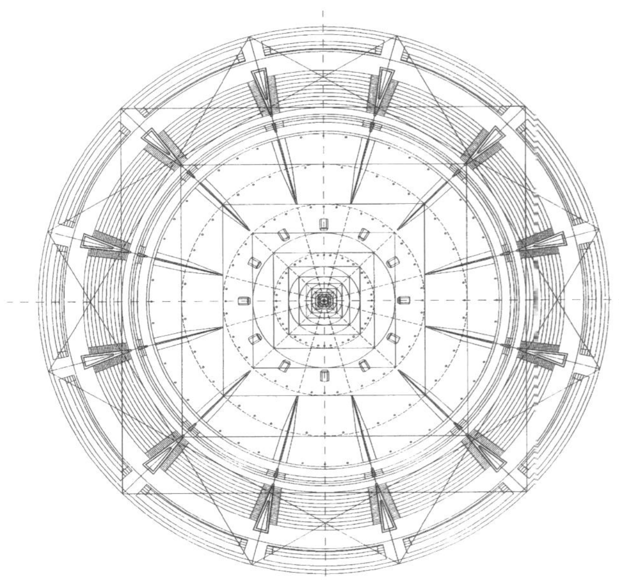

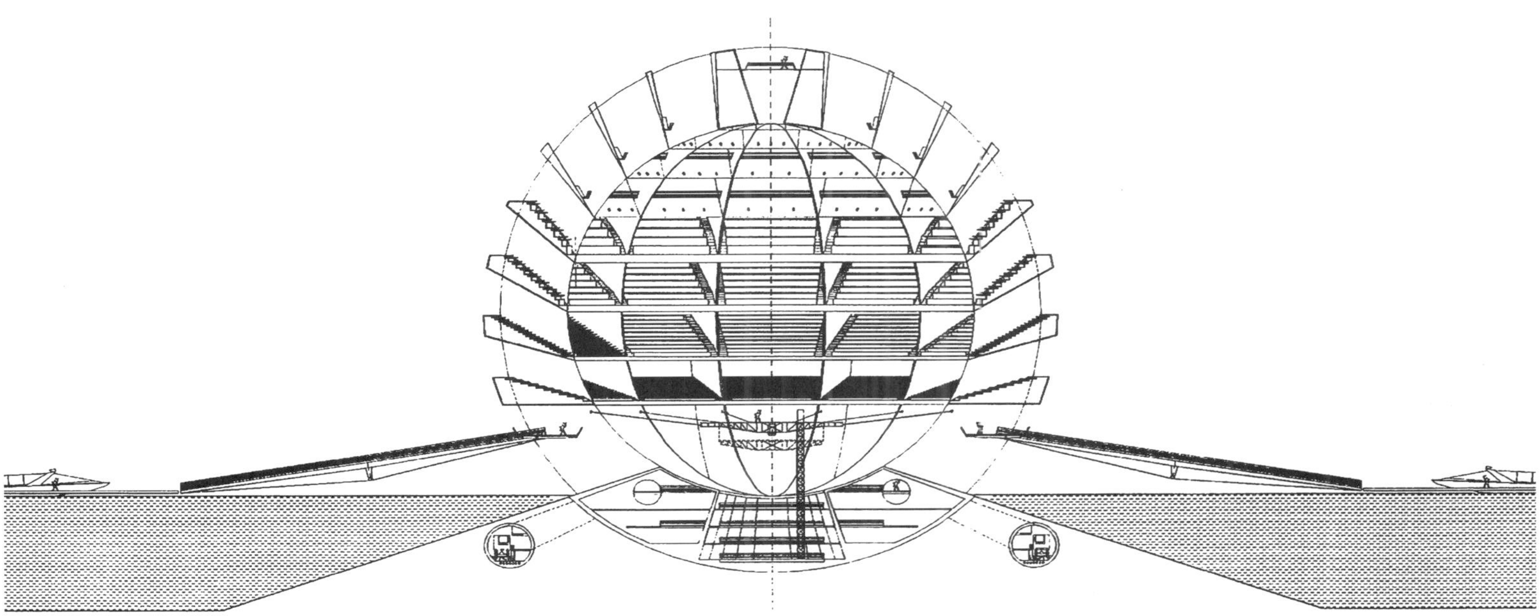

Bays

Library in Guadalajara

With— Juan Palomar

Guadalajara / 2005

— The Exeter Academy Library is a sphere within a cube, a total space that throws function into relief. Inspired by this work, we drew up a proposal for the library of the Universidad de Guadalajara.

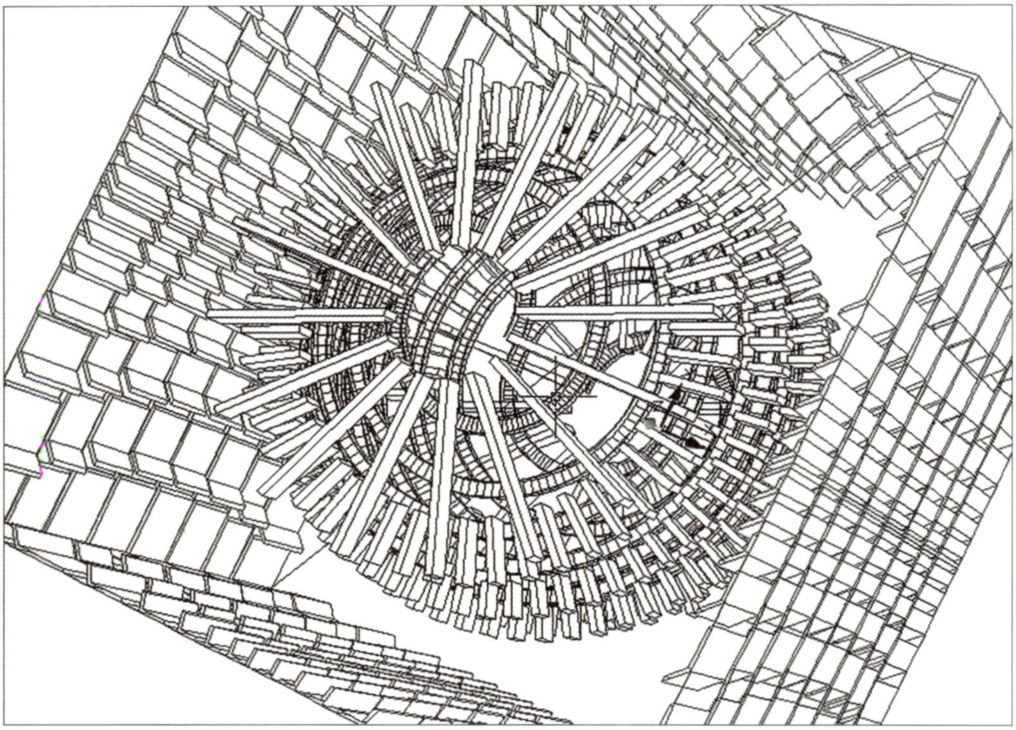

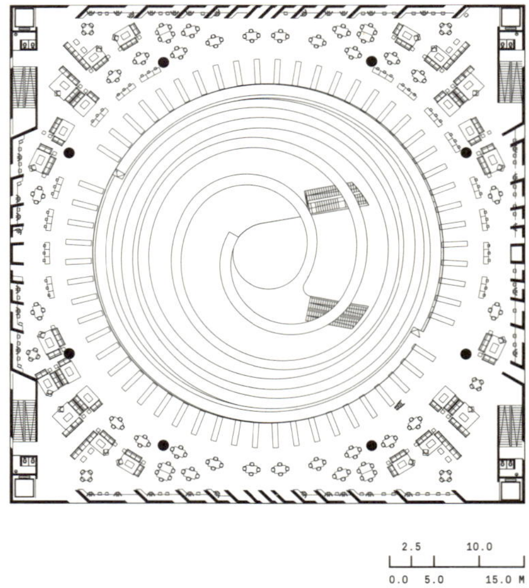

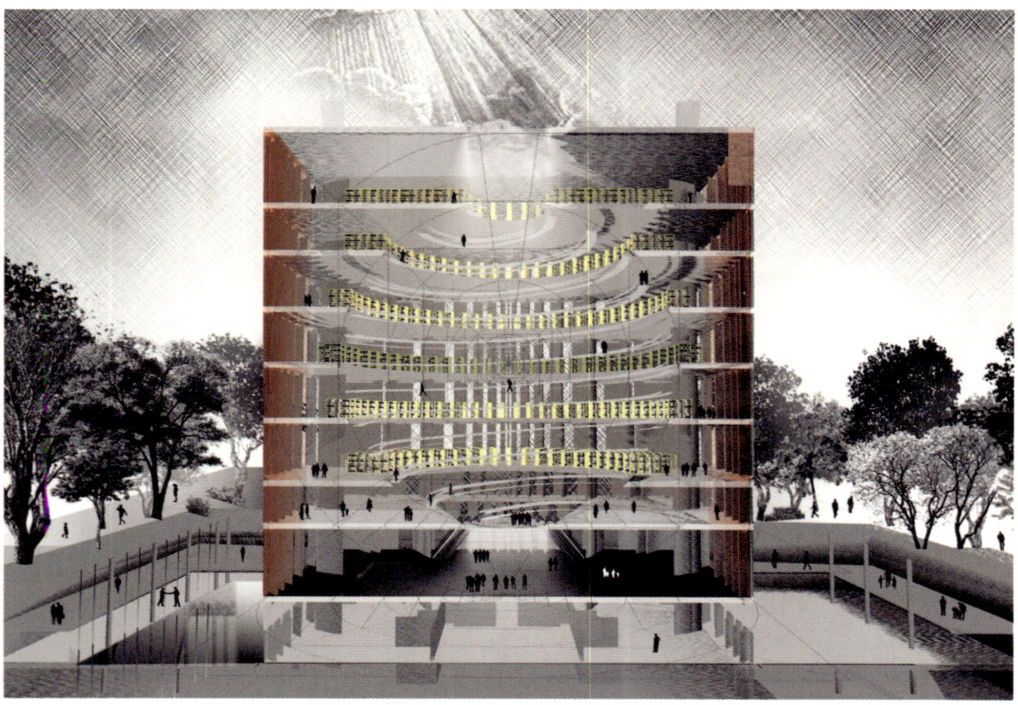

Louis Kahn. Exeter Academy Library (1971)

Maguen David Synagoge

With— Felipe Buendía, Anja Flesh, Julio González, Juan Palomar, Adriana León, and Gustavo Lipkau

Mexico City / 2005

Louis Kahn. Hurva Synagogue (1968), Jerusalem

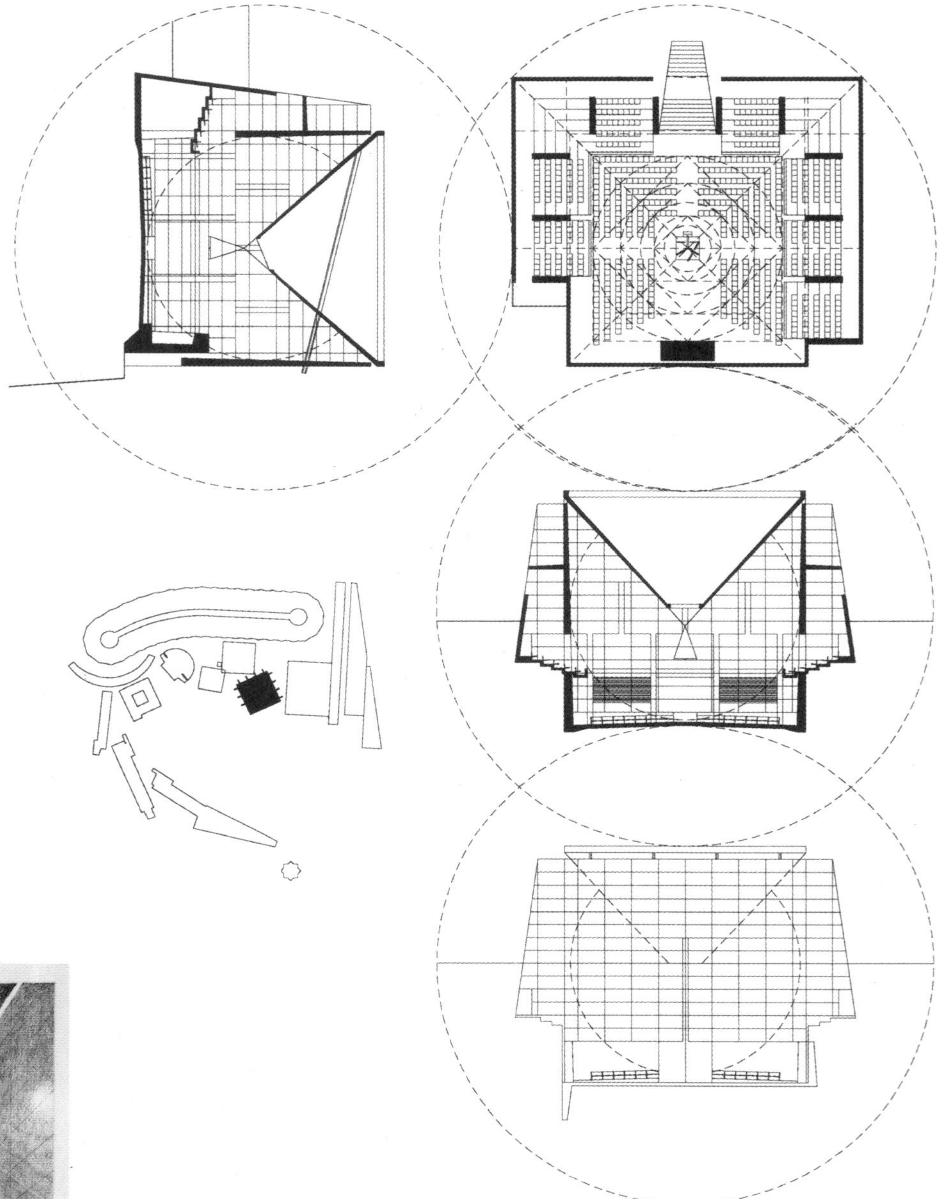

Insectarium

With— Iván Ramírez

Mexico City / 2008

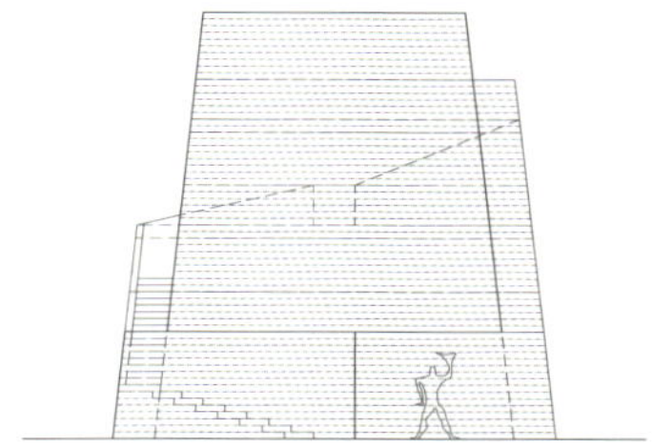

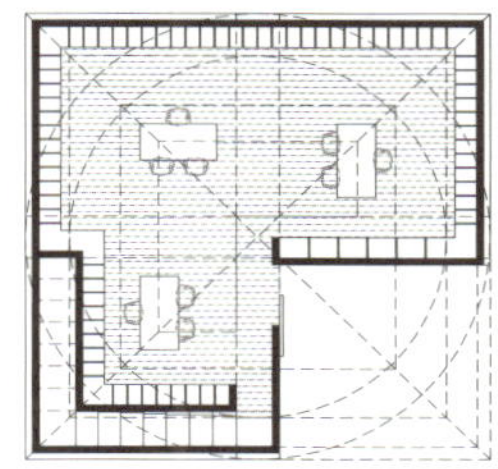

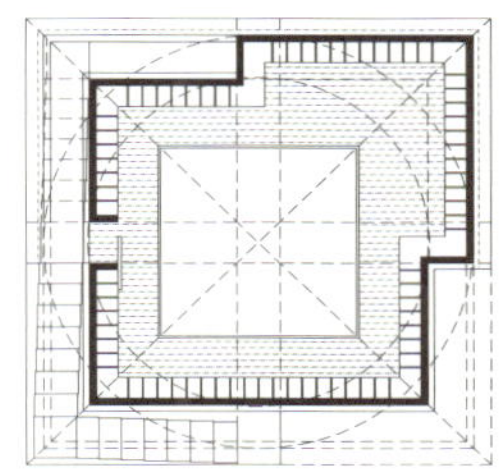

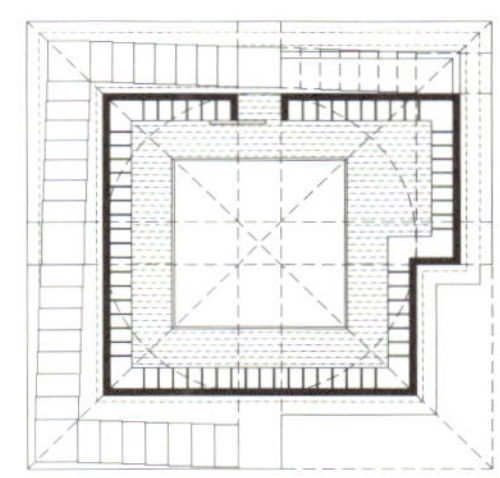

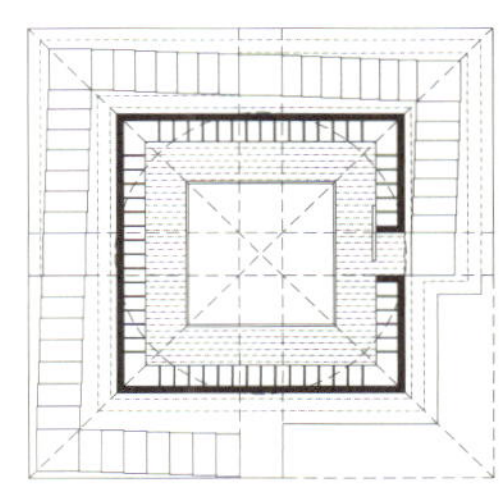

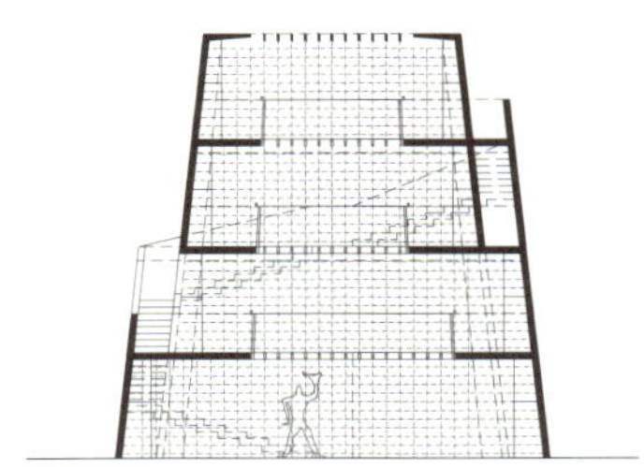

0.0 2.5 5.0 10.0 M

Monte Sinaí Synagoge

With— Alberto Kably and Jair Laiter

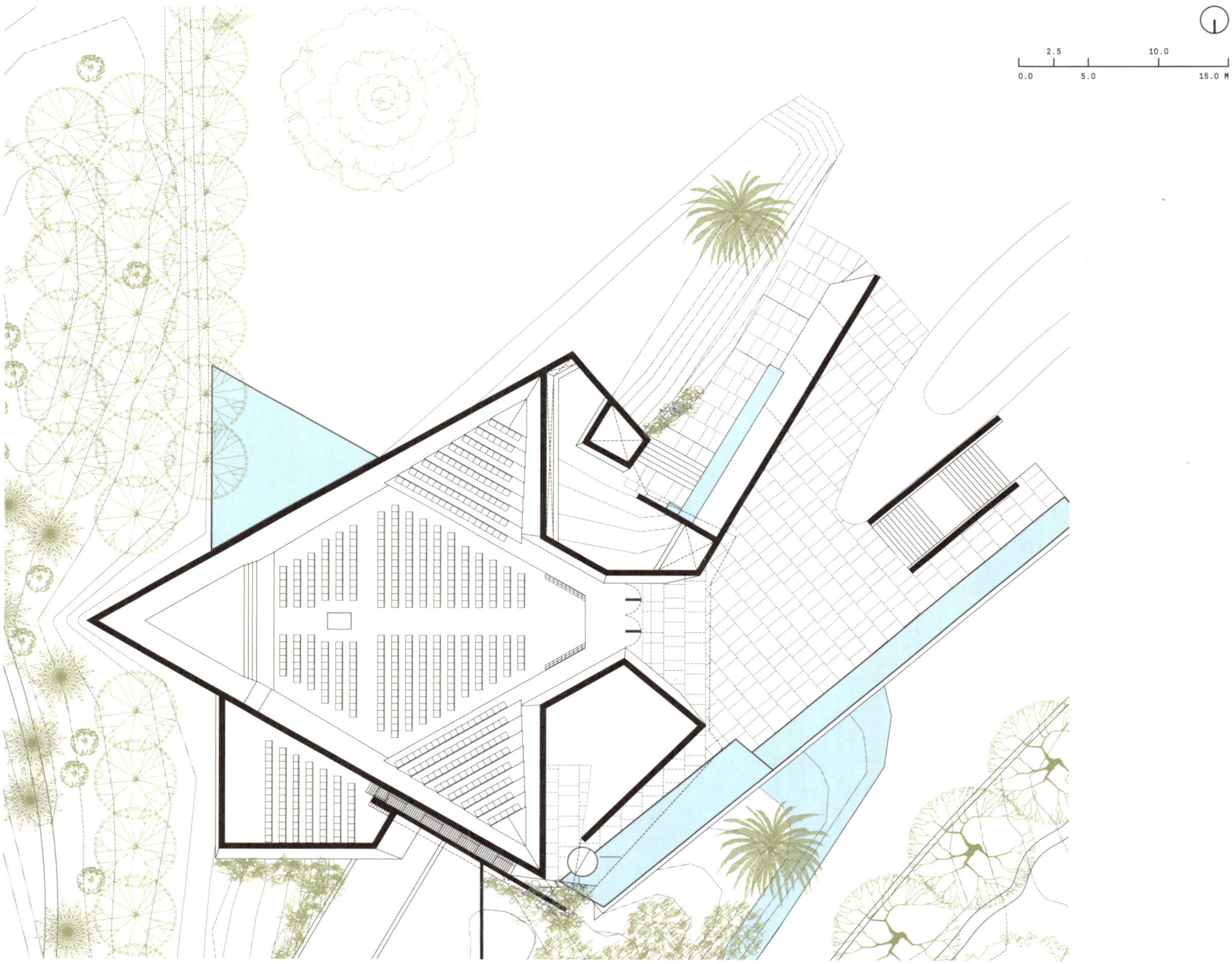

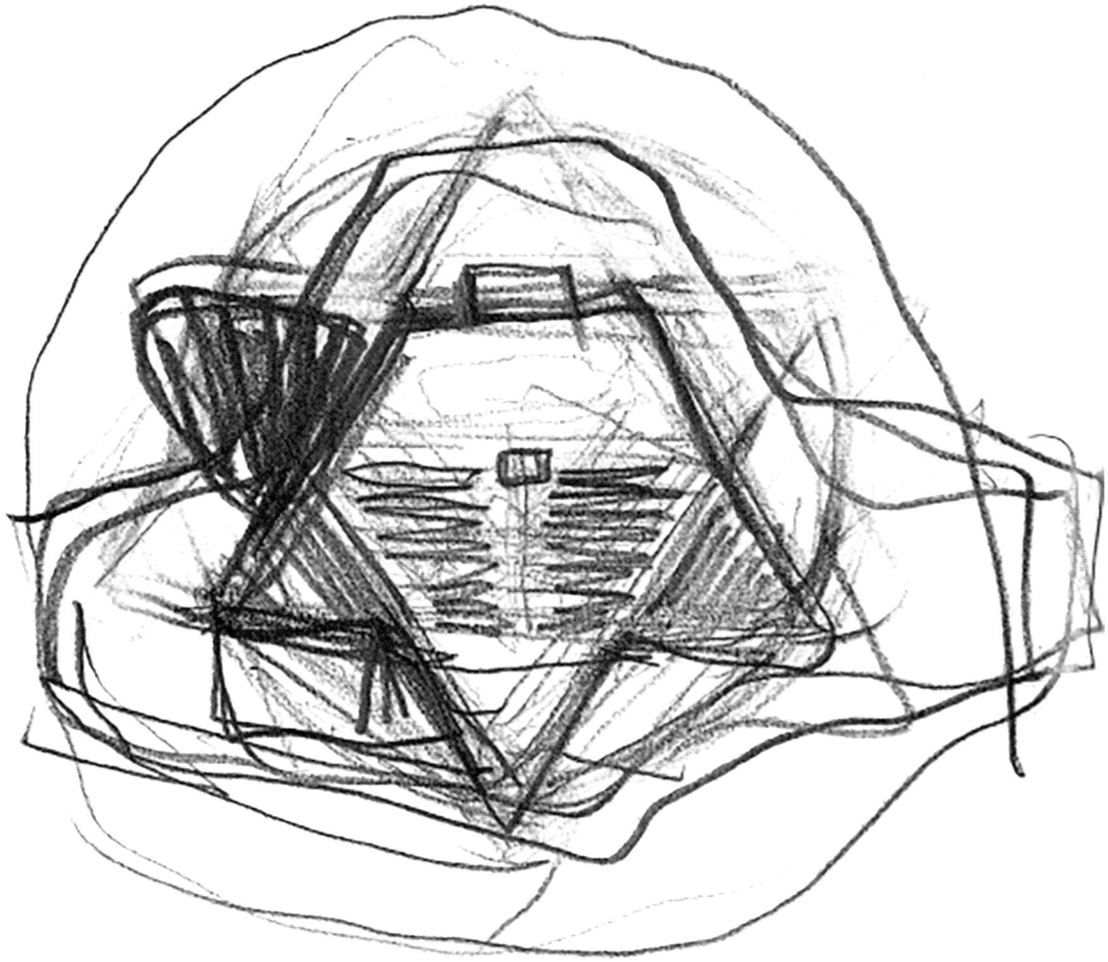

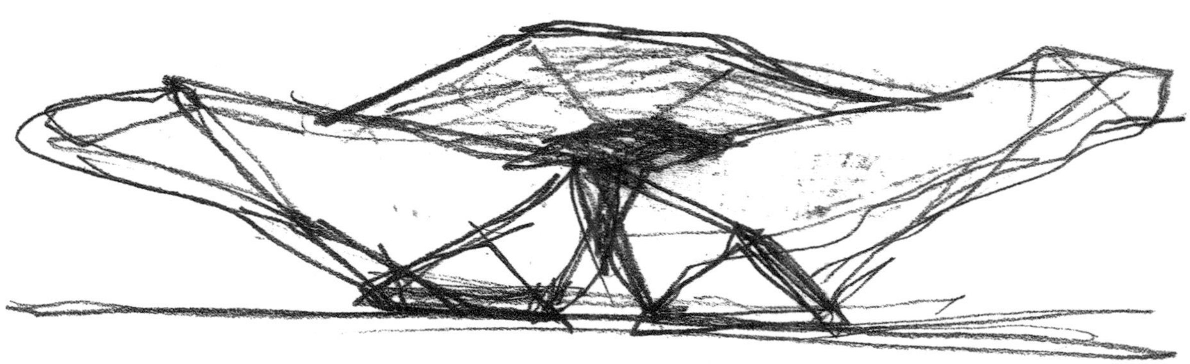

Q-1 Church

Querétaro / 2015

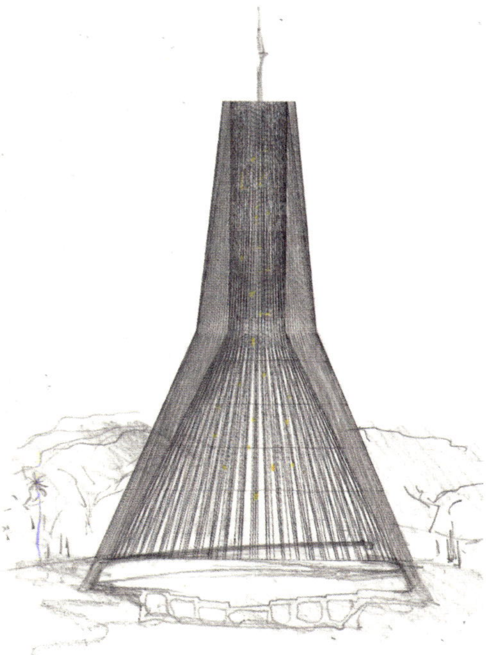

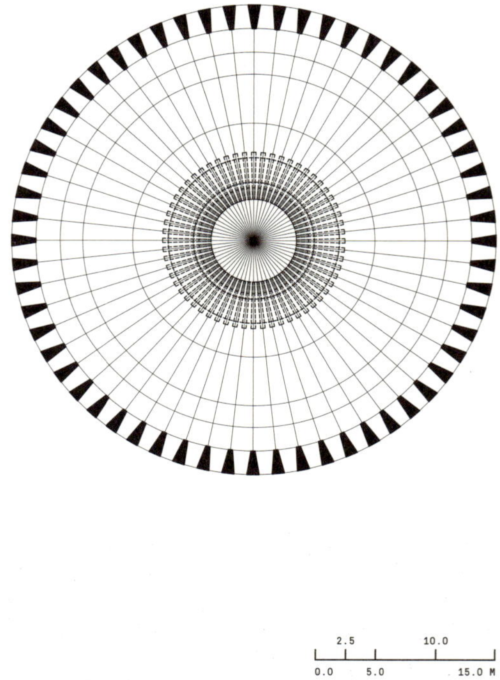

Q-2 Church

— A cathedral in a mountain in the city of Querétaro, in central Mexico. The plan and structure are determined by structural cylinders of reinforced concrete, arranged in a geometrical pattern. The cathedral offers a majestic spectacle of natural light flooding in.

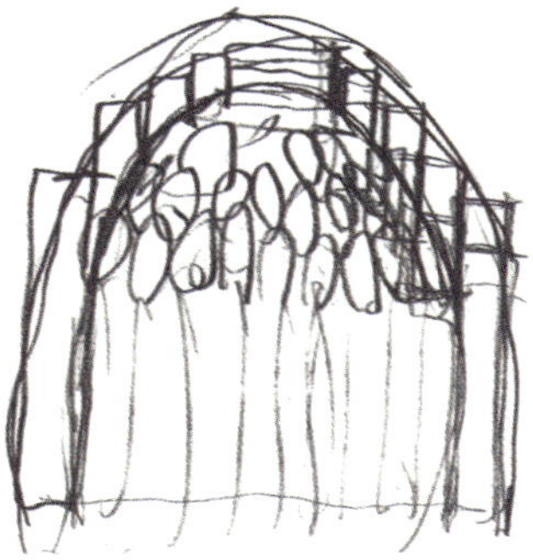

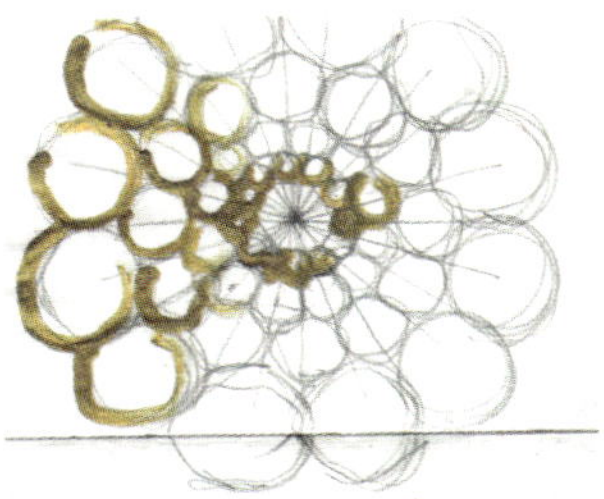

Meditation Space

With— Xavier González and Raquel Font

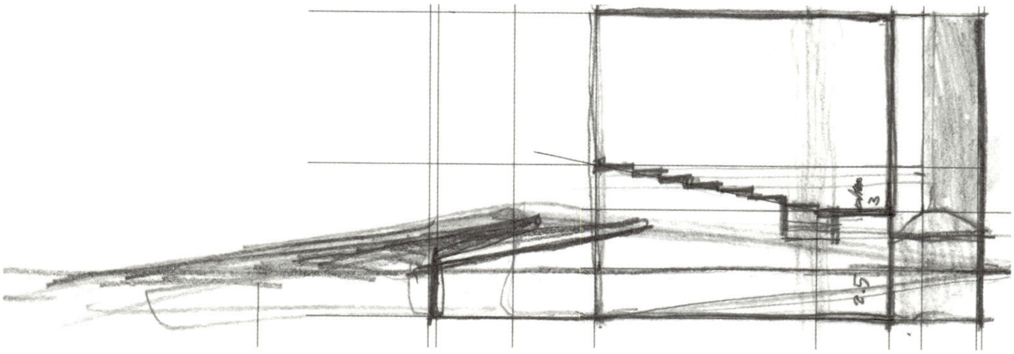

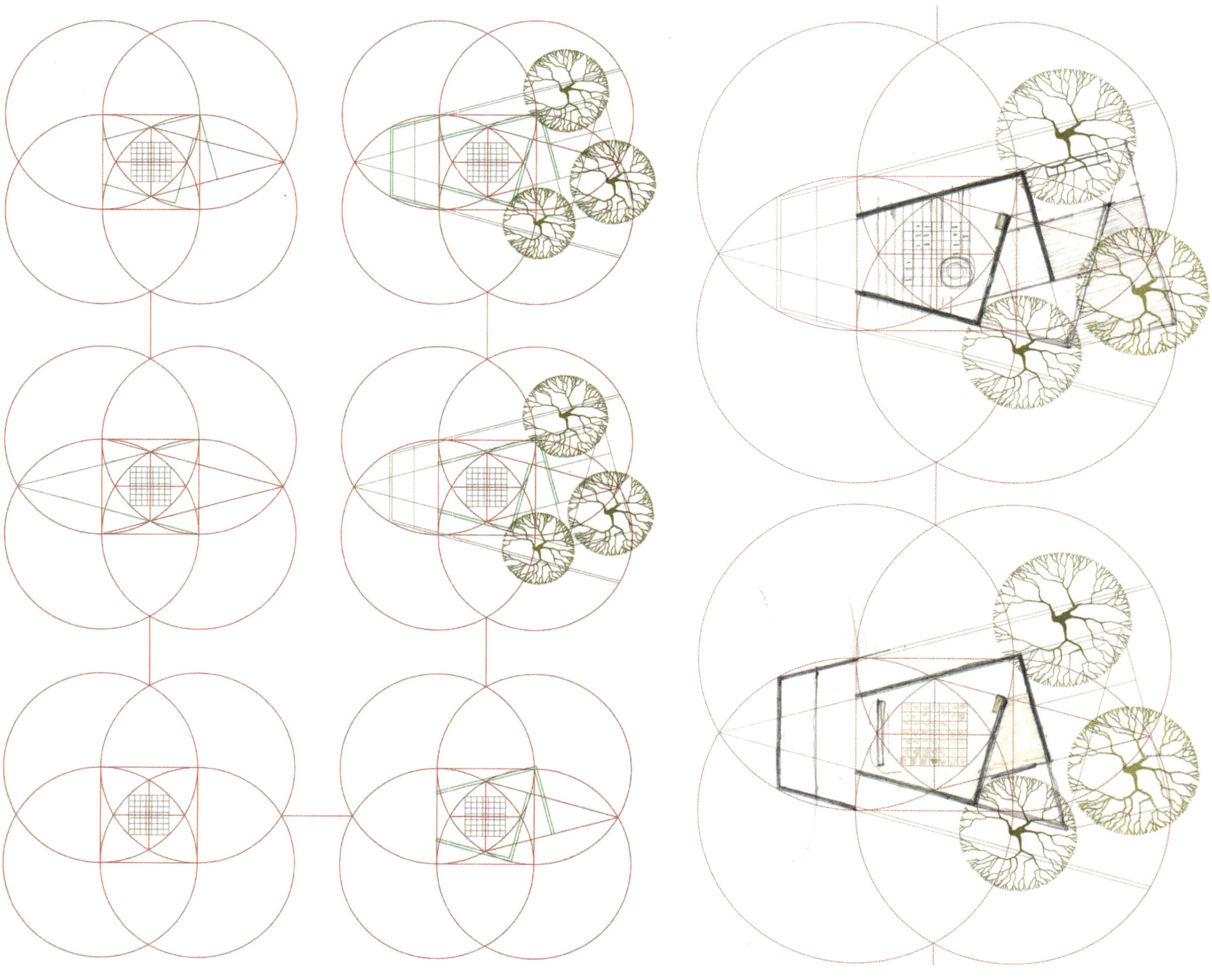

The meditation space is, above all, an observatory of views and framings of the distant mountains, as well as of the changing light of its interior.

Toscano Theater
in memoriam Nacho Toscano

With— David Garza

Oaxaca / 2019

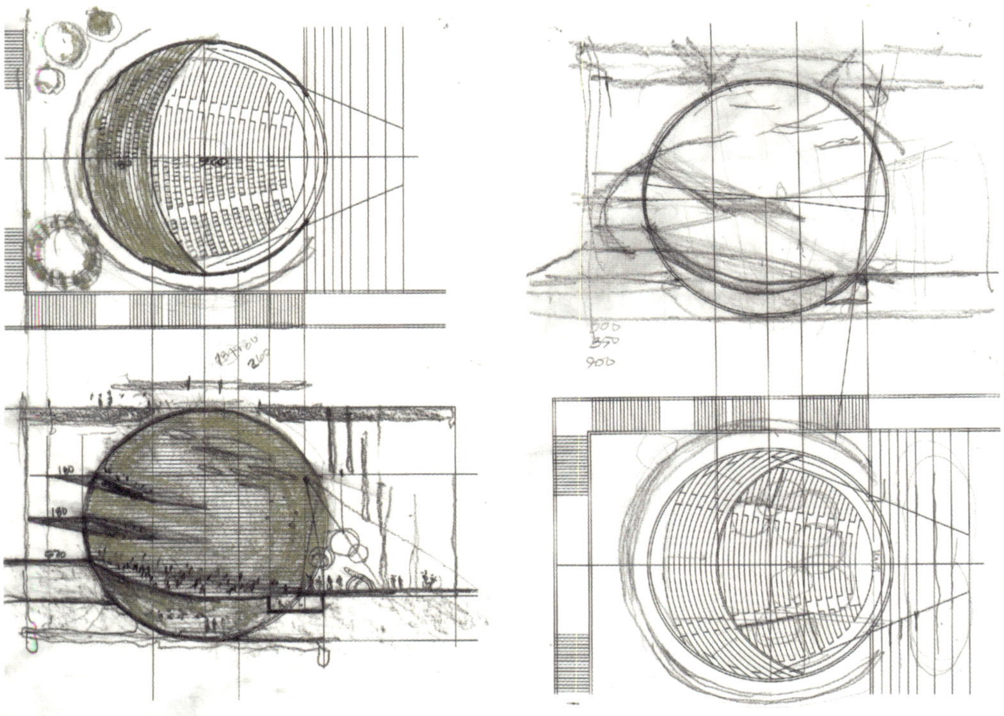

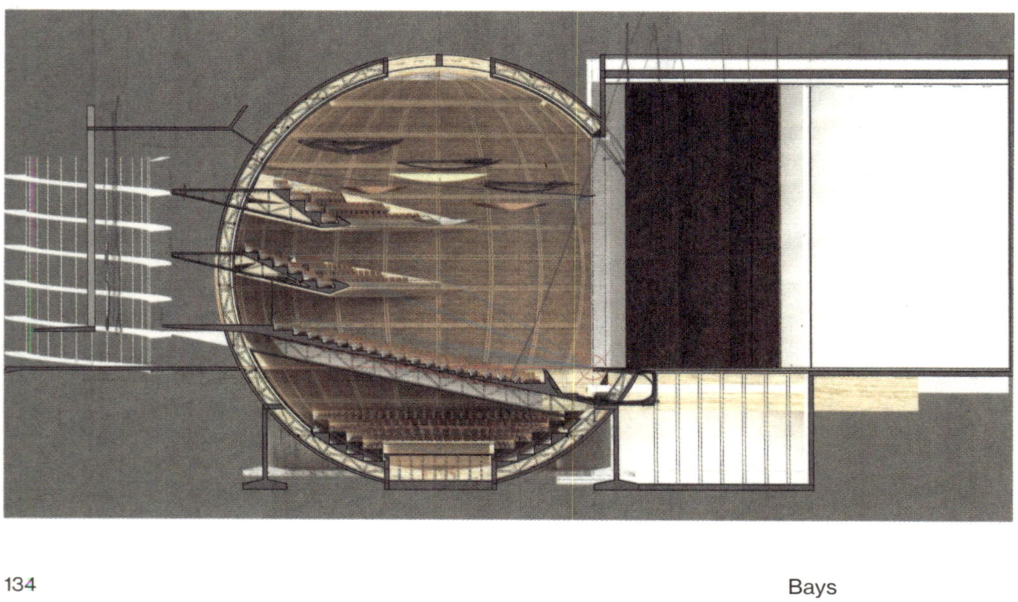

Mijares Variations

A series of buildings derived from the geometry and expression of a single material: exposed concrete brick. The result of the presence of a local brick factory, they are also inspired by the arches of Roman baths (*thermae*) and the mosques of Istanbul, where Ottoman architecture meets the European Renaissance, by Bruno Taut's glass pavilion and the catenary structures of Antoni Gaudí, by the patios of Rogelio Salmona and, above all, by the compositional logic of Carlos Mijares.

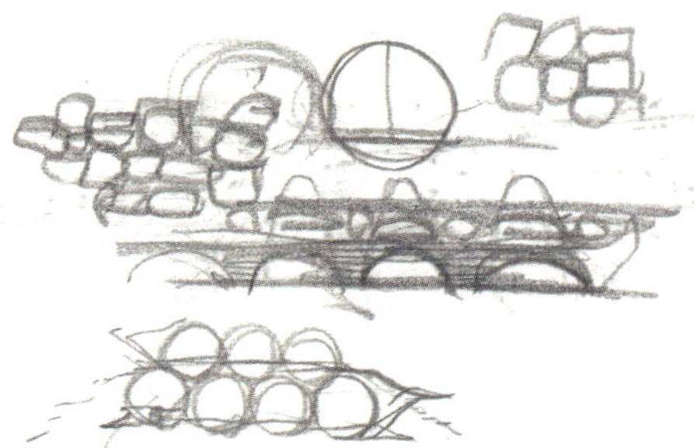

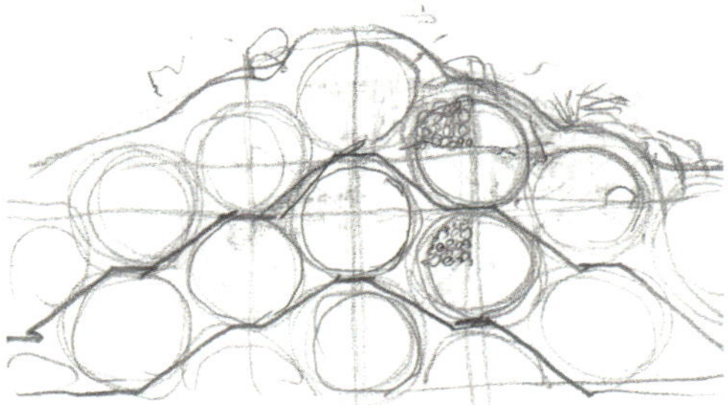
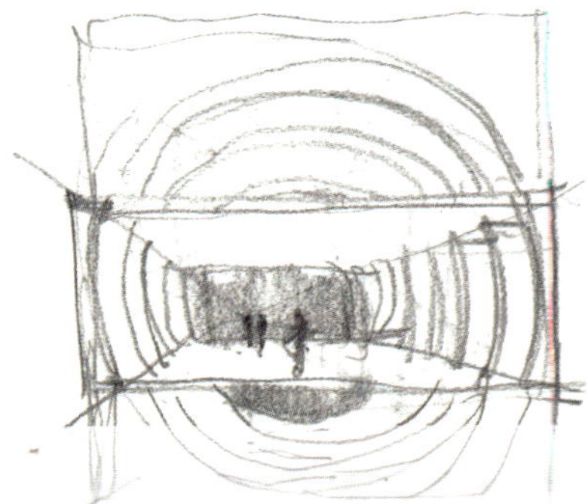
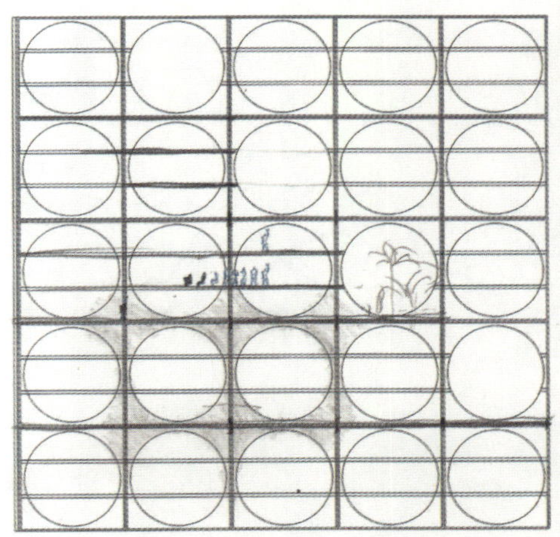
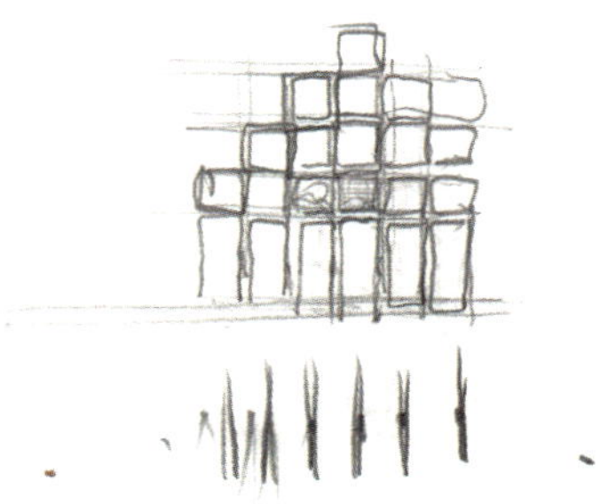

Santa Cruz Chapel

Con— Roberto Silva

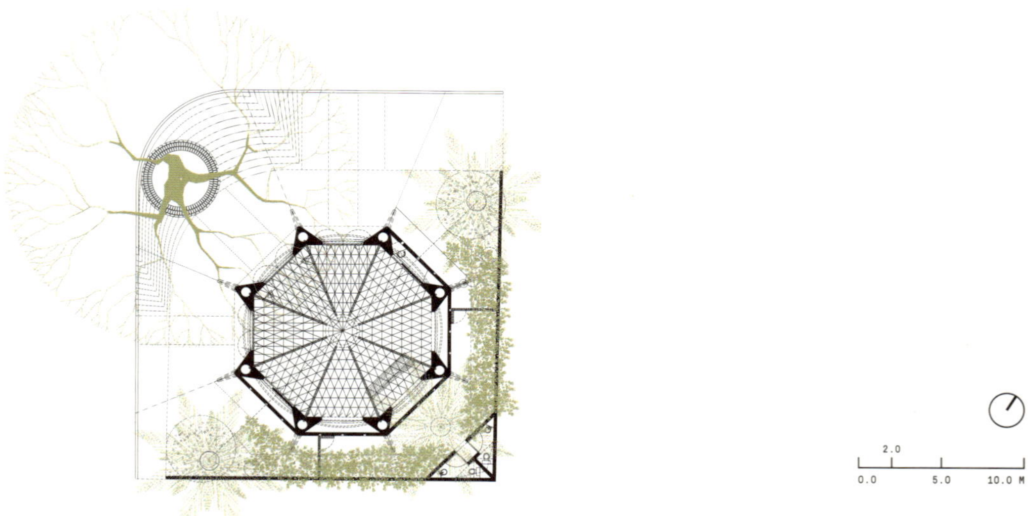

Emiliano Zapata Primary School

With— Roberto Silva

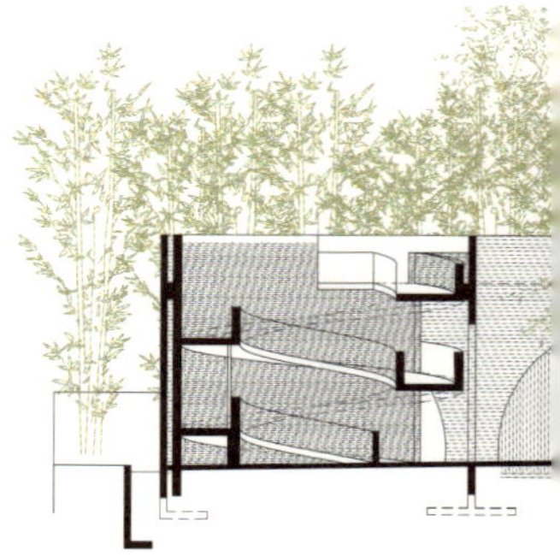

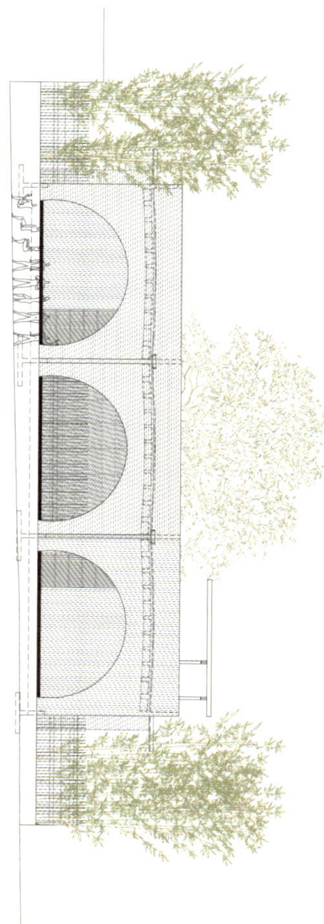

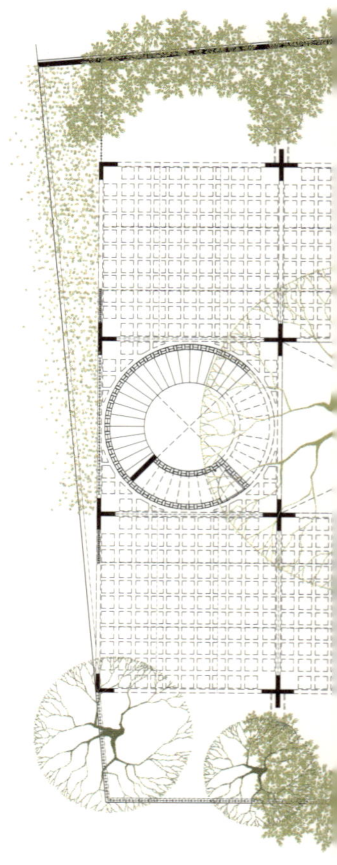

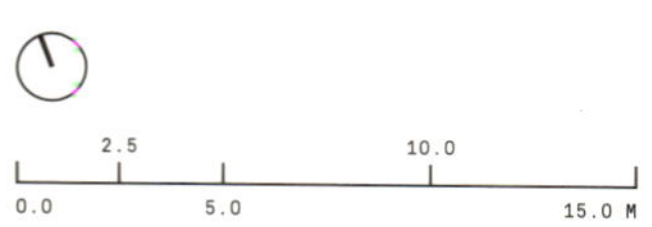

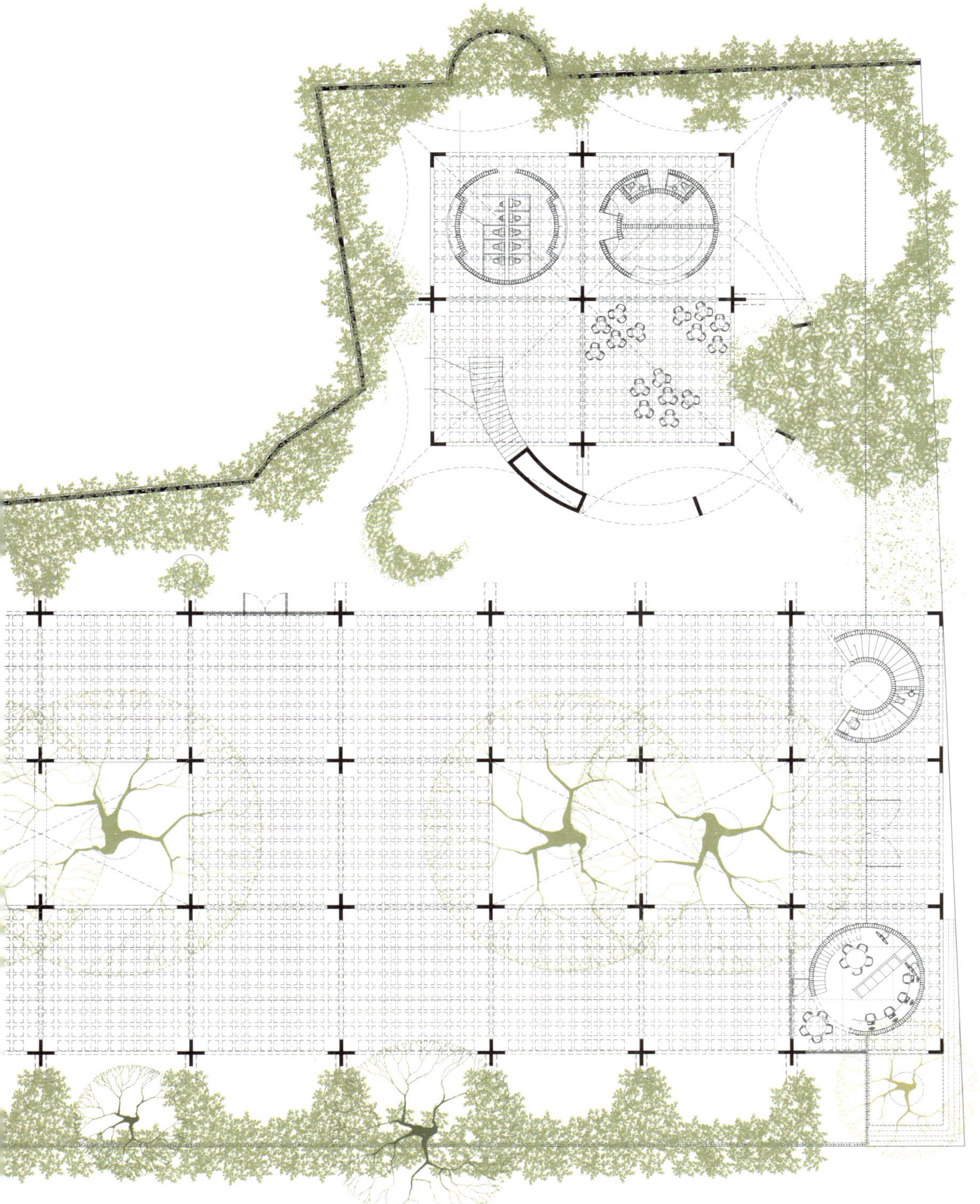

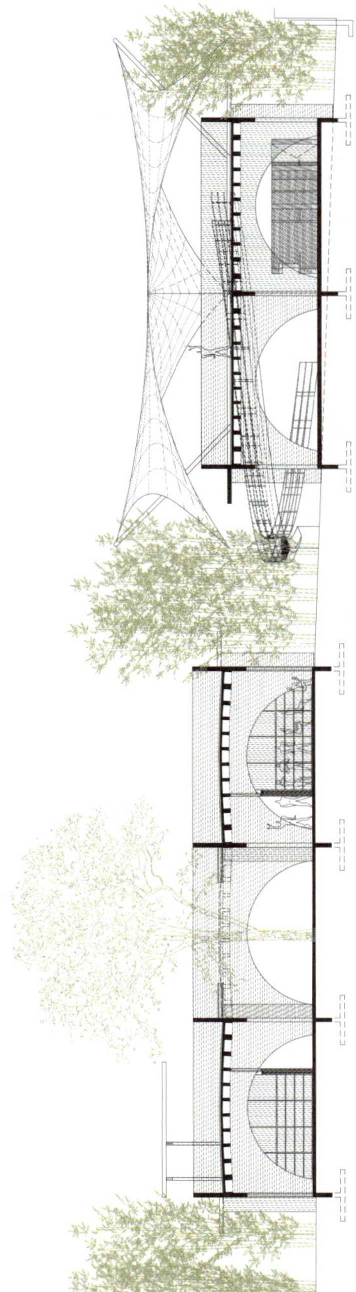

Many towns and villages in Mexico were strongly impacted by the September 2017 earthquakes. In Jojutla, Kalach built a chapel and school to replace the one that, although it did not collapse, was damaged. The challenge was to design a highly resistant structure that was in no danger of collapsing. A framework of concrete arches extends in both directions, defining the form of the new school, with central patios and classrooms around the sides.

Pilares La Pulga

With— Edgar Ojeda and María Kalach

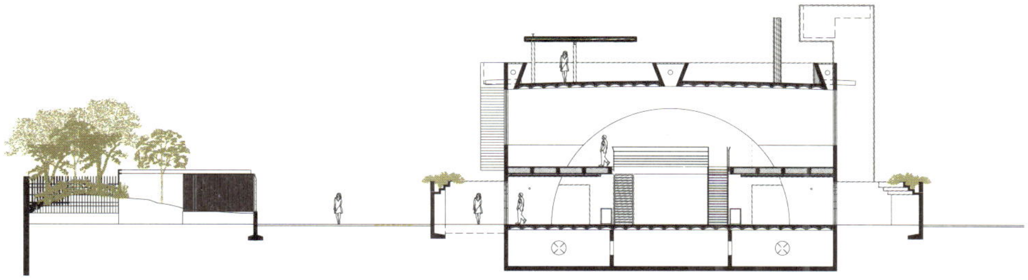

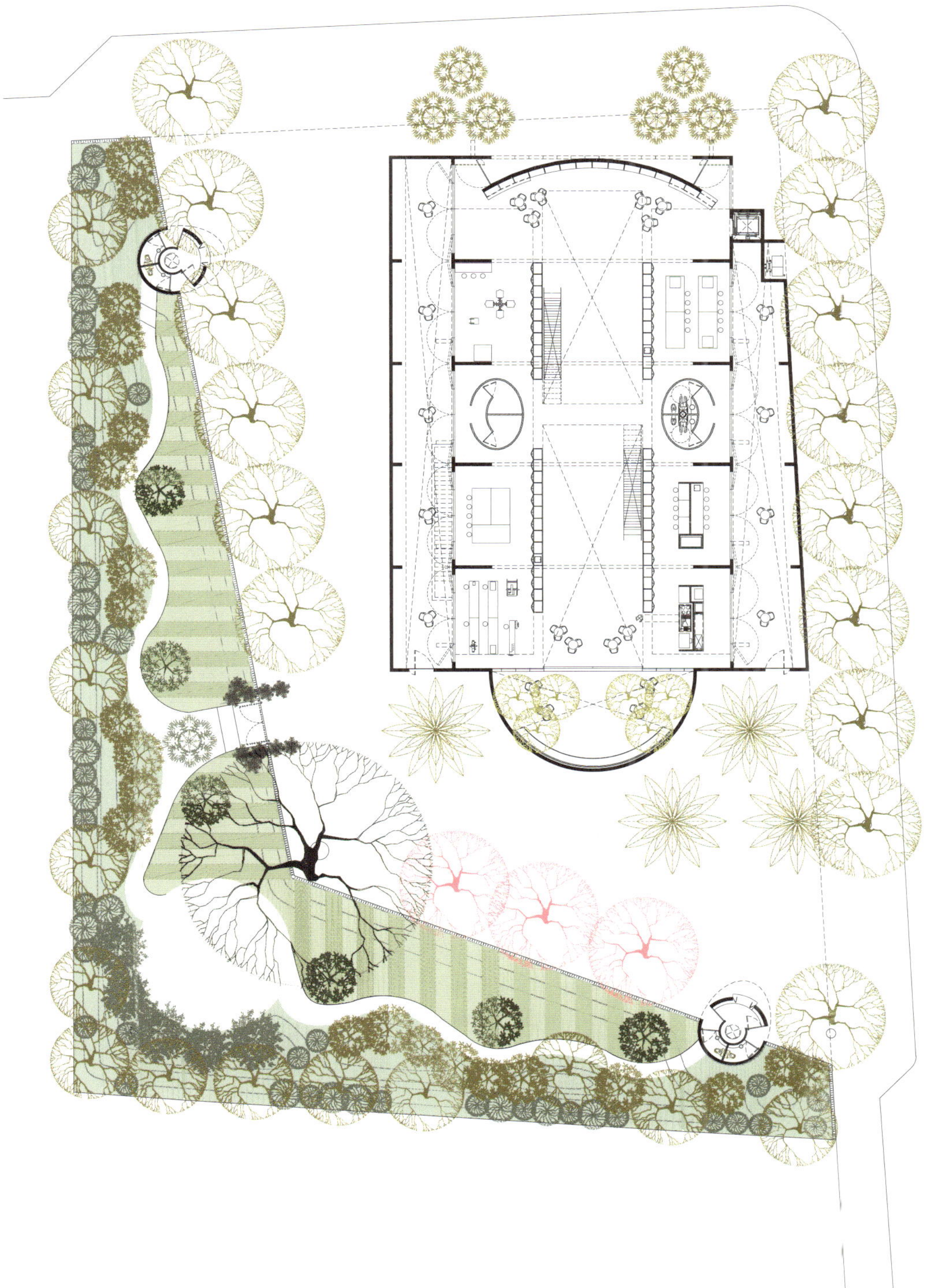

2.5
10.0
0.0
5.0
15.0 M

Housing

— If the city is an organism, the house is the basic cell of the urban tissue. Repeated over and over, it makes up the primordial mass of the city: connected in chains or weaves. When the houses are constructed back to back or side by side, or in collective projects, or when they constitute denser units, these may function as cloisters, as borders, or as minor pieces that complete city blocks.

Collective housing is the weave or fabric that fills in the framework of the city. It is the magma of which our urban conglomerates are made. Collective housing can be analyzed from two vantage points: as cell and as system of growth. Studies of the urban habitat show that, as if it were a living organism, housing can be approached in terms of typology (the unit) or in terms of systems of connected dwellings (the project). In both cases, the production of Albert Kalach is both prolific and important, at times generating, at times completing the urban and territorial fabric.

In typological terms, his designs are bursting with freedom, finding solutions where no one ever thought to look for them: at times increasing the height of a domestic space, so that the sense of luxury is felt by the total resulting space, and not by the square footage; at others extending the area of the residence outdoors, by means of ample terraces full of greenery, which provide residents with the experience of nature even as their privacy is protected. With faultless logic, Kalach proposes polyvalent floor plans whose singularity is the section, providing even reduced spaces with the maximum possible height, making for more volume and for central overhead spaces in the service areas, or generating fluid spaces that blur the differences of level.

The repetition of inhabitable cells defines the range of different strategies for connecting them. A new building may take its place between preexisting neighbors, completing a block or filling in a piece that was missing in the urban fabric. In this sense, Kalach is constantly on the lookout for unused lots in the urban layout, where he can undertake to "make city" where others saw only unusable space. In territorial contexts, the aggregation of cells may form collective blocks of housing, dwellings set side by side or back to back or in towers, neighborhoods whose genealogy recalls chains or weaves, creating cloister-like conglomerations or redefining the metropolitan borders between city and countryside.

Alberto Kalach has largely drawn on the arsenal of still valid ideas and typologies of architectural modernity, meeting the needs of contemporary collective housing by contributing typological, distributive, and functional variants. In this way, he proposes systems that will define the future growth of our cities in terms of housing.

One More Room

With— Juan de la Rosa

/ 2015

"One More Room" was designed in response to an initiative by Carlos Zedillo, as director of research of the Infonavit, Mexico's low-cost housing institute, to follow up on the promise eventually to expand thousands of houses constructed by the government. This prototype is for a light but spacious construction that can be put together in a period of two weeks. This room has been set up in several town plazas and also installed in an actual residence.

With— Gustavo Lipkau

Mexico City / 1997

MAL House

Mexico City / 1997

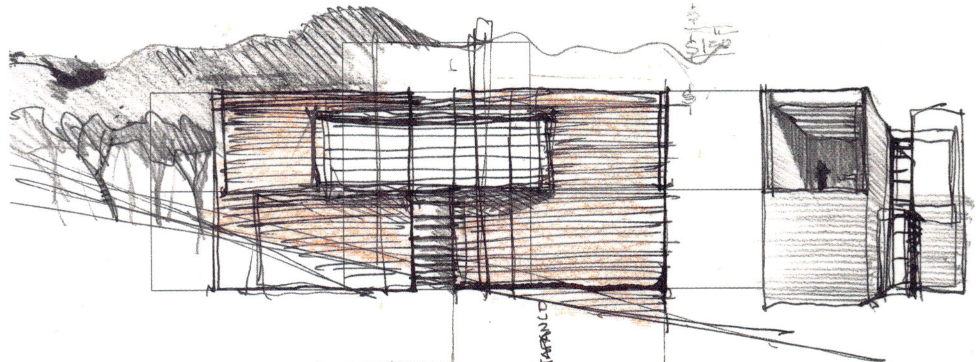

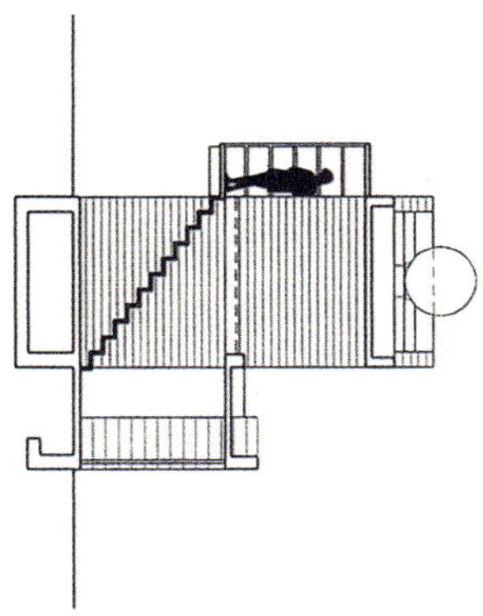

CORTE TRANSVERSAL

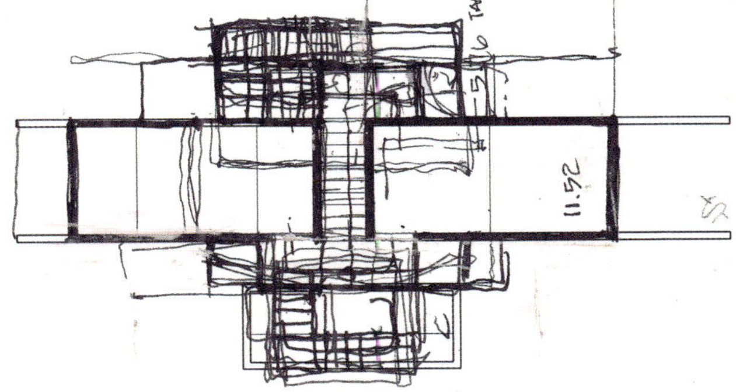

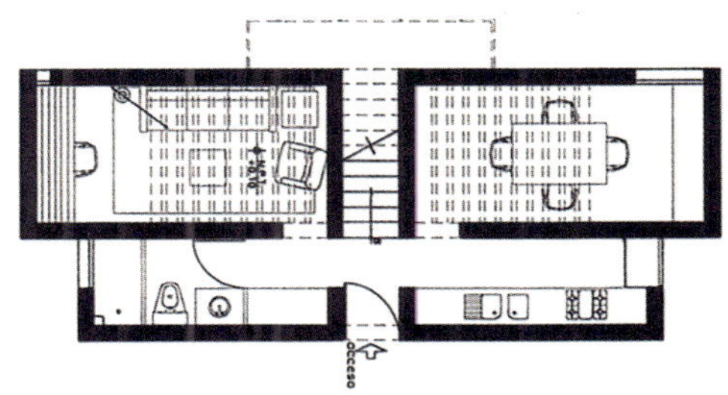

PLANTA BAJA

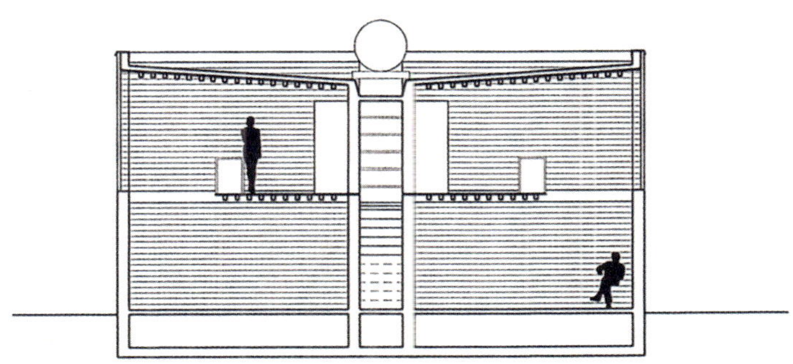

CORTE LONGITUDINAL CL-1

— VIC House and MAL House are experiments in low-cost housing, basic cells of the urban tissue. The built version, based on concrete blocks with integrated reinforcements and wooden floor slabs, facilitates construction. Cost: US$5,000.00.

Rodin

With— Daniel Álvarez, Salvador Ferreiro, Felipe Buendía, and Axel Arañó

Mexico City / 1993

The Rodin and Adolf apartment buildings are contiguous with their respective neighbors, with a third façade that completes the continuity of the urban grid.

— Thousands of lots mutilated by the widening of adjacent thoroughfares offer extraordinary possibilities for re-densifying and dignifying the surrounding streets.

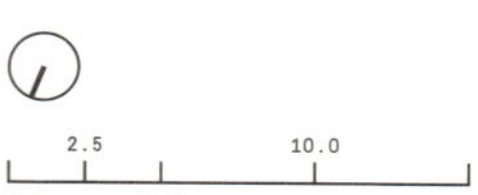

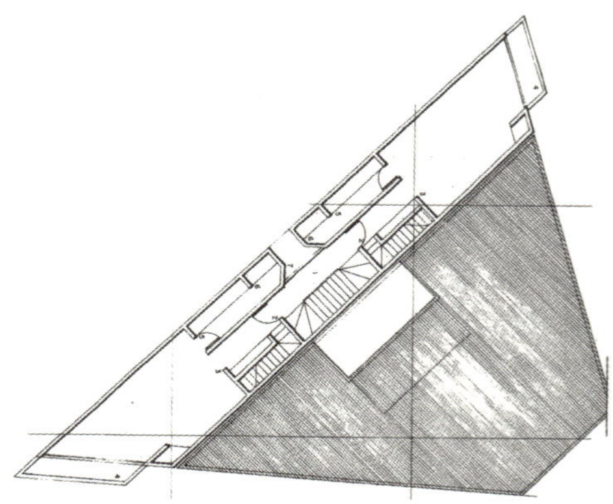

Adolf

With— Daniel Álvarez, Axel Arañó, and Rosa López

Mexico City / 1993

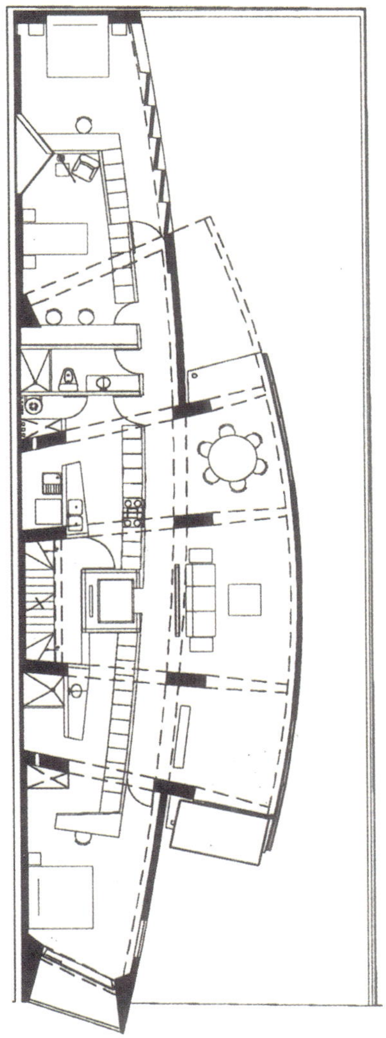

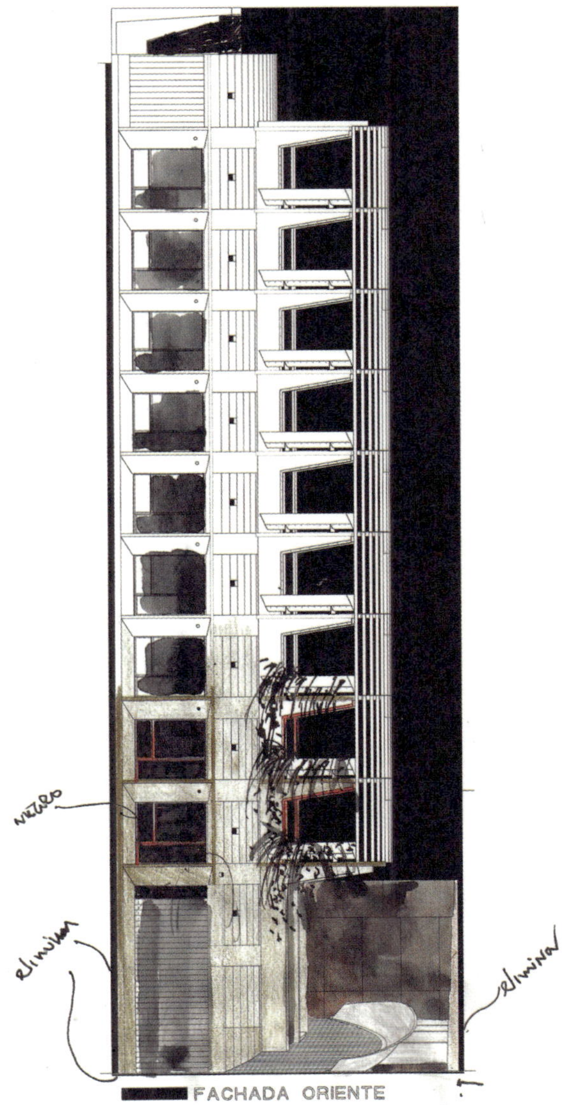

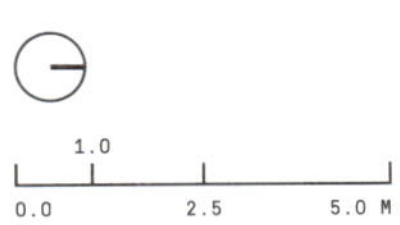

Fresas

With— Daniel Álvarez and Salvador Ferreiro

Mexico City / 1991

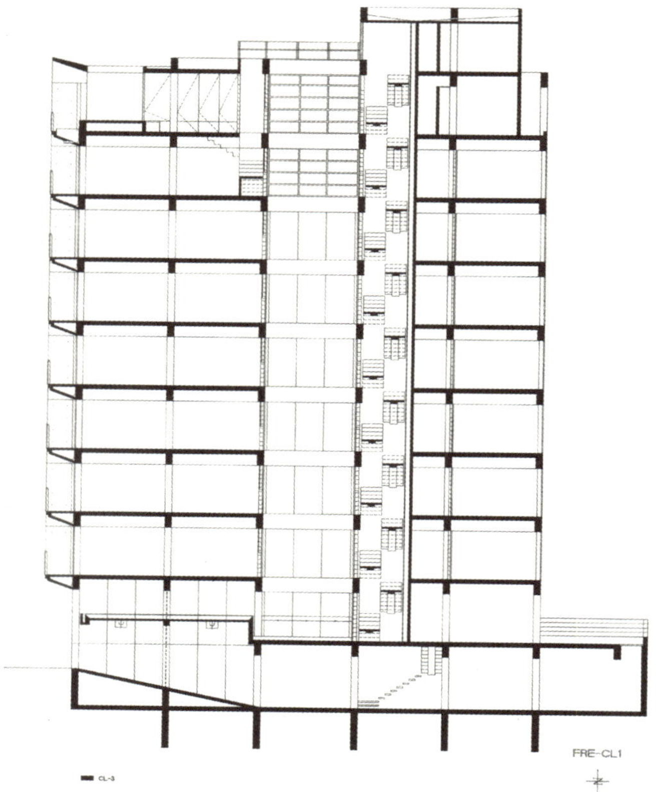

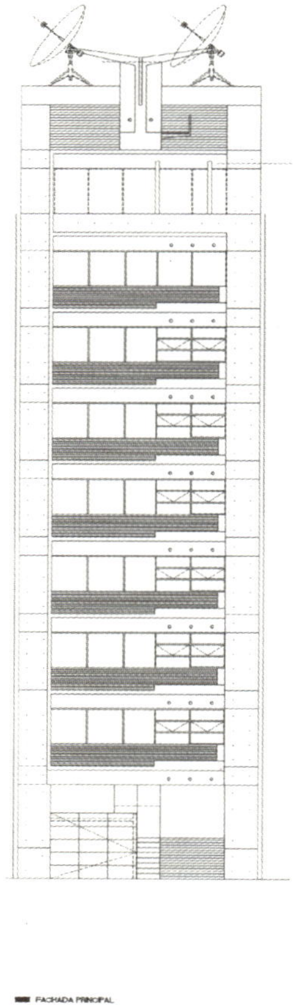

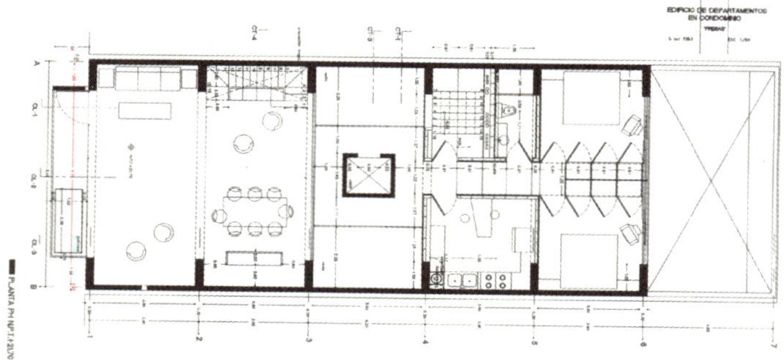

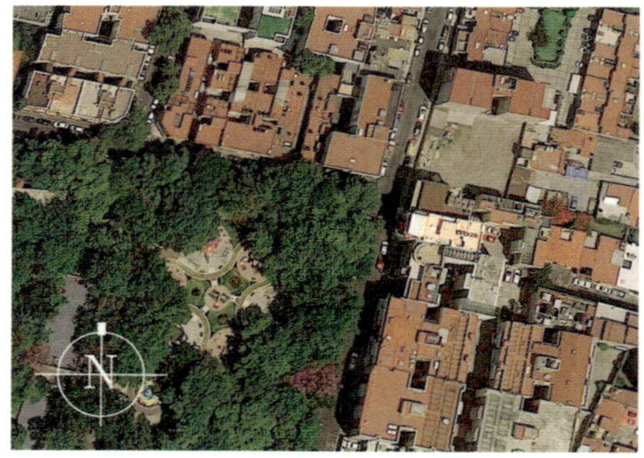

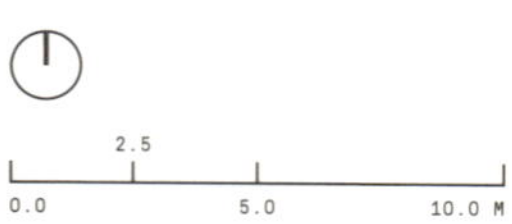

Holbein

With— Daniel Álvarez, Salvador Ferreiro, and Patricia Prieto

Mexico City / 1991

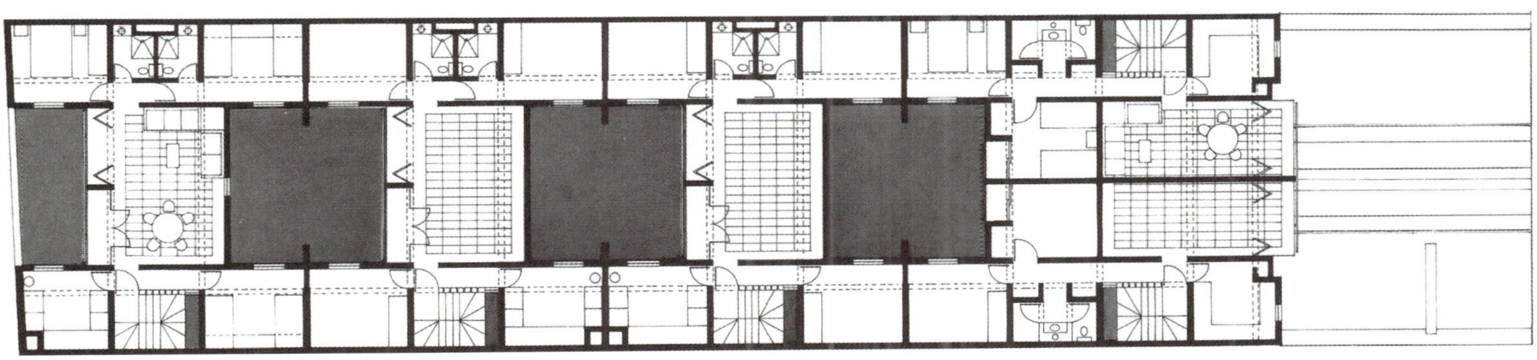

— The Karl Marx Hof in Vienna, designed by Karl Ehn, and the apartment building in Mexico City by Carlos Mijares are in the DNA of this construction.

NY 21st

With— Adriana León and David Martínez

New York / 2014

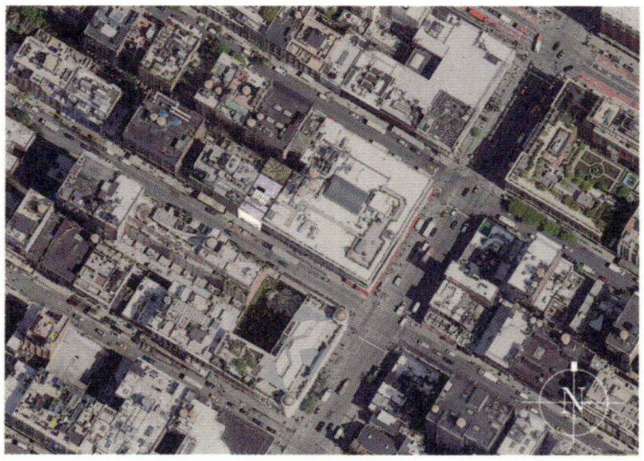

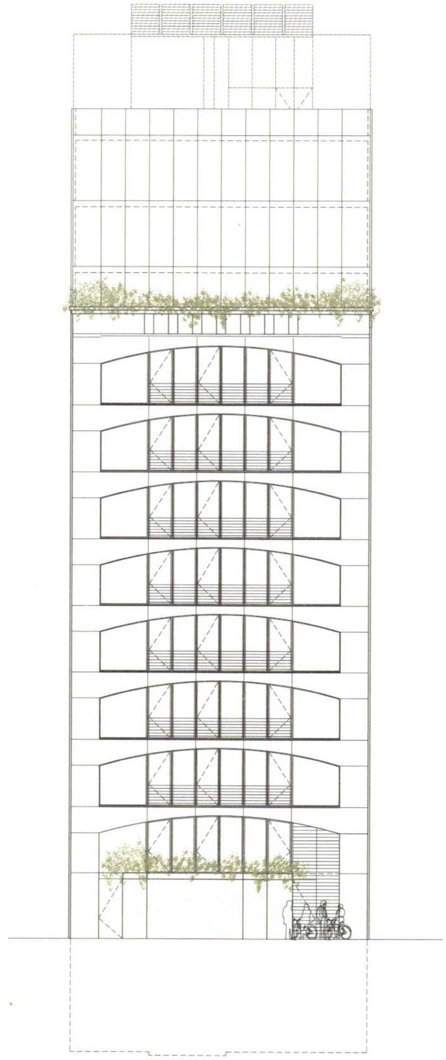

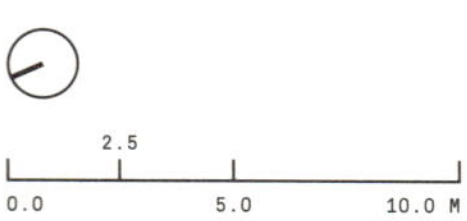

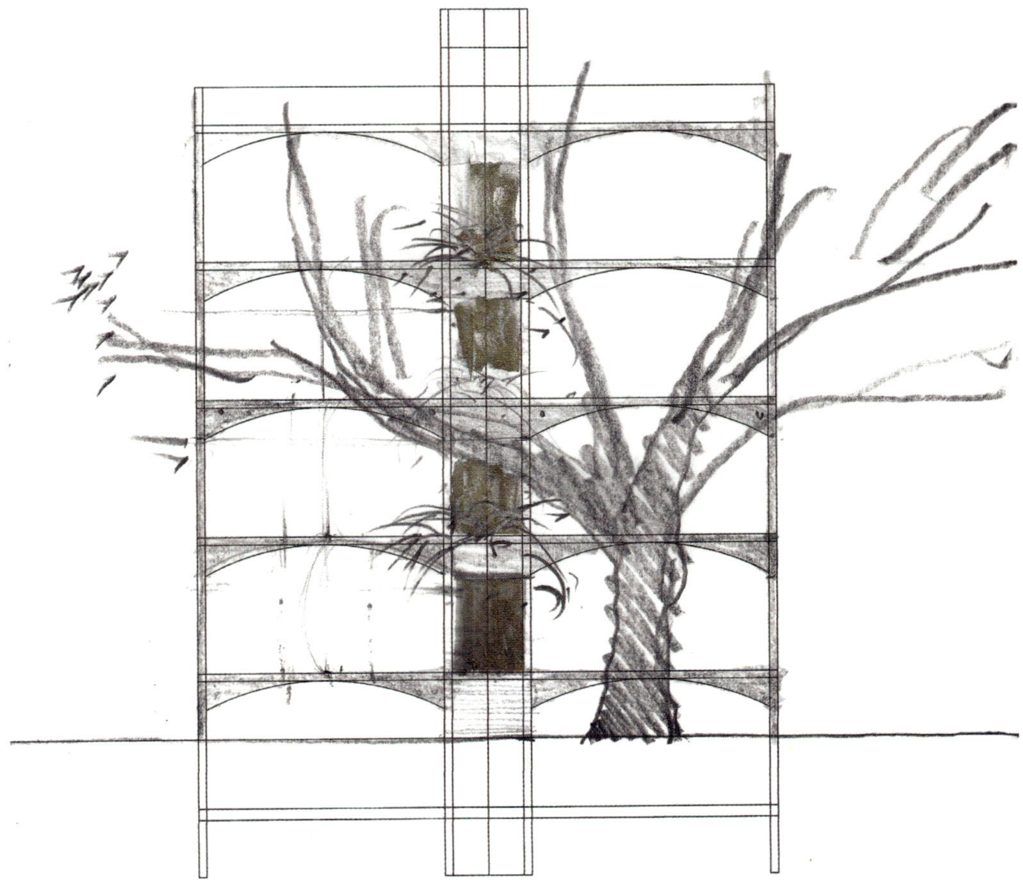

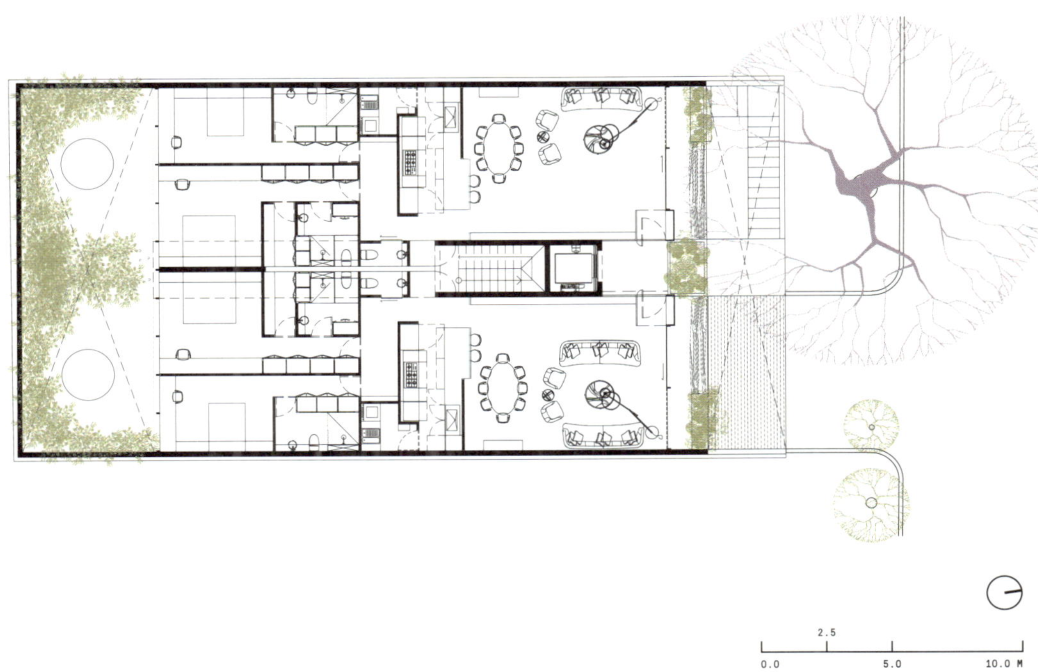
2.5
0.0
5.0
10.0 M

Coahuila 46

With— Nathalie Franquebalme, Mariana Manjarrez, and Lucas Elizondo

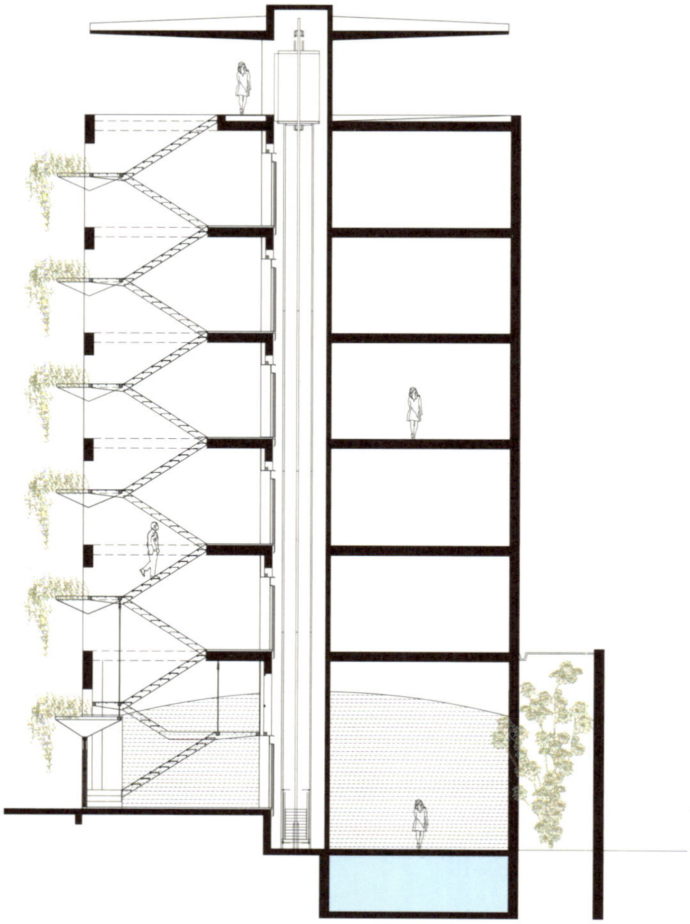

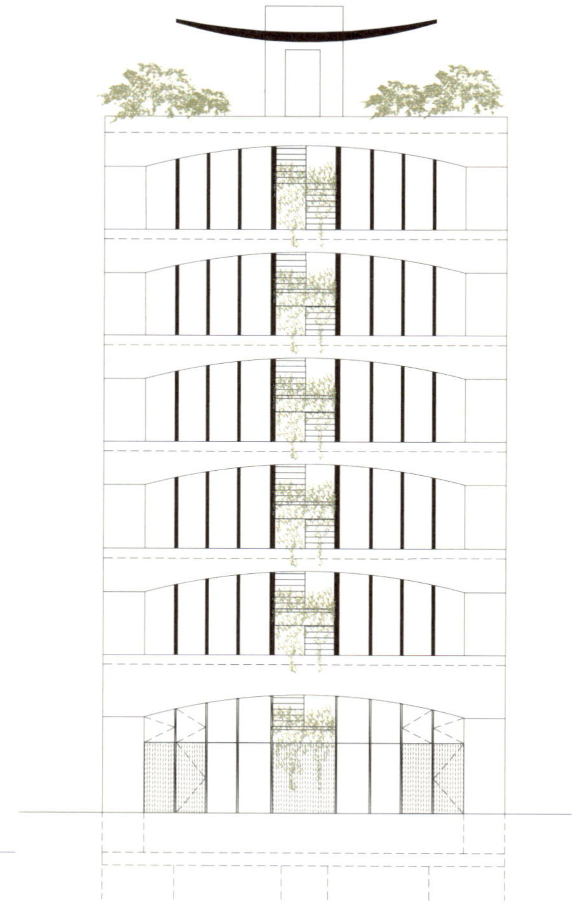

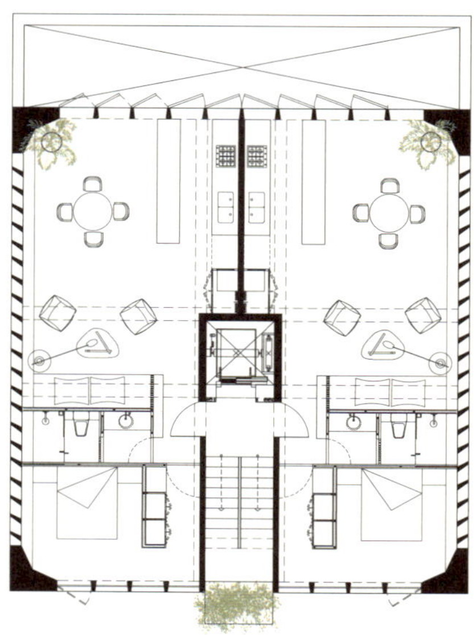

Sombrerete

With— López Baz y Calleja

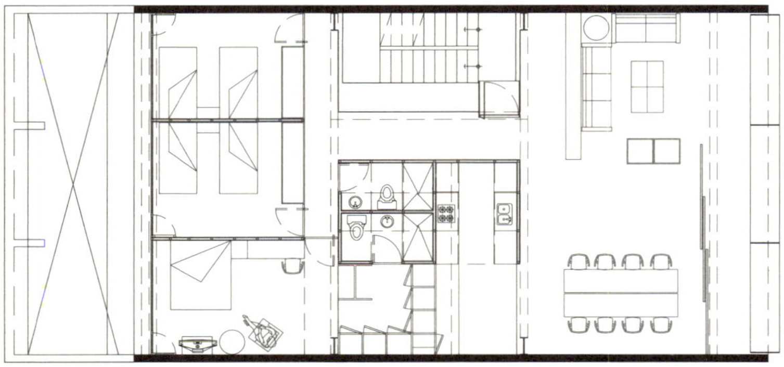

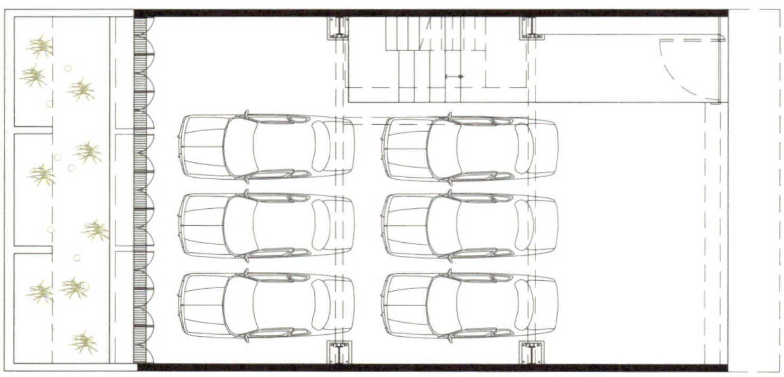

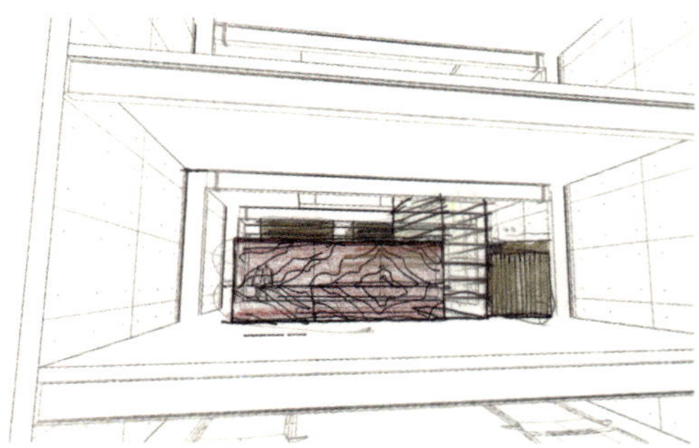

Parroquia

With— Daniel Álvarez

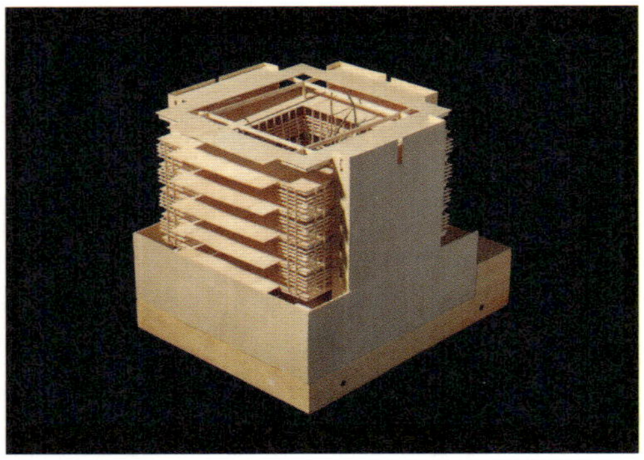

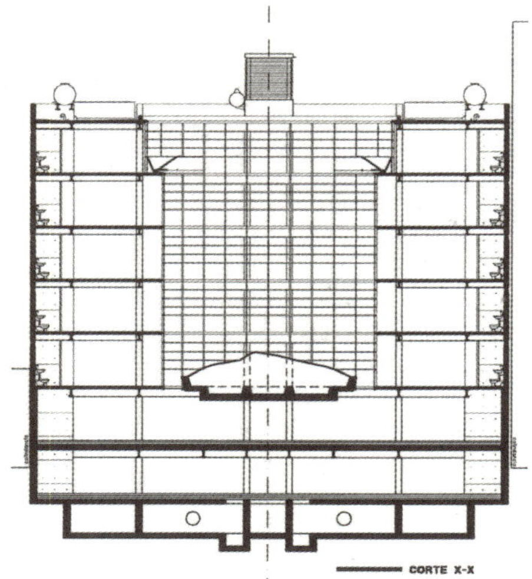

Parroquia 1

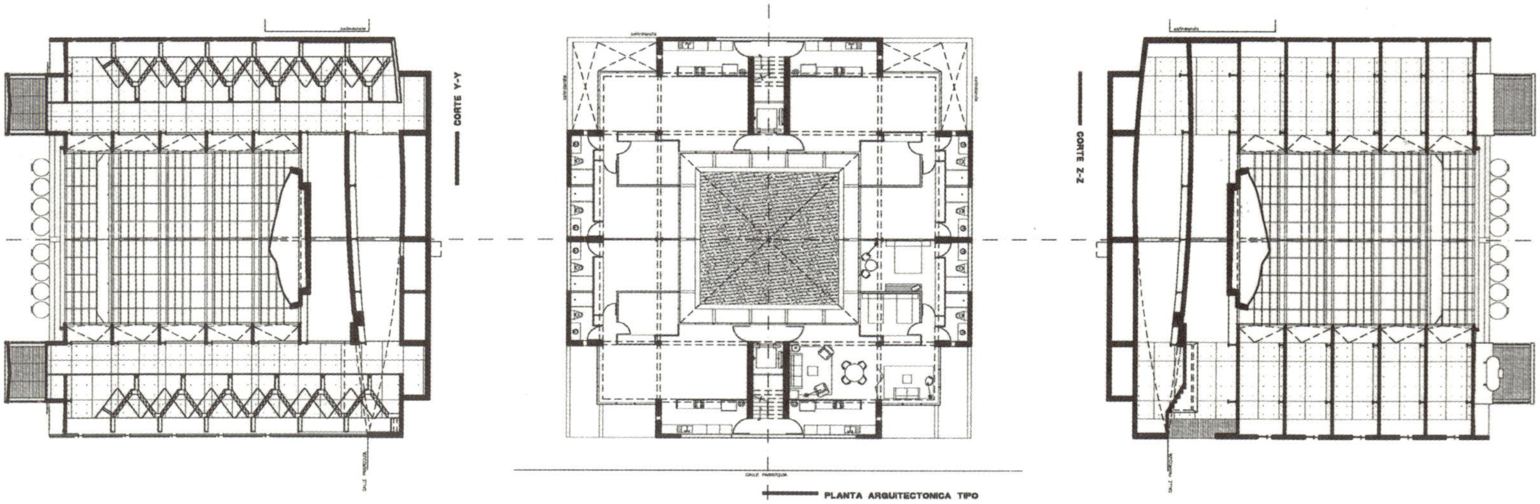

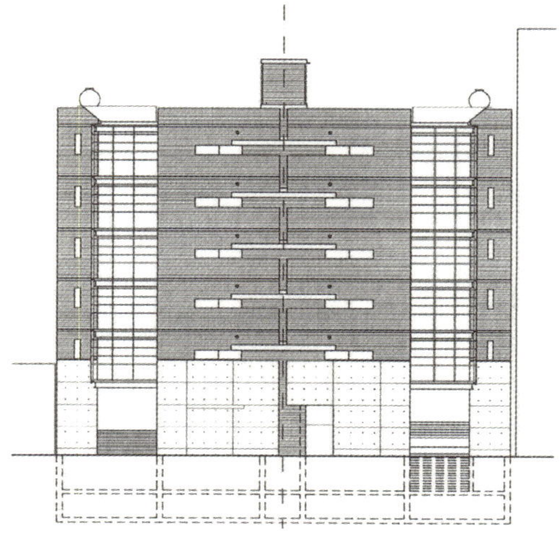

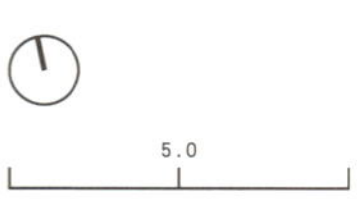

Parroquia 2

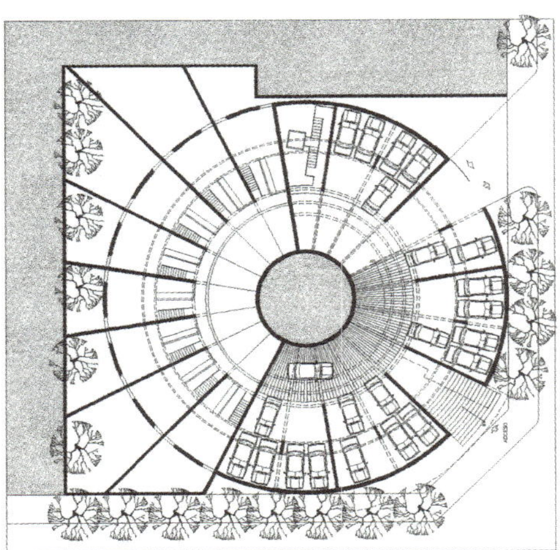
p. baja

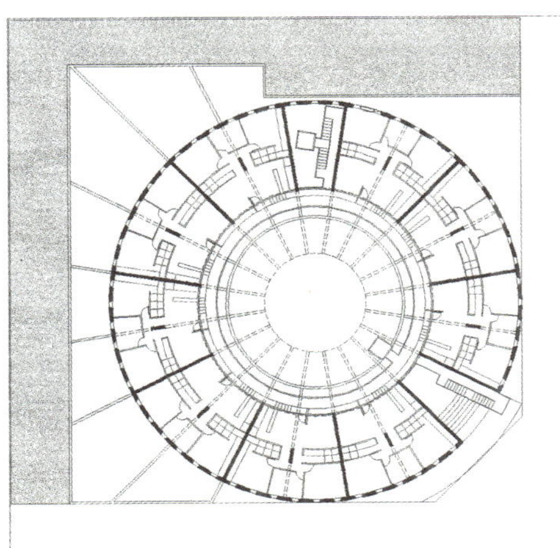
p. tipo

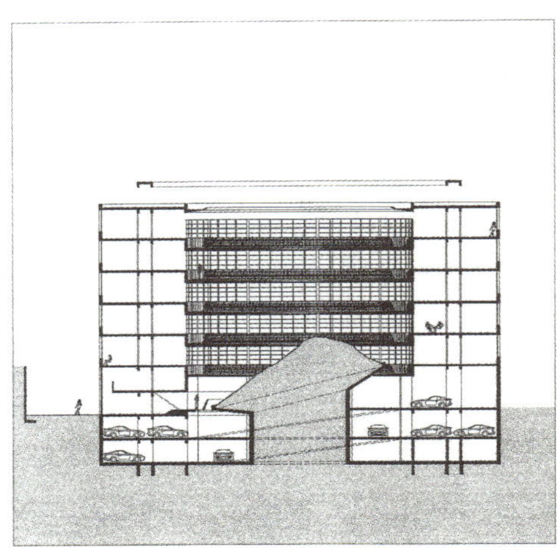
corte

Parroquia 3

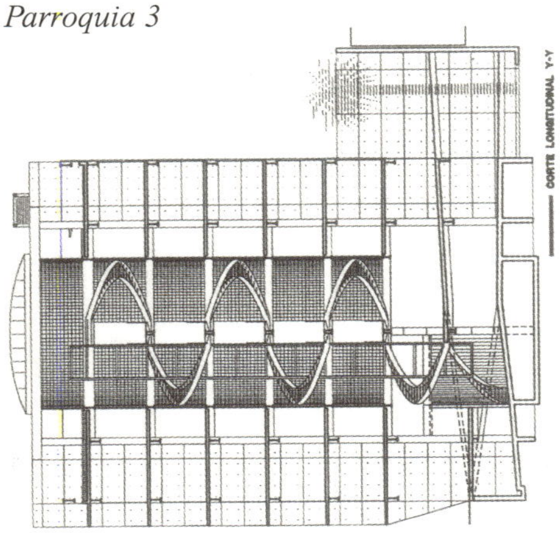
CORTE LONGITUDINAL Y-Y

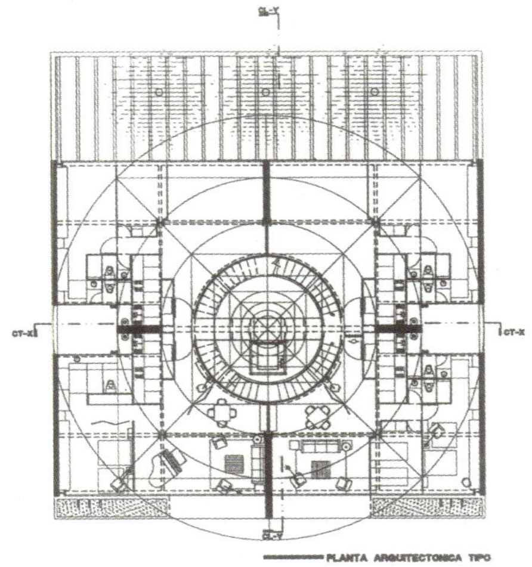
PLANTA ARQUITECTONICA TIPO

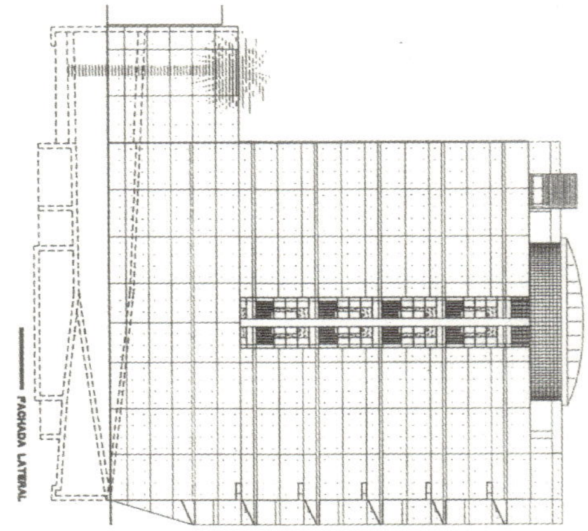
FACHADA LATERAL

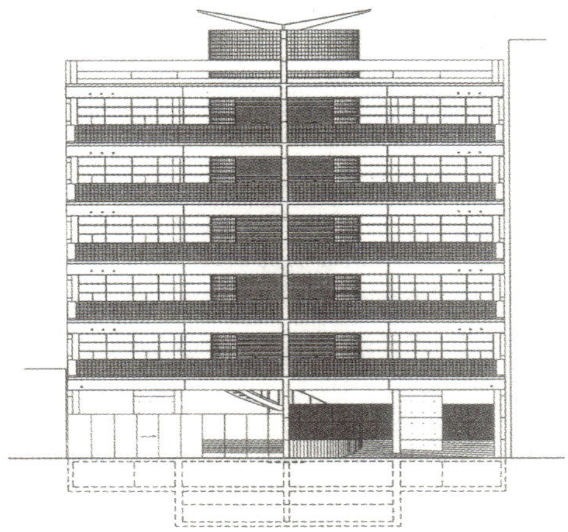

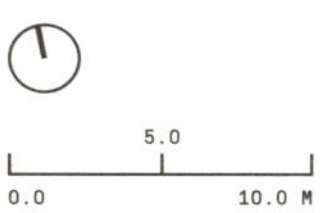
5.0
0.0
10.0 M

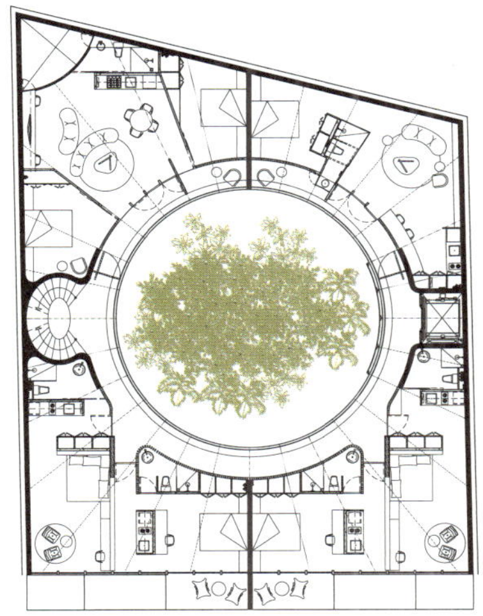

2.5
0.0
5.0
10.0 M

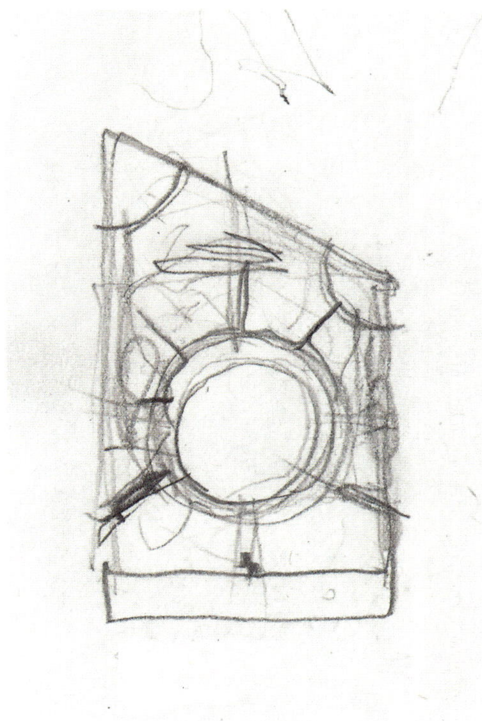

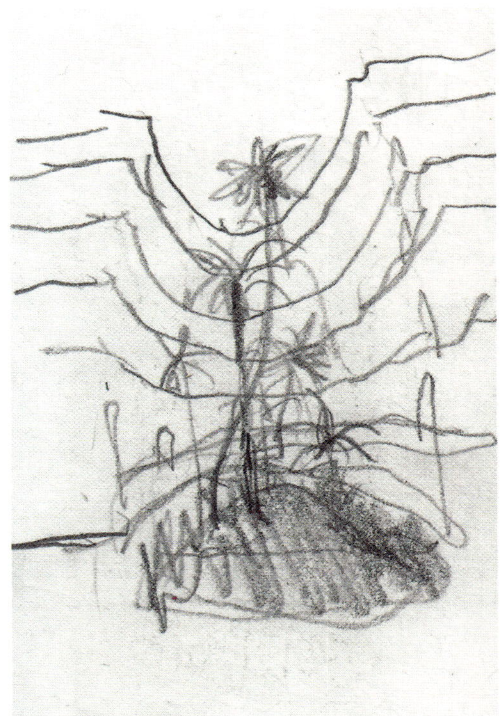

Tonalá

With— Héctor Módica
and Emmanuel Ramírez

Mexico City / 2005

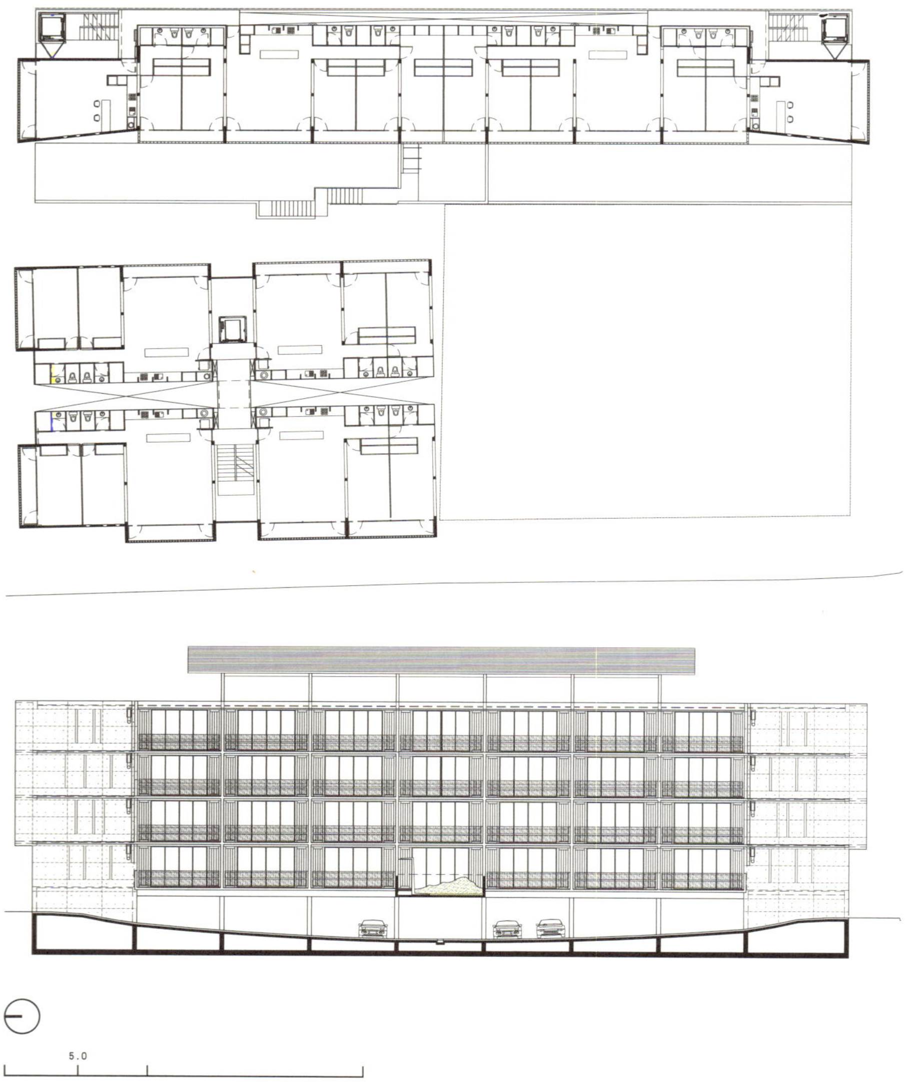

Some apartment buildings, most of them in Mexico City, function as pieces integrated into the urban fabric to complete a city block, sometimes on an irregularly-shaped lot, at other times on a corner location: blocks contained by the city and yet surrounded by greenery.

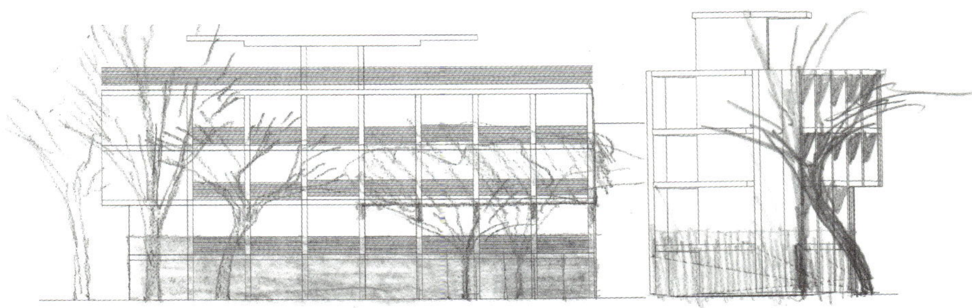

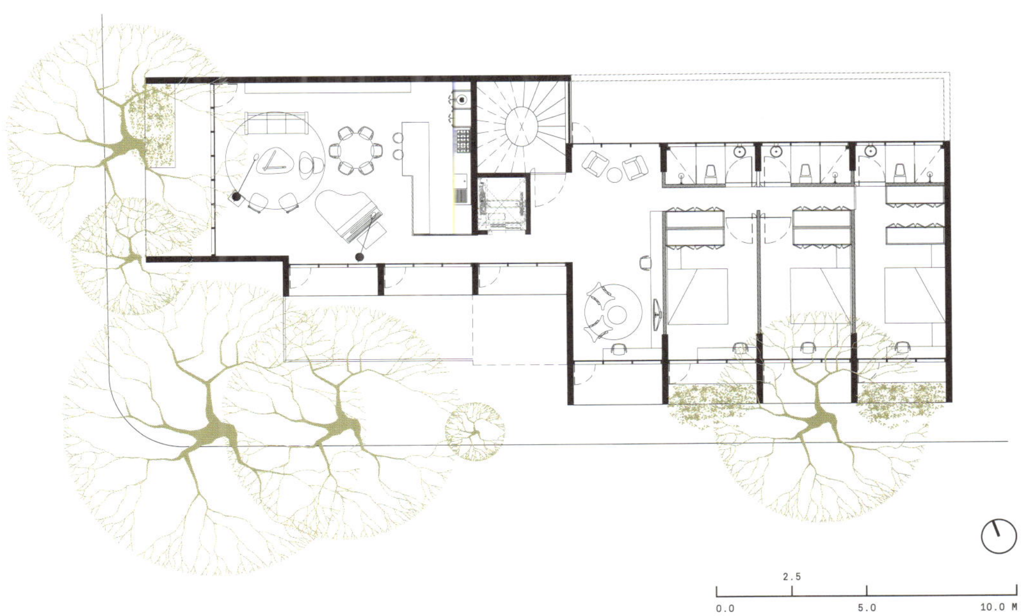
2.5
0.0
5.0
10.0 M

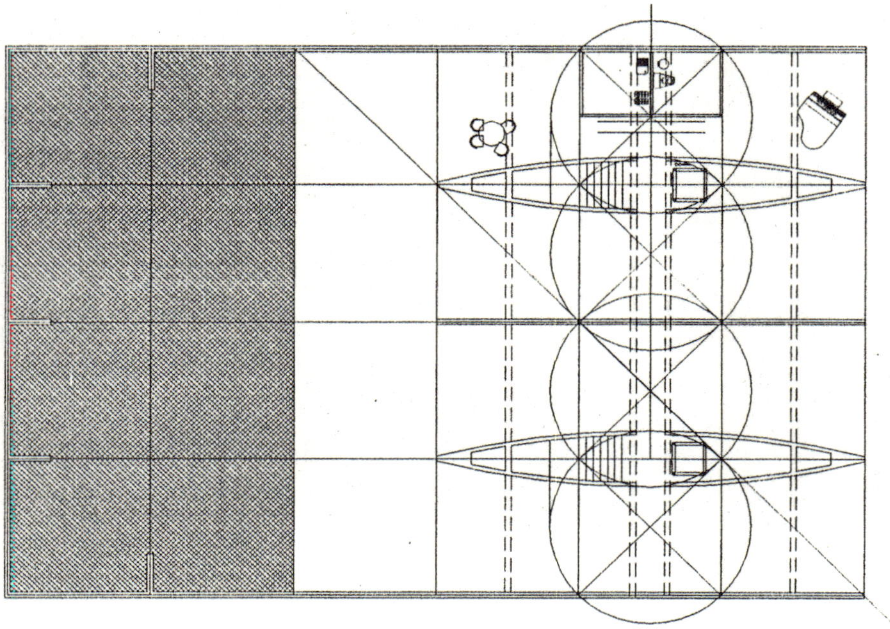

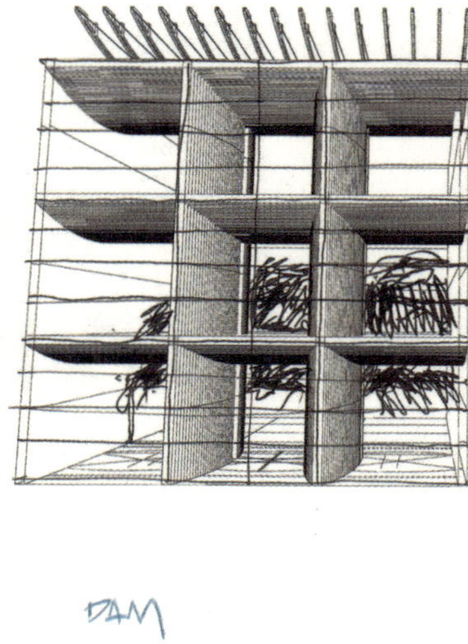
DAM

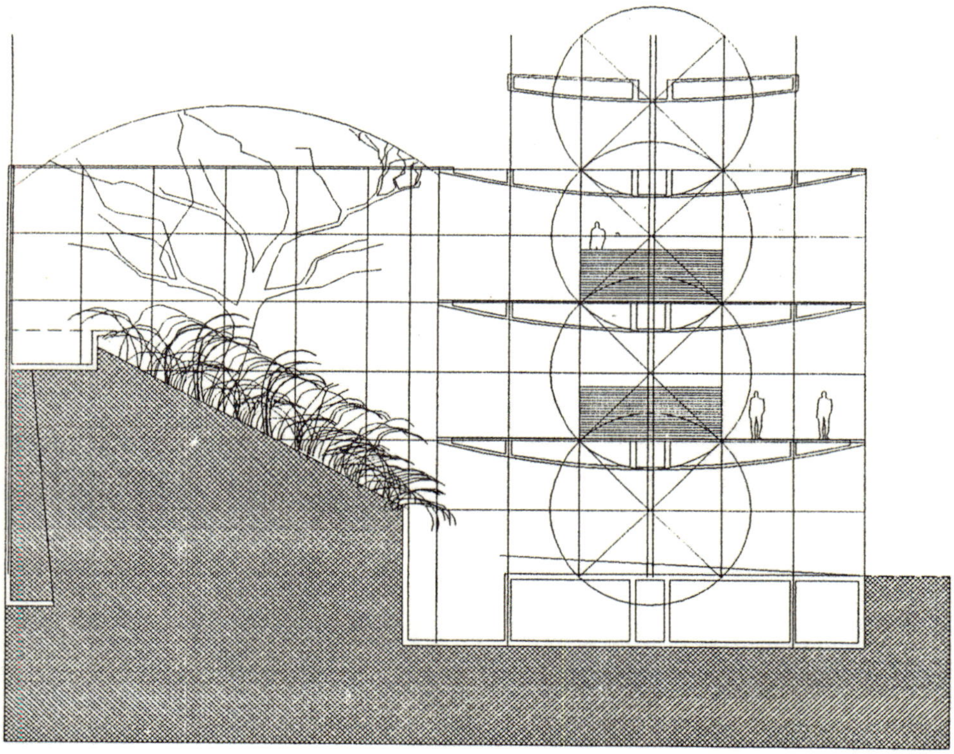

AMSTERDAM
8 DEPTOS
1 JARDIN

Garibaldi

With— Iván Ramírez

Guadalajara / 2008

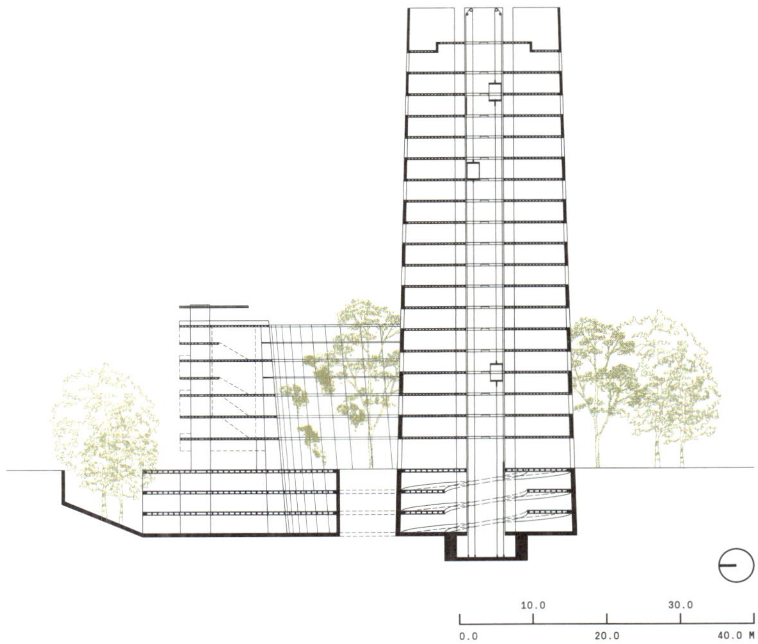

2.5
0.0
5.0 M

Nuevo León

With— David Garza

Mexico City / 2020

Vertientes

With— Moisés Becker and Humberto Ricalde

Mexico City / 2005

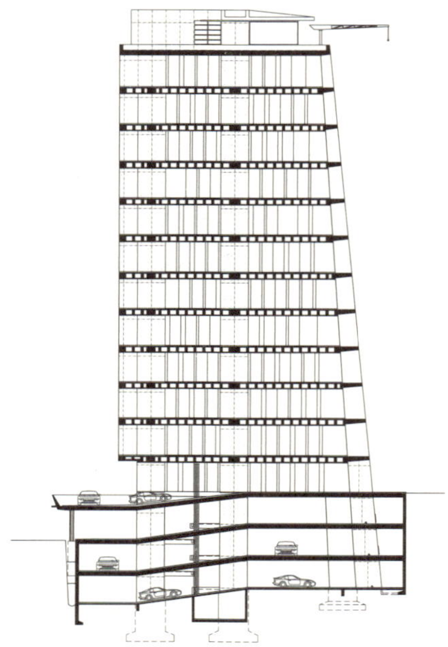

Rebollar

With— Priscila Lozano and Roberto Silva

Mexico City / 2017

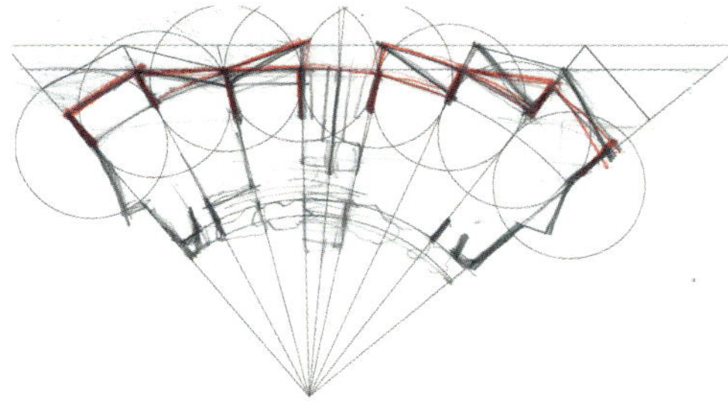

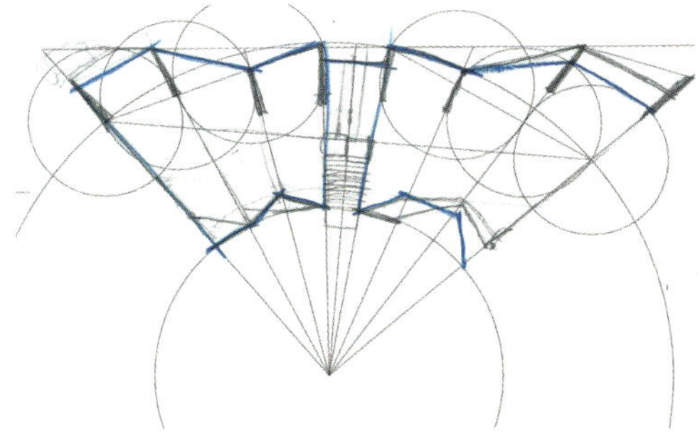

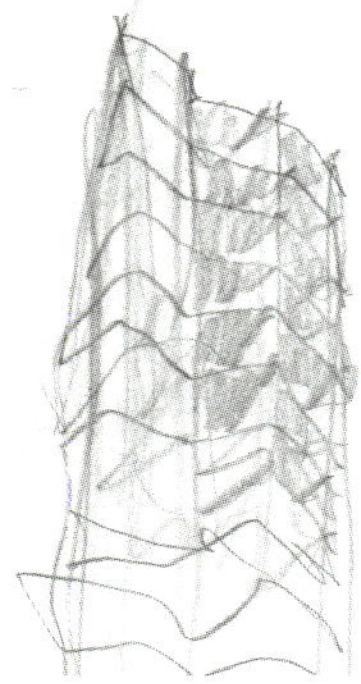

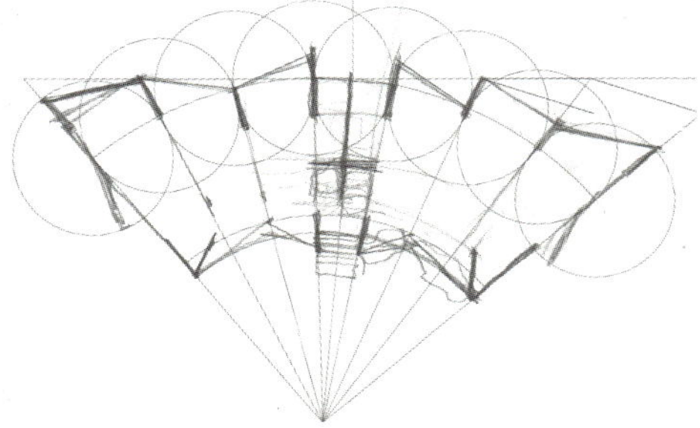

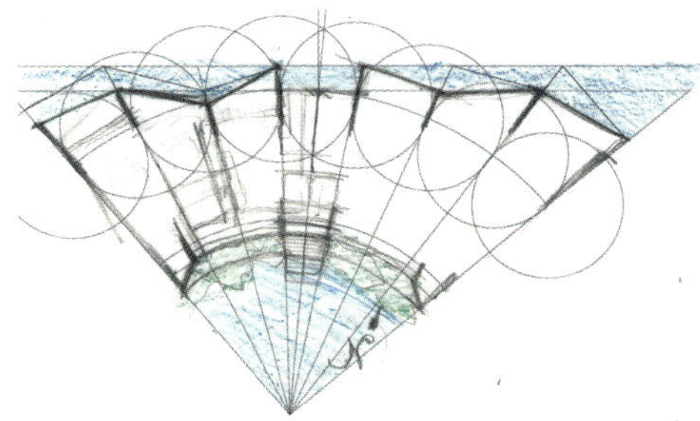

Santa María la Ribera

With— Héctor Módica and Iván Ramírez

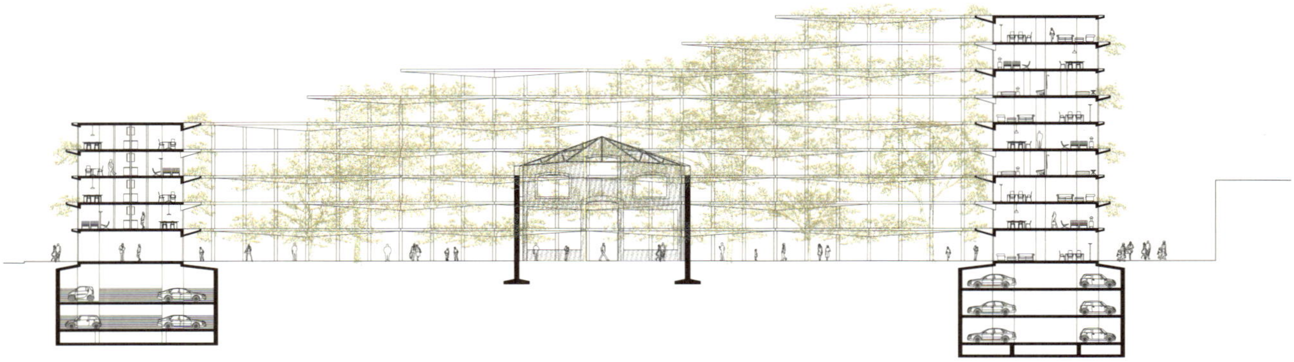

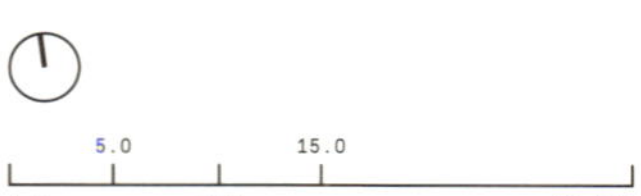

N

Tláloc

With— Daniel Álvarez, Salvador Ferreiro, Moisés Miserachi, Axel Arañó, Felipe Buendía, Rebeca Cotera, and Julio González

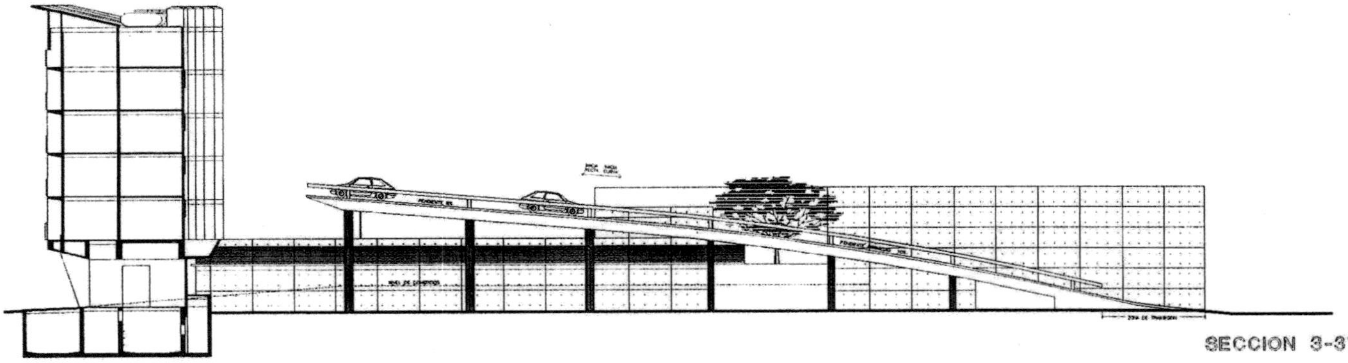

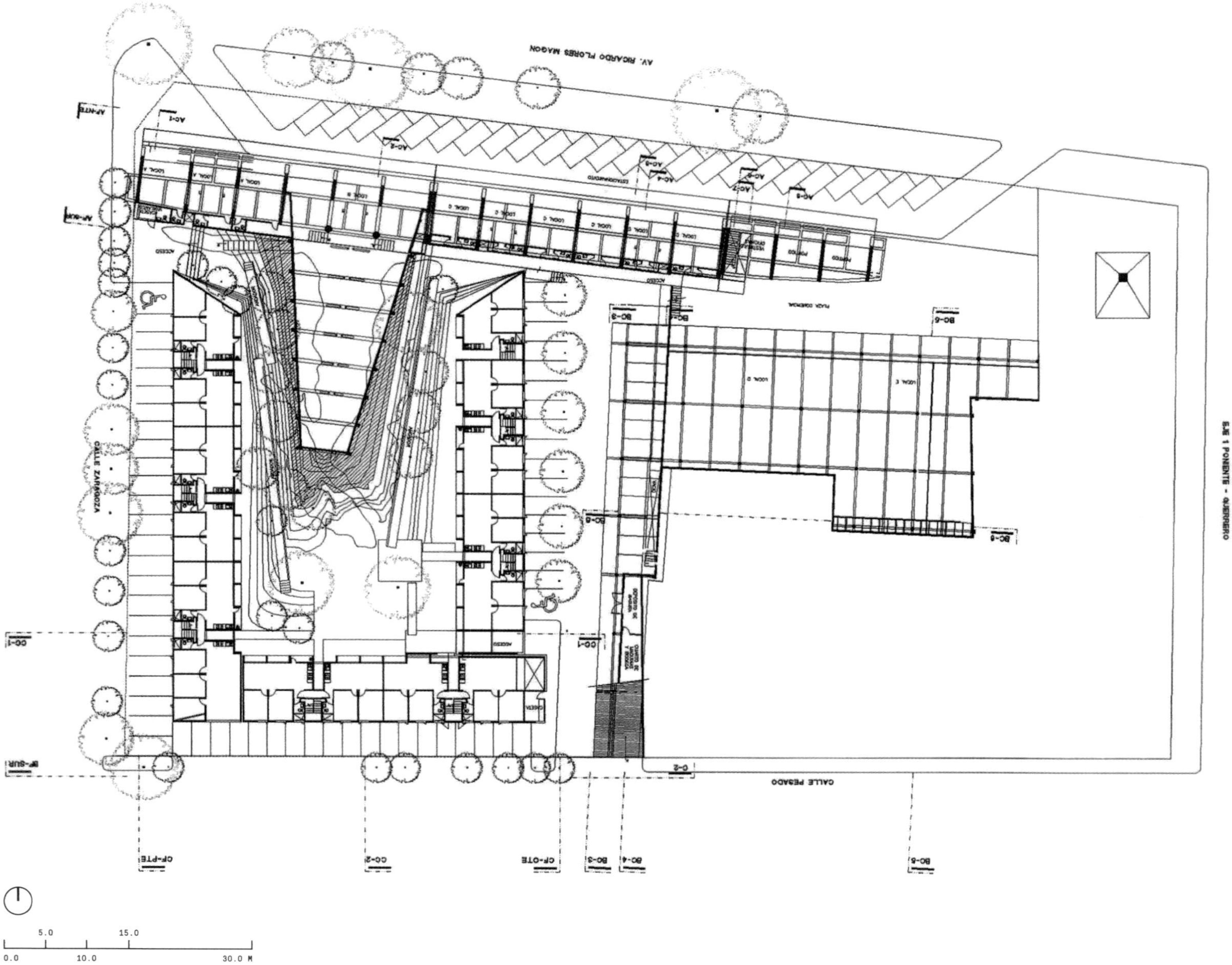

Zurich

With— Héctor Módica, Takemune Takuma, and Iván Ramírez

Zurich / 2009

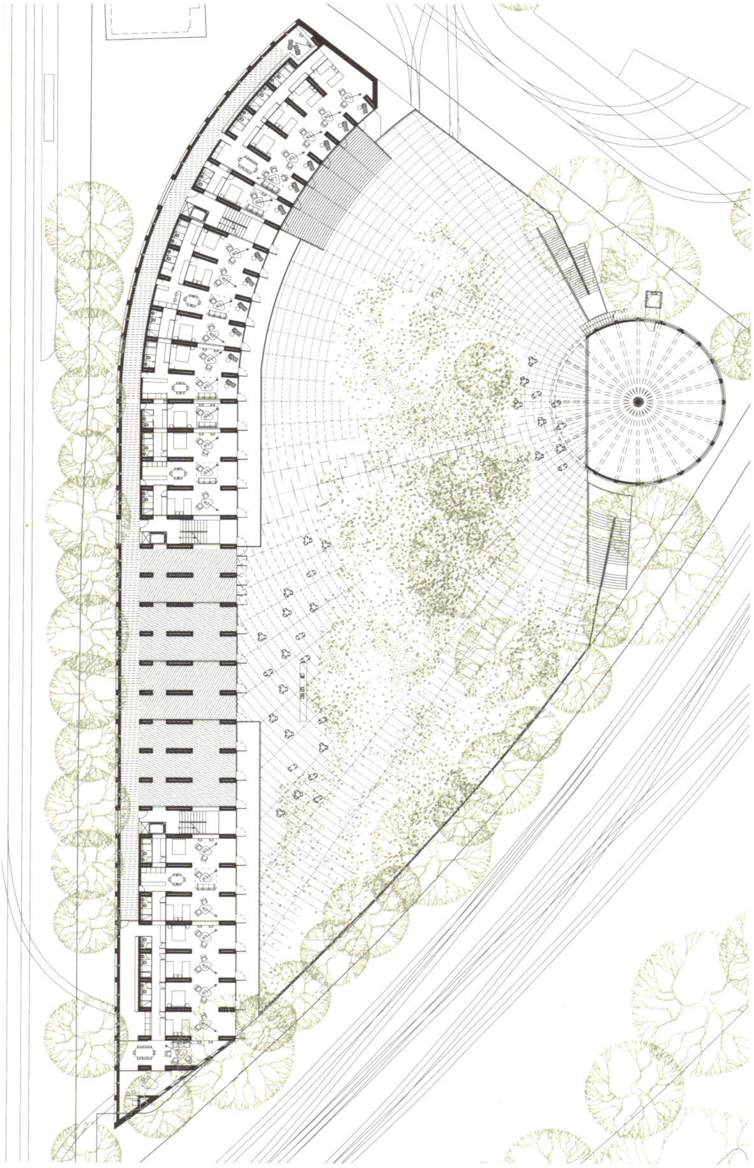

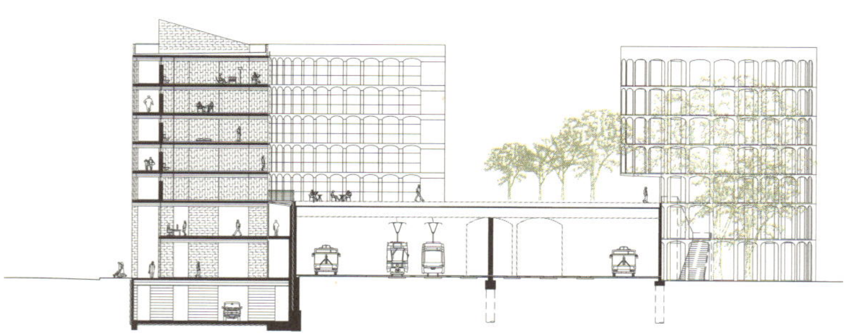

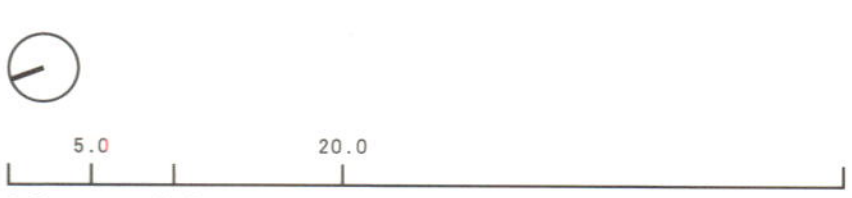

Rosedal

With— José Luis Reyes

Mexico City / 2009

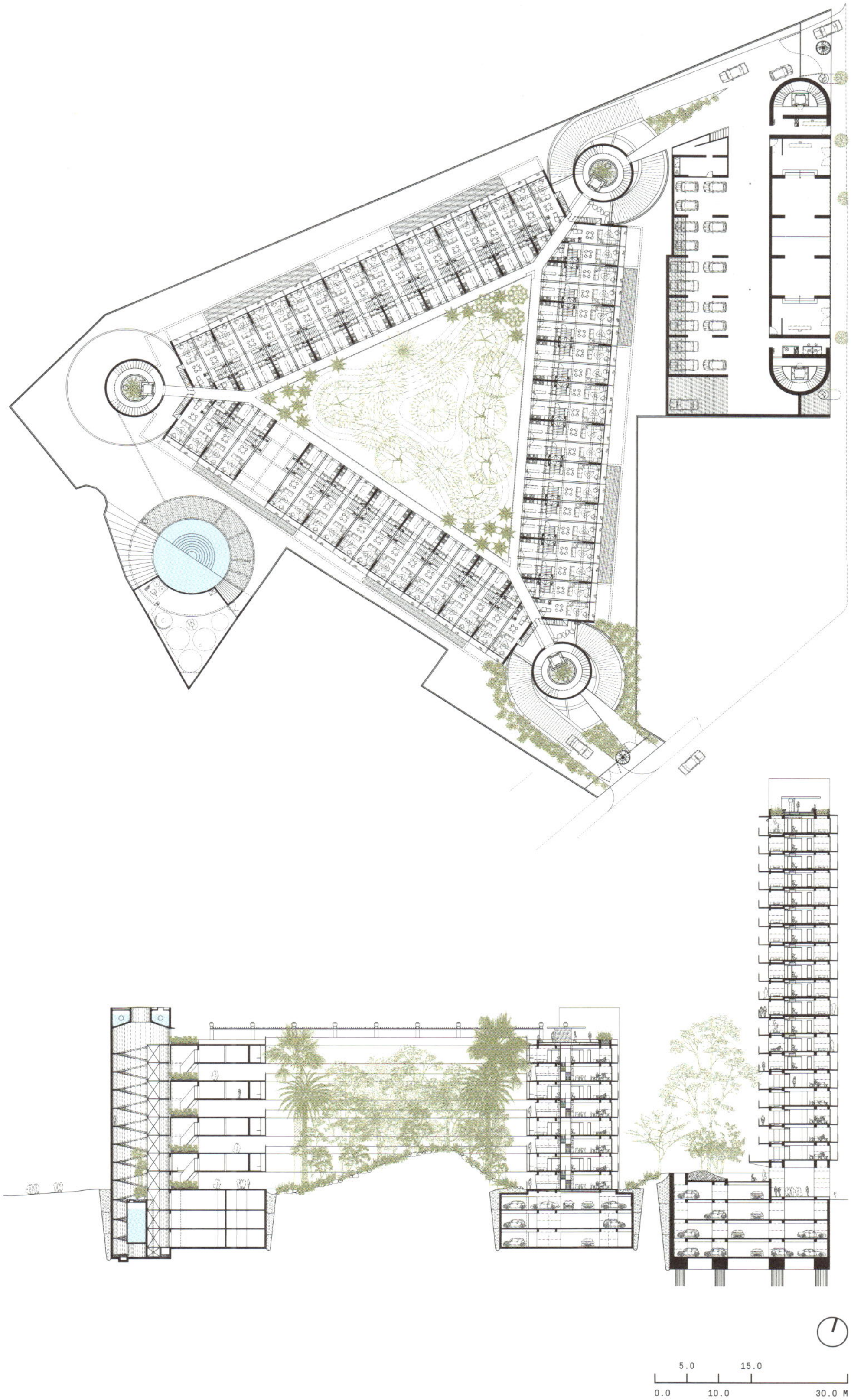

Monjes Capuchinos

With— Héctor Módica

Mexico City / 2013

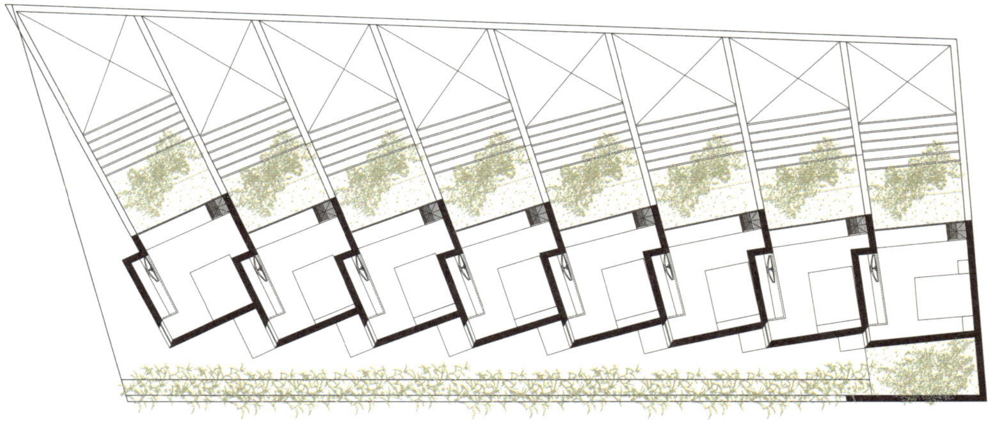

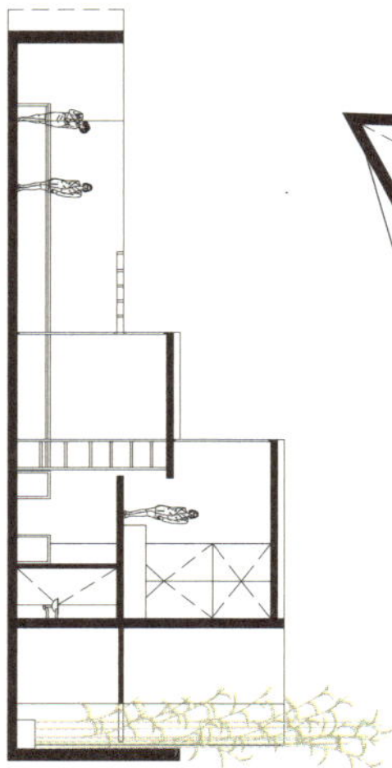

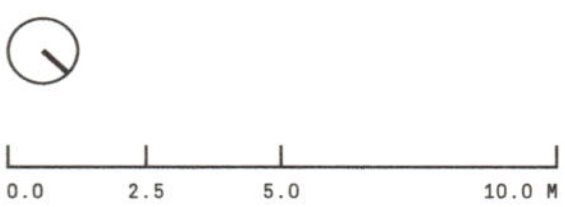

In open environments, with natural surroundings, Kalach proposes housing units arranged side by side to form chains or tissues. These group are integrated with the topography and oriented toward lakes, mountains, or green areas.

Cano 13

With— Héctor Módica

Mexico City / 2012

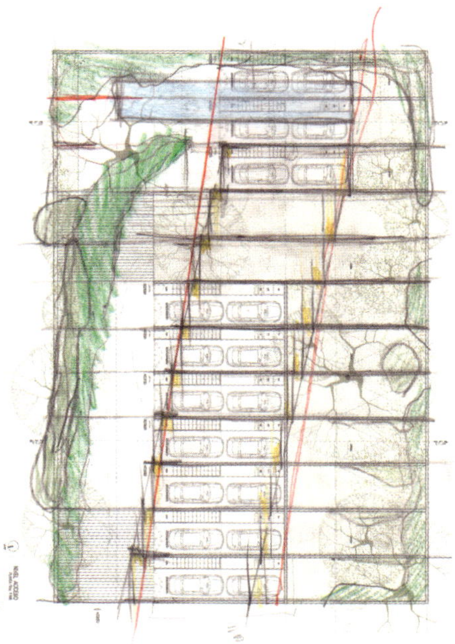

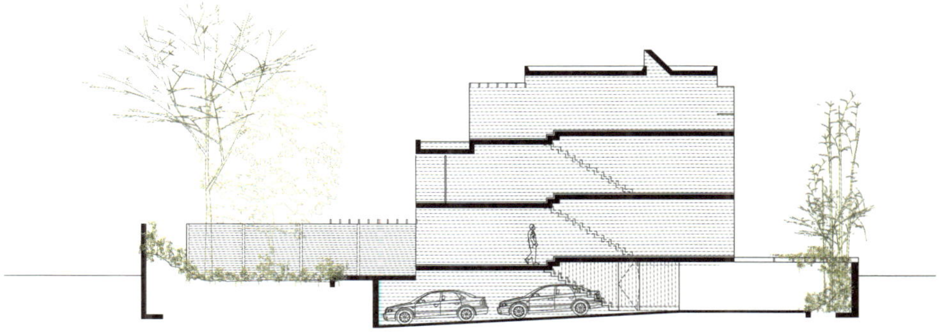

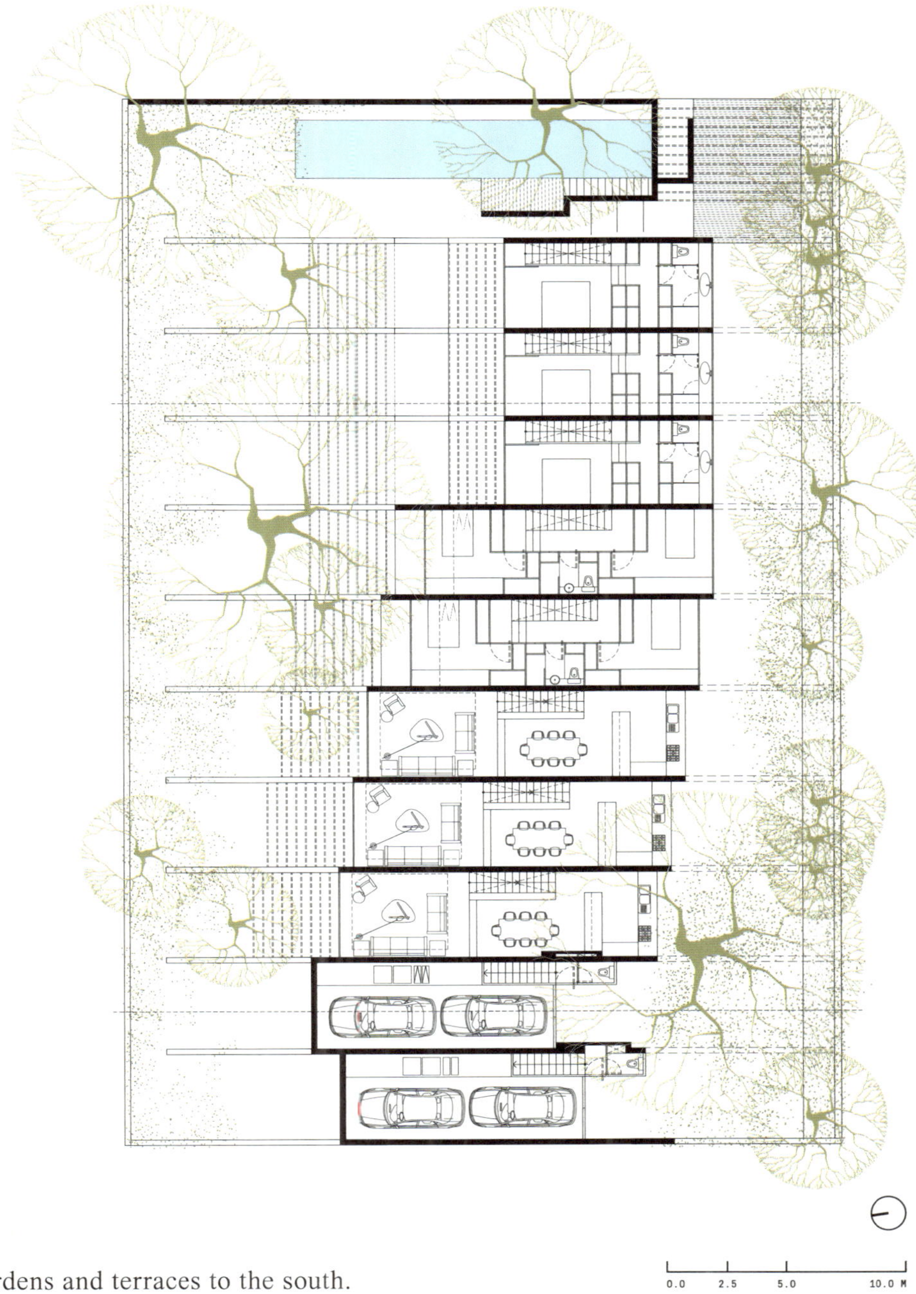

— Gardens and terraces to the south.

Barranca Valle

With— Iván Ramírez

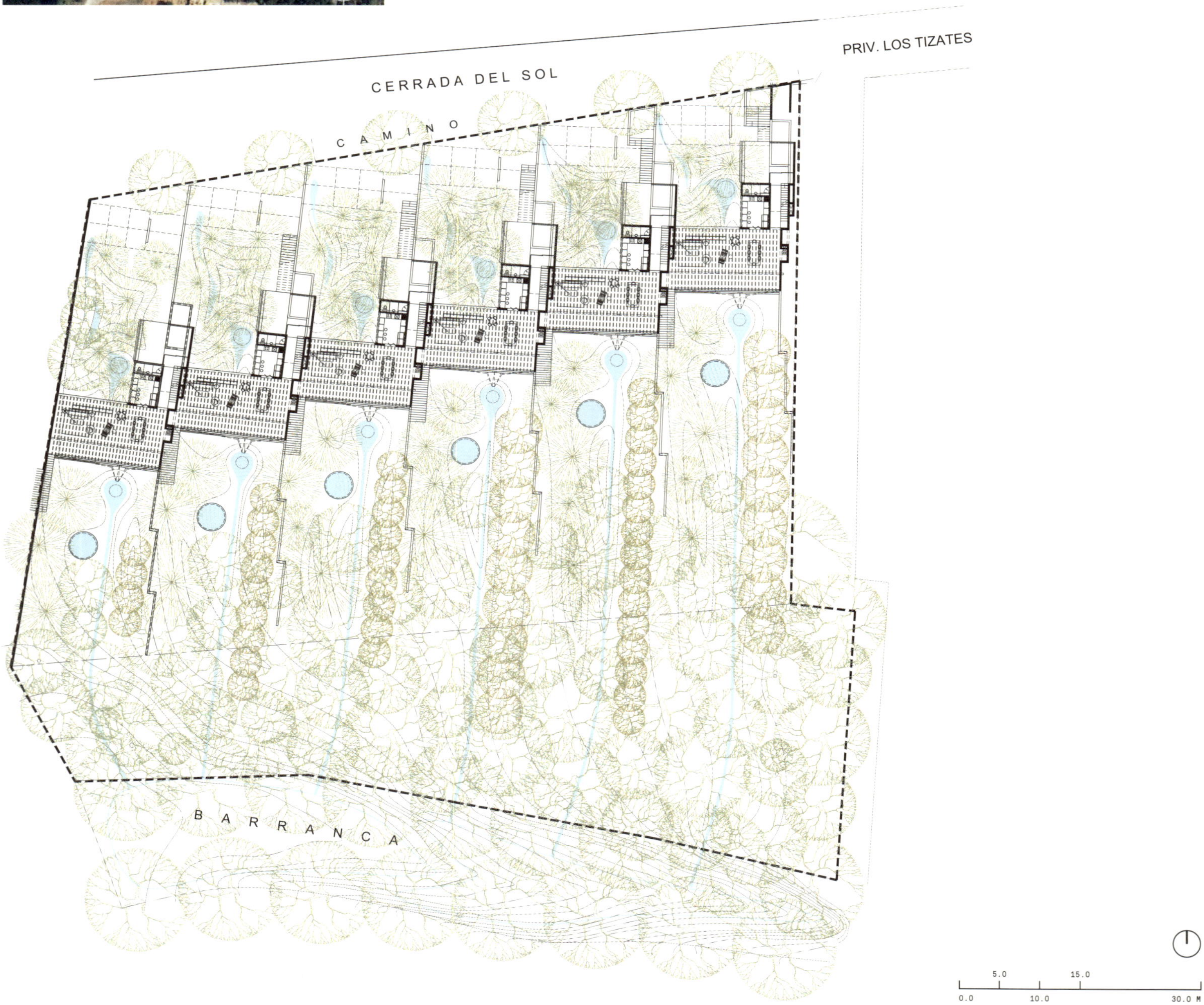

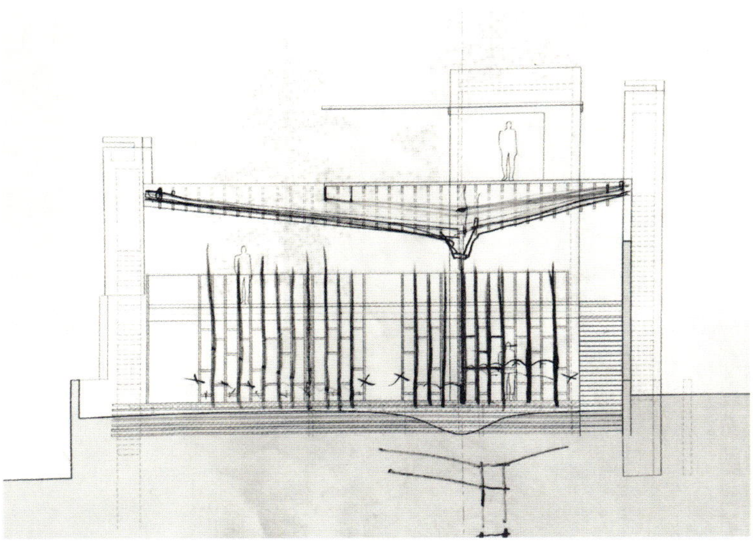

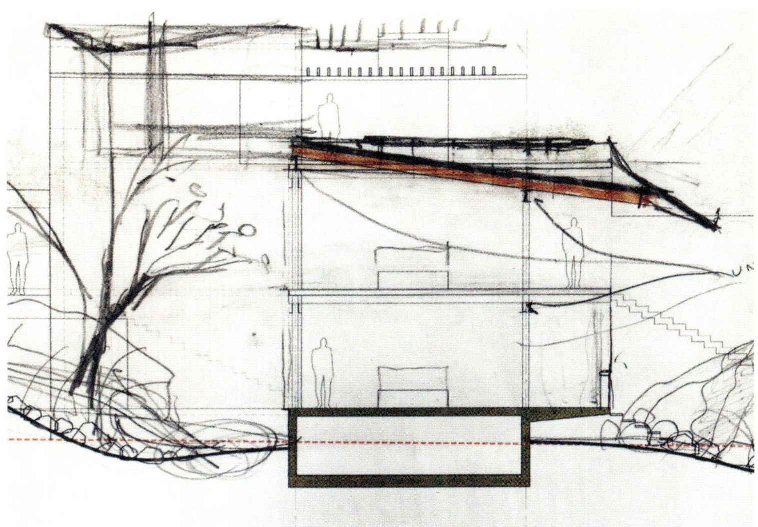

Casitas Valle

With— Iván Ramírez

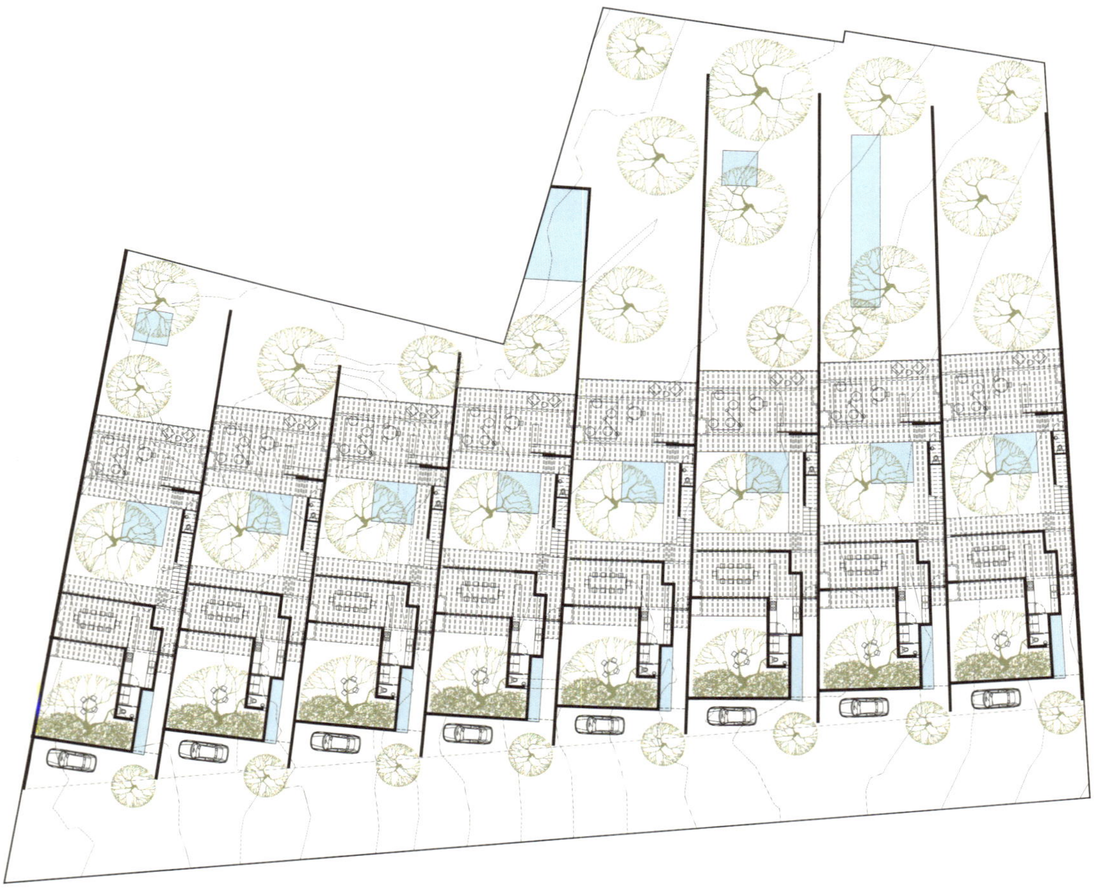

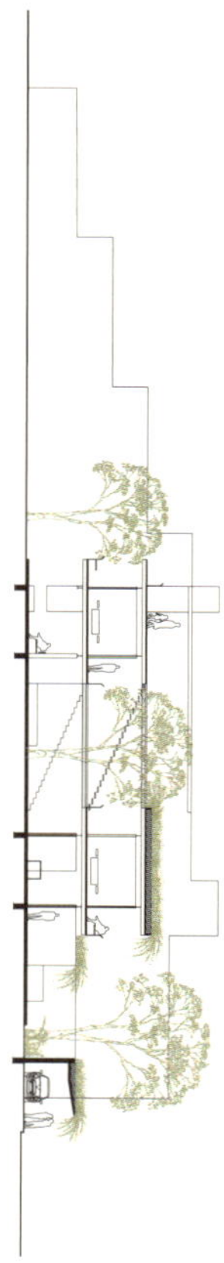

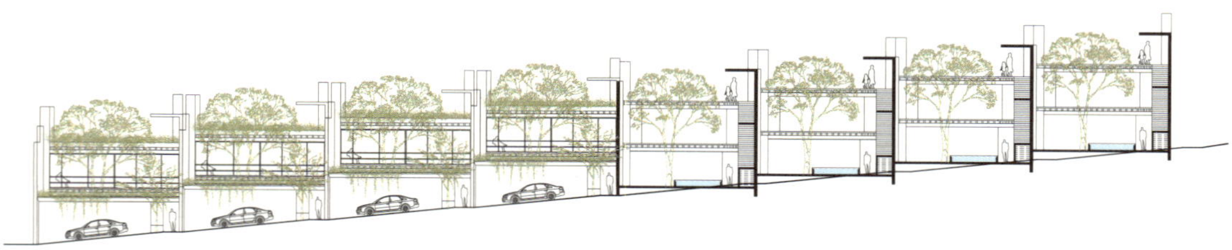

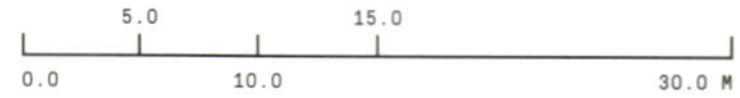

CERRADA DEL SOL
NORTE

Hermosillo

With— David Martínez

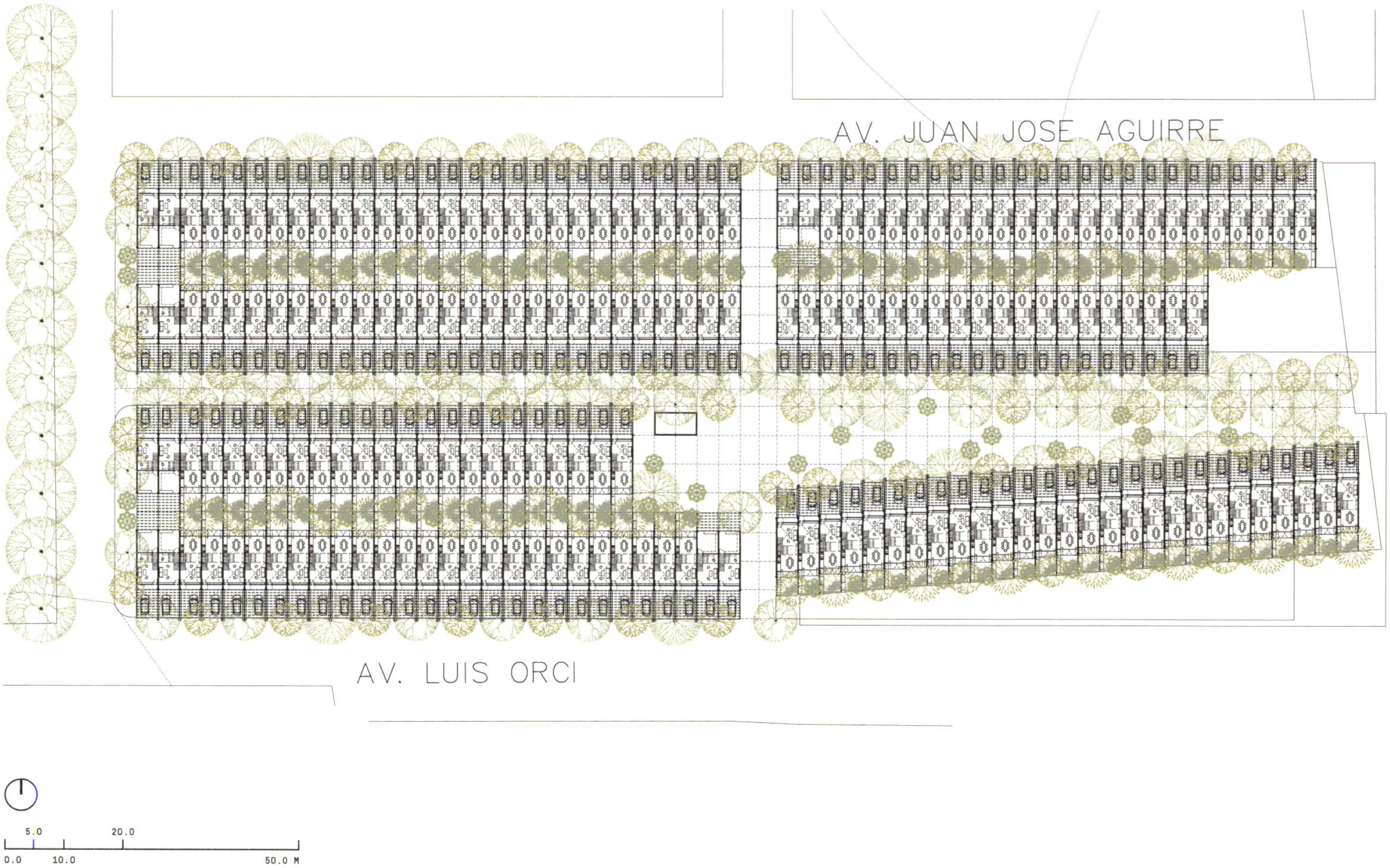

The Ten Commandments of the Hermosillo Housing Project

1. Intra-urban
2. Woven on the weft
3. Narrower, more densely treed streets
4. Narrower and deeper lots
5. Contiguous constructions
6. Green roofs
7. Solar control
8. Cross ventilation
9. High ceilings
10. Continuous space

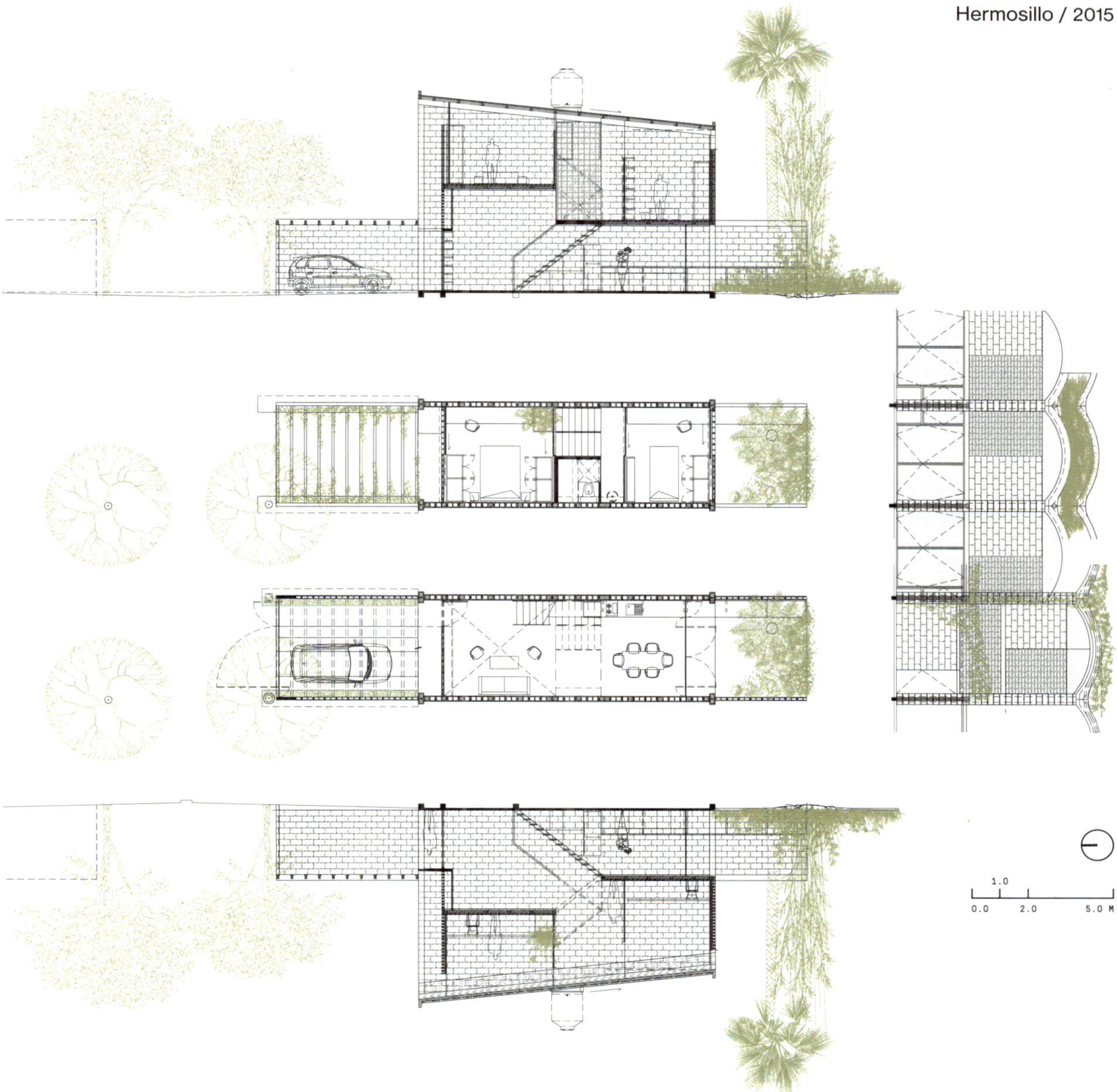

The low-cost housing project constructed in Hermosillo is based on previous experiments carried out in an intra-urban context, woven into the urban fabric by a set of narrow, densely treed streets. The individual lots are narrow and deep, with the result that the residential units –3.50 meters wide– stand side by side. The extreme climate of the area is offset by green roofs and windows with solar controls, which also favor cross ventilation. Inside each house, the ample heights define a continuous space, the different areas configured by a central structure containing the stairway, bathroom, and closets. With the vehemence that characterizes his practice, Kalach has managed to fit 180 single-family units into a one-hectare lot on which he was asked to design eighty. He converted the 45 m² required for each unit into 70 m², reducing construction costs without increasing total investment in the project. He also improved thermal efficiency without in the least affecting the program demanded. Each residential unit still has its own driveway and back patio, as well as the usual program of living room, dining room, kitchen, bathroom, and two bedrooms.

Guaymas

With— Xavier González

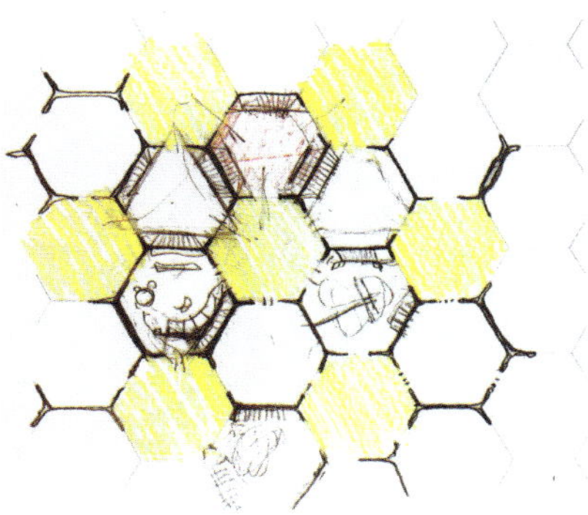

Tijuana

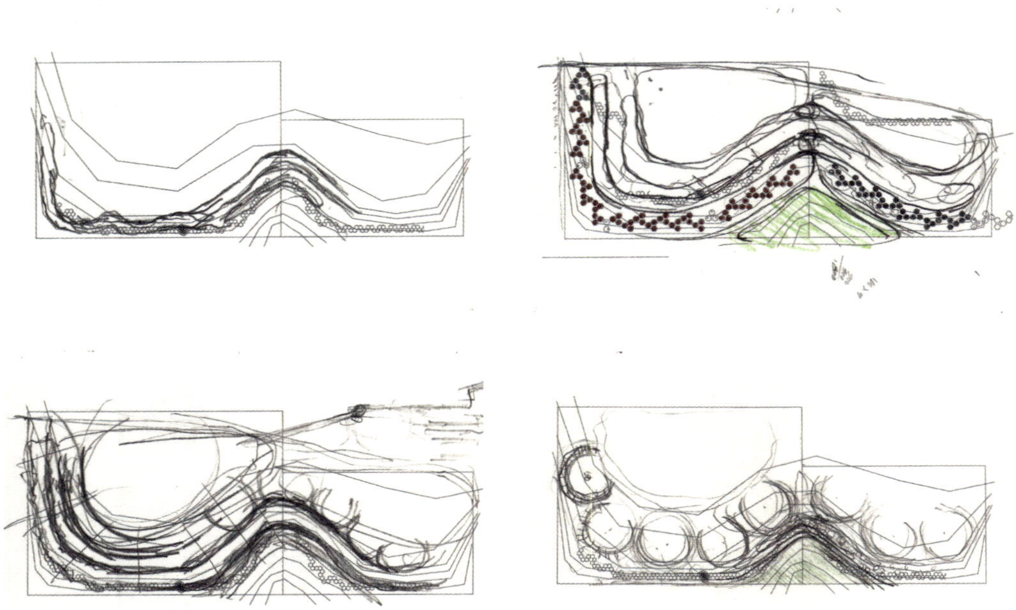

— This image illustrates the conventional housing that occupies 100% of the lot vs. urban development sensitive to the natural surroundings, occupying only 18%. The latter keeps the same number of housing units, in small buildings of three, four, or five levels. We have reduced the traces of occupation by buildings and streets to only 28% of the site. This makes for an environment of densely treed parks and gardens, permeable soils, and pleasant vistas.

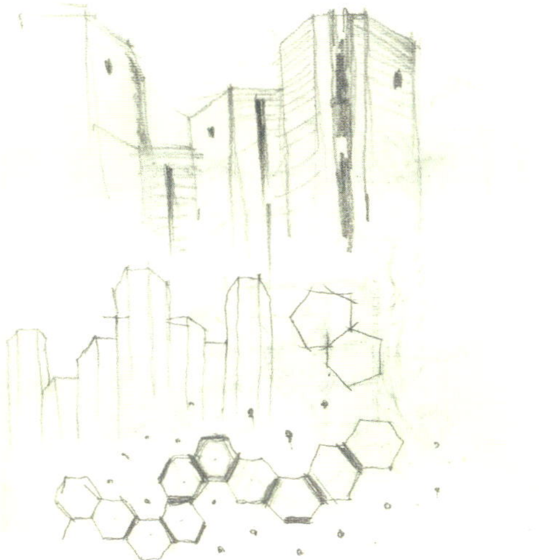

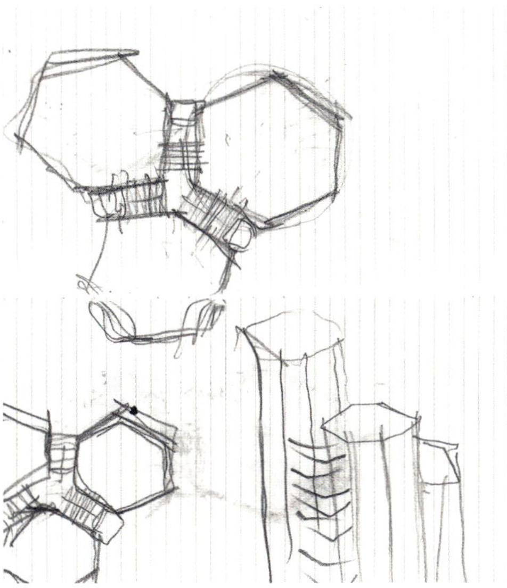

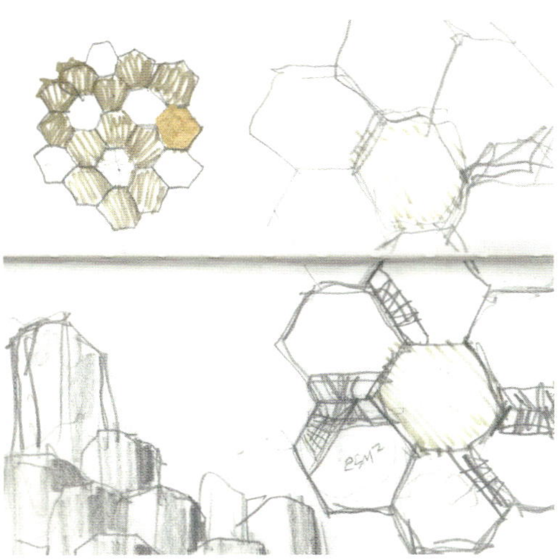

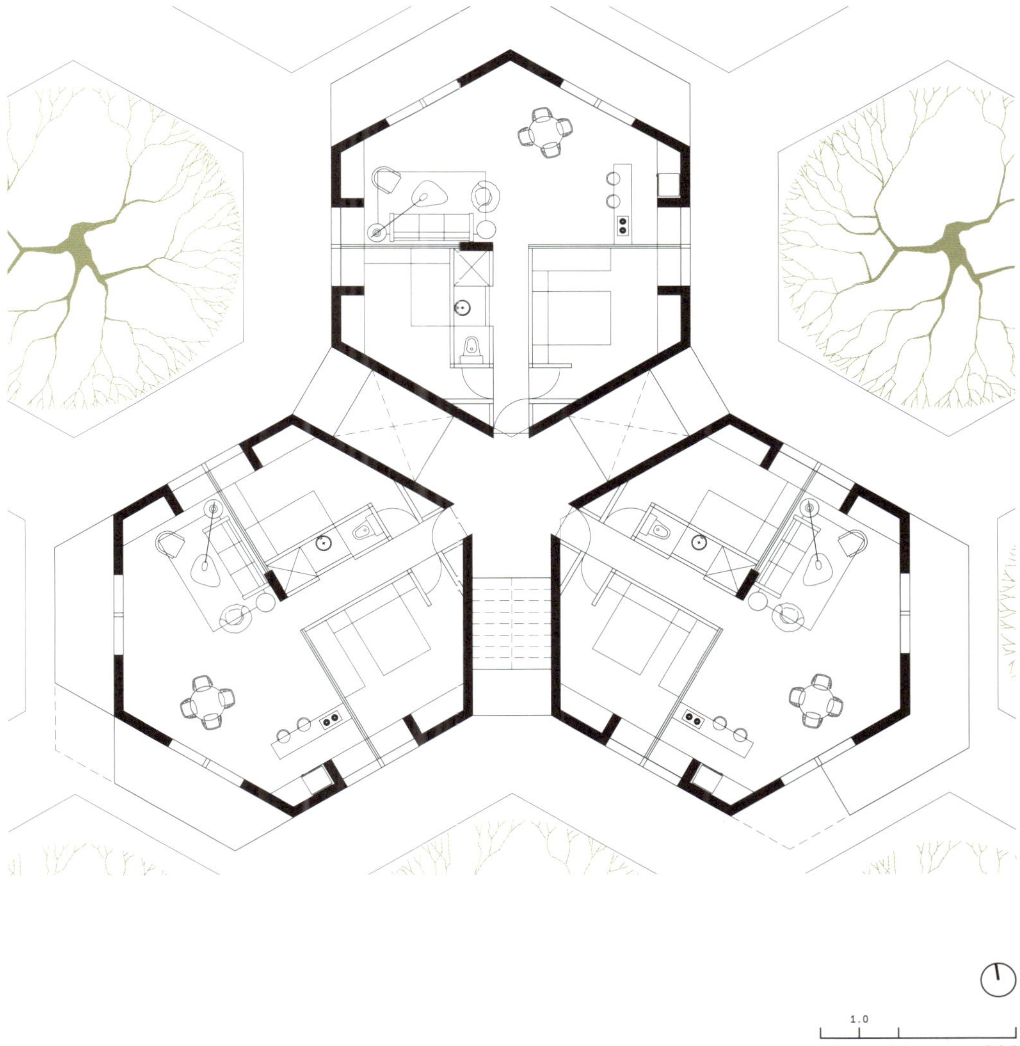
1.0
0.0
2.0
5.0 M

Ajusco
edge of the city

With— Susana Pantoja

Mexico City / 2013

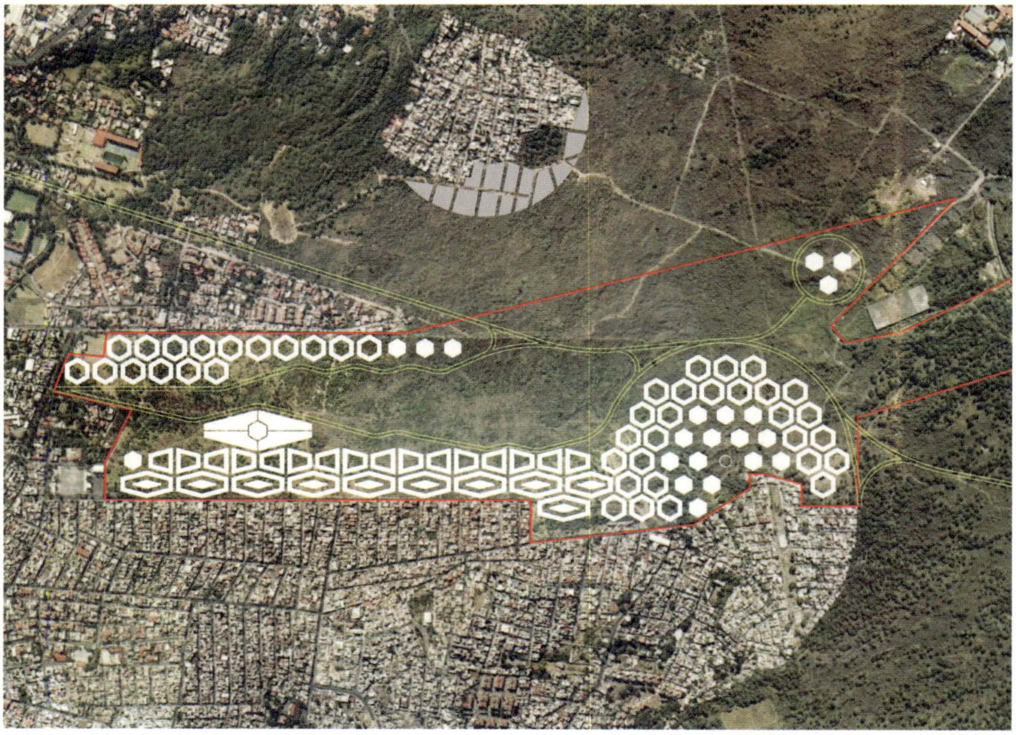

El Salado

With— Axel Arañó, Emilio Cohen, Rebeca Cotera, Julio González, Walter Lingard, and Rosa López

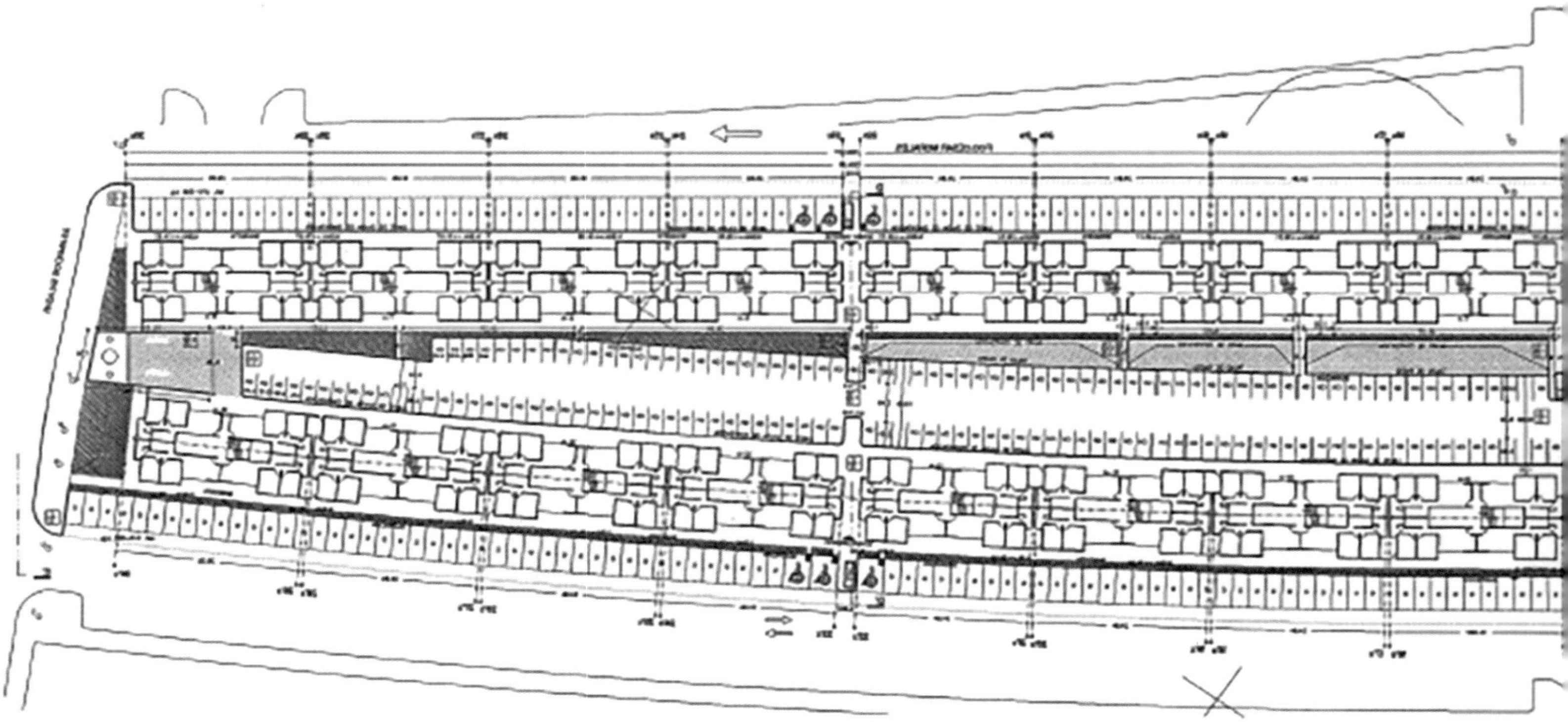

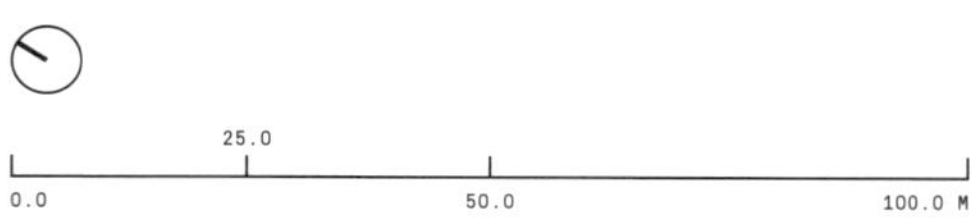

— The creation of dense but efficient block allows the creation of border areas alongside the new parks and public spaces the city requires.

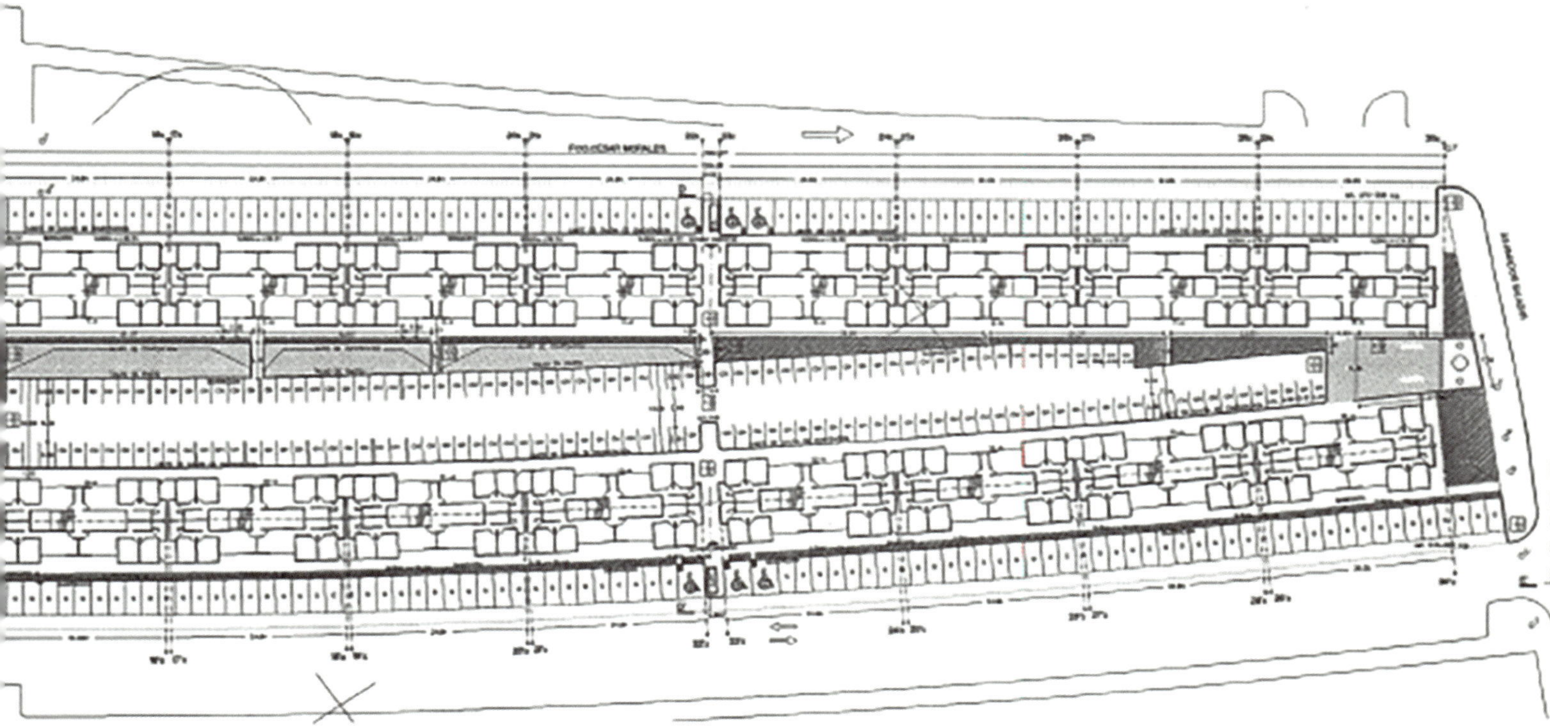

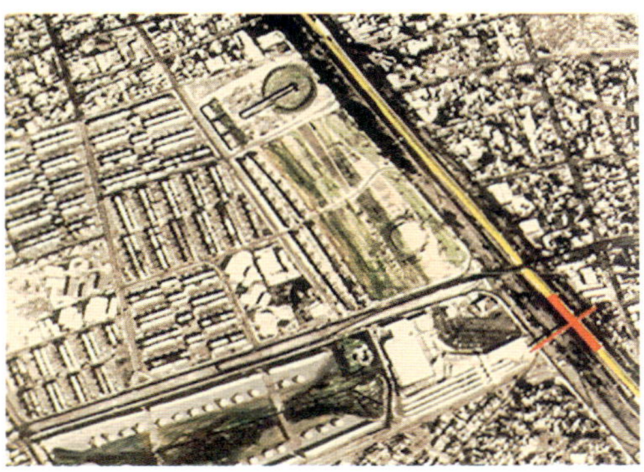

Perinorte

With— Armando Oliver

Estado de México / 2004

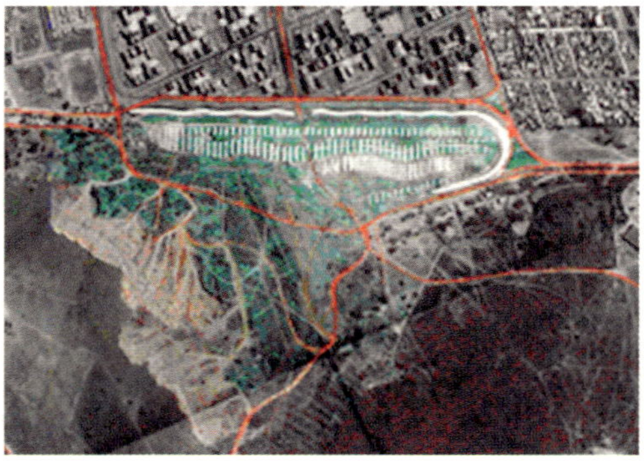

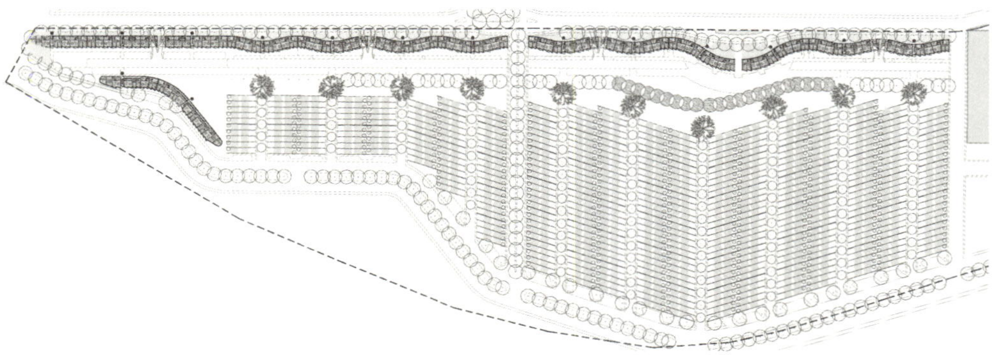

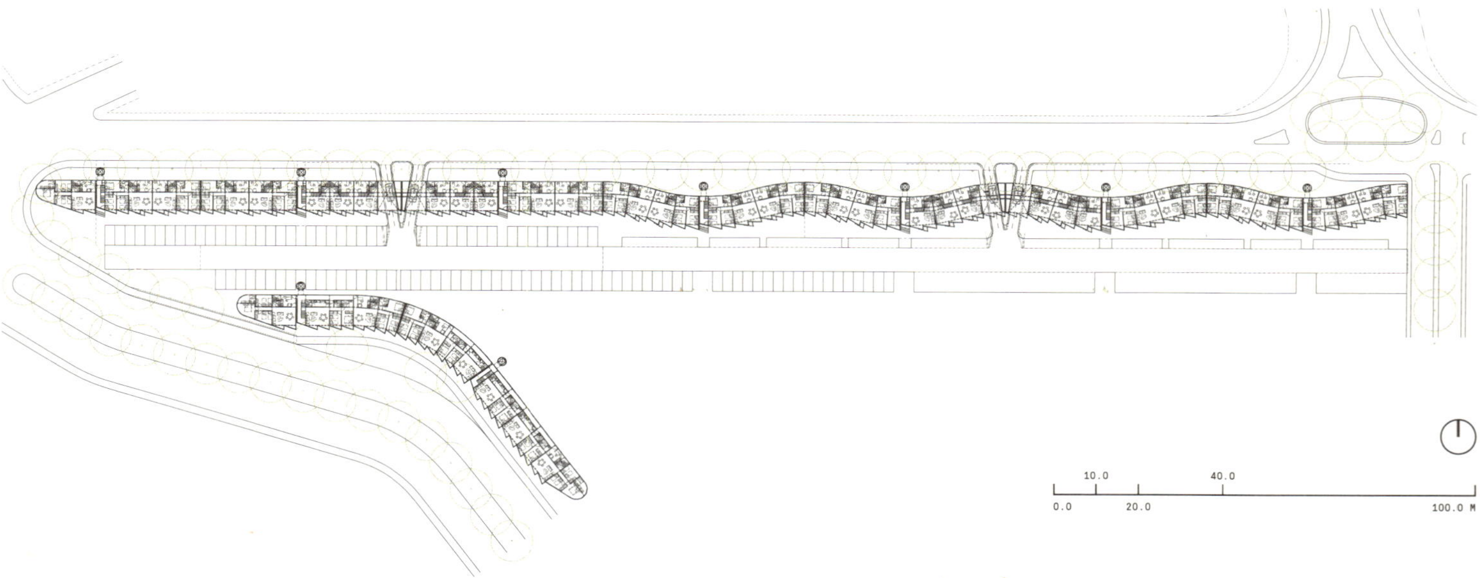

— A gentle slope, a slight angle, a variation in color help to break the monotony.

Ahijones Castilla

With— Héctor Módica and Iván Ramírez

Spain / 2008

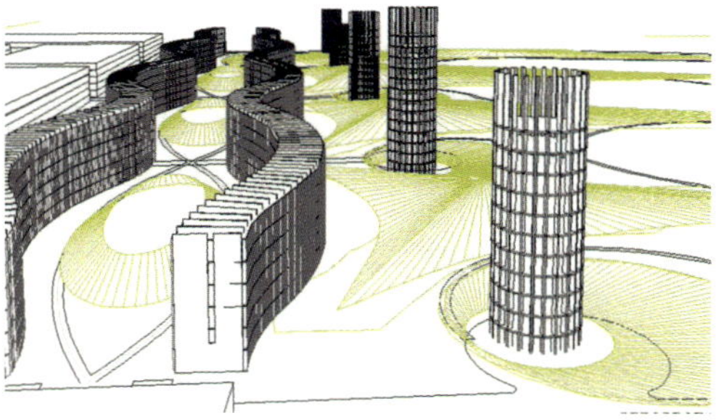

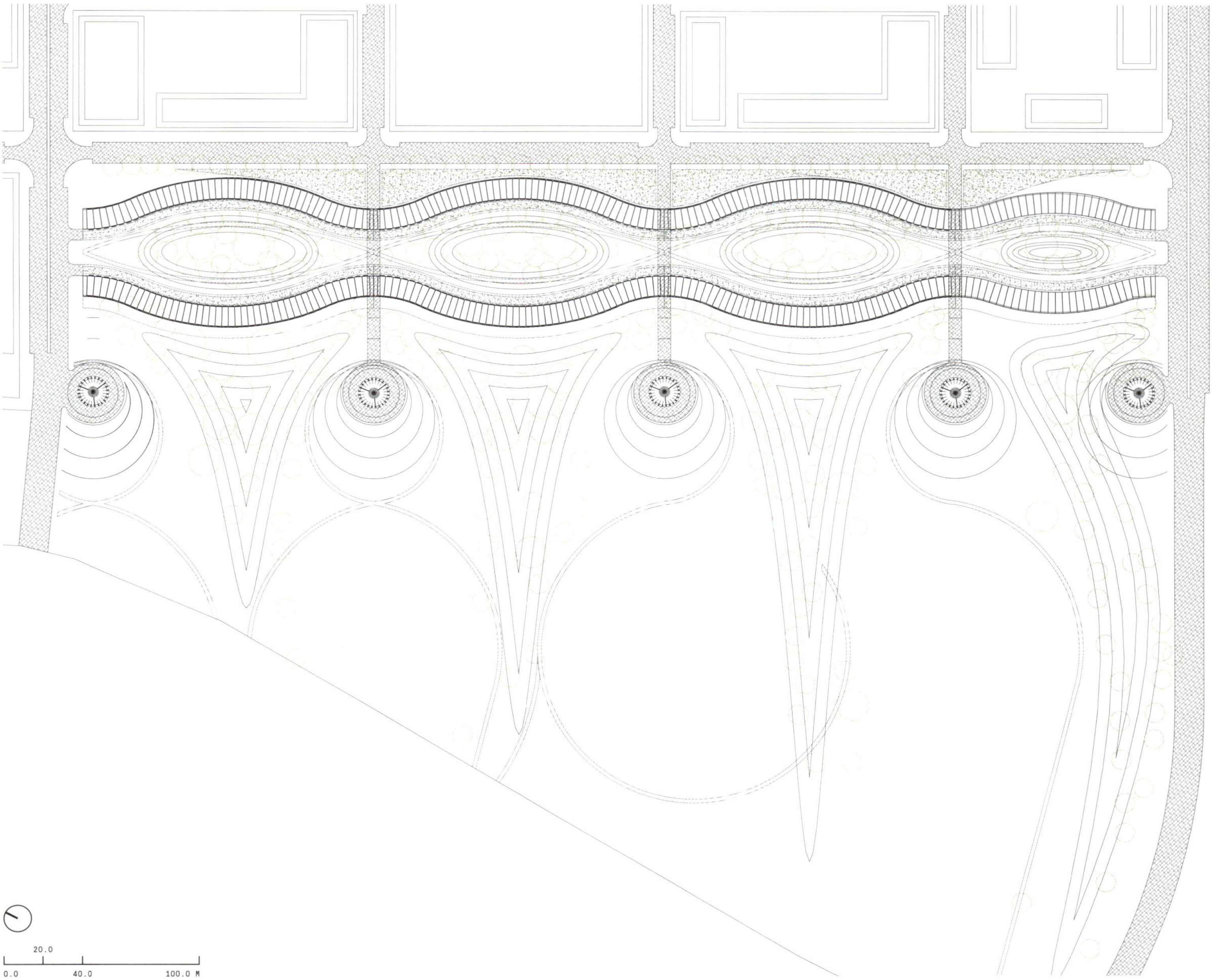

Cerro de la Estrella

With— Cecilia Solís

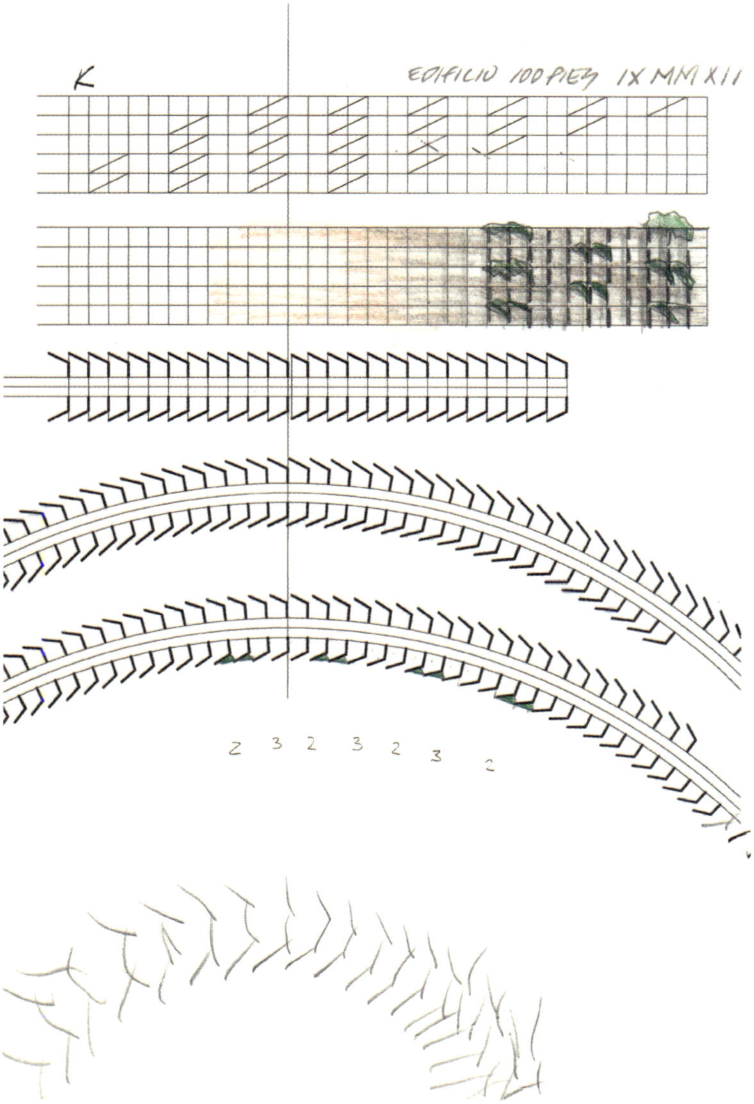

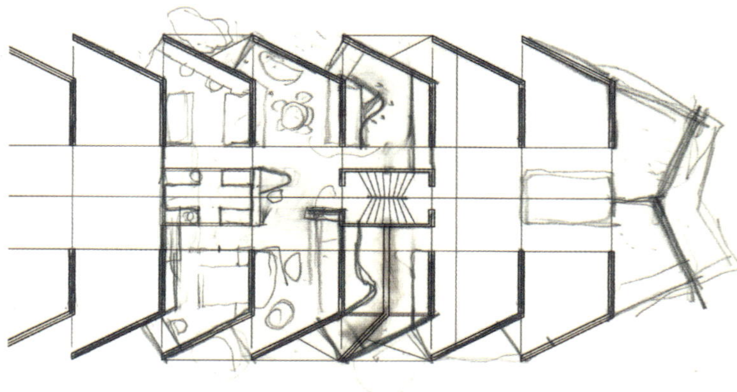

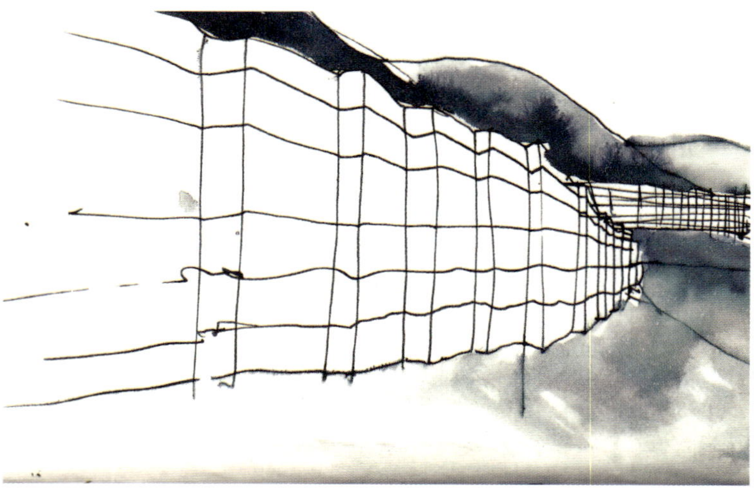

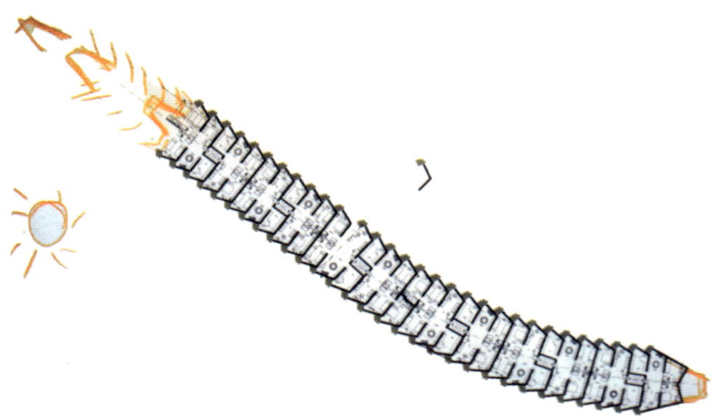

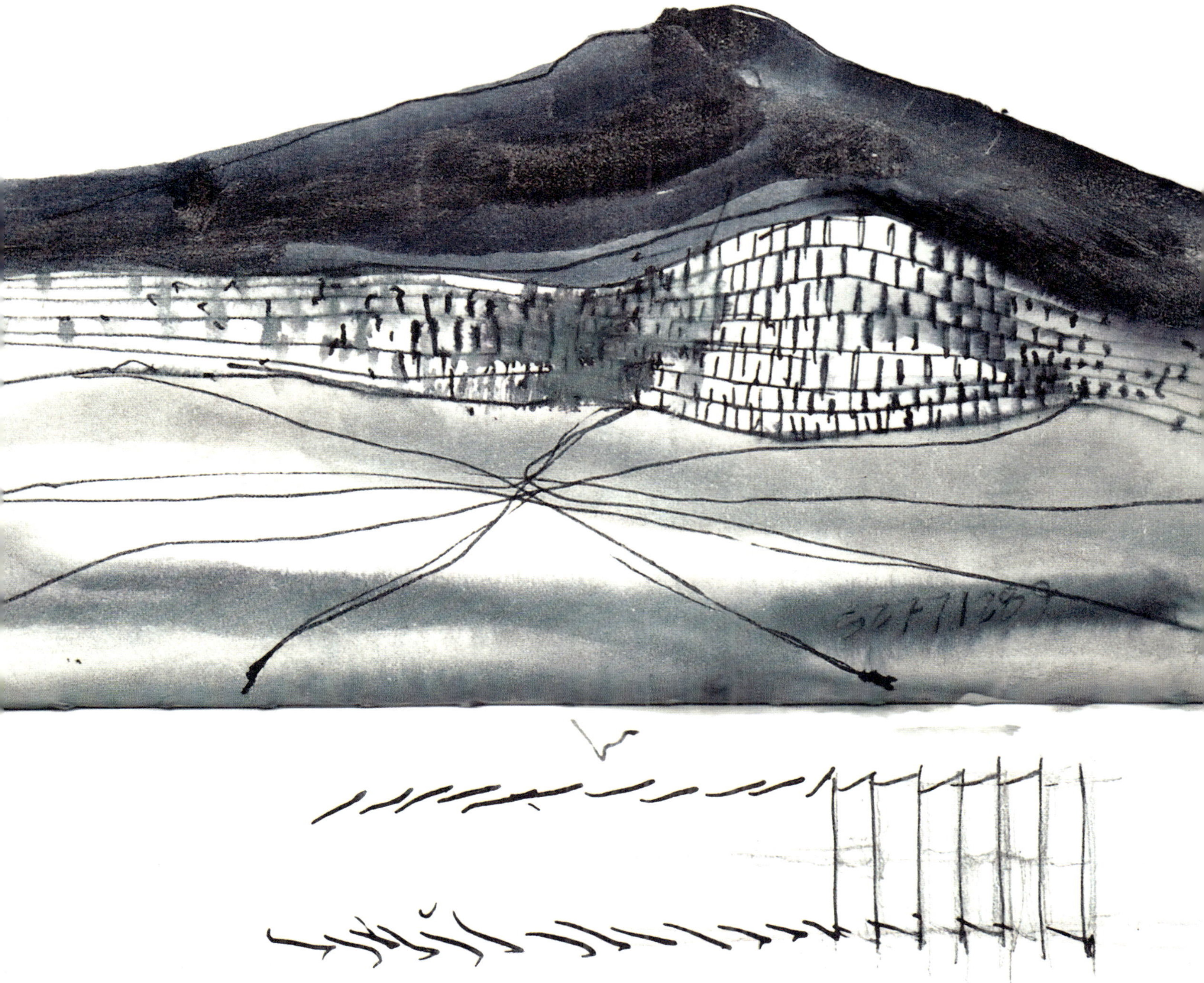

— Many natural areas are constantly invaded by the expansion of the city. Stalwart, dense, and efficient buildings that serve as delimiting walls: urban on one side, rural and natural on the other.

Housing and Territory

— Housing and territory are closely interconnected. The one affects the other. Woodlands, fields, towns, and villages all form part of a single landscape, a single place.

I suppose that, out of thoughtlessness, we have not yet planned our territory. The urban and territorial plans we have devised do not really embrace very much. Few cities or states in Mexico have urban development plans. Our country has been deforested, the countryside has been neglected, and chaotic urban sprawl devours the landscape. There are many highways to be built, railways to be reactivated, seaports and airports to be built or improved. The development of alternative energy sources is another pending challenge.

It is instructive to fly over countries like Holland, France, or England (even by means of Google Earth) in order to understand how a territory can actually be controlled. There we see strictly delimited urban conglomerations, living side-by-side with farmland and natural surroundings.

We have to wisely limit the extension of our cities and towns while at the same time reforesting wild areas and cultivating farmland.

Our case study, Milpa Alta, is complicated by its proximity to Mexico City, making it subject to deforestation processes and rapid, unorganized urban growth. The most serious issue is the fact that the zone is of the utmost importance to replenishing the water table that supplies Mexico City.

We propose, therefore, to impose a limit on each built-up area, made up of houses backing one another to form a large rampart: on one side, the urban settlement; on the other, the countryside and the landscape.

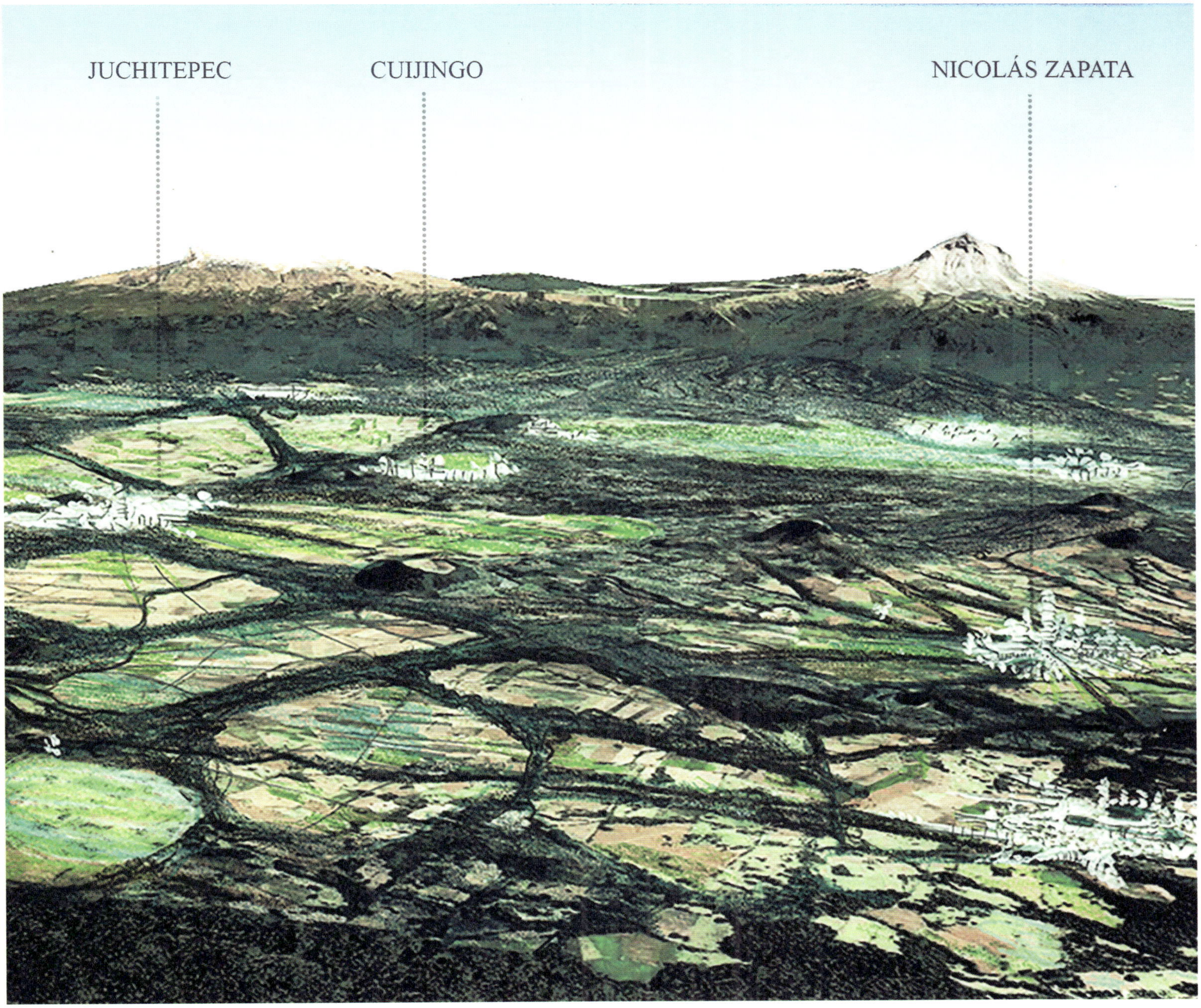
JUCHITEPEC
CUIJINGO
NICOLÁS ZAPATA

JUCHITEPEC
CUIJINGO

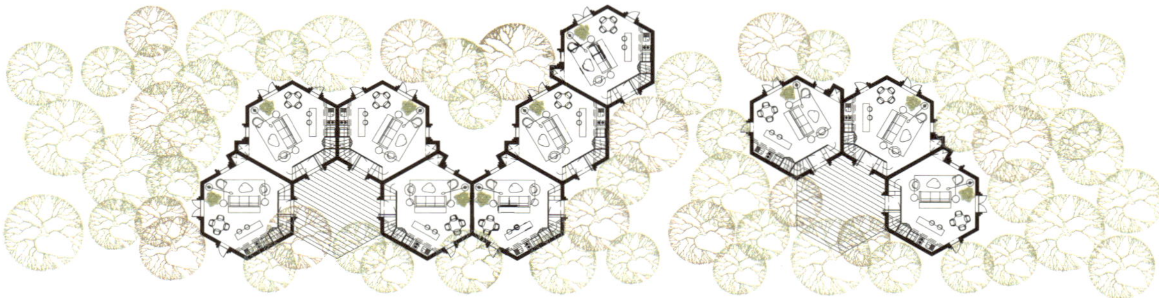

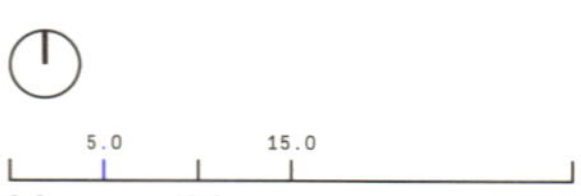
5.0
15.0
0.0
10.0
30.0 M

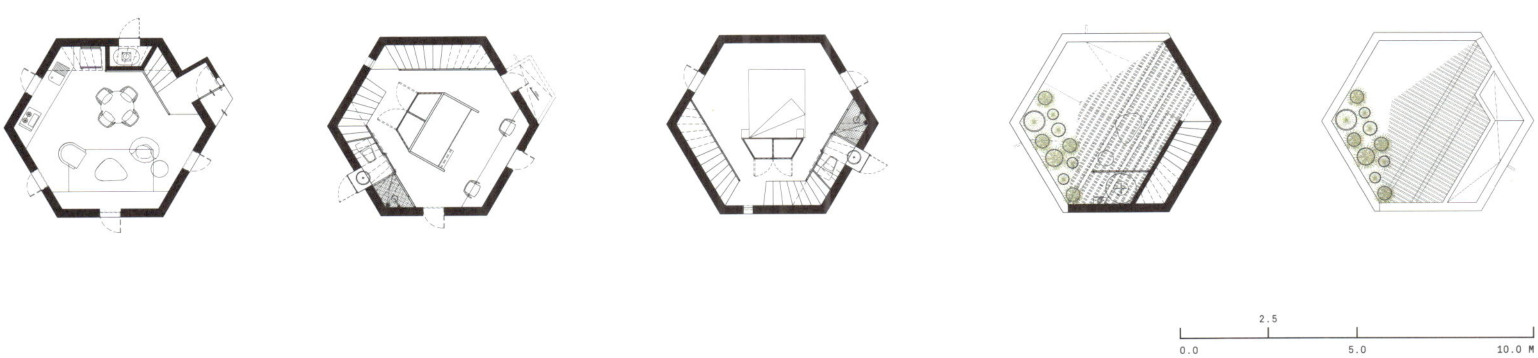
2.5
0.0
5.0
10.0 M

Peñón Paraíso

With— Emilio Cohen

Mexico City / 1994

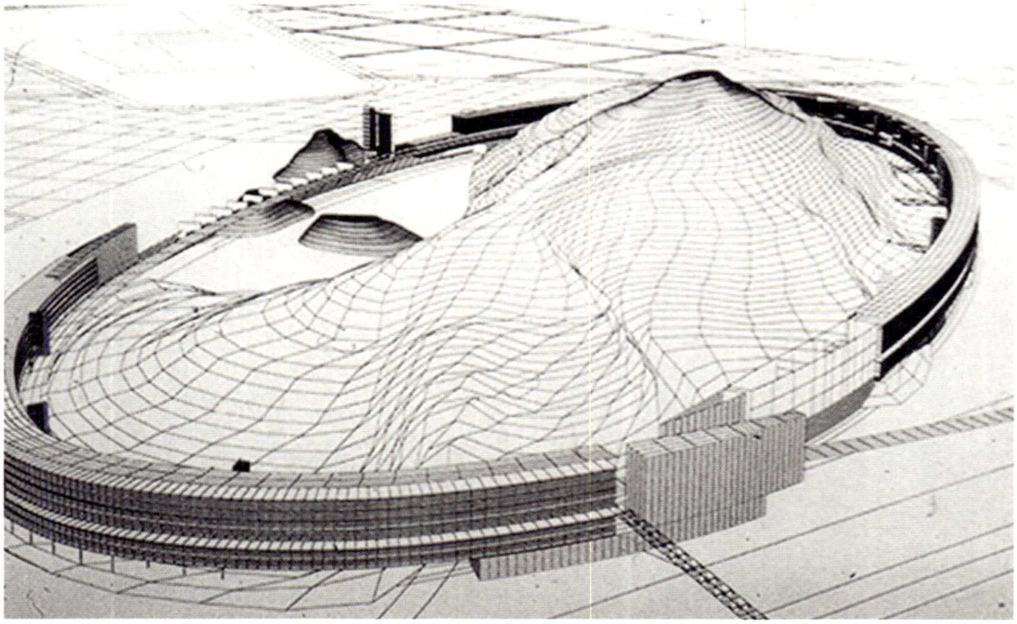

MX-Puebla

With— Roberto Gómez

Mexico City / 1995

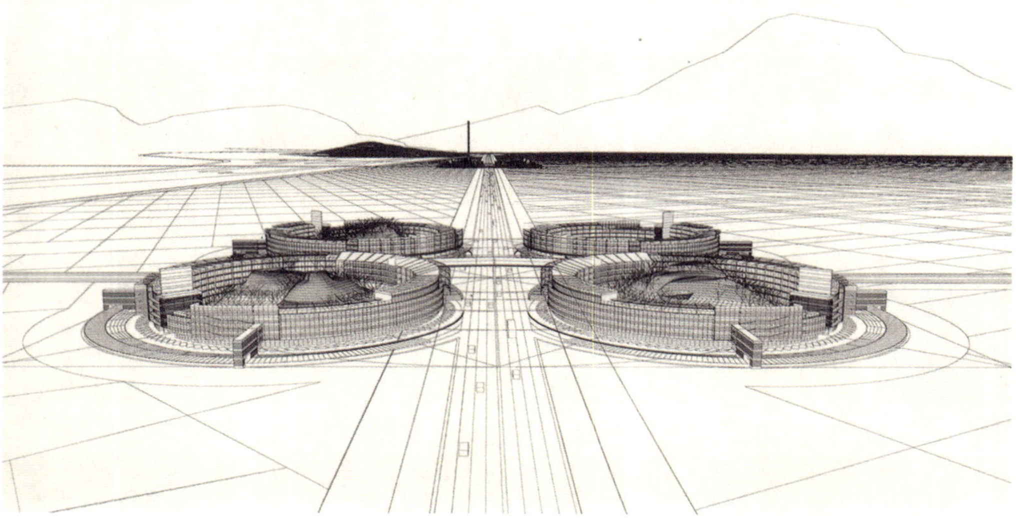

Another one of Kalach's typological explorations is the cloister: radial housing that serves to contain the urban conglomerate and protect it from the natural surroundings.

Peñoles

With— David Martínez

Torreón / 2014

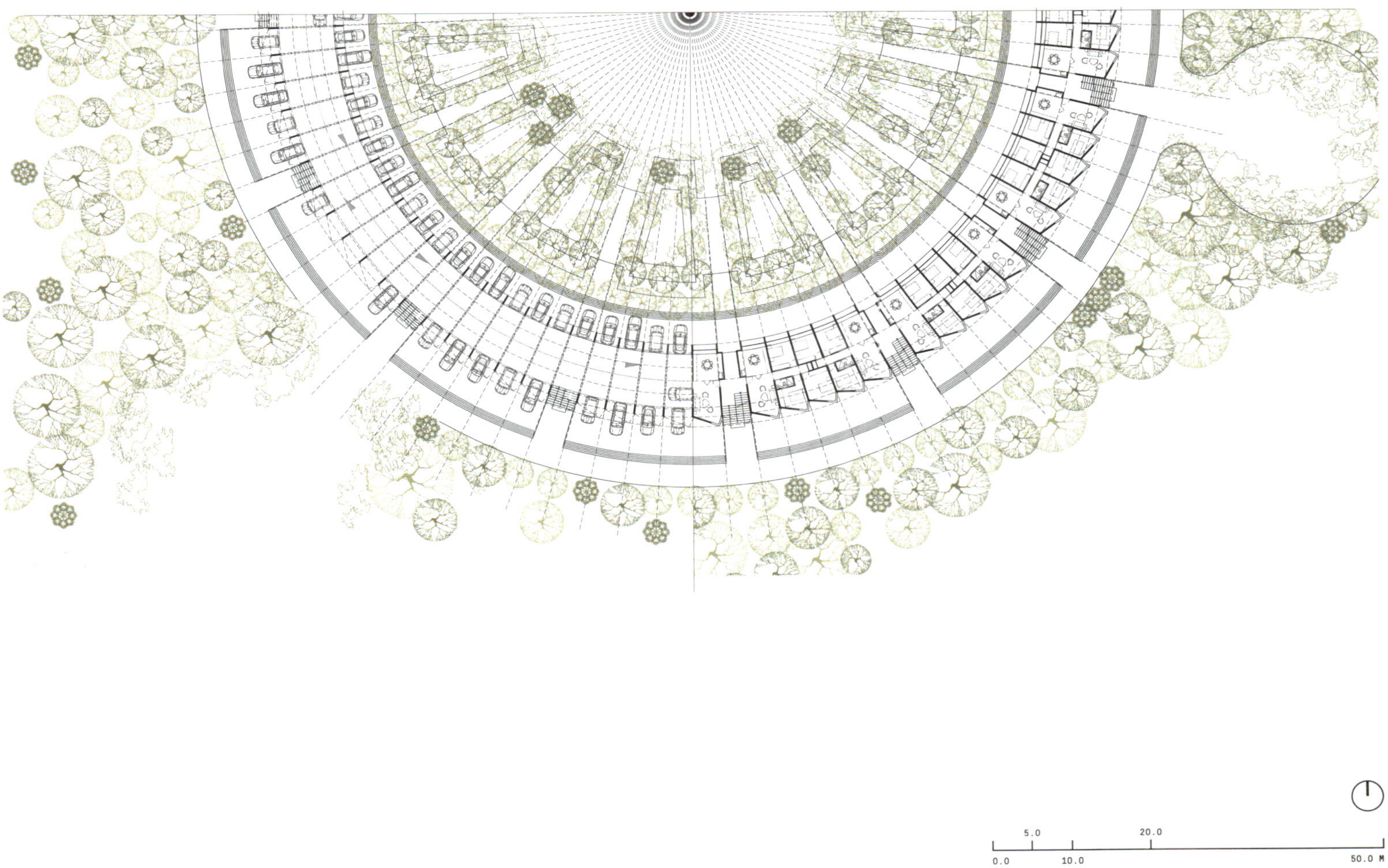

Reynosa

10.0
0.0
20.0 M

City-State

/ 2012

— It is thrilling to discover that there are still ancient city states, like those in the Bible and the *Iliad*. Little cities contained within themselves, amidst cultivated fields and natural landscapes, which preserve their size and layout, their streets and plazas, their monuments. However much the architecture may have been transformed, the spirit and essence of the whole remain.

With their tangle of narrow winding streets, these towns are the seeds of the ideal polities conceived of by our utopian dreamers: Campanella's City of the Sun, Thomas More's Utopia, Francis Bacon's New Atlantis.

Just forty years ago, León Krier, with his magical drawings, insisted on small towns that could be covered by walking.

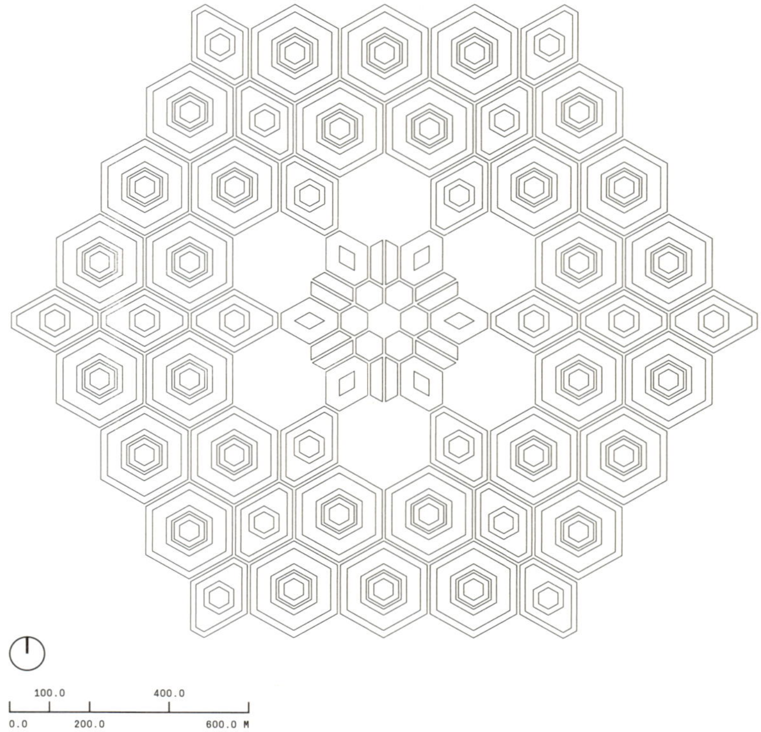

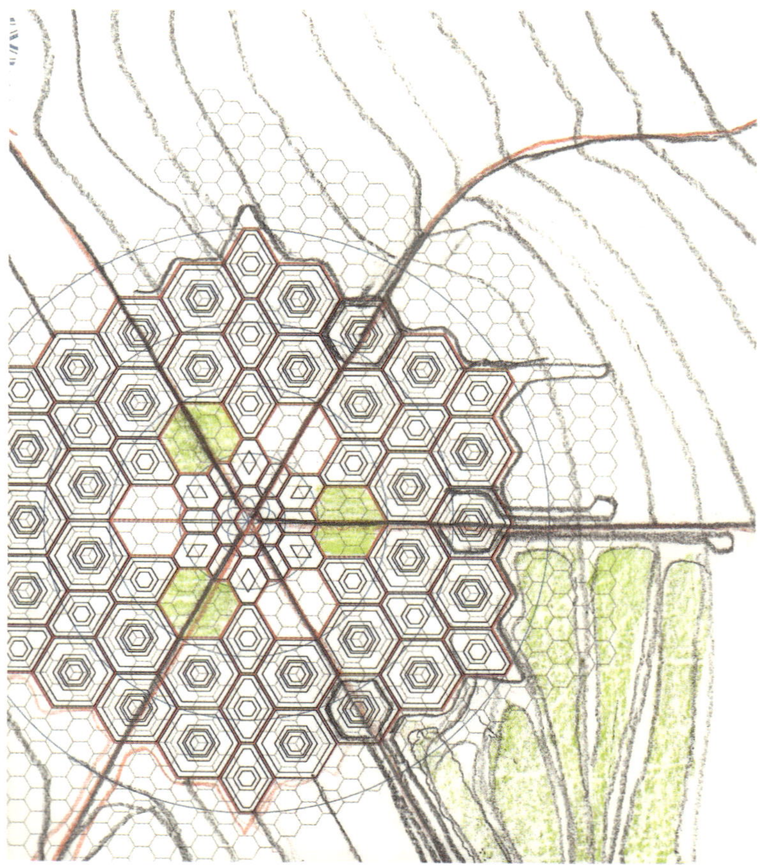

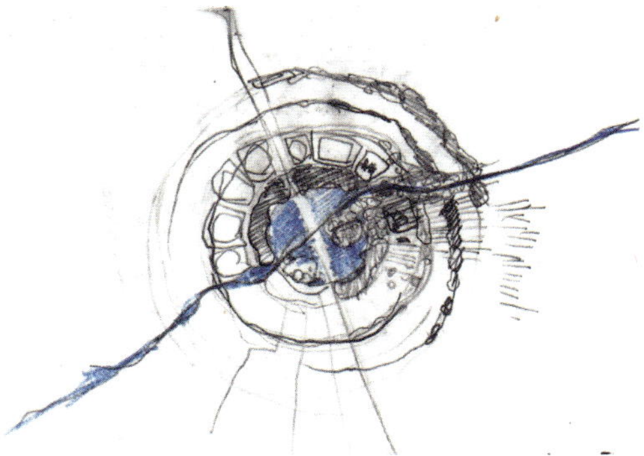

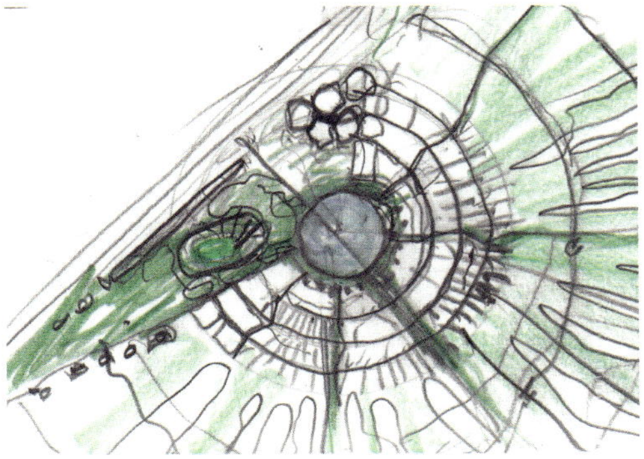

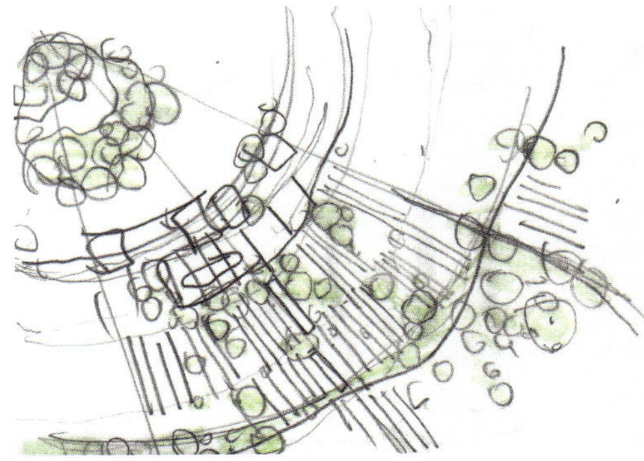

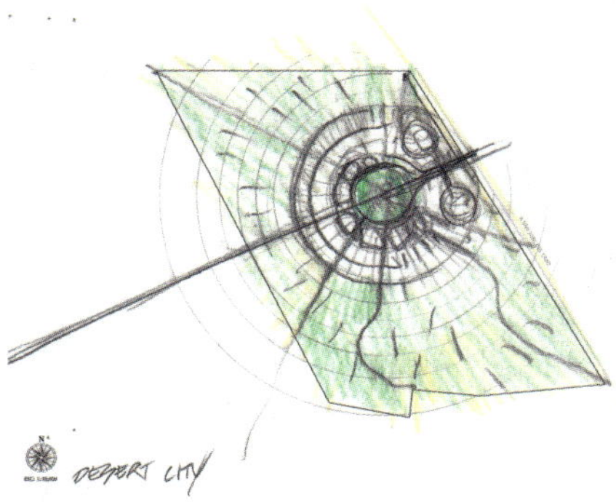

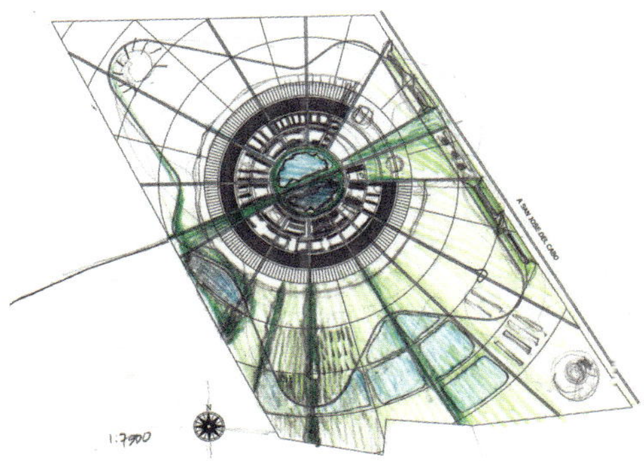

Houses and Gardens

— There are houses set like pieces in the landscape, when the landscape is beautiful and sings.
There are houses conceived as labyrinths, to hide in, to be lost and found in.
There are venerable old houses, recycled with new forms of life.
There are houses concealed as terraces in gardens.
There is a garden that Barragán designed as a house and an idea that Le Corbusier sowed as a seed, which went on to conquer the world.

Alberto Kalach recalls that José María Buendía – one of the few masters he acknowledges – preferred "sensorial experience... to conceptualism; sequence rather than the single space; the narration of a fantastic tale and not the demonstration of a genial idea; the labyrinth versus the glass box."[1] That is what happens in his houses, where the architectural elements that enclose the spaces are grafted onto the terrain, to be embraced by nature. The designs of this visionary architect emerge from the repetition of lines that allow one to imagine a promenade or the penetrations of light. Thus, the design frees itself from the reiterated lines that give form to the spatial idea. The essence of architecture emerges from its skeleton, prevailing in its ultimate expression. The structure is both proto-architecture and ruin. His domestic spaces are defined by concrete walls and slabs, with all expression yielded, in some projects, to the structure, as in Le Corbusier's Dom-Ino House.

The limits between nature and artifice, between vegetation and construction, are gradually blurred, in order to intensify the perception of the natural world, combining space, light, and nature. Intuition, in alliance with time, replaces geometrical rigor. And the architect who wanted to be a gardener acts as a geomancer, interpreting the marks on the earth and its telluric energies. Inert mineral matter is assumed as a support, as a generator of habitable space and limits, while the architect allows the vegetal world to fill space with time. Kalach would agree, perhaps, with Tadao Ando, that "natural phenomena like light and water need to be 'architecturalized' by geometry and the idea, if we wish the hidden spirit, concealed behind 'nature,' to be revealed."[2] In his most recent houses the tensions between what belongs and what doesn't, between the radical approach, without concession, and empathy with nature, disappears.

[1] Alberto Kalach, "Paradise is a Garden," in *Alberto Kalach*, edited by Miquel Adrià (Barcelona: Gustavo Gili, 2004), p. 22.

[2] "Naturaleza hecha abstracción," interview with Tadao Ando. *El Croquis* 44 (Madrid, 2000), p. 95.

House in Tepoztlán

With— Alejandro Sánchez

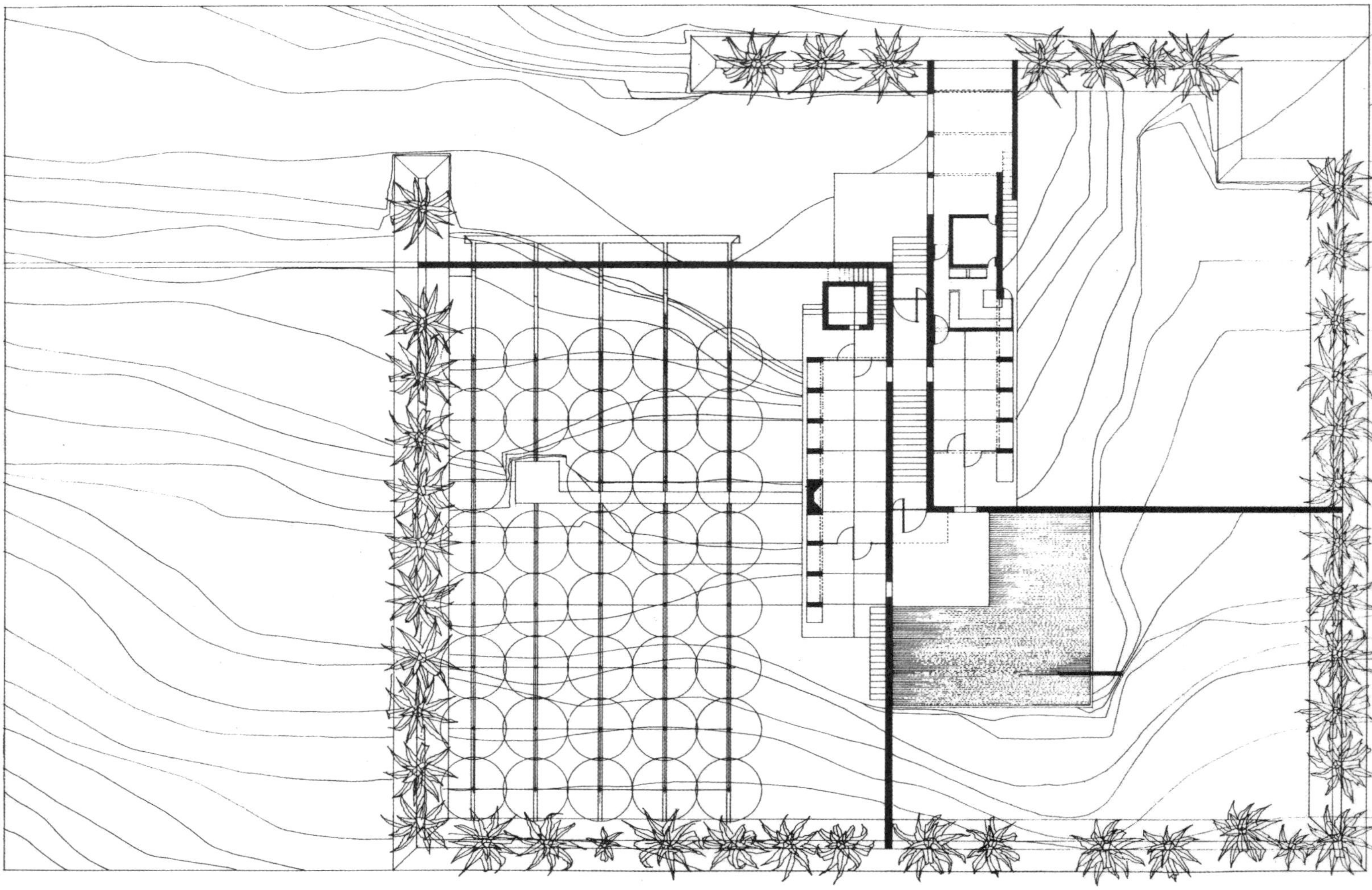

— One bright youthful morning, as my dear friend and teacher Alejandro Sánchez ("El Mánchez") and I were smoking a few joints on a gentle slope at the foot of the imposing Tepozteco, we imagined four different gardens to be enjoyed from the raised terraces of the house.

Palmira House

With— Daniel Álvarez

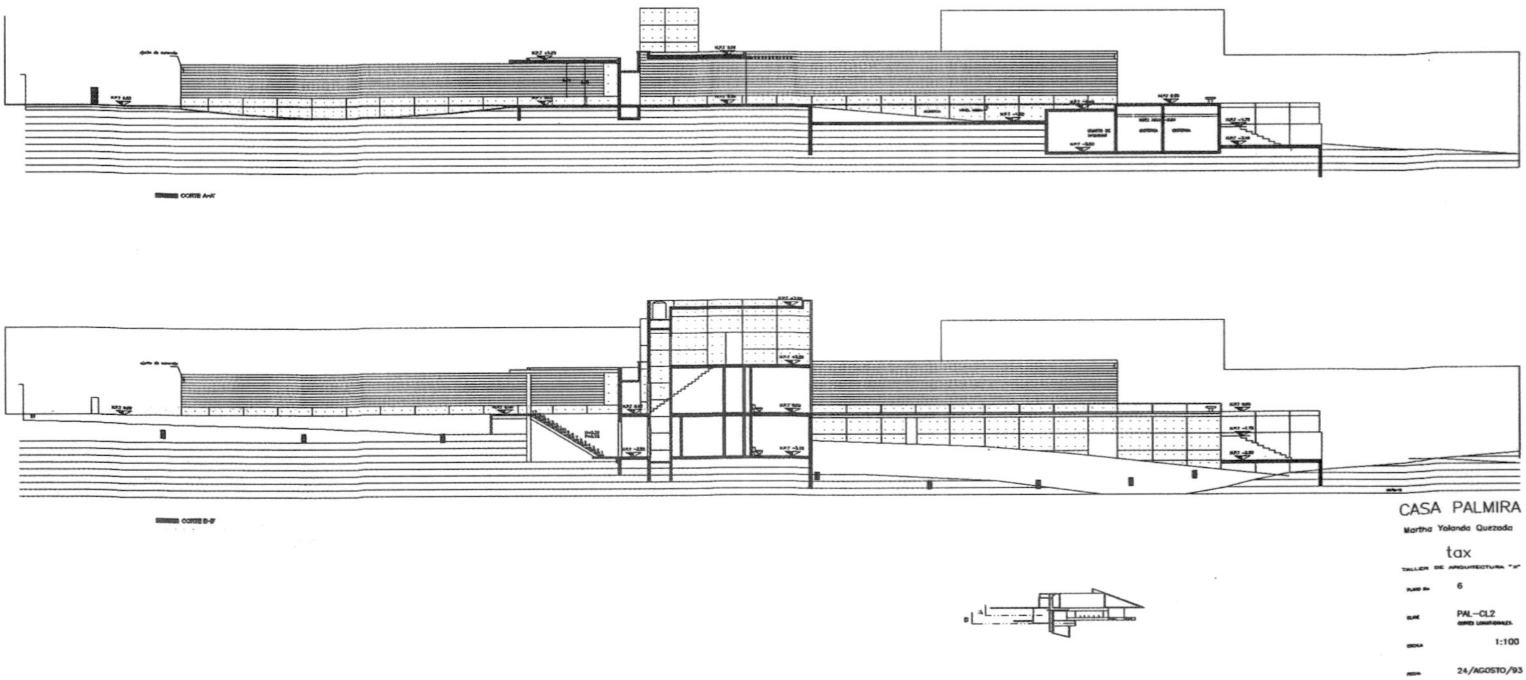
CASA PALMIRA
Martha Yolanda Quezada
tax
6
PAL-CL2
1:100
24/AGOSTO/93

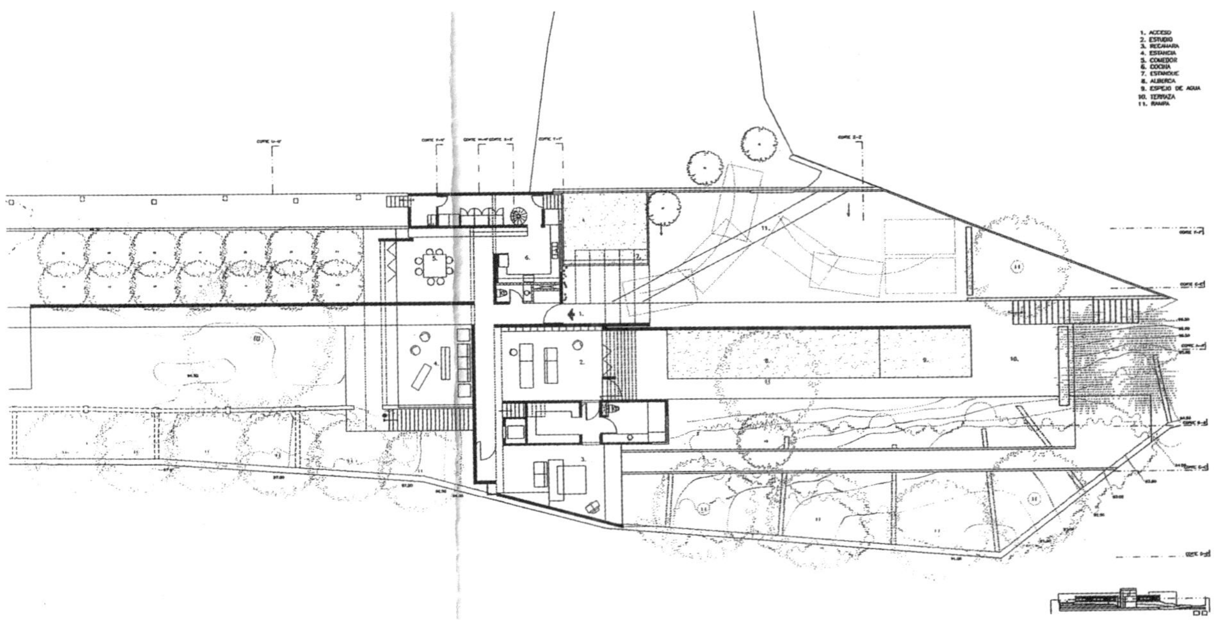
1. ACCESO
2. ESTUDIO
3. RECAMARA
4. ESTANCIA
5. COMEDOR
6. COCINA
7. ESTANQUE
8. ALBERCA
9. ESPEJO DE AGUA
10. TERRAZA
11. RAMPA

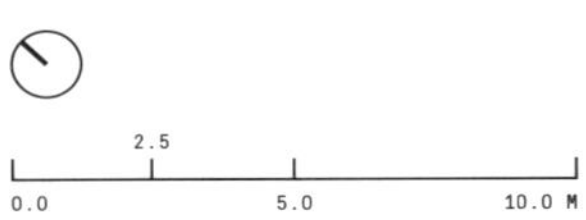
2.5
0.0
5.0
10.0 M

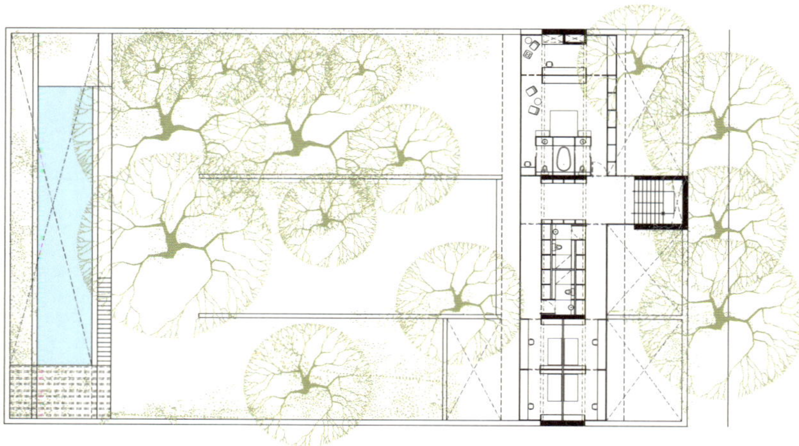

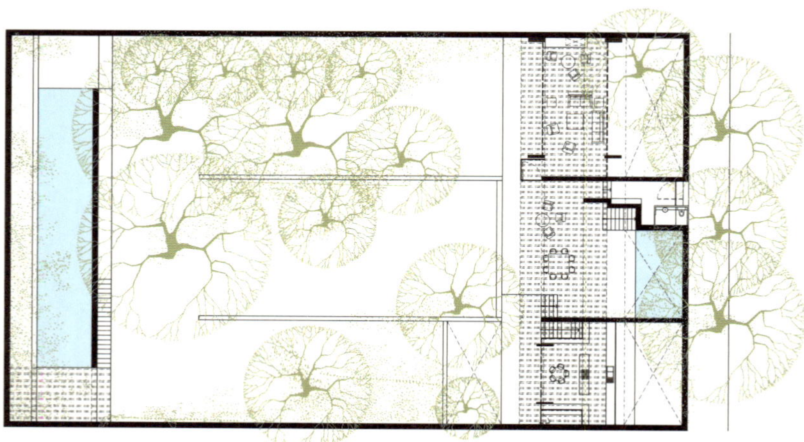

5.0
0.0
10.0
25.0 M

Vera House

With— Héctor Módica

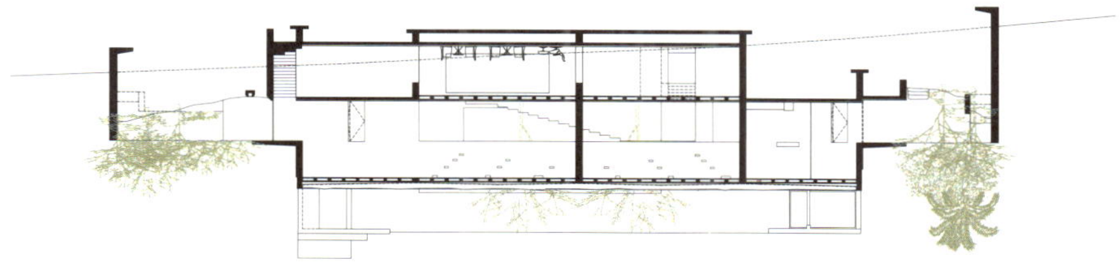

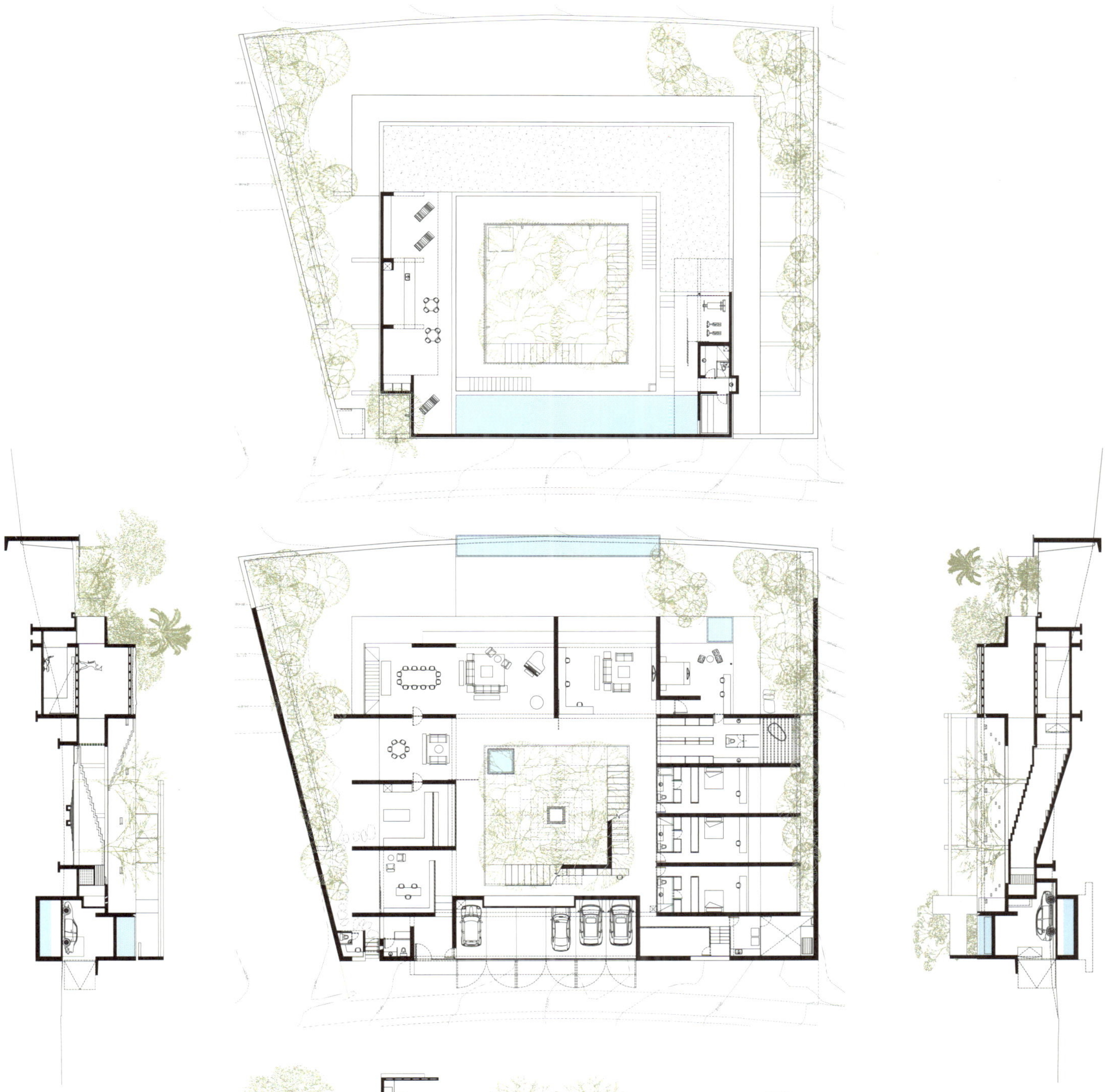

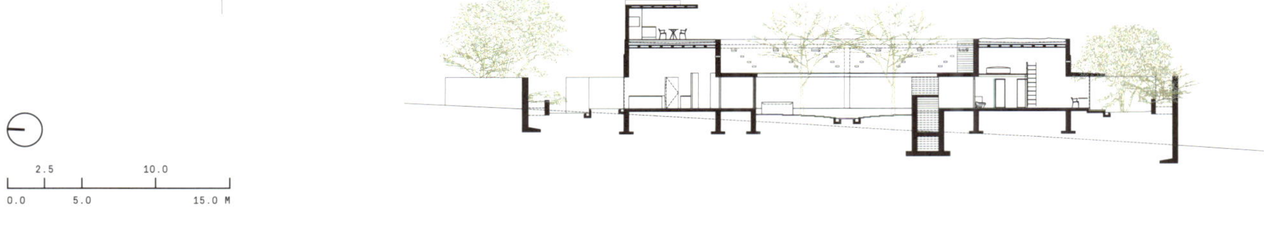
2.5
10.0
0.0
5.0
15.0 M

Valle House

With— Adriana León and María Kalach

In the house in Valle de Bravo, four platforms project from the slope, looking southeastward over the valley, before vanishing into the garden that is the house.

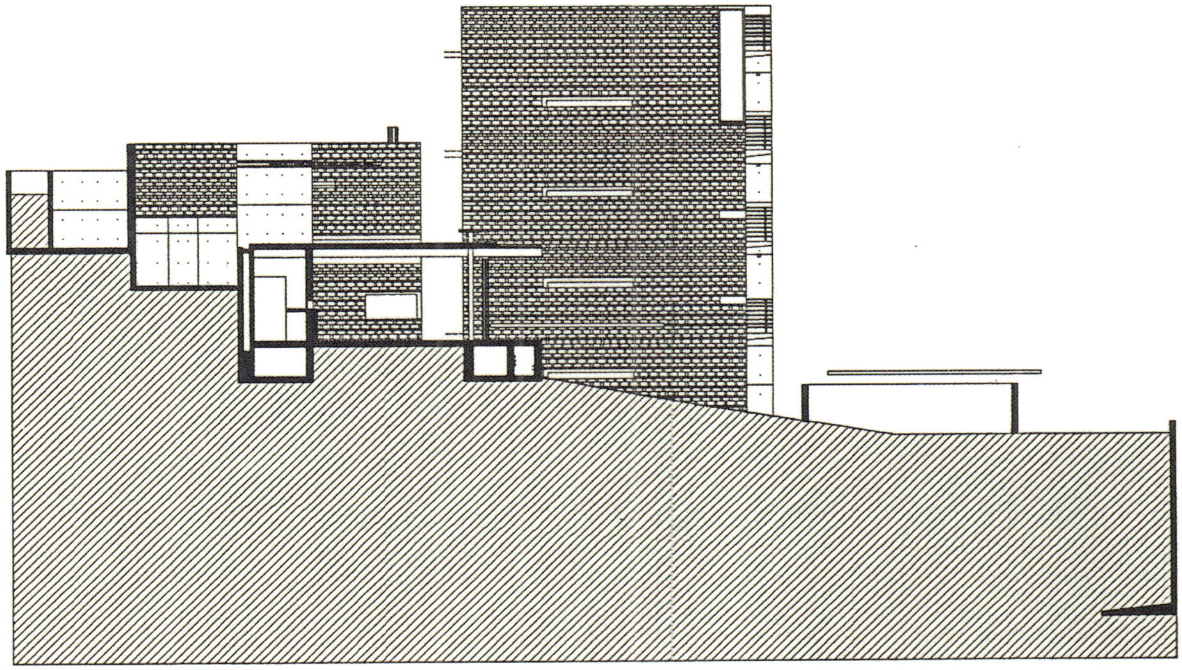

CORTE LONGITUDINAL "A".

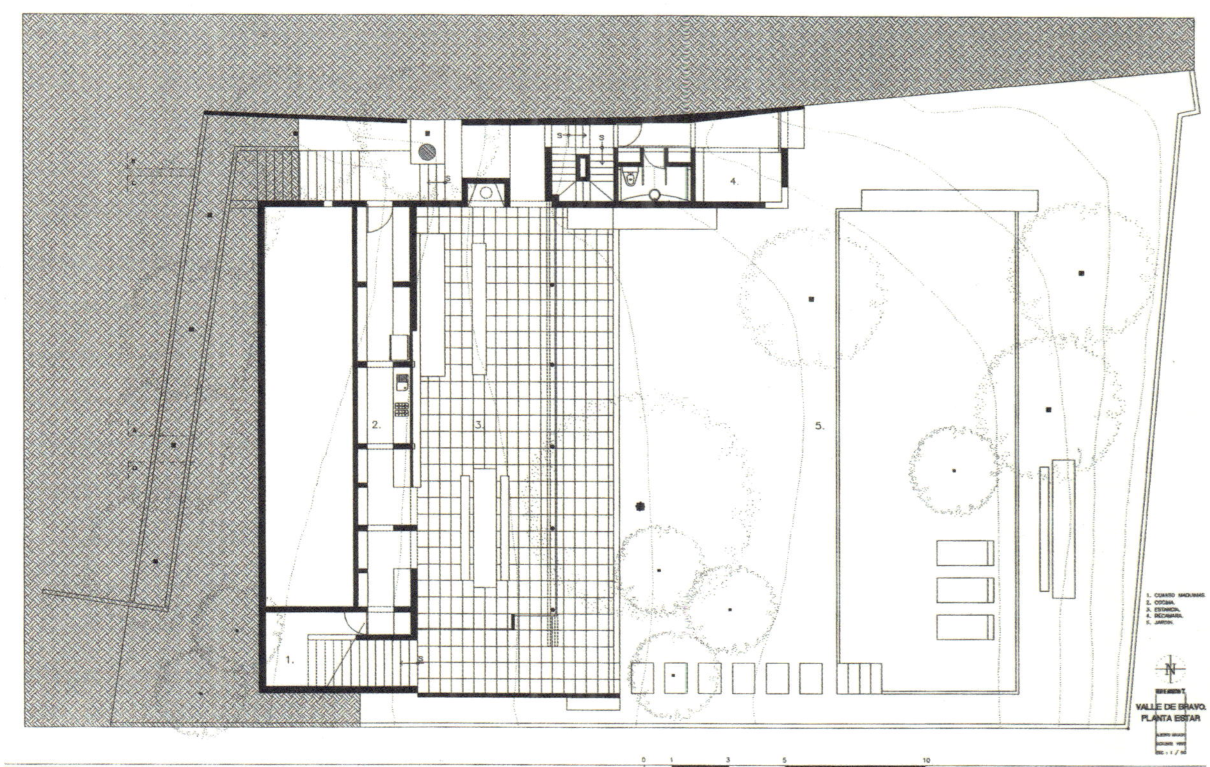

Homo
Deus

Tonda House

With— Héctor Módica

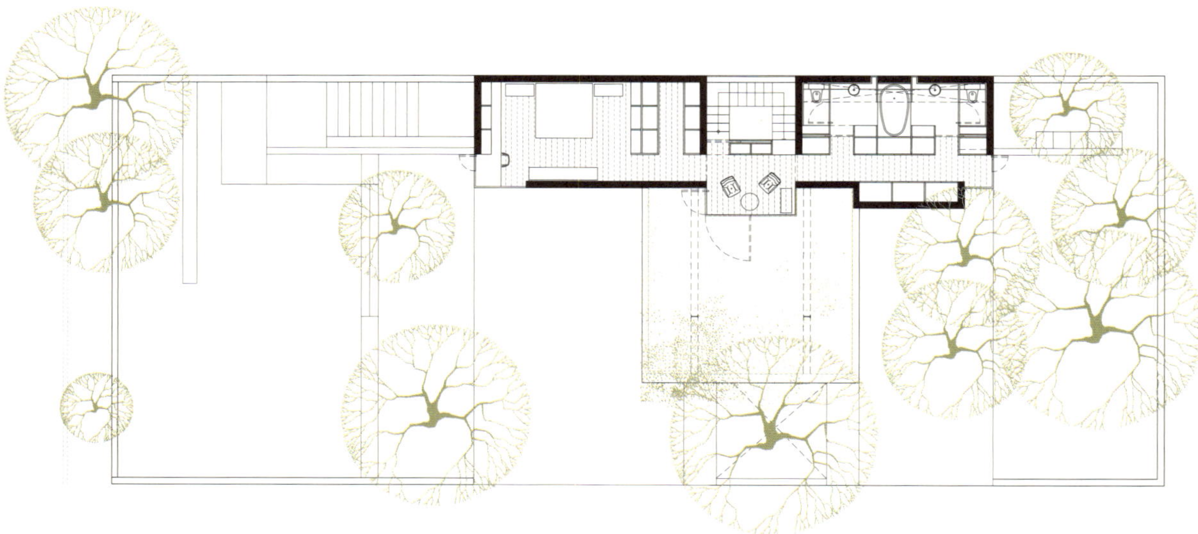

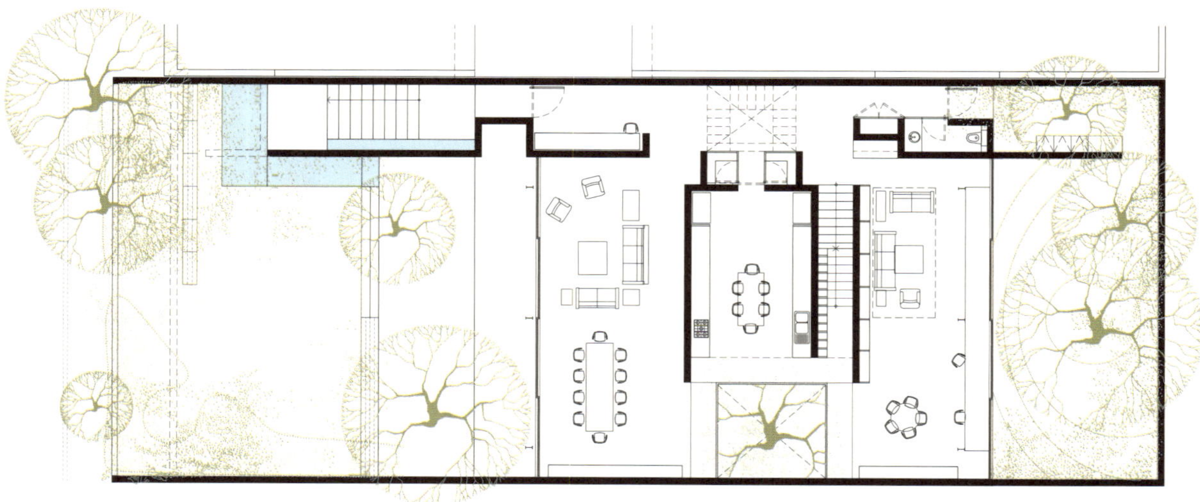

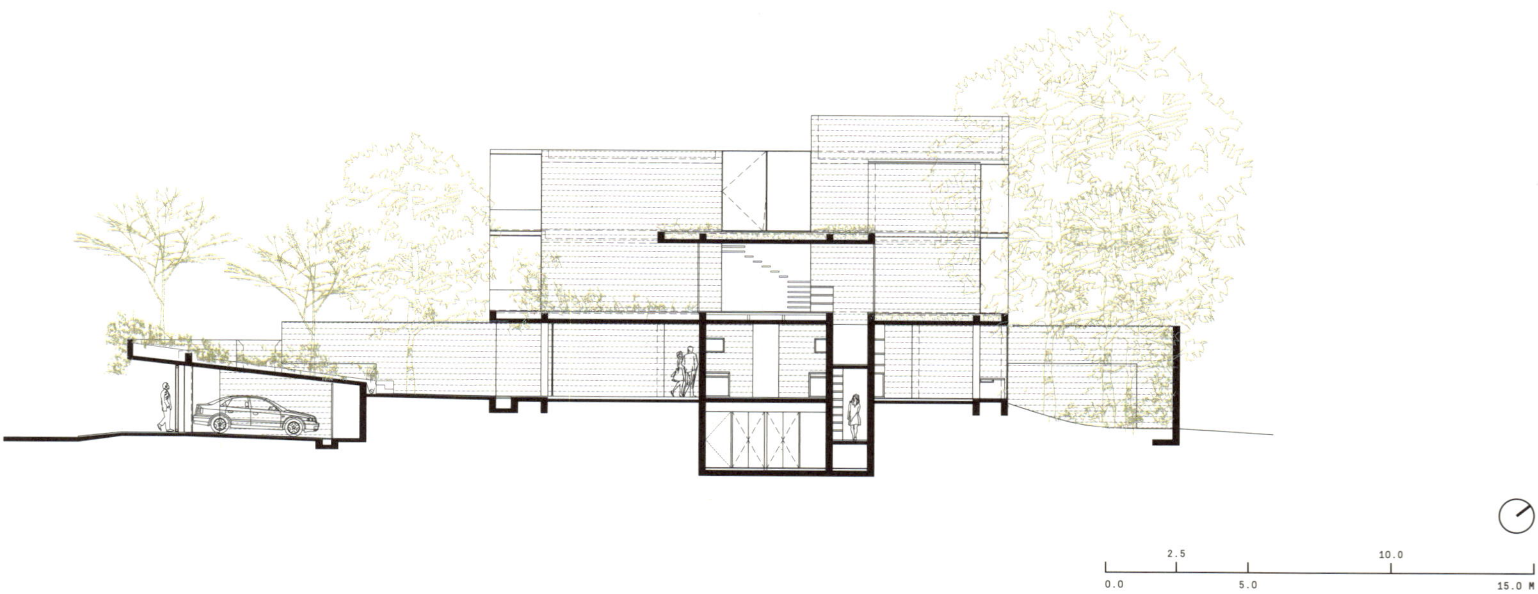

CASA T 04 · 2010

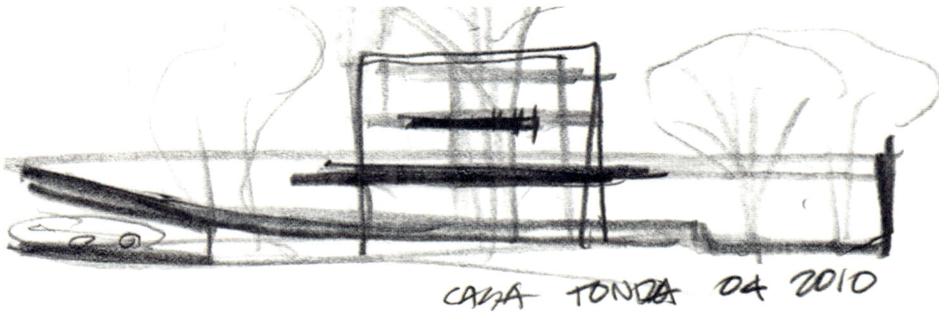
CASA TONDA 04 2010

CASA T.
04 2010

Tec de Monterrey House

With— Adriana León and Xavier González

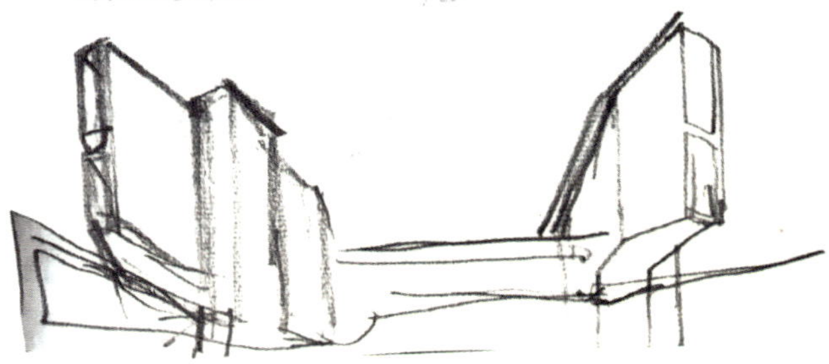

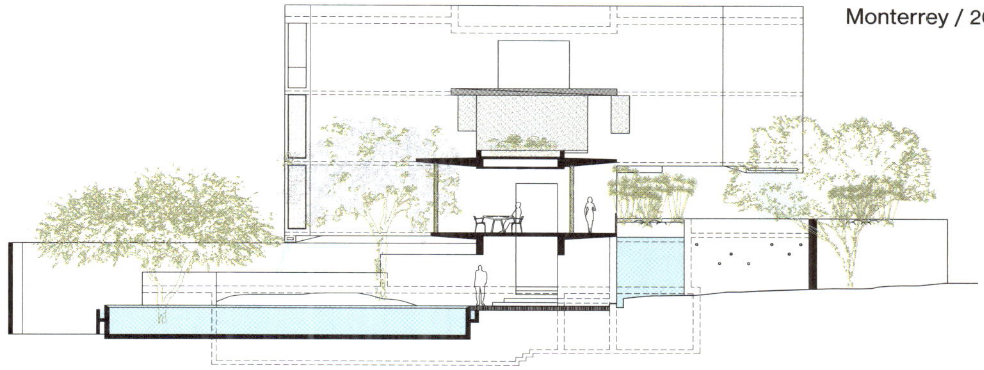

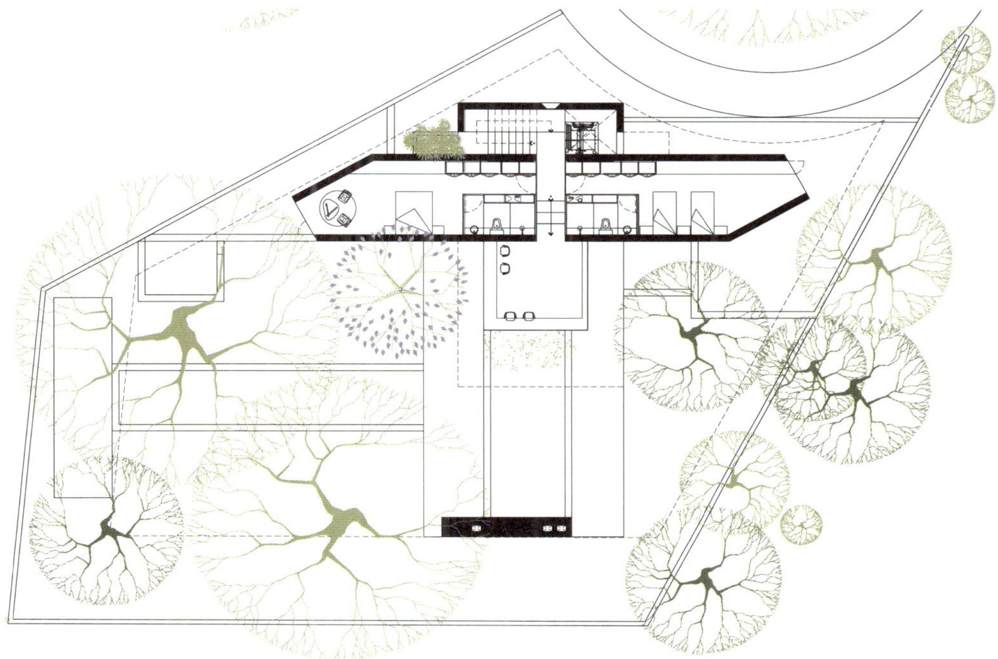

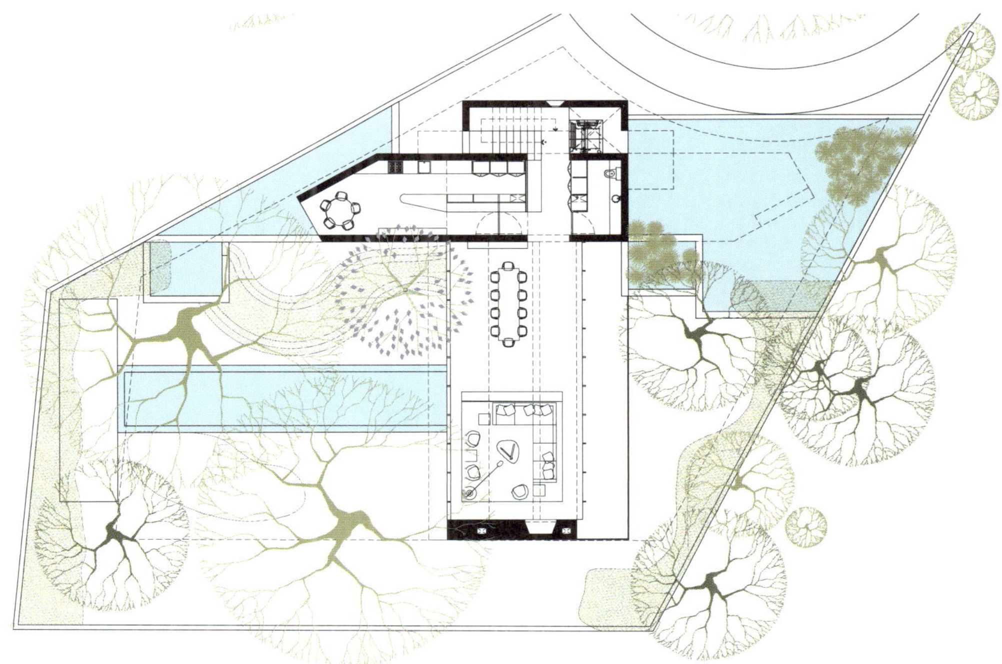

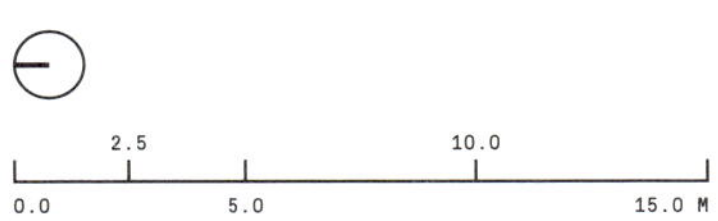
2.5
10.0
0.0
5.0
15.0 M

Workshop for Sergio Hernández

With— Héctor Módica

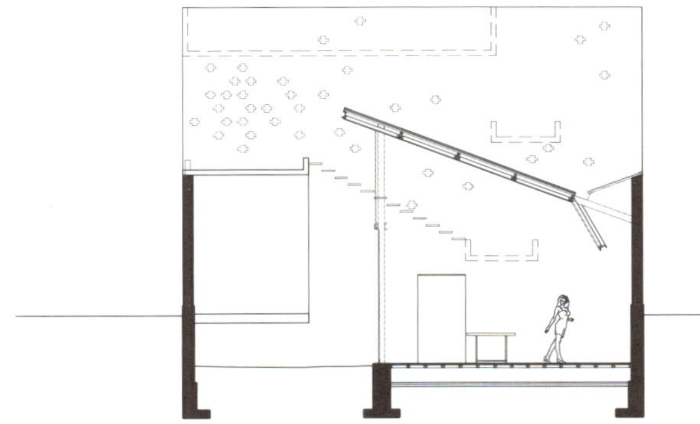

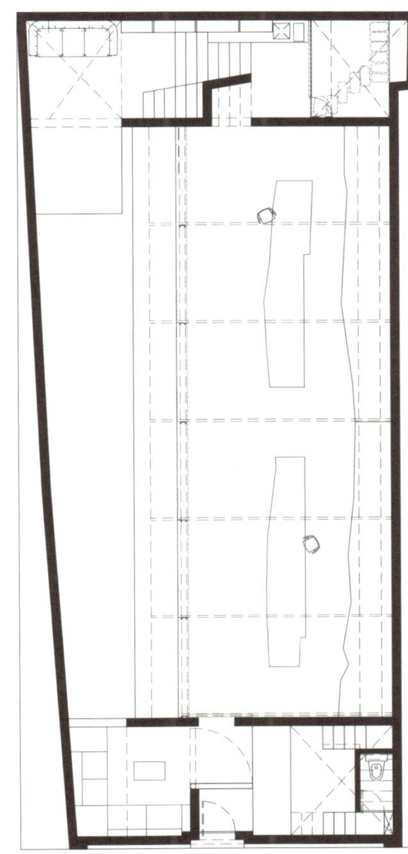

2.5
7.5
0.0
5.0
10.0 M

Cima House

With— Adriana León and Ignacio del Río

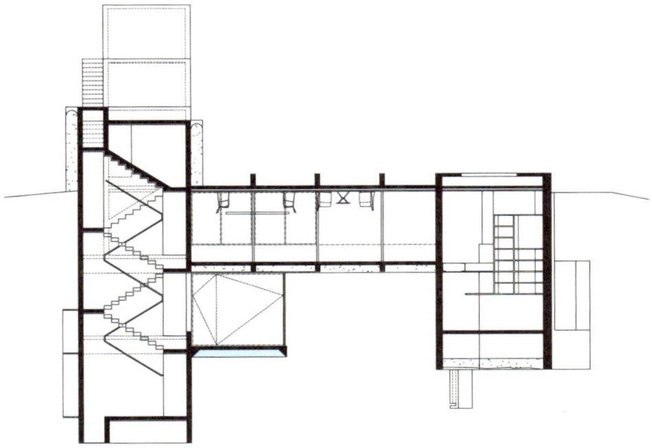

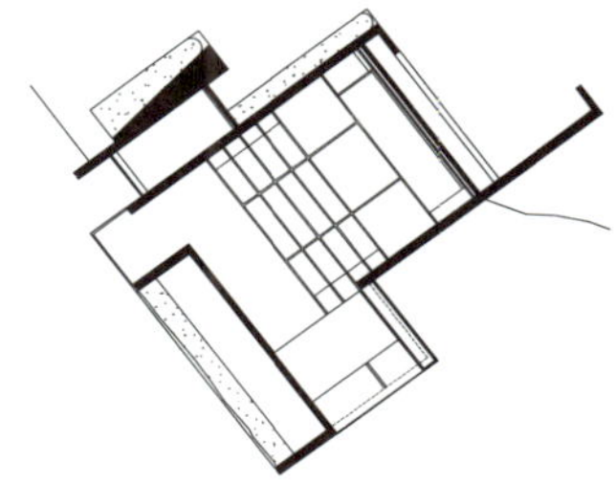

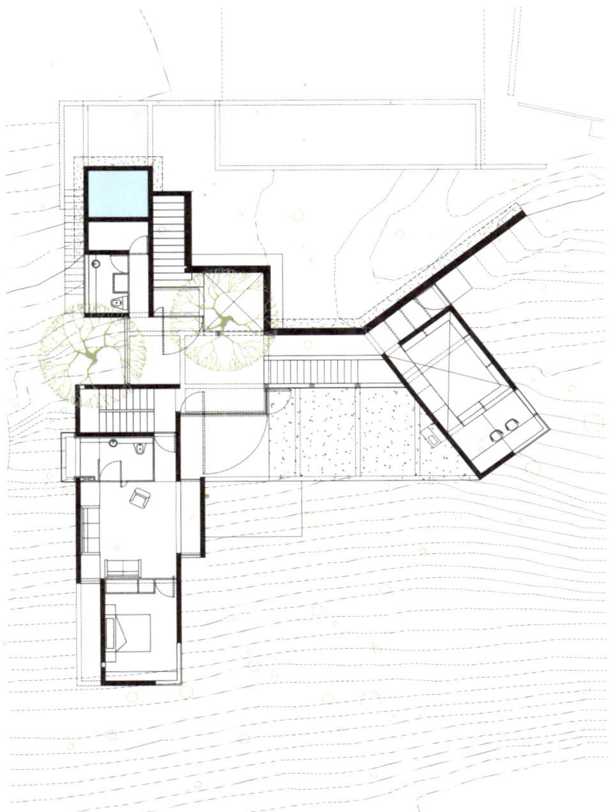

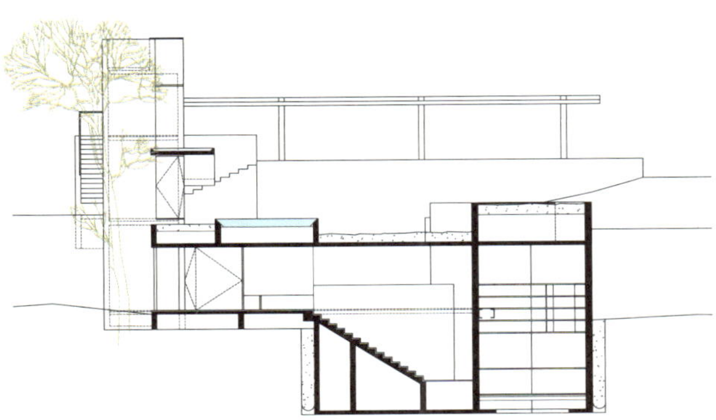

2.0
10.0
0.0
5.0
15.0 M

GGG House

With— Félix Madrazo and Guillermo González

Mexico City / 1995

— Set within a chaotic context of warehouses, residential buildings, and houses, the labyrinth draws back, gaining in privacy while offering long vistas of the neighboring gardens.

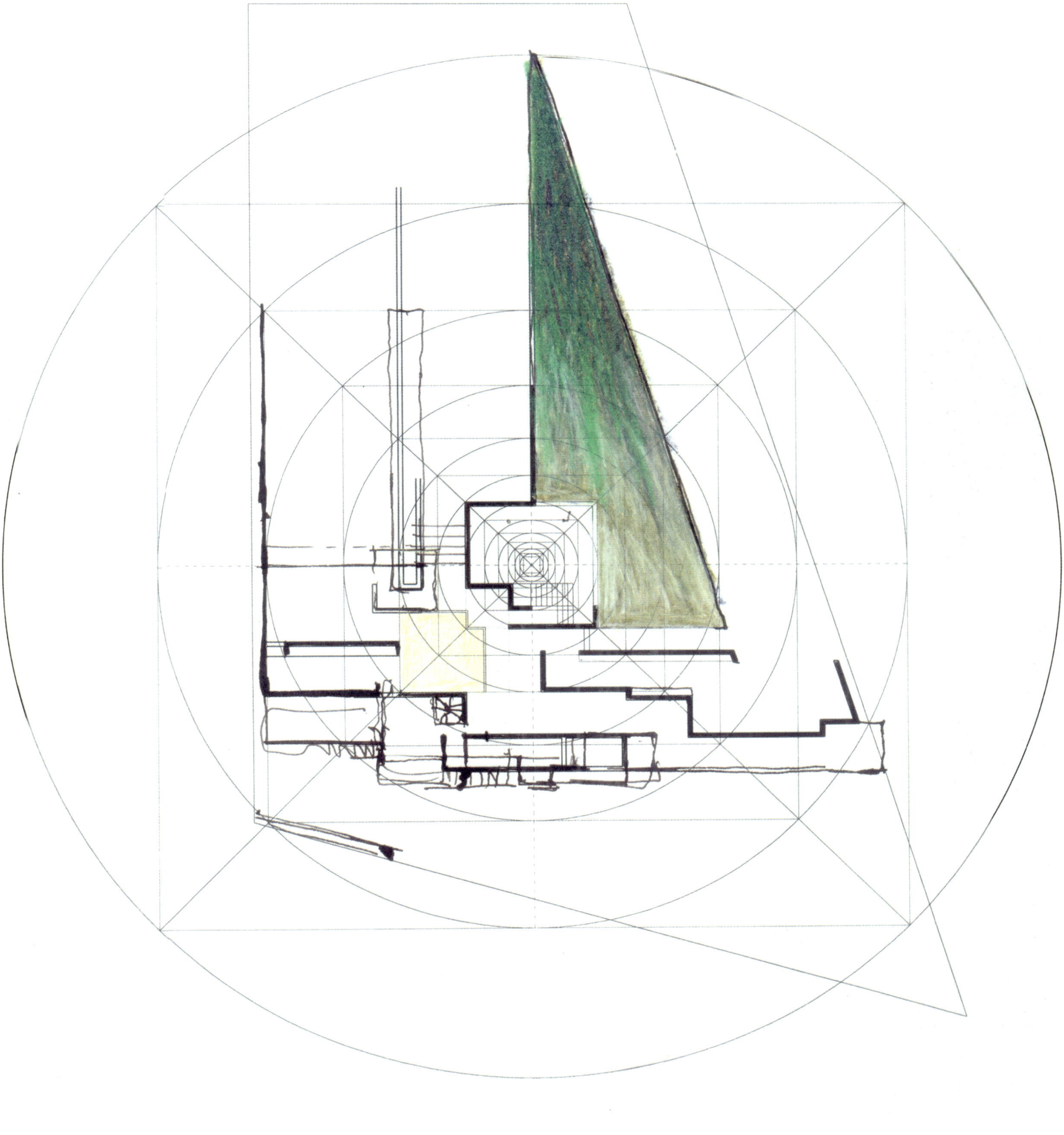

The GGG House, inspired by the work of sculptor Jorge Yazpik, freely explores the possibilities of form and spatial organization. It is part of a concrete monolith fragmented geometrically within a virtual grid. Light filters in through the cracks, flooding the spaces and marking the passage of time. Gardens, pools, pavilions, and alcoves are intercommunicated by means of niches and concealed spaces that fragment the monolith into multiple circuits.

Mojada House

With— Adriana León and Ignacio del Río

Mexico City / 2005

— The "damp house" [*casa mojada*] was given its name by Ian, the youngest resident of it. It withdraws from the neighboring constructions, concealed in a ravine with a small creek running by.

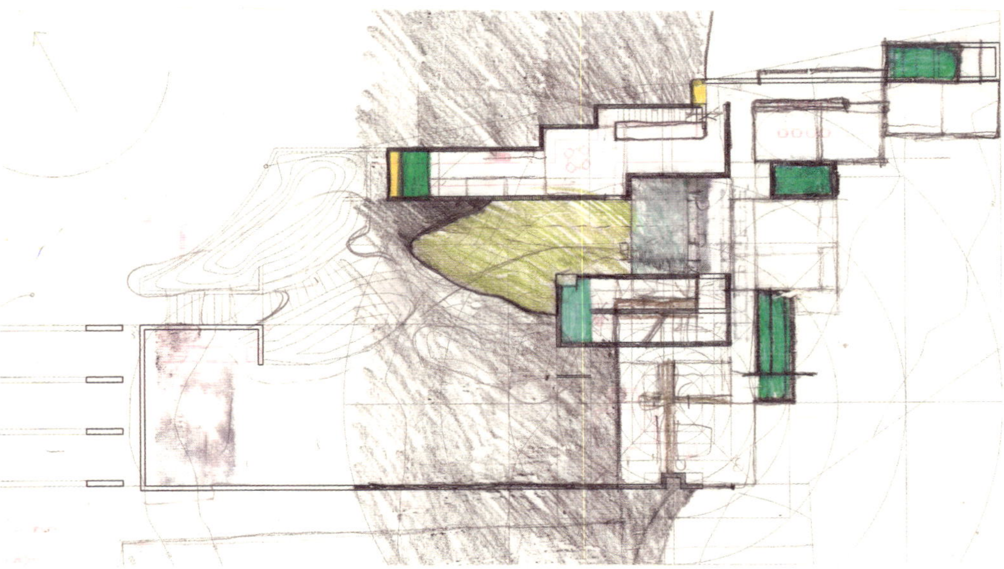

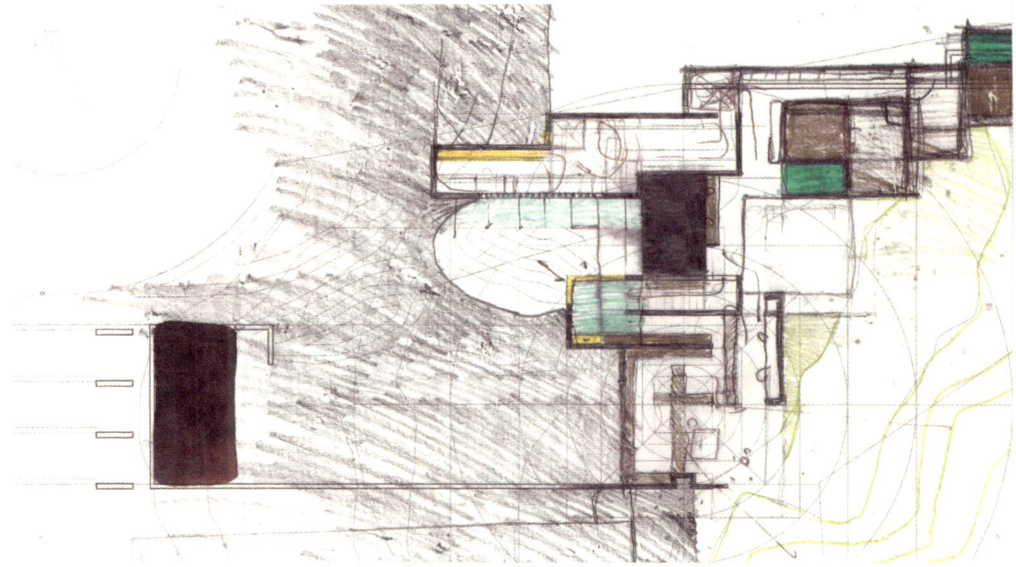

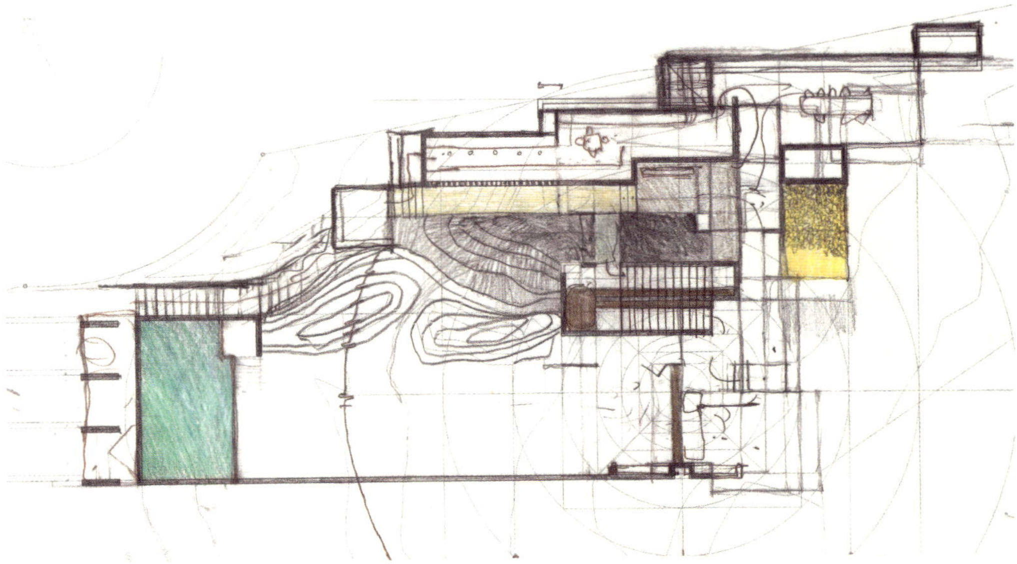

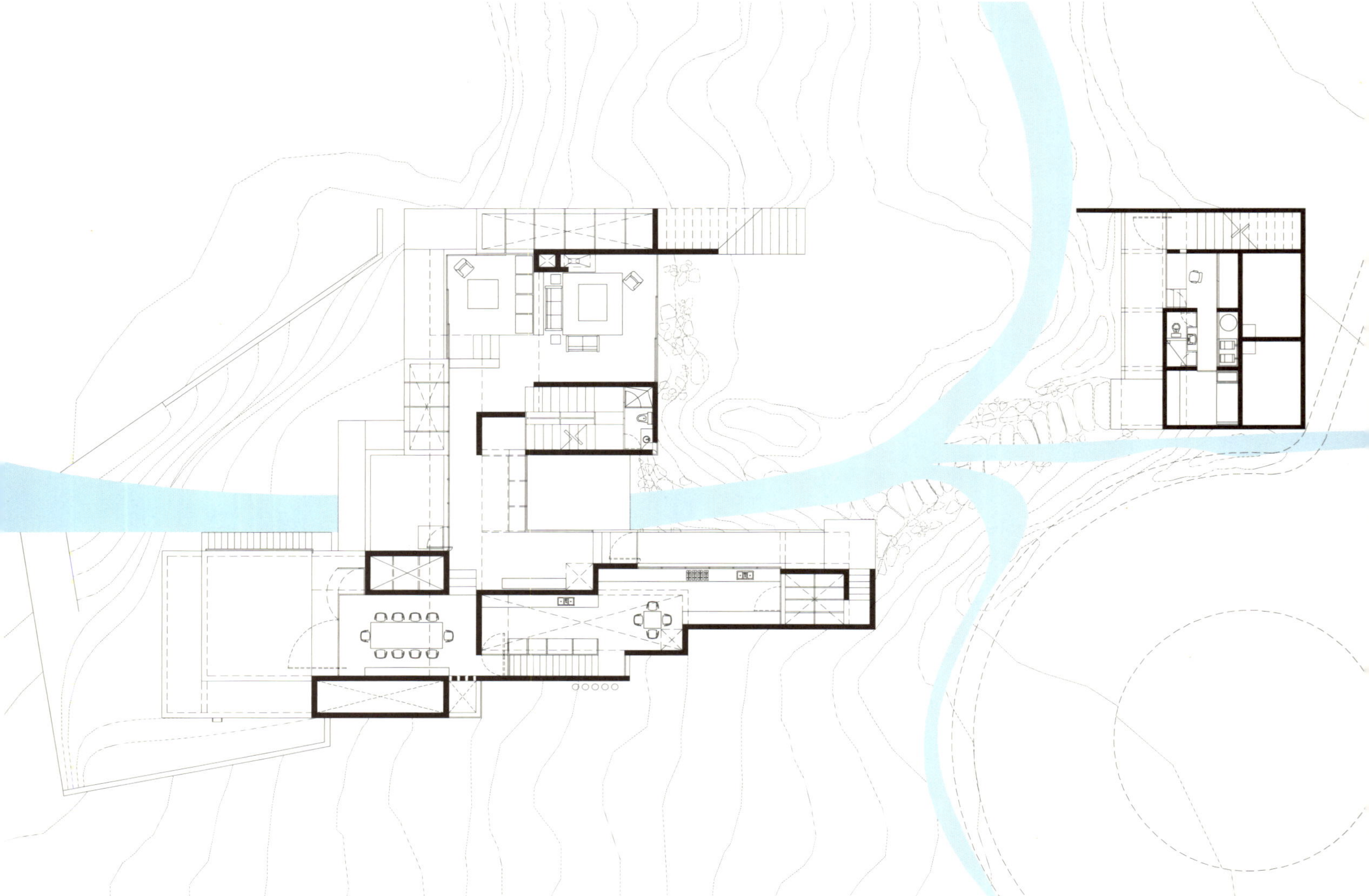

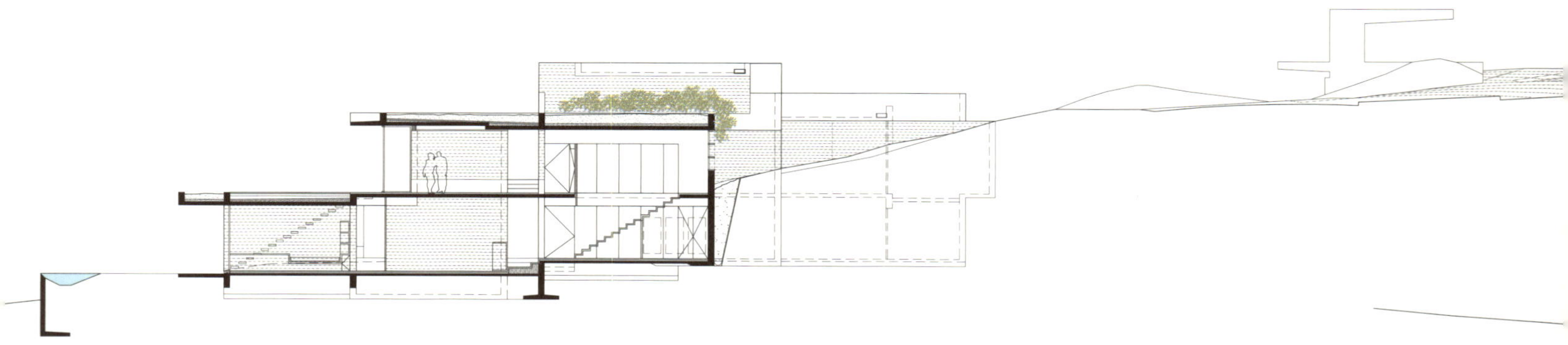

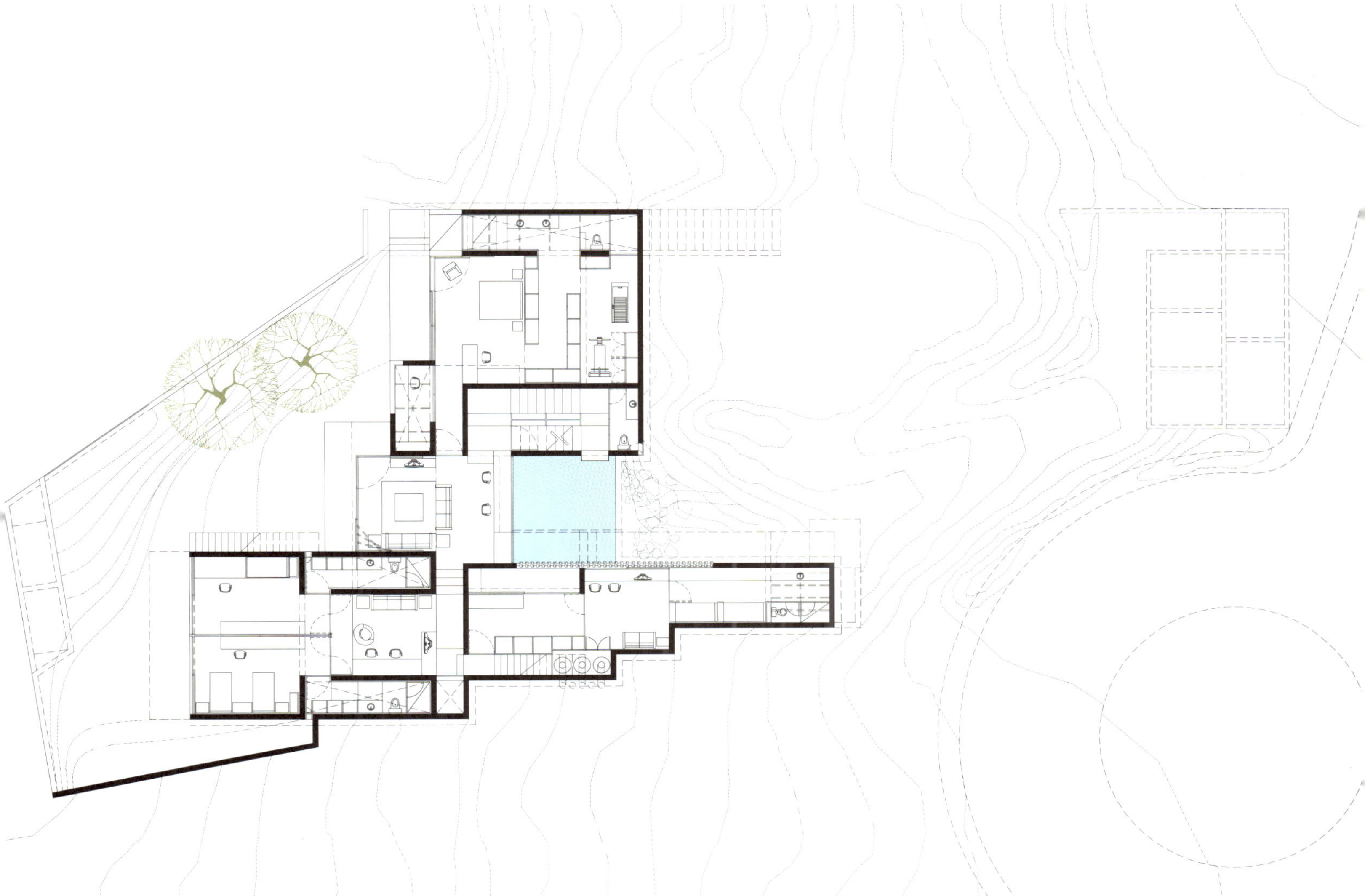

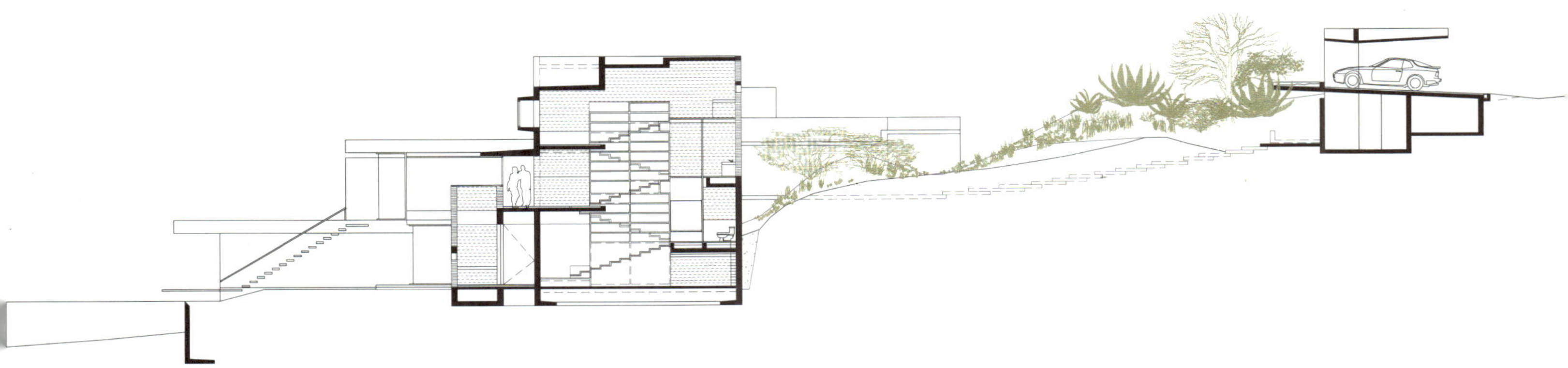

2.5
10.0
0.0
5.0
15.0 M

Negro House

With— Daniel Álvarez and Gustavo Lipkau

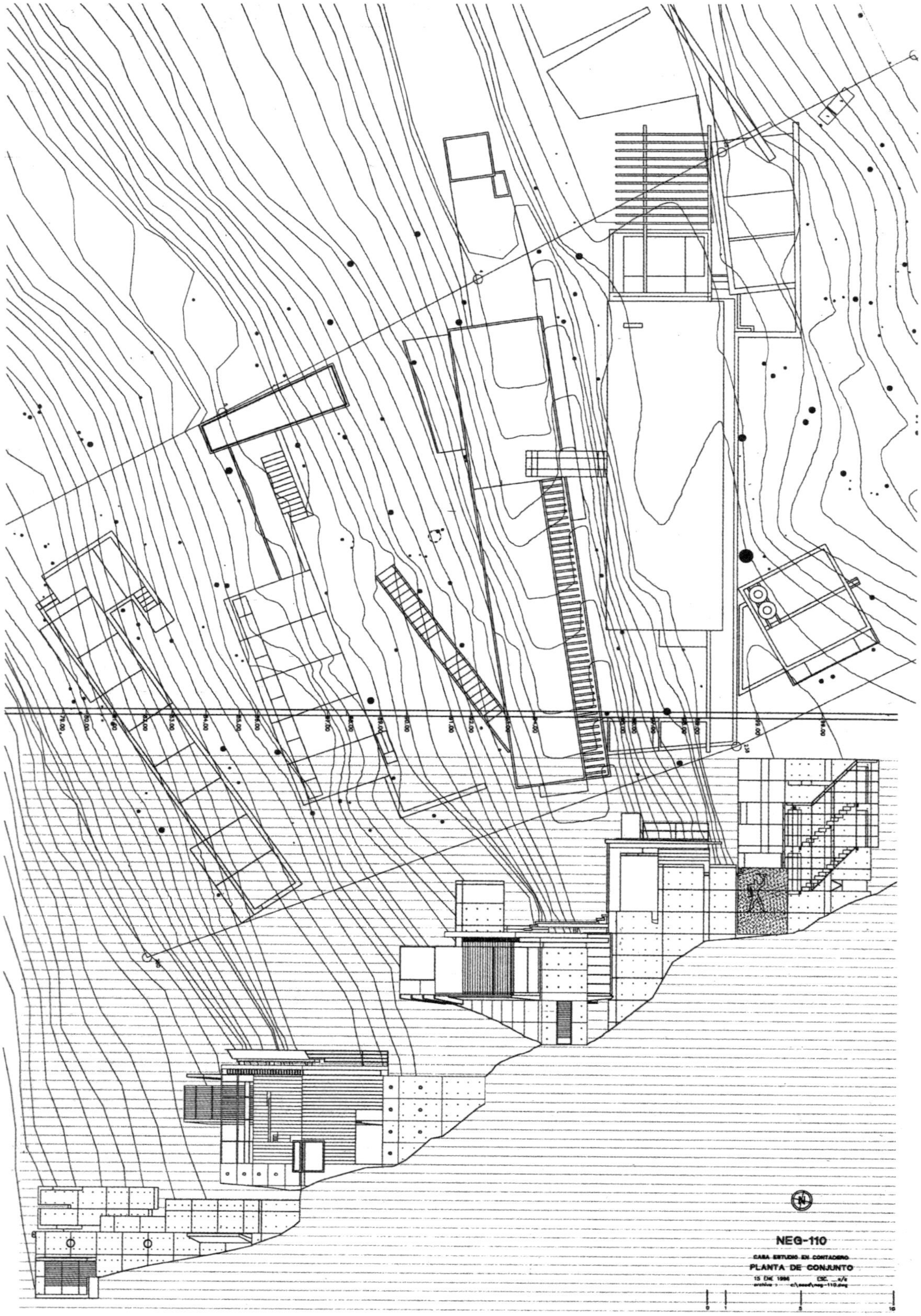

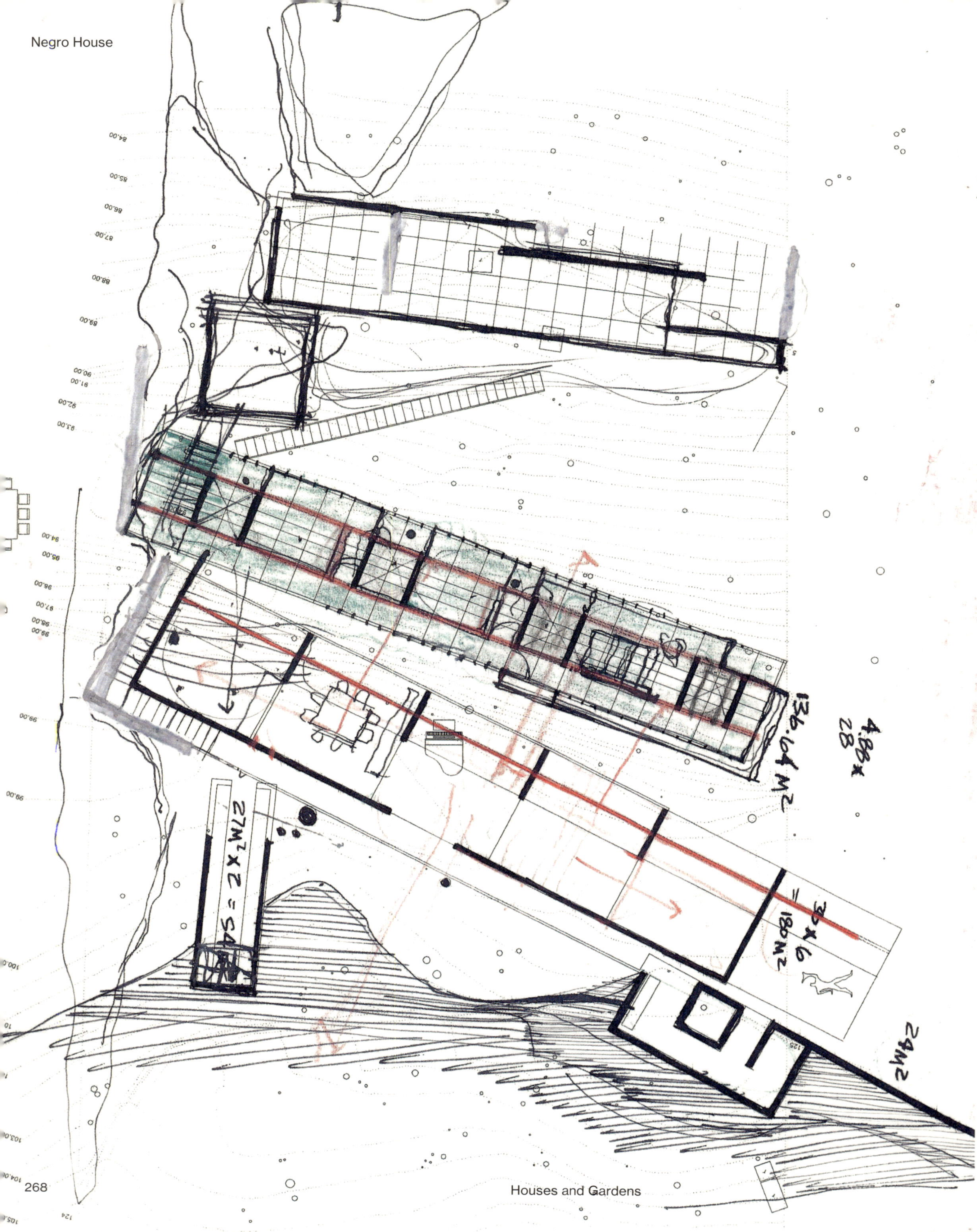

The five volumes of the Negro House rest like the fingers of a hand on the south-facing slope, thickly dotted with oak trees and tepozanes. Each one of these volumes houses a part of the program: the kitchen and services in one, the entry, the living room, and dining room in another, the bedrooms in the middle volume, and the last two containing the studio and the swimming pool. The concrete walls pursue their own discourse, their laws, their calligraphy. Nature has also followed her course, camouflaging over the course of twenty years a residence which, like many archaeological sites, can now only be recognized from the air.

NEG- 100A 24 DIC 95

Seaside House

With— Adriana León, Emmanuel Ramírez, and Gustavo Lipkau

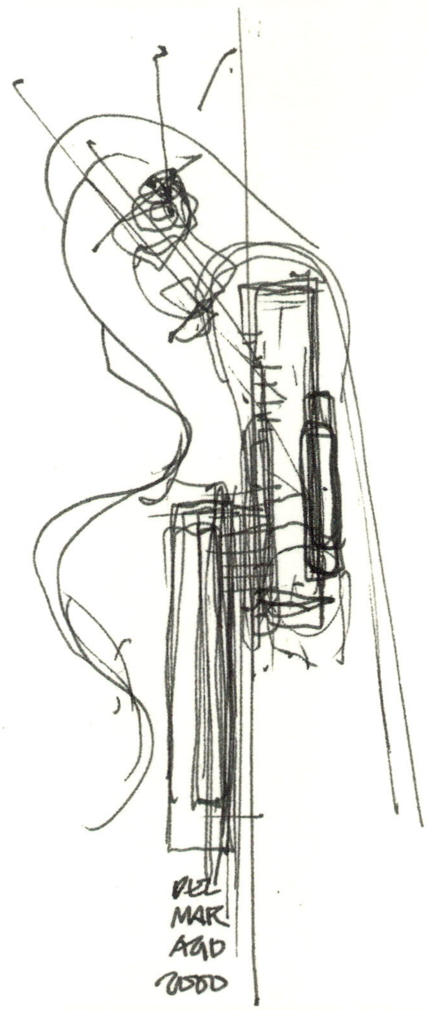

In the Seaside House, the domestic programs are organized into platforms and pavilions inserted into the landscape, out of which gardens, greenhouses, amphitheaters, and even ruins emerge, enriching the habitable spaces with subtlety and complexity, even as they adapt to the lot, seeking out different vistas, atmospheres, and promenades.

California / 2001

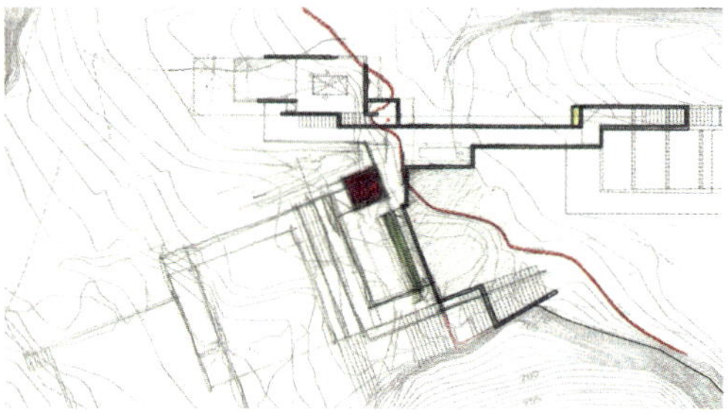

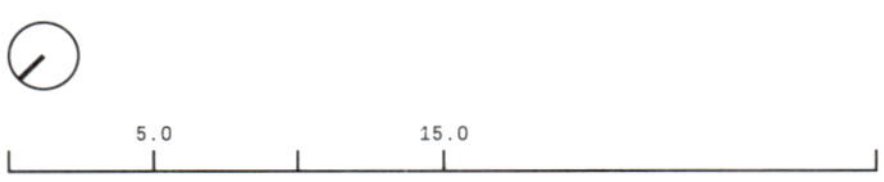

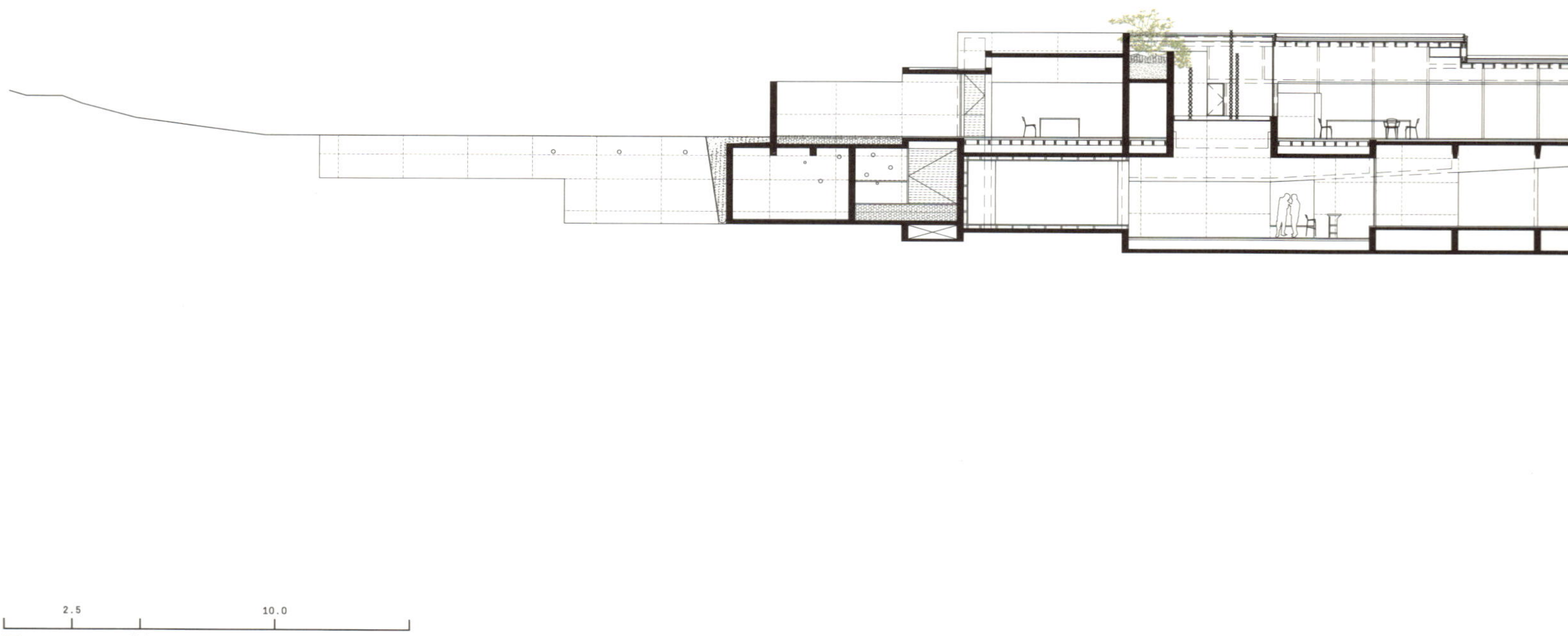
2.5
10.0
0.0
5.0
15.0 M

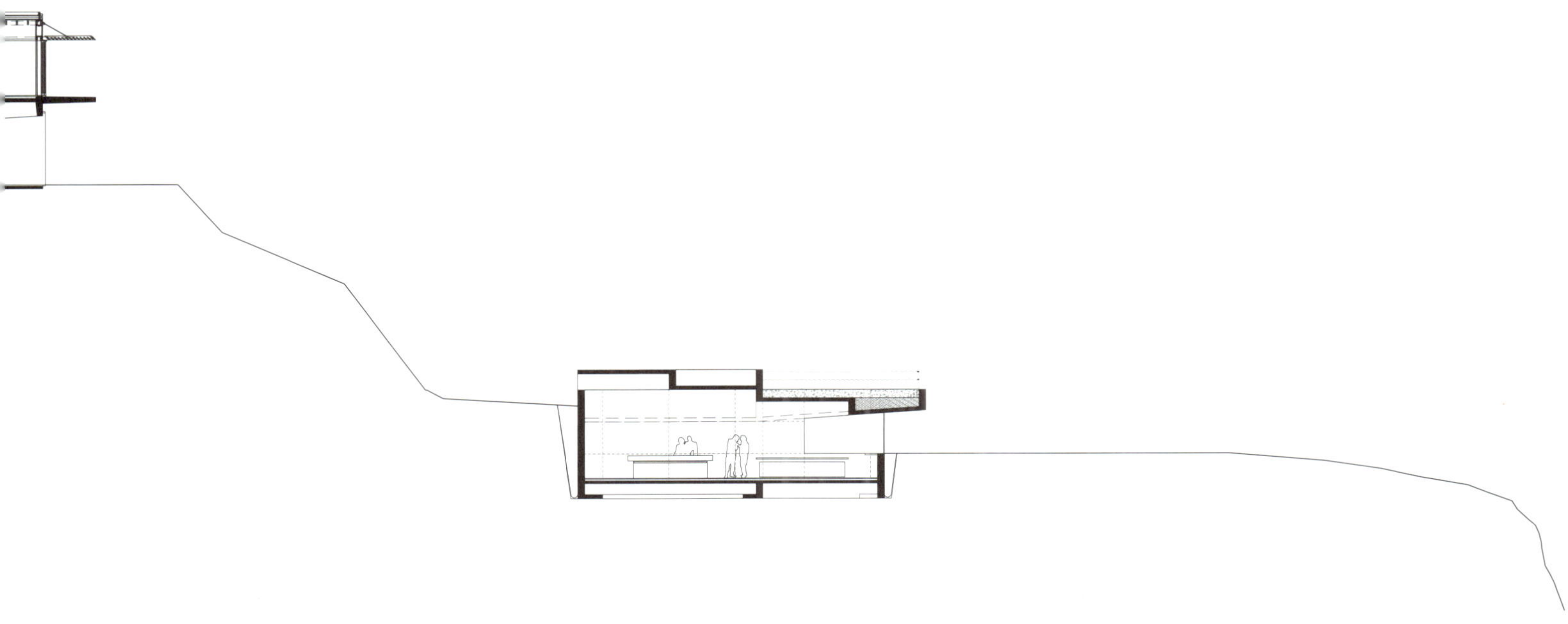

Romany House

With— Adriana León and Ignacio del Río

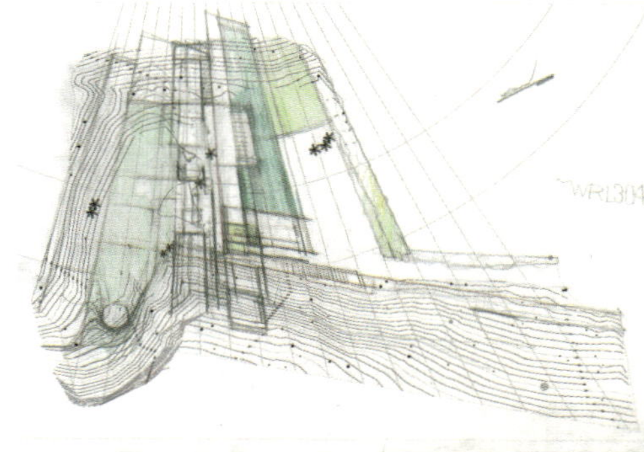

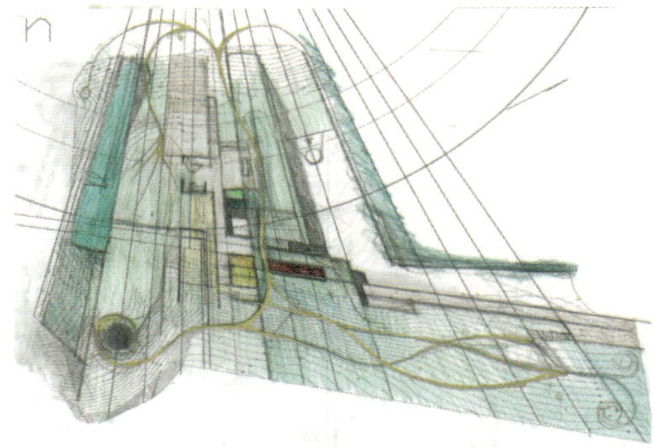

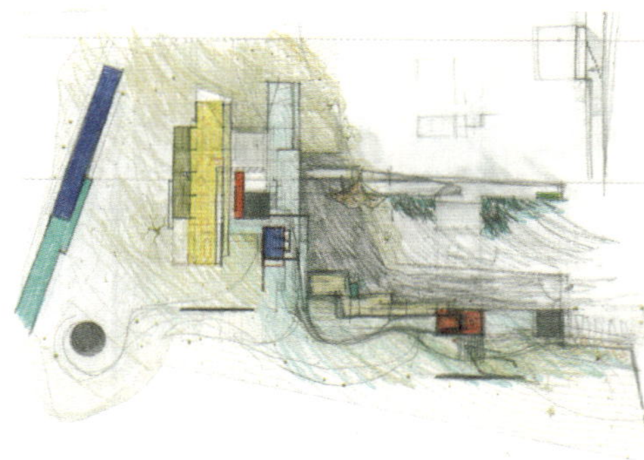

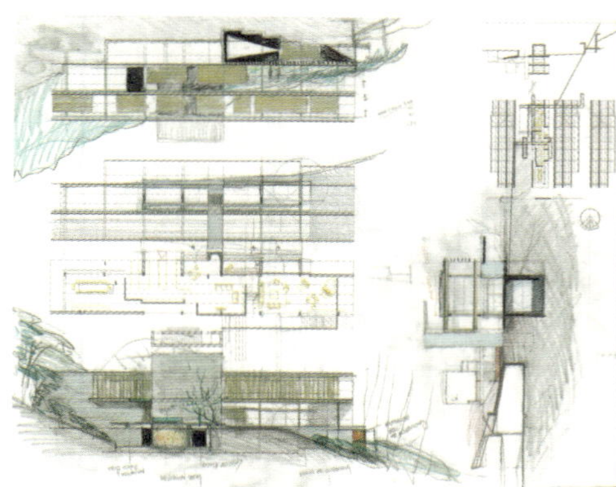

2.5
10.0
0.0
5.0
15.0 M

Serpentine House

With— Adriana León and Iván Ramírez

— Variations on a house adapted to the beauty of the topography.

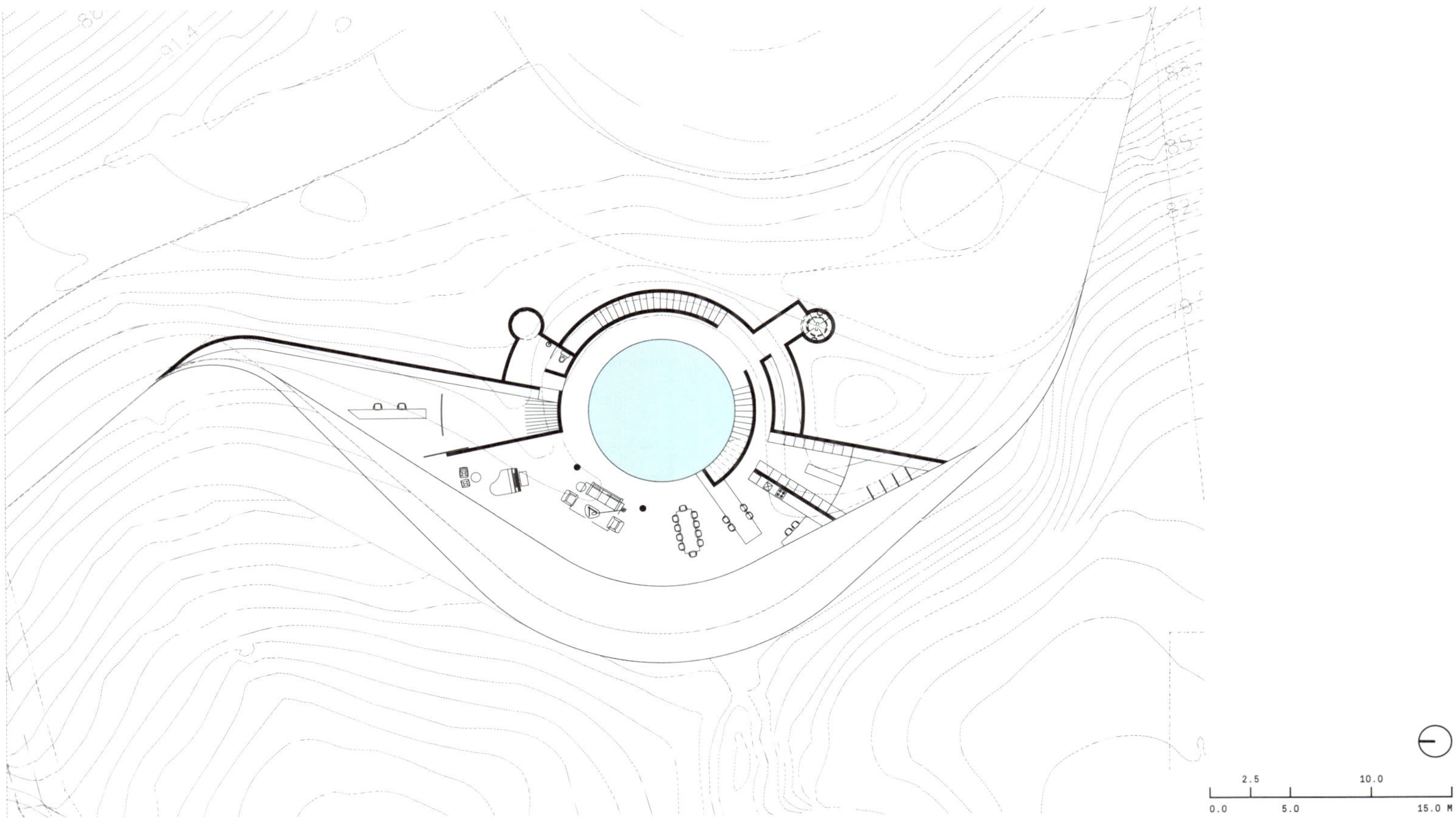
2.5
10.0
0.0
5.0
15.0 M

Green House

With— Hidemasa Hirosawa and María Kalach

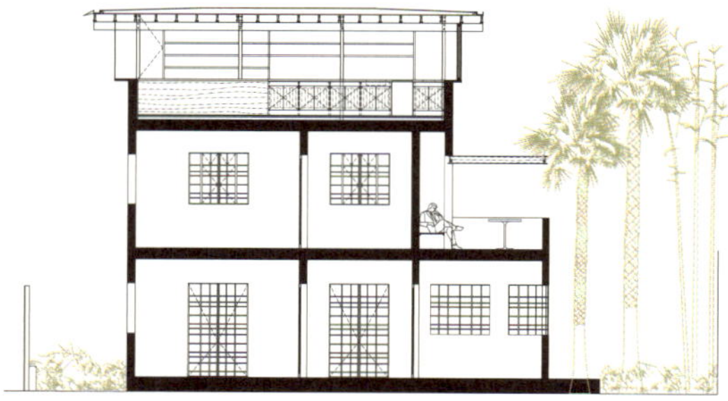

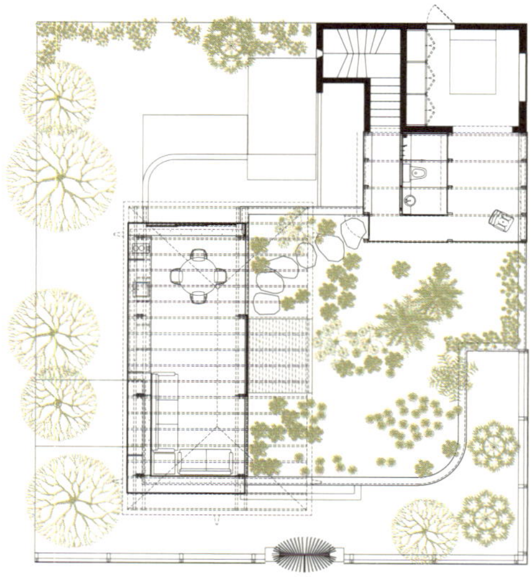

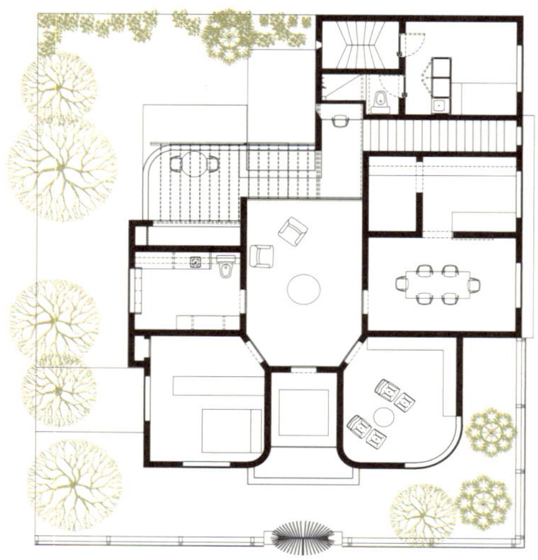

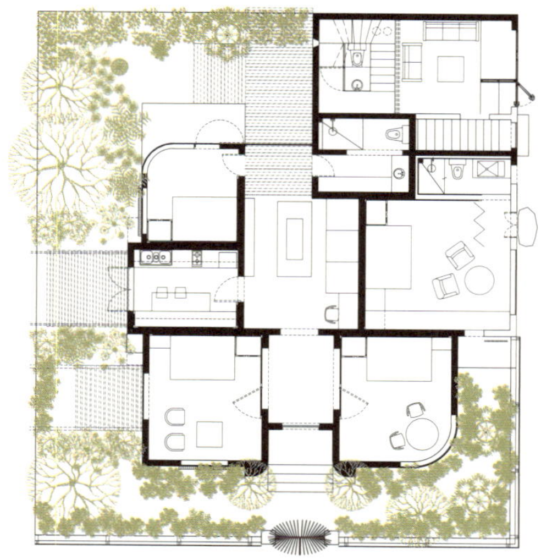

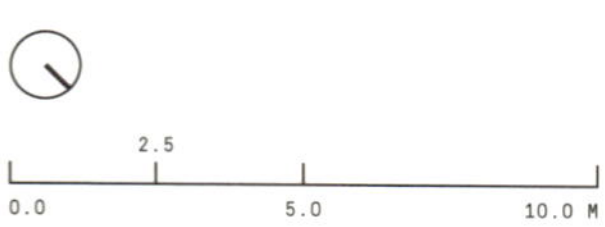

Recycling

— This charming house, constructed in 1930 by the engineer Cota, is a genuine lesson in architecture. A small "main living room" in the middle of the house irradiates out to the four cardinal directions. Five years later, the same engineer elegantly transformed the single house into two. He must have had a firm grasp of future demographic trends. Eighty years later, the house was renovated again and divided into four residences, with a light wooden addition on the rooftop and minimal adjustments to the versatile floor plan.

Casa Wabi
Santa María la Ribera

With— Héctor Módica

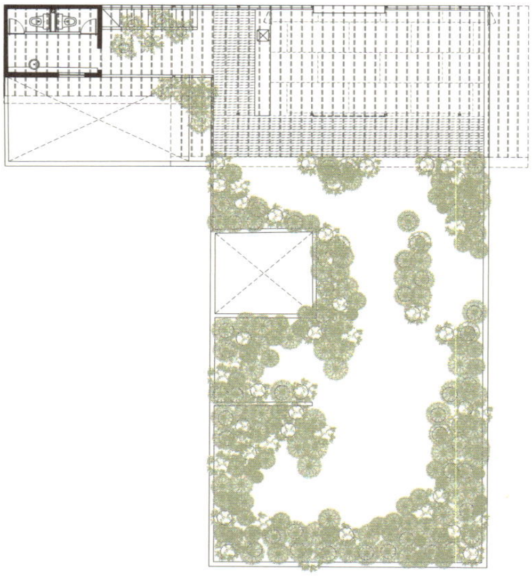

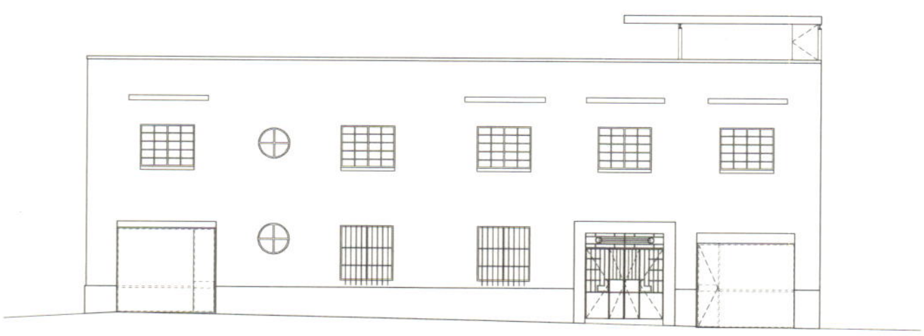

House in Zicatela

With— Juan de la Rosa and Iván Ramírez

The house in Zicatela consists of two unfinished volumes, of three and five levels, separated by a street. Four columns suffice for each of the two volumes, with solid floor slabs joined by a stairway. Each part of the program – bedroom, living room, kitchen – occupies a single level, with elegance and austerity. The very few architectural elements, such as stairways, railings, and brise-soleils, are also reduced to the minimum.

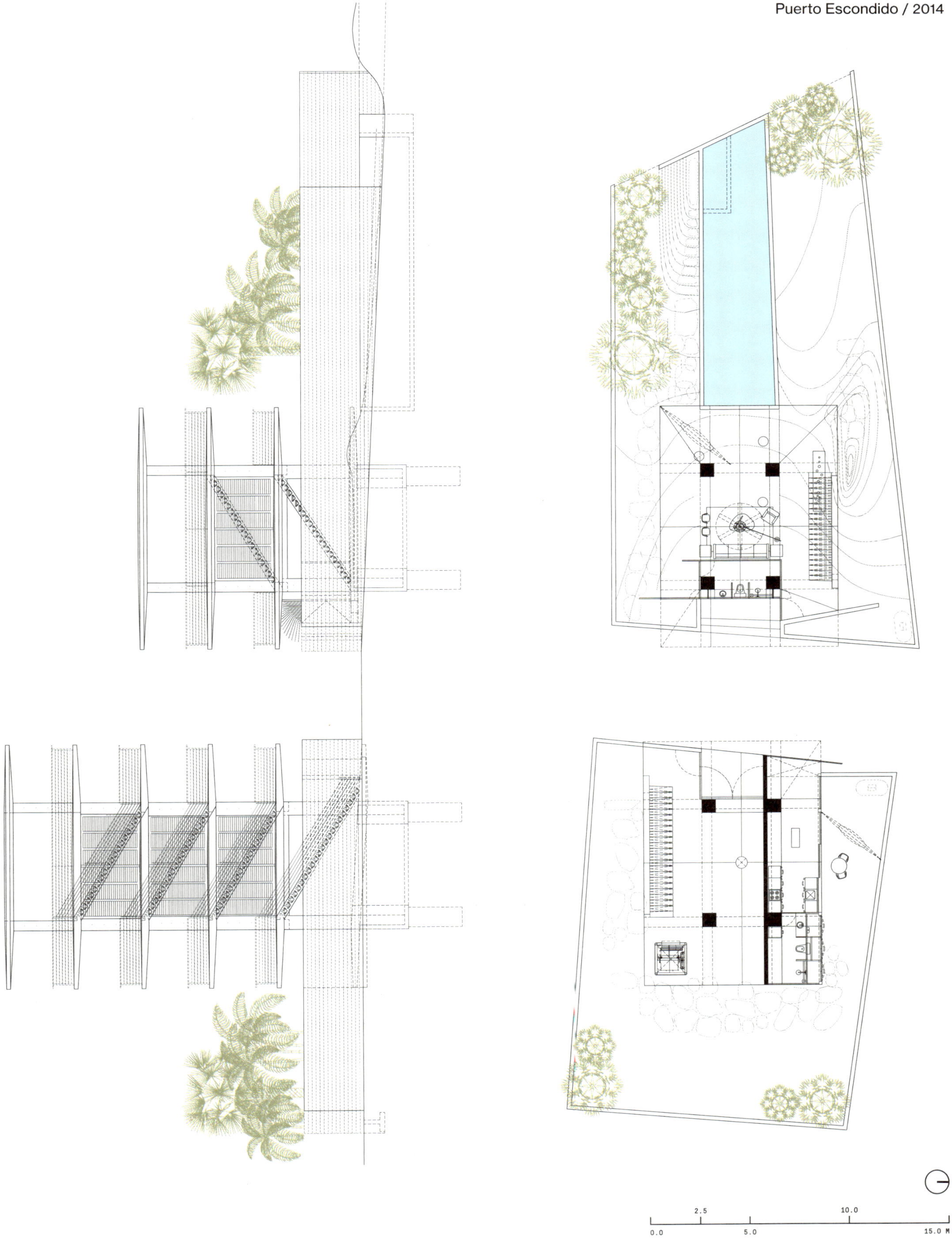
2.5
10.0
0.0
5.0
15.0 M

Tzalancab

With— Susana Pantoja, Ingrid Montes, and Hidemasa Hirosawa

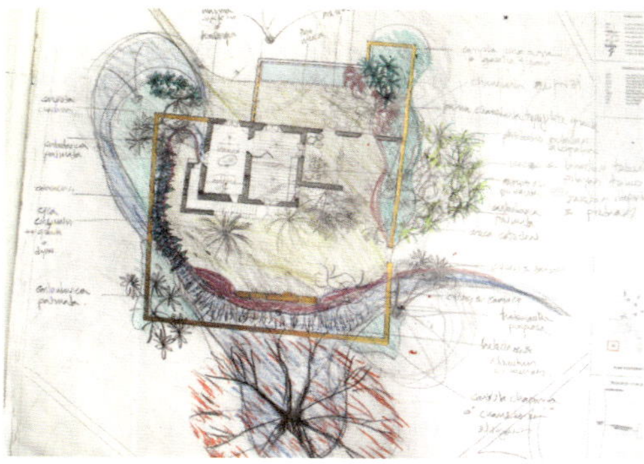

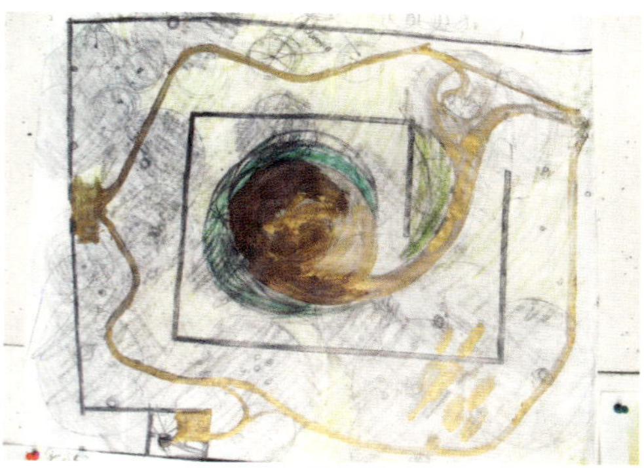

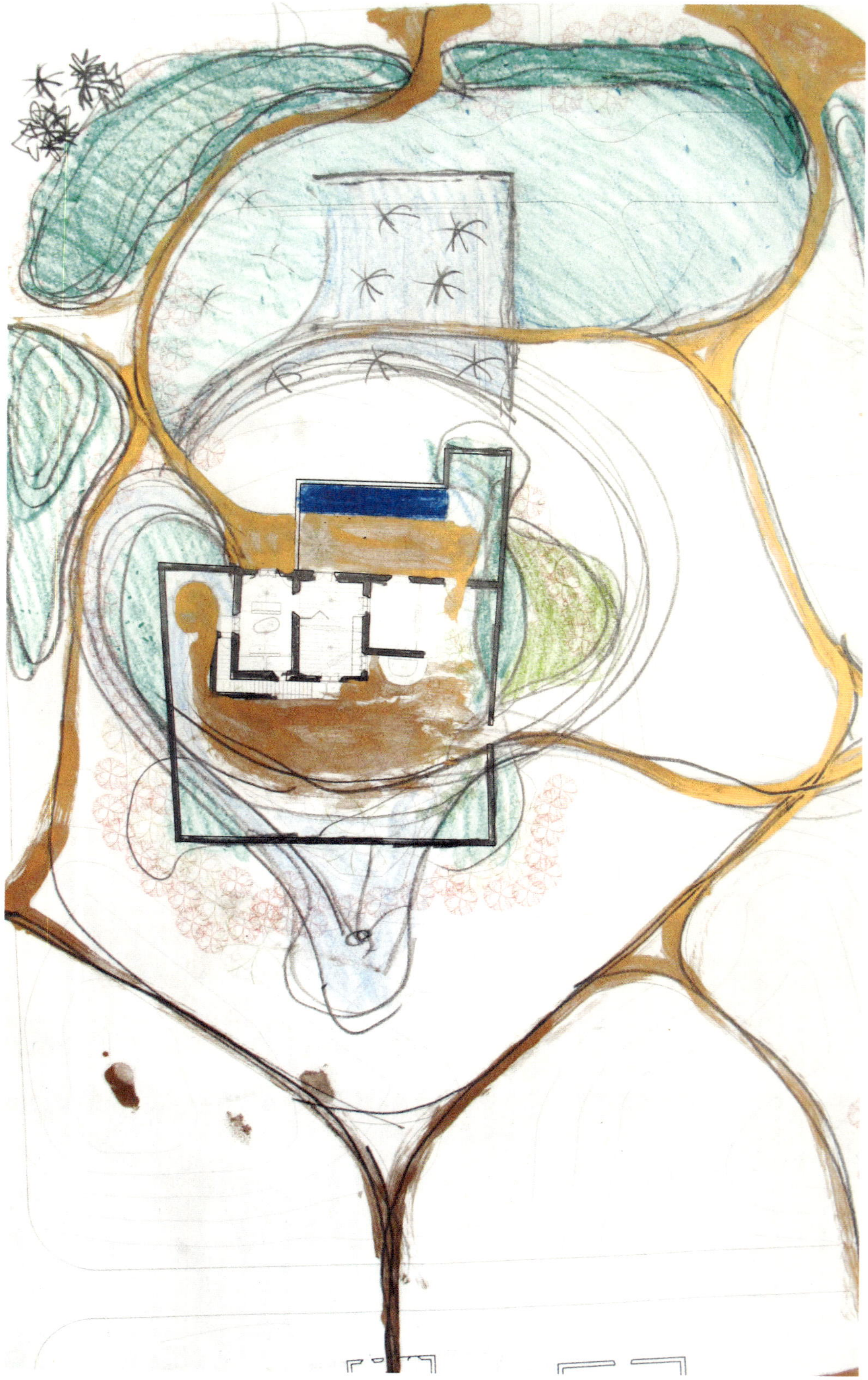

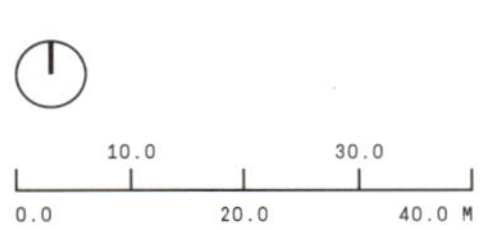

In the Tzalancab hacienda, where the Maya Houses 1 and 2 come together in the Mestiza House, the ruined constructions and preexisting trees were accepted as a part of the design. There is no need to impose one's own language, to exacerbate the Rousseauian naturalism, and still less to favor the archaeological treatment of obsolete walls. Both concrete slabs and dried palm leaves are used for roofing; pergolas blink out their reflections; a pool runs out from the back; and the stairs continue, climbing to form a new ziggurat.

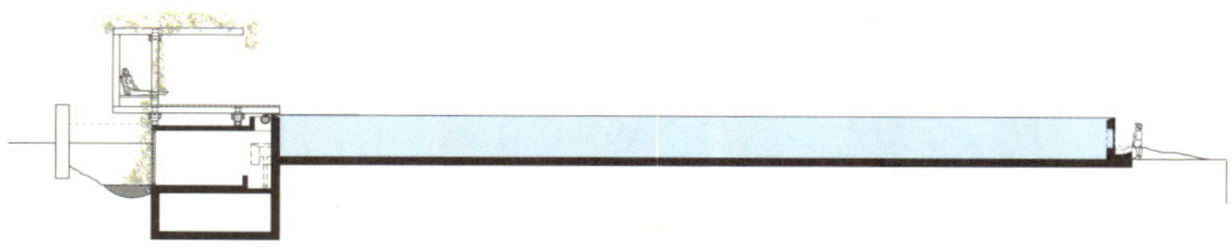

2.5
10.0
0.0
5.0
15.0 M

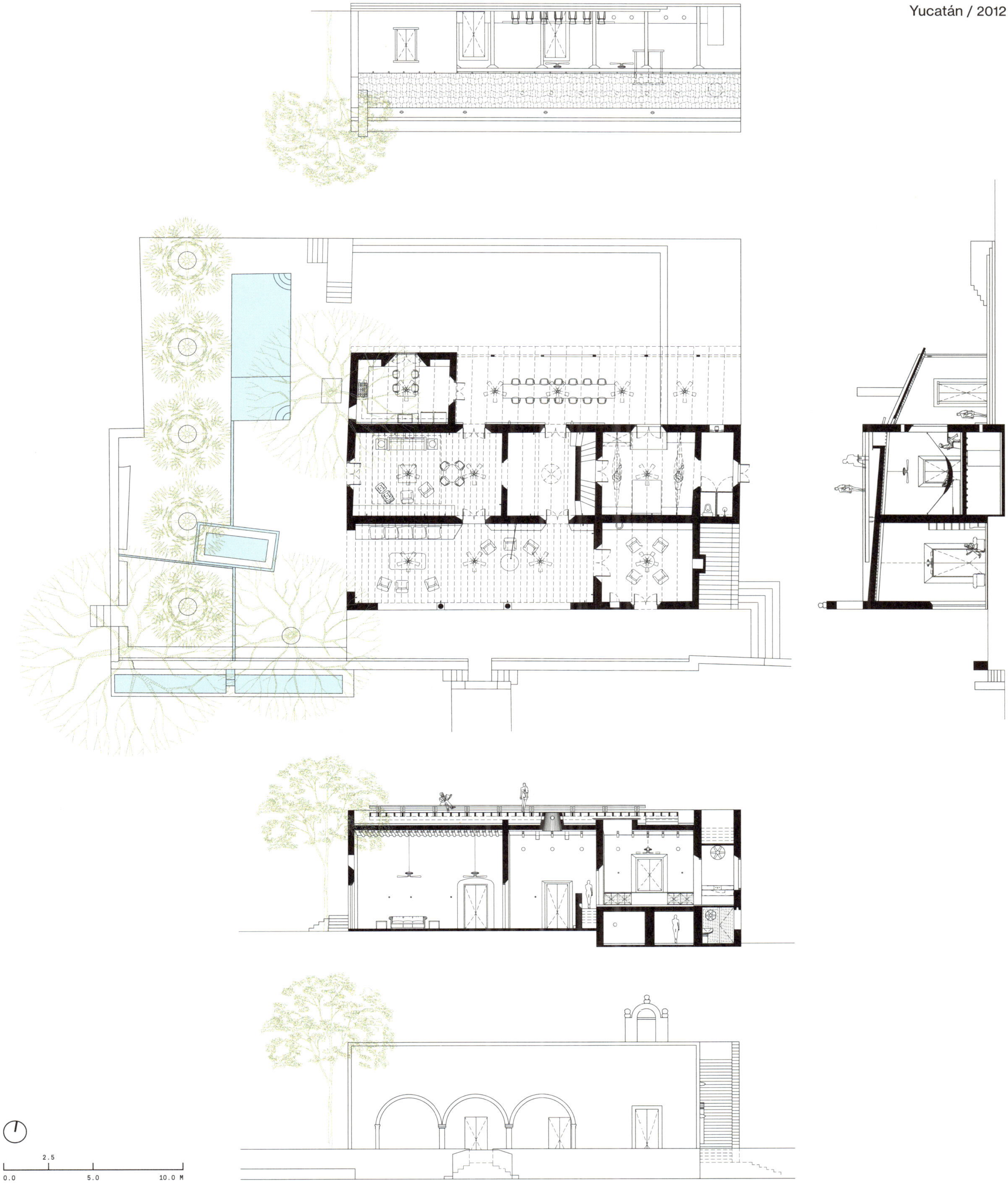
2.5
0.0
5.0
10.0 M

La Platanera

The preexisting context of an abandoned mansion in the San Miguel Chapultepec neighborhood of Mexico City —the construction invaded by the surrounding vegetation: both walls and trees— has been fully accepted and integrated. Architectural oxymorons —enclosed light, interior garden, peeling walls— recreate the quality of a domesticated garden, reclaimed from the wild and belonging again to the *domus*. The new roof does not touch the preexisting walls, while providing plenty of light from above, and the library-studio floats above the garden between the two wooden planes of floor and ceiling.

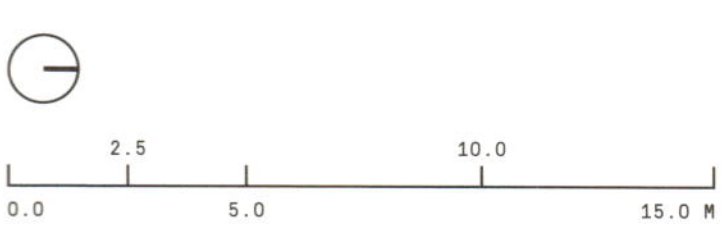

Barragán Garden

— In the year 2000, for six intense months, our workshop occupied the magical Jardín 17 of Luis Barragán. We were installed at the back of the deep lot and, in order to get to the workshop, it was necessary to pass through the garden, like an immersion in a dream of blue and indigo, shot through with green light.

Just halfway along, behind a wall that divides the garden into two "periods," there was a border of loose stones and earth, where I imagined that Barragán must have imagined a pool.

Fifteen years later, after the garden had been neglected and abandoned, we restored it, respecting Barragán's palette of plant life and integrating a number of guest species. We also finally added the pool that I had always imagined Barragán imagining.

Towers

— Towers will proliferate throughout the city, along circulation corridors and wide avenues, near to or above major transport hubs, creating new urban centers. Borders to protect green areas or alongside large parks. Vertical constructions pose a challenge to natural forces: first and foremost is the structural theme. While a house can be conceived in terms of privacy and exposure to sunlight, or a theater in terms of vantage points and acoustics, in a tower everything is governed by structure, conceived in terms of its particular spatial organization and orientations. If the major intellectual and constructive effort is put into the structure, then this must be thought of as the very expression of the building.[1]

The future of our cities depends on re-densification. We must "increase the number of inhabitants without expanding the surface area, improving or making the best possible use of existing services and infrastructures. Making the city denser, having it grow in height but not in extension, has obvious advantages: we destroy fewer natural areas, we reduce travel time, we make the most of existing infrastructure, and we improve safety and neighborhood quality of life. It is obvious, therefore, that tall and medium-height buildings will be increasingly a focus of reflection and exploration for architects, engineers, and urban planners. Some will study their insertion and ideal location within the urban fabric; others will concentrate on the quality of their spaces and the logic of their structures."[2]

The logic of the tower derives from its structure, which generates the efficiency of its loadbearing forces, its installations, and its flows of circulation, as well as the formal result. Unlike the glazed prisms and curtain walls of architectural modernity, the structure is neither concealed nor diluted as part of the façade, but rather defines the width of the perimeters and is expressed in terms of brise-soleils and series of columns, outlining triangulations that render more efficient its loadbearing capacity and resistance to earthquakes, or freeing up large voids in the lower sections. The logic of the classical column, with base, shaft, and capital, is accepted, so each tower has a beginning and an end, a sense of proportion. And different solutions are explored, with the service core in the middle or along the edges, allowing for all possible distributions and all manner of interior layouts.

[1] Alberto Kalach, "Torres de la ciudad," *Reforma 27* (Mexico City: Arquine, 2012) p. 28.

[2] *Ibid.*

Tower in Tijuana

Moon Tower

With— Héctor Módica and Iván Ramírez

Tijuana / 2017

— Ever since the time of Abraham, the structural efficiency of the cone, used in constructing pyramids and ziggurats, has been well known. A crazy gringo —a real estate developer and a distant descendant of the Patriarch— approached us with a request to design the highest tower in the Tijuana - San Diego metropolitan area, at a central location that seemed suitable to me. The fantasy is never-ending.

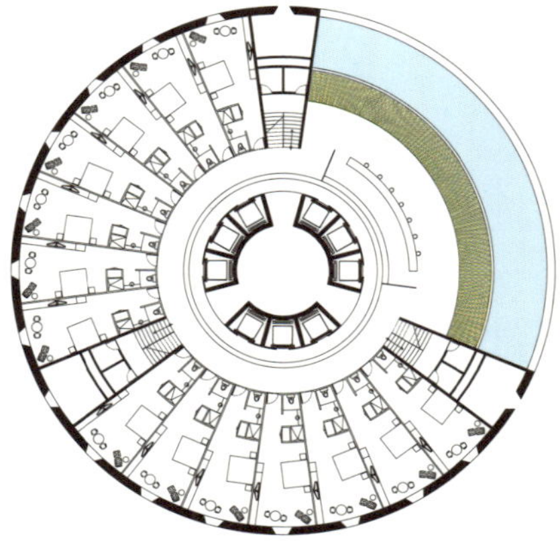

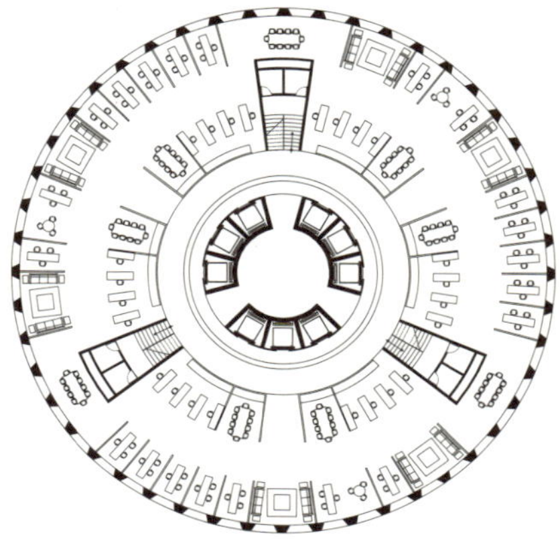

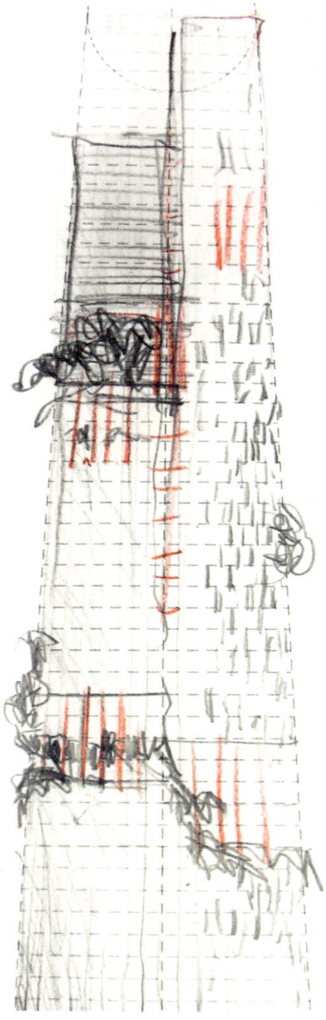

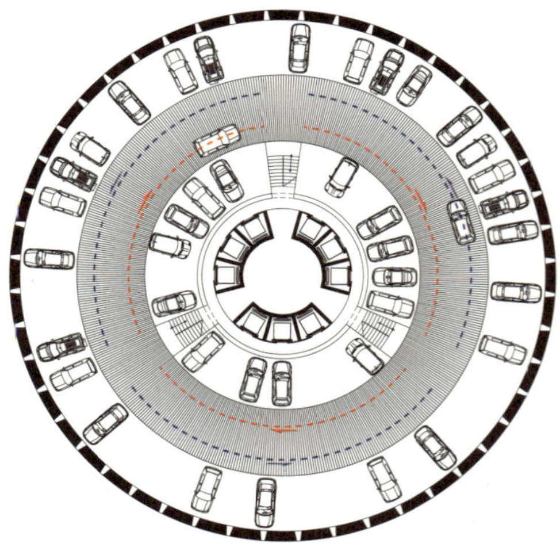

The universal character of the column is tried out on different scales and in different locations. In the designs for the Tijuana and ICA towers, a series of exterior columns constitutes the exposed structure of the cylindrical towers.

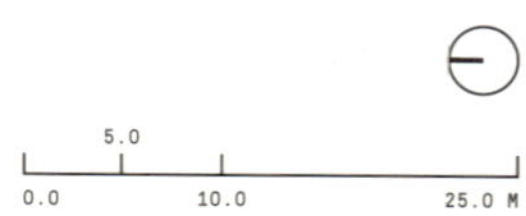

ICA Tower

With— Héctor Módica and Takemune Takuma

Mexico City / 2007

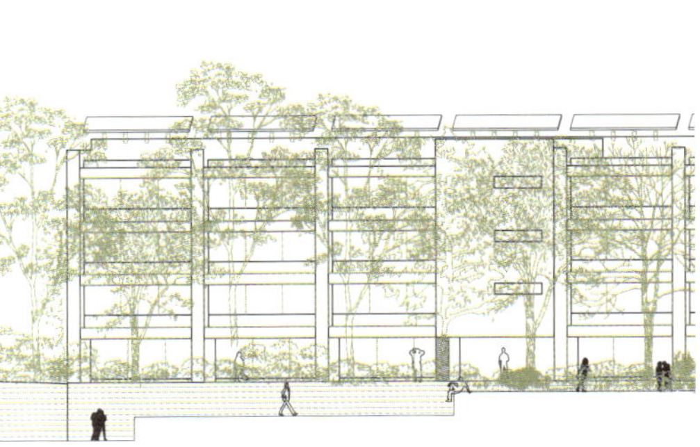

Q Tower

With— Héctor Módica

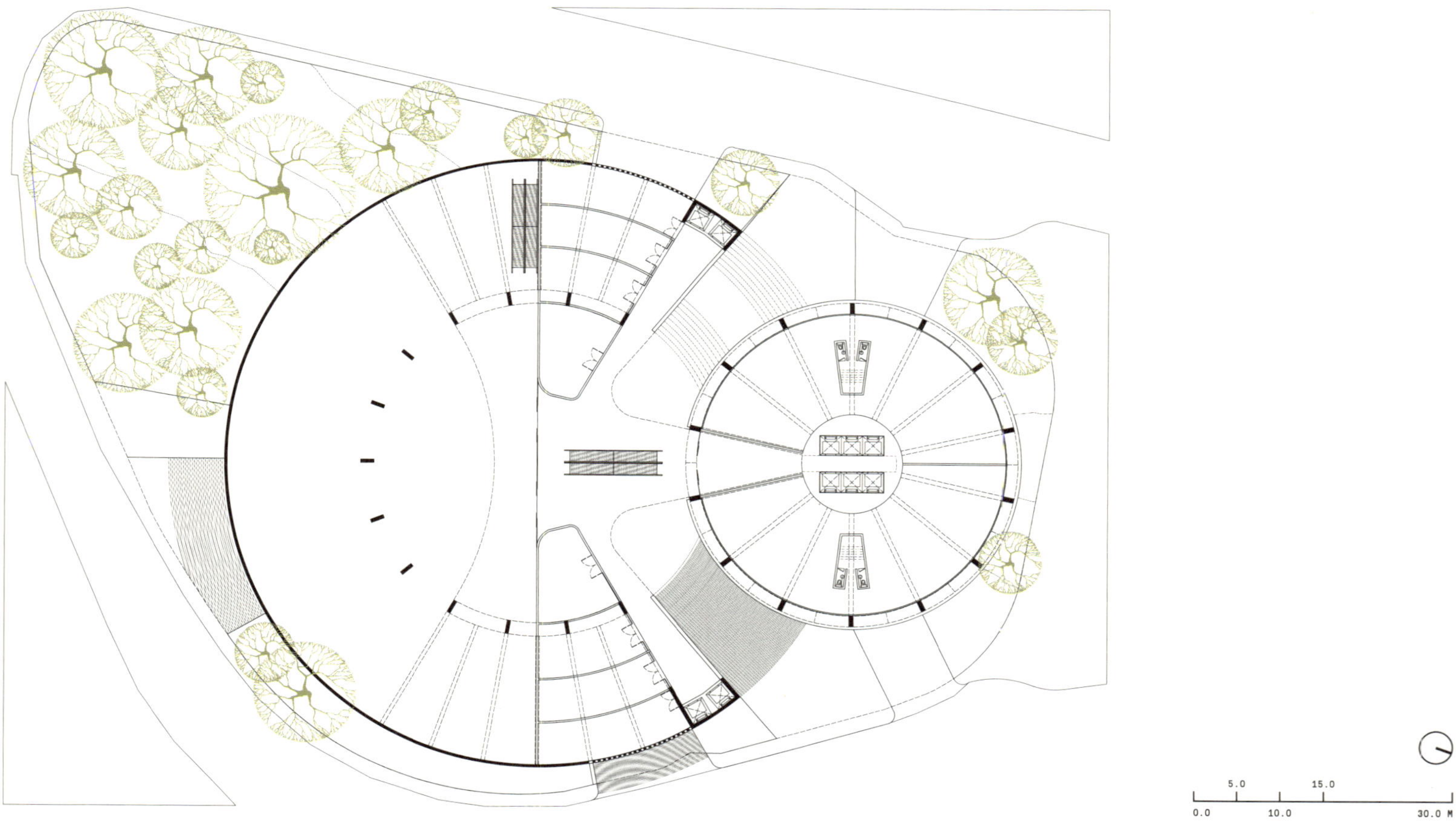

C3 Tower

With— Héctor Módica

— There is an amusing story behind this design, which is a tribute to Oscar Niemeyer. We had been invited to participate in competition of ideas for the C-3, the science center of the Universidad Nacional Autónoma de México, to be located at the southern end of the campus, within the zone of the natural reserve. Our proposal, logical enough, was to design a tower occupying the smallest possible surface area, in order to preserve the landscape of rocks and exotic plants, as well as to create a visible urban landmark. We restricted cars and other vehicles to already existing parking areas. The jury, made up of "distinguished architects," rejected our design on the grounds that it exceeded the height of the university concert hall. What a relief!

A few days later, we got a call from the administration of the university. The design had captivated them, but they proposed locating the tower on the far northern edge of the campus, at the end of Avenida Revolución. Again, the group of "distinguished architects" who held sway in the university undertook to prevent construction.

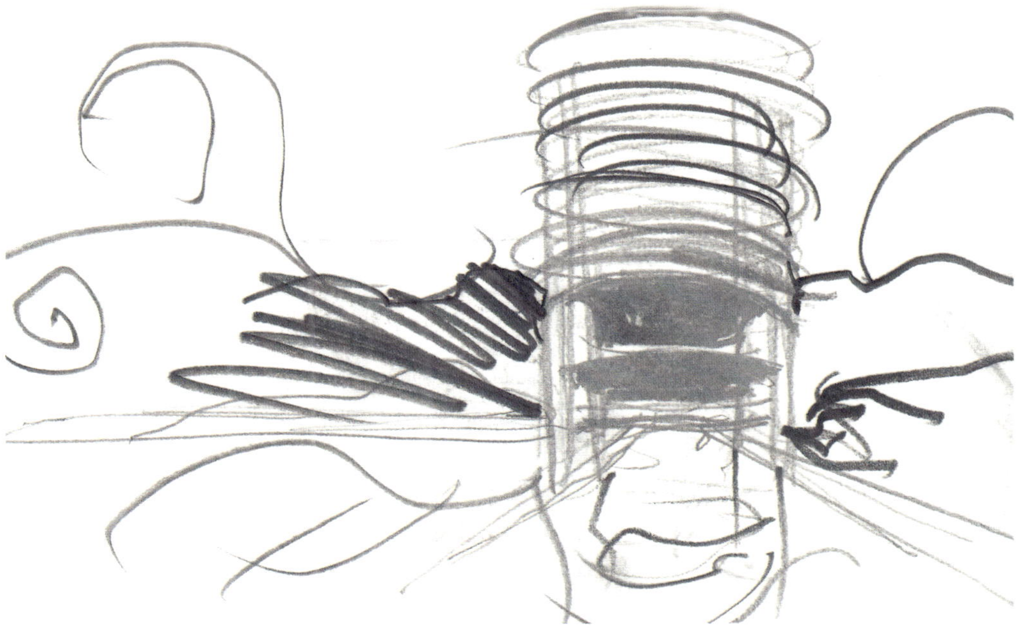

preservar paisaje natural
máxima conservación del área natural

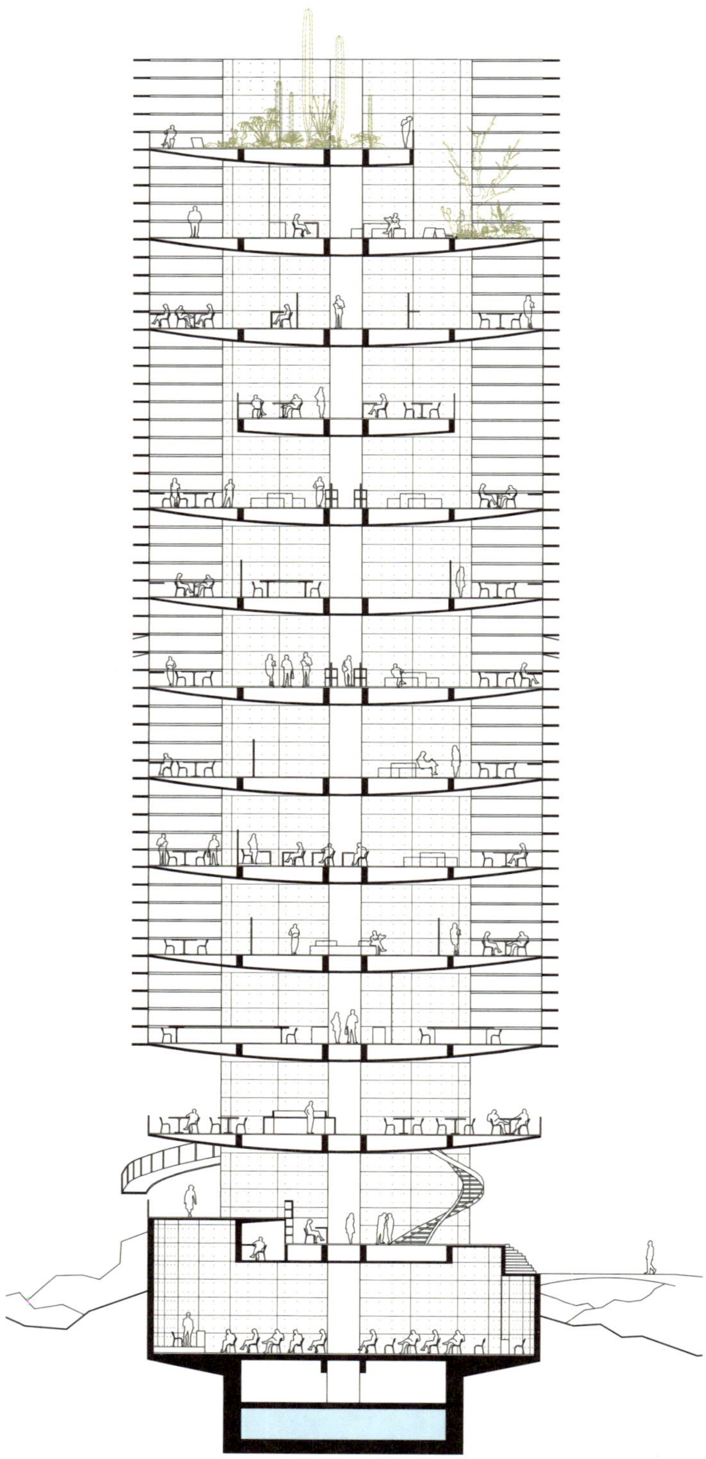

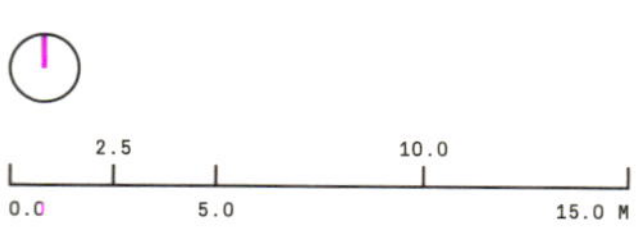
2.5
10.0
0.0
5.0
15.0 M

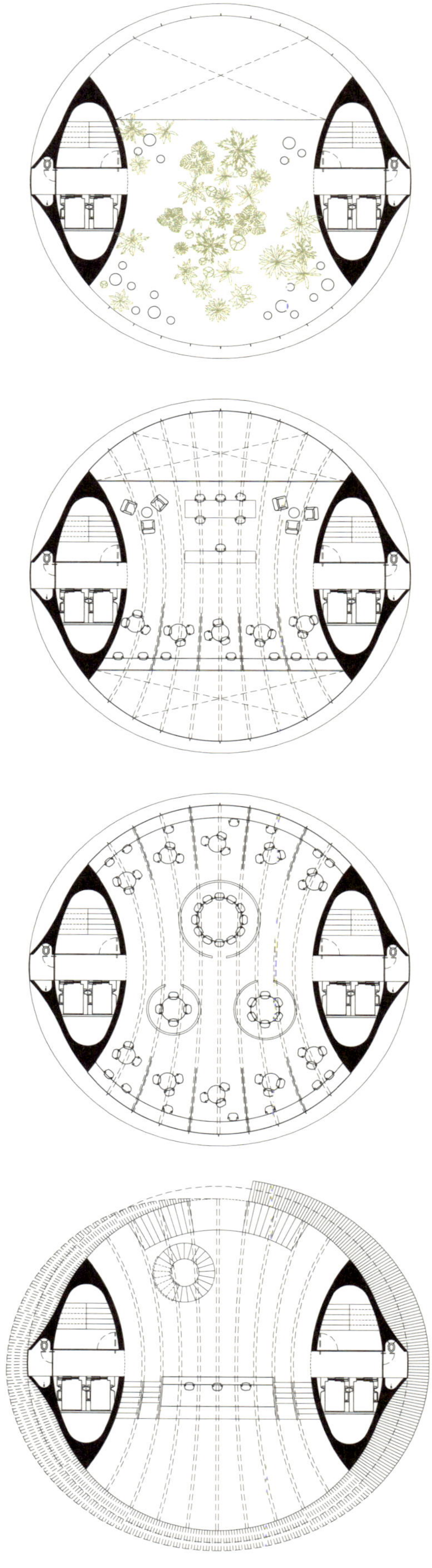

Telecom

With— Héctor Módica

Taiwan, China / 2011

The most audacious of Kalach's variations on the tower typology was the design for a Telecom telecommunications tower in Taiwan. Convex arches in a circular plan are crowned, asymmetrically, by a virtual slanted plane.

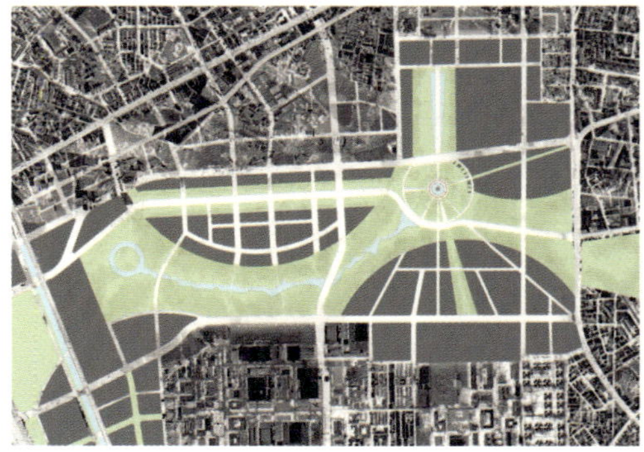

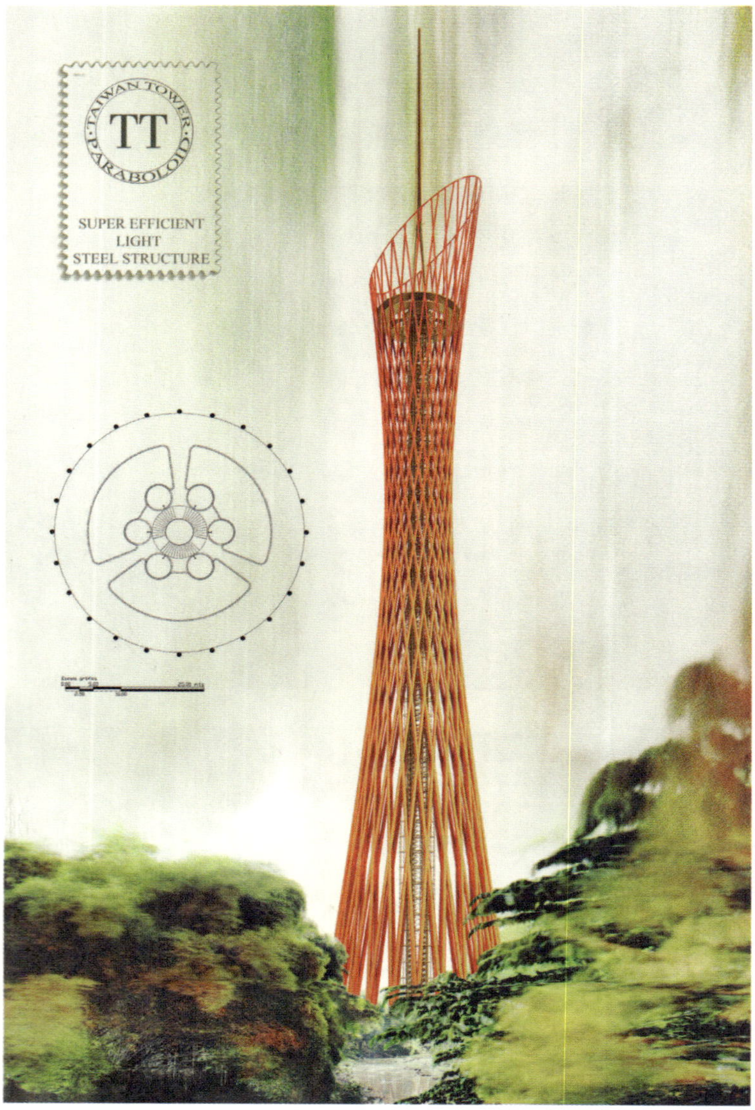

Lafayette Lighthouse

With— David Garza

Guadalajara / 2019

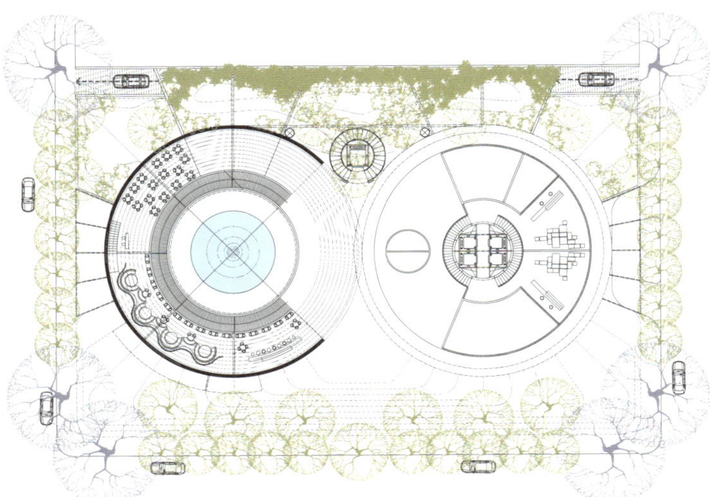

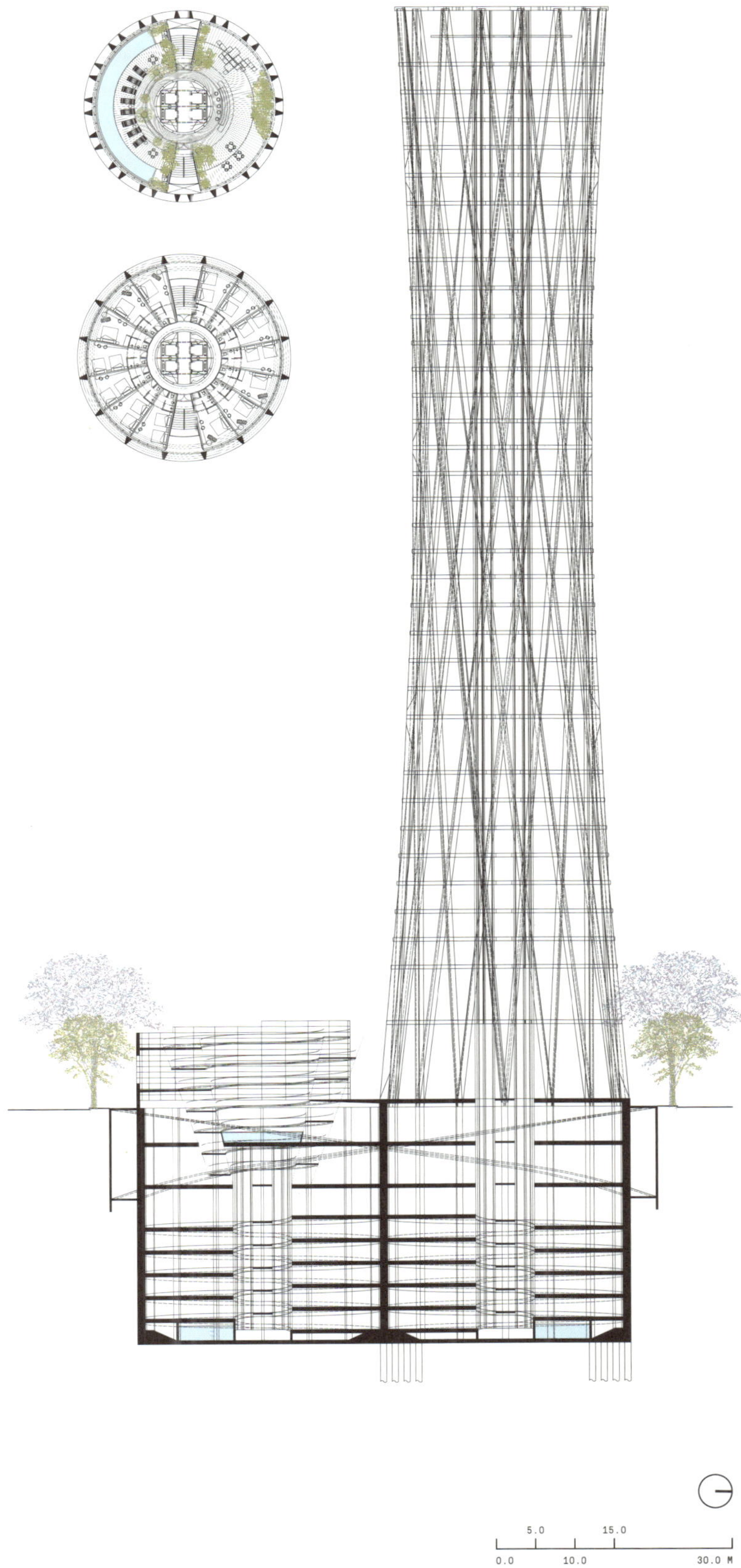

Hotel in Houston

With— Gonzalo Mauleón

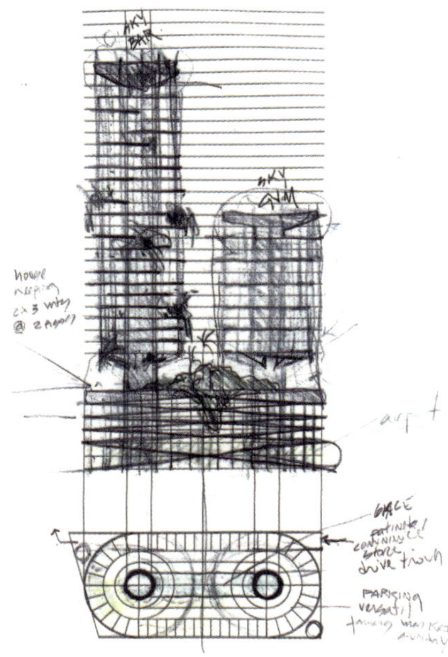

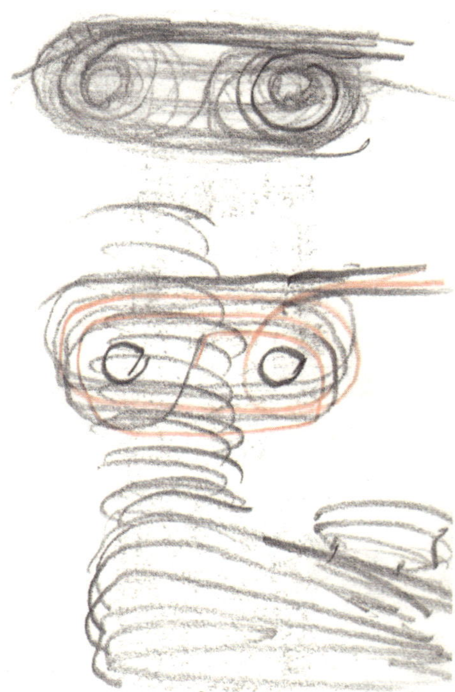

Reforma 27

With— Bolívar Garrido, José Luis Reyes, Héctor Módica, Iván Ramírez, Susana Pantoja, Ana María Martínez, Patricia Galdós, Adriana León, Julieta de la Portilla, and Marco Kalach

This 25-story apartment tower is aligned alongside the Paseo de la Reforma, with deep loadbearing façades in the form of grids that create inhabitable niches. The structural façades, of red-pigmented reinforced concrete, make for suitable thermal mass and allow for free plans. The tall ground-floor portico integrates the tower with the street, while the one that crowns the building connects it visually to the urban skyline. The programmatic elements include a lobby, a parking area, a gymnasium, a swimming pool, gardens, and five types of apartments of one, two, and three bedrooms. The program is organized into two parallel residential blocks separated by an elevator core in the center and open patios on both sides, defined by convex façades that open onto the surrounding urban vistas.

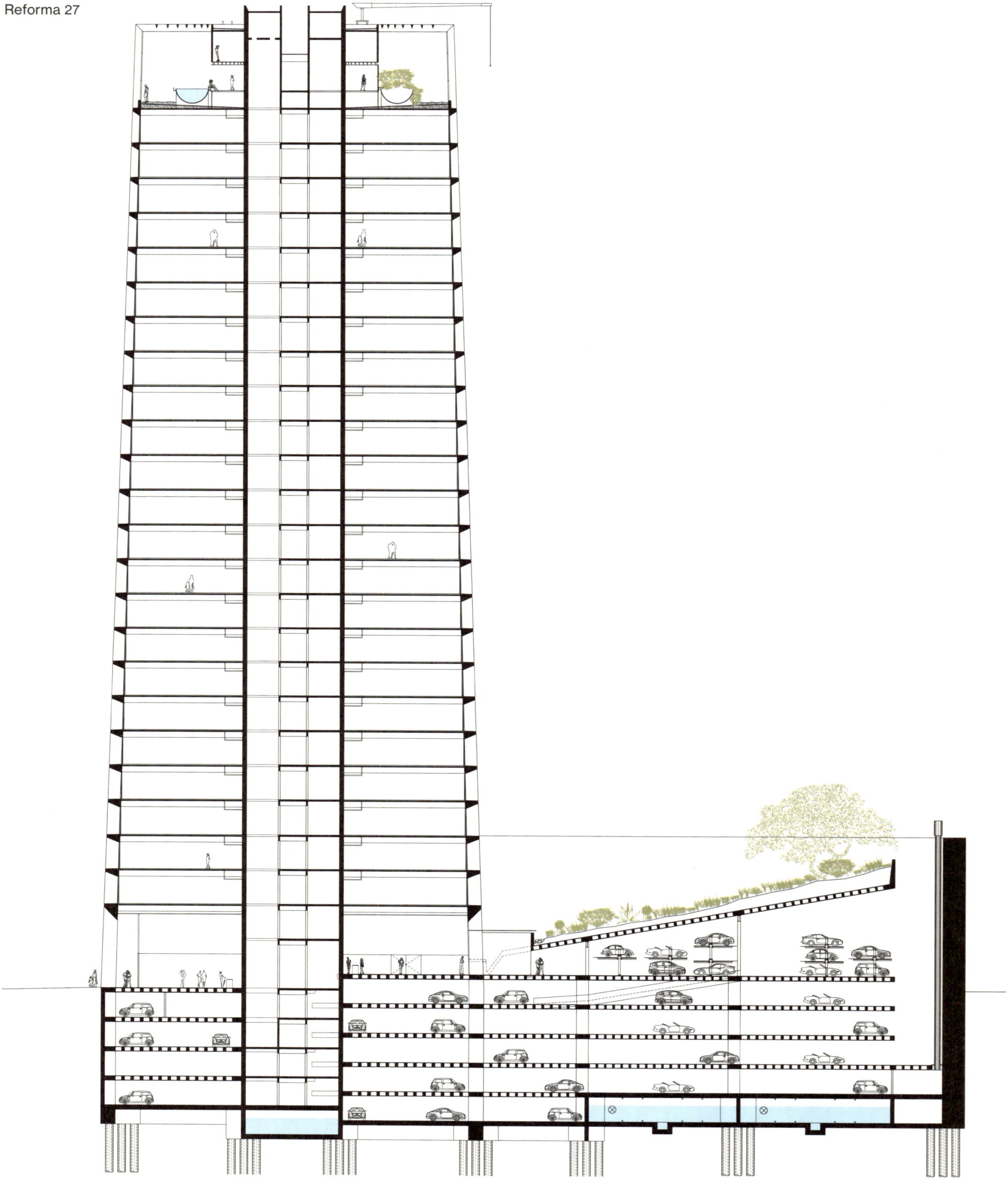

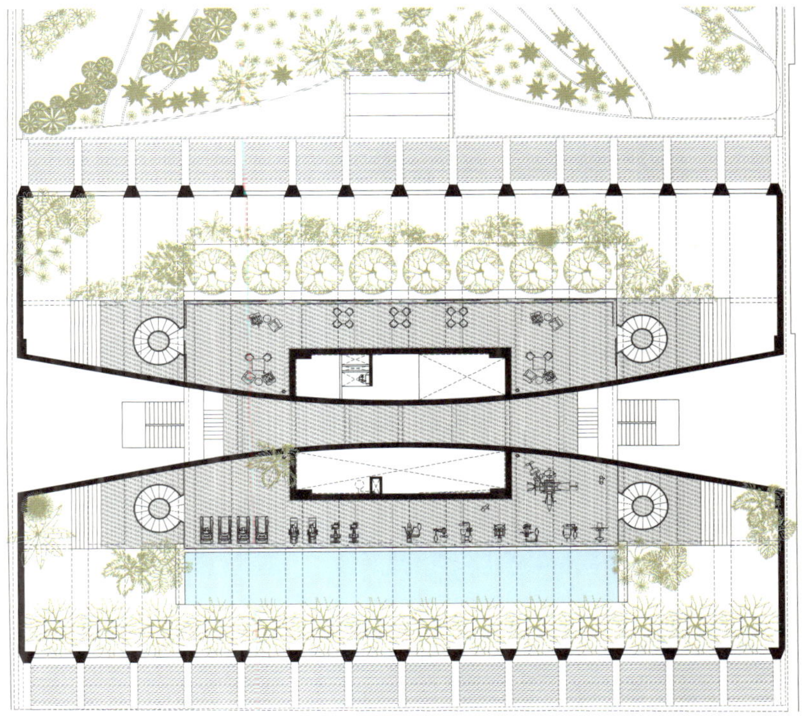

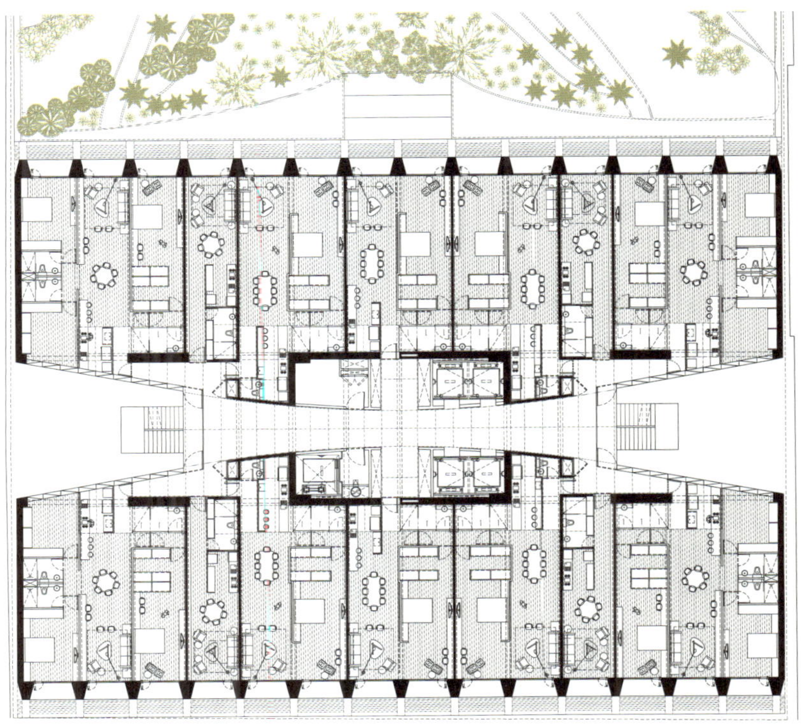

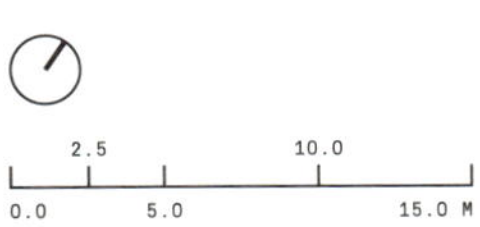
2.5
10.0
0.0
5.0
15.0 M

Towers

Reforma 90

Mexico City / 2007

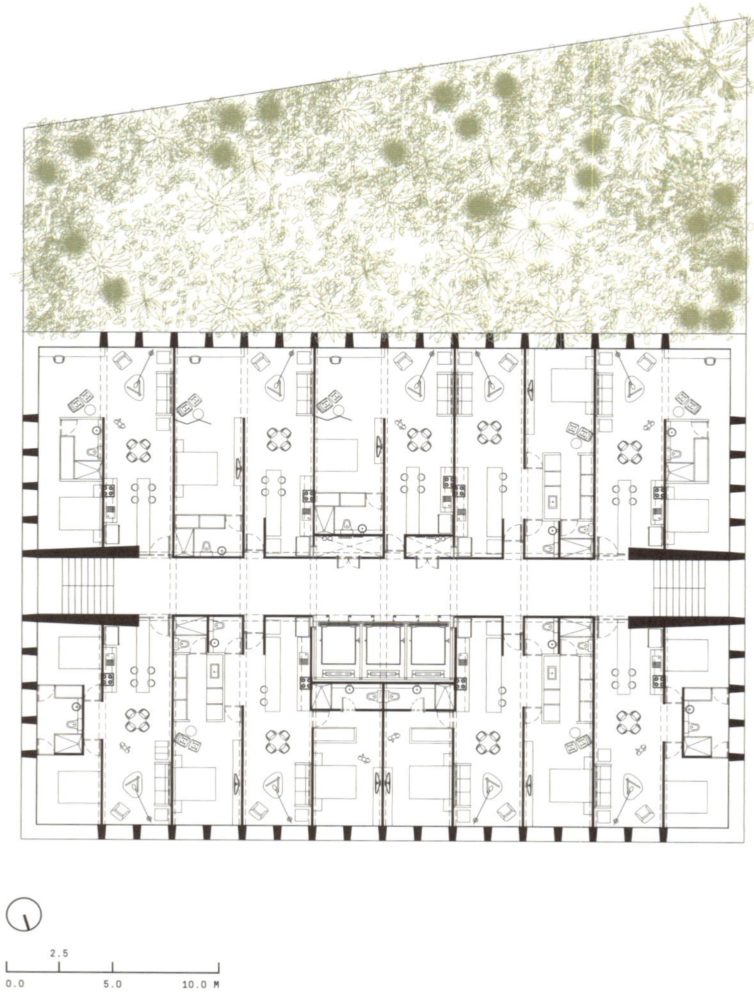

This tower, the immediate forerunner of the one at Reforma 27, with a grid-like structural façade, has a portico on the ground floor and another, with a more compact plan, at the top of the building.

Tower in Caracas

With— Héctor Módica and Takemune Takuma

Caracas / 2008

Bansí Tower

With— Héctor Módica

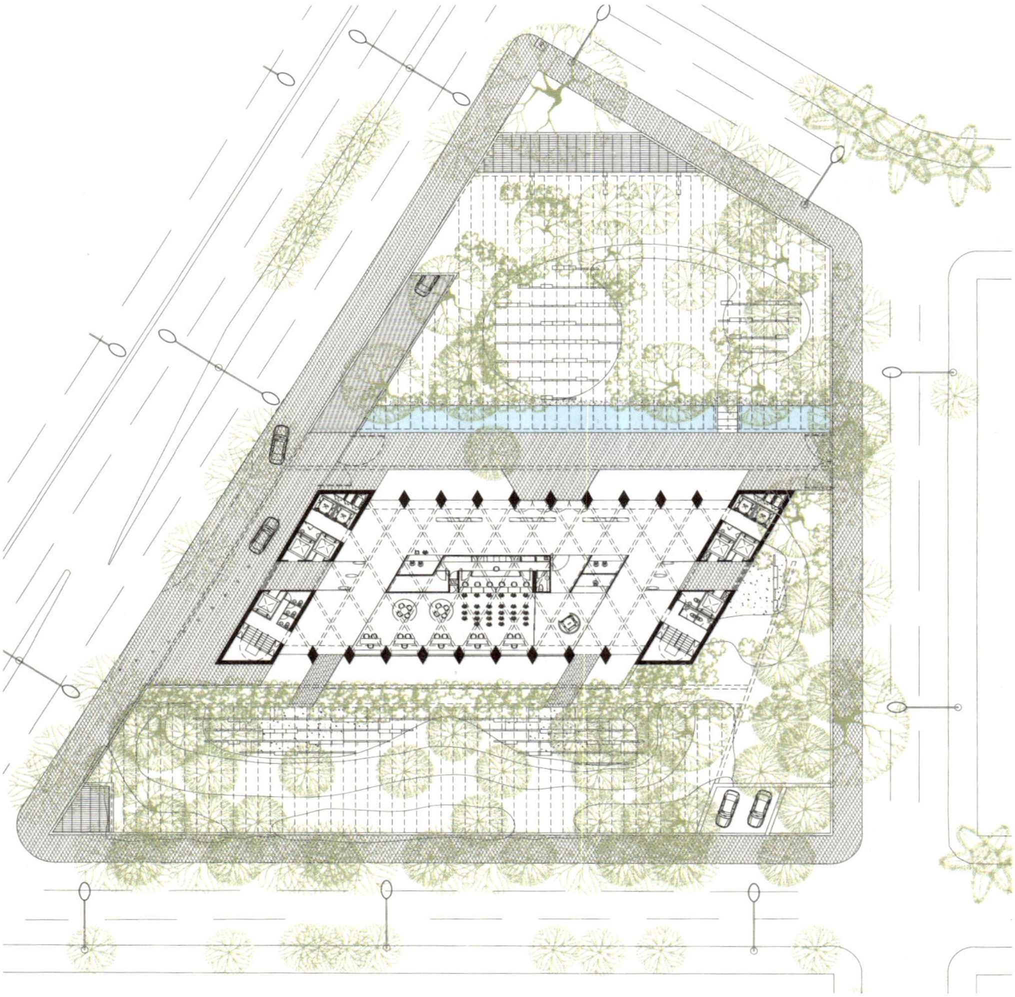

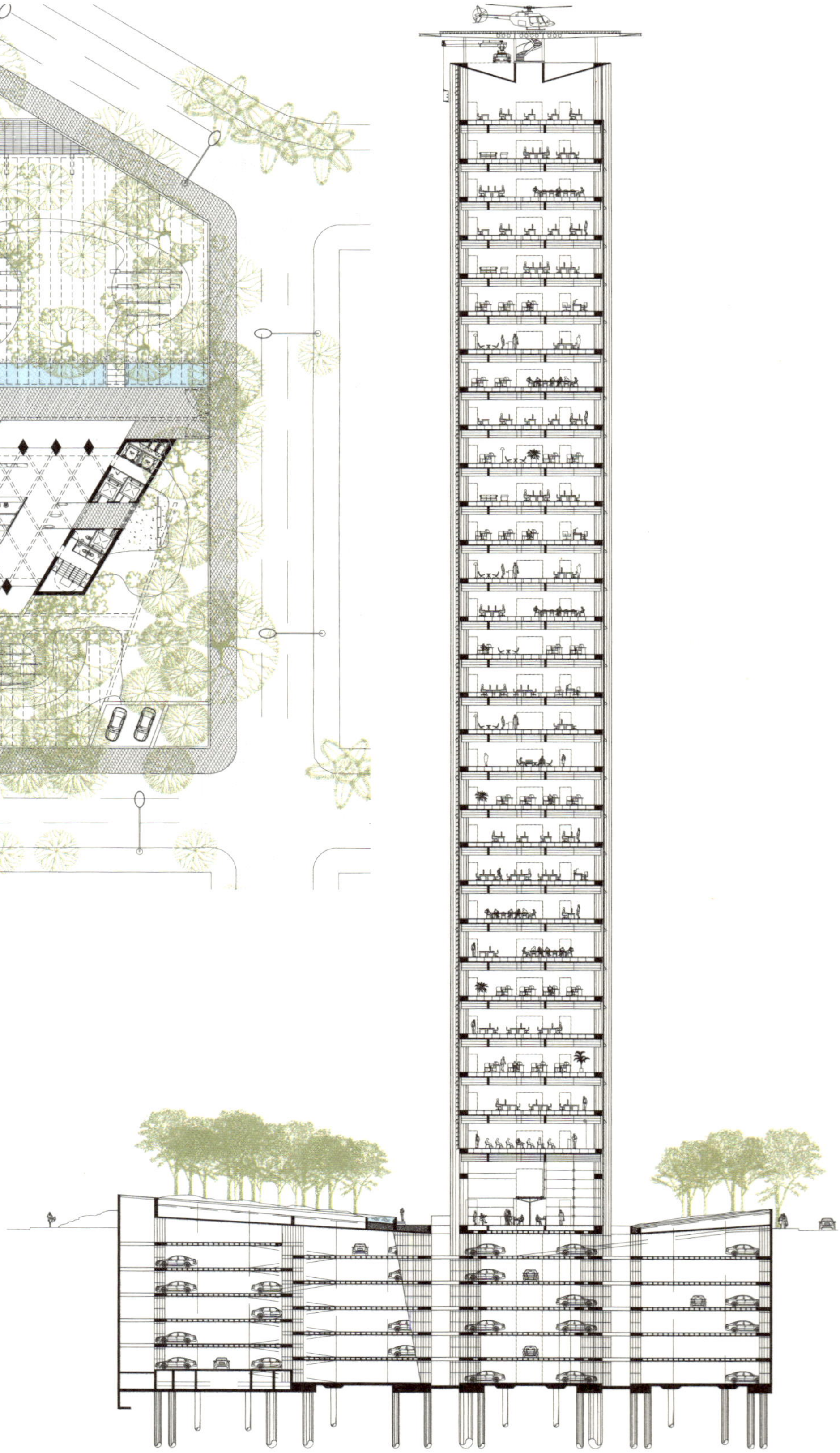

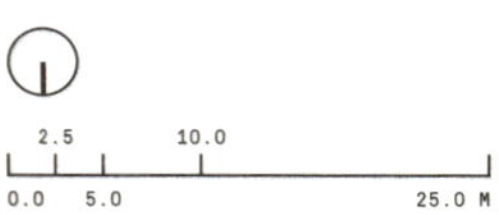

Santander Tower

With— Héctor Módica, Takemune Takuma, and Iván Ramírez

Monterrey / 2009

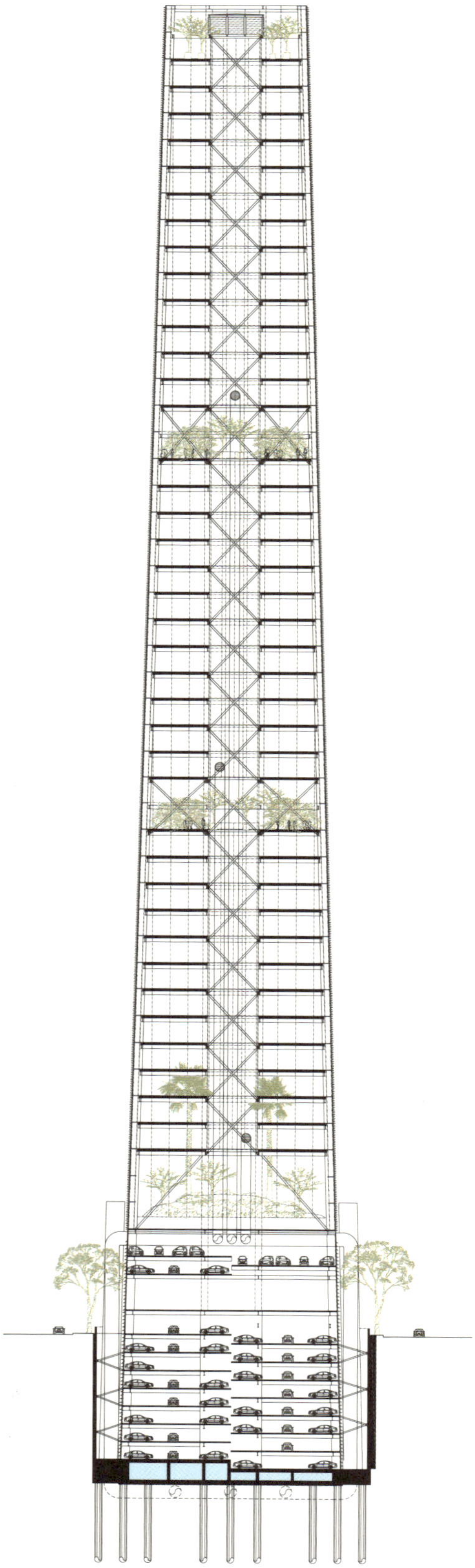

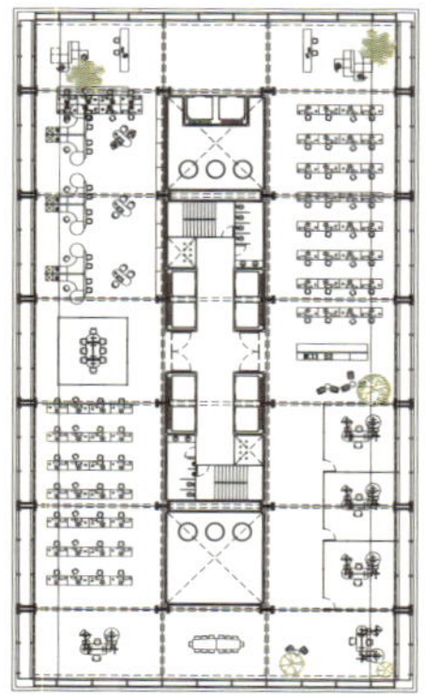

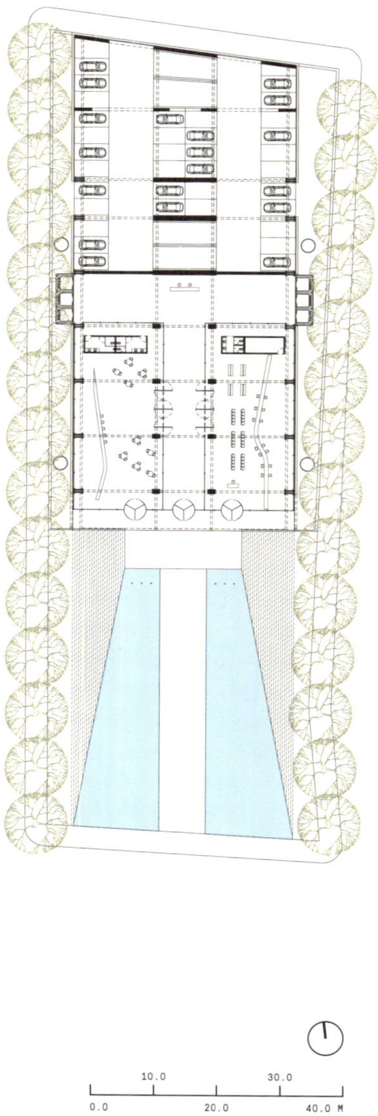

Rey Maxtla Tower

With— Toshiyuki Kobayashi and Nathalie Franquebalme

Mexico City / 2017

This is a variation on the typology of Reforma 27, designed to incorporate an open public market on the ground floor, with columns slanting outwards.

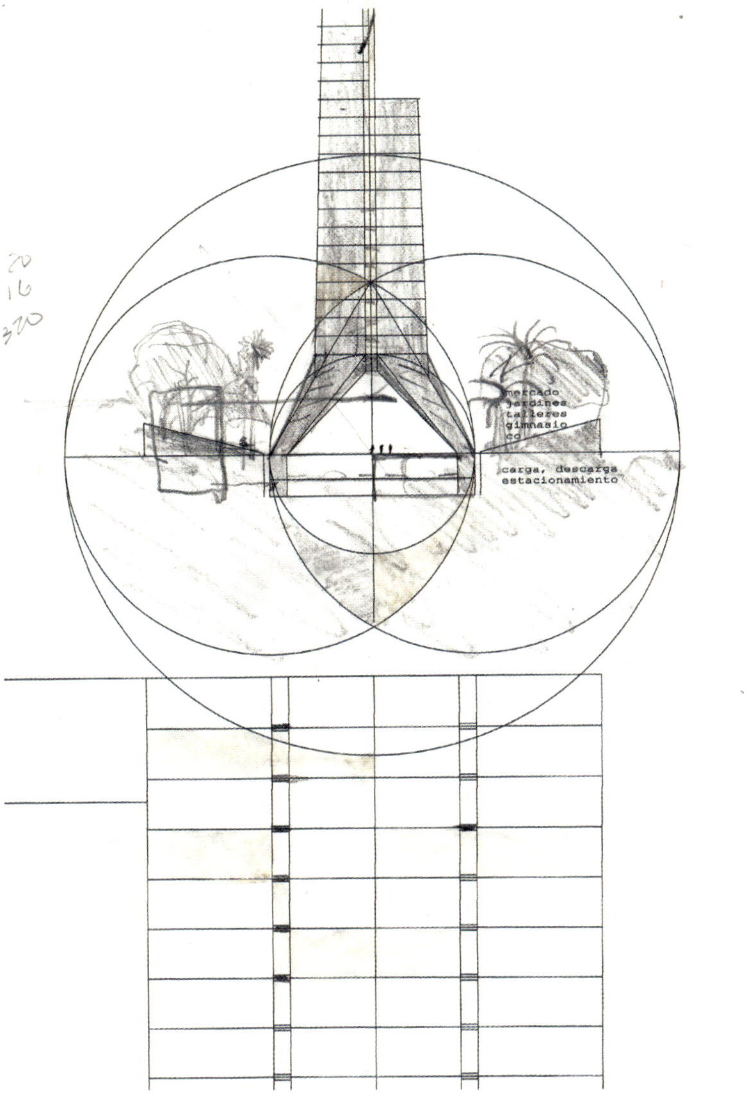

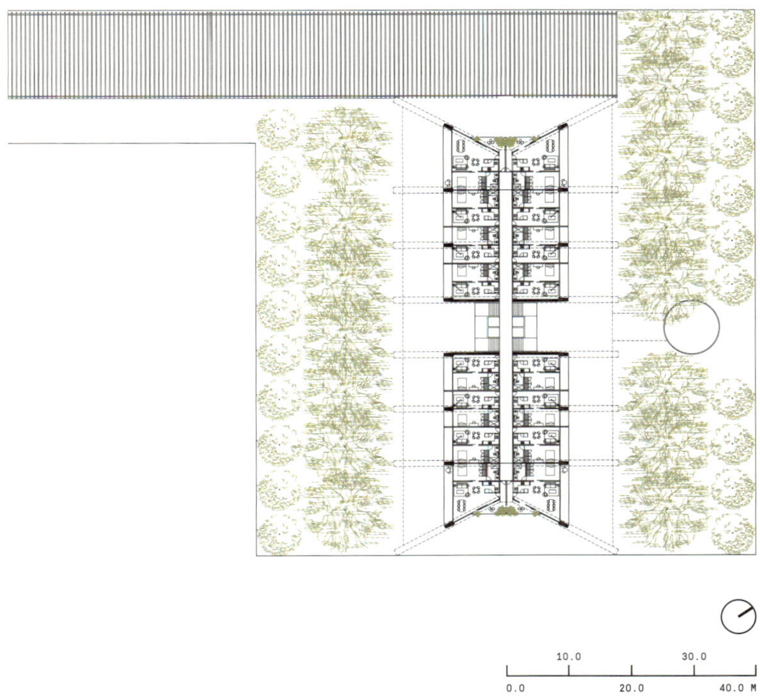

Punta Ixtapa

With— López Baz y Calleja and Emmanuel Ramírez

Tropical Towers

A series of projects along the tropical coastline of the Pacific Ocean was the opportunity for a typology that seeks to make the slightest possible intervention into the context. Uprights driven into the jungle hillsides resolve the vertical communications through the structure, while at the same time providing support for a series of partially occupied platforms, transformed into spectacular apartments with 360-degree vistas. Landmarks mirroring each other in the landscape, with organic morphologies inspired by natural ones, but on another scale.

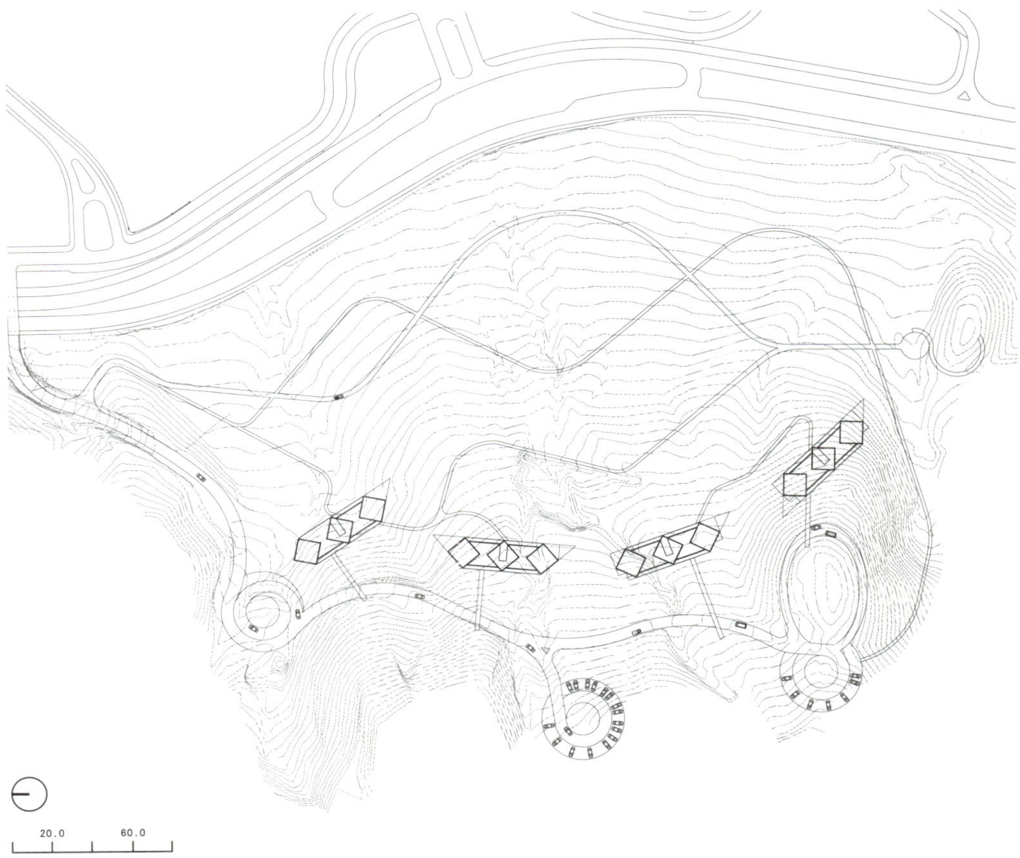

Towers

Tower in Vallarta

With— Héctor Módica and Iván Ramírez

Puerto Vallarta / 2012

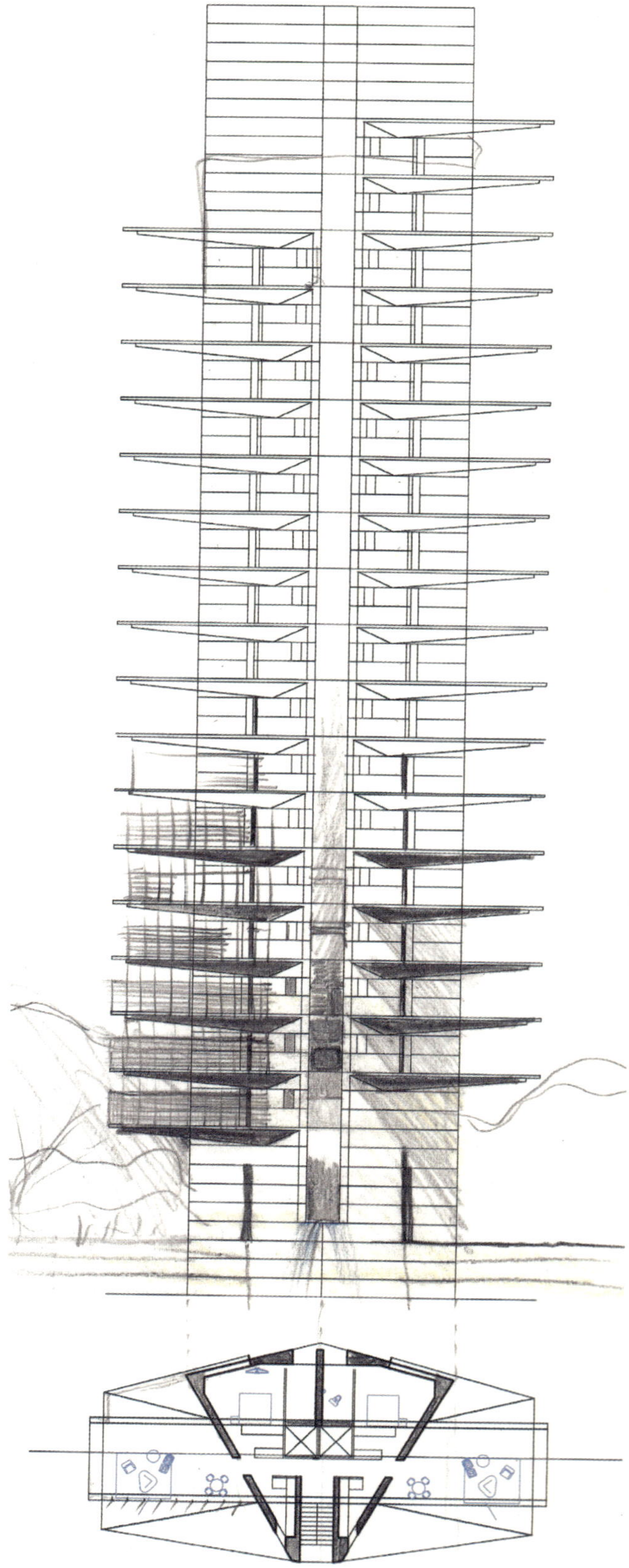

Tree Tower

With— Héctor Módica and Iván Ramírez

Baja California Sur / 2012

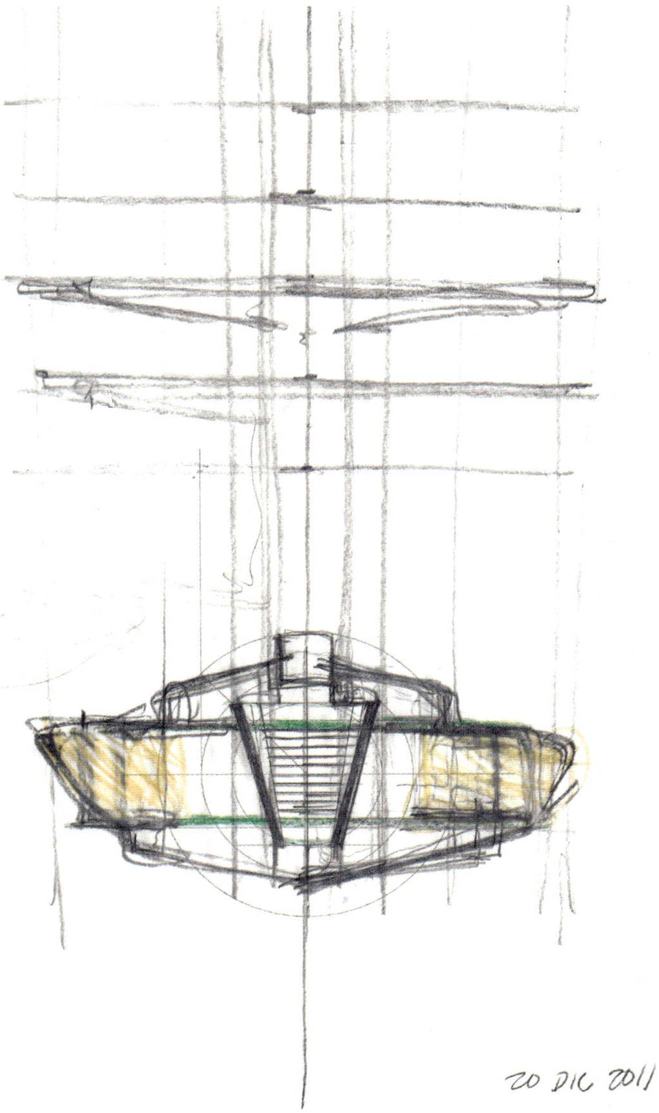

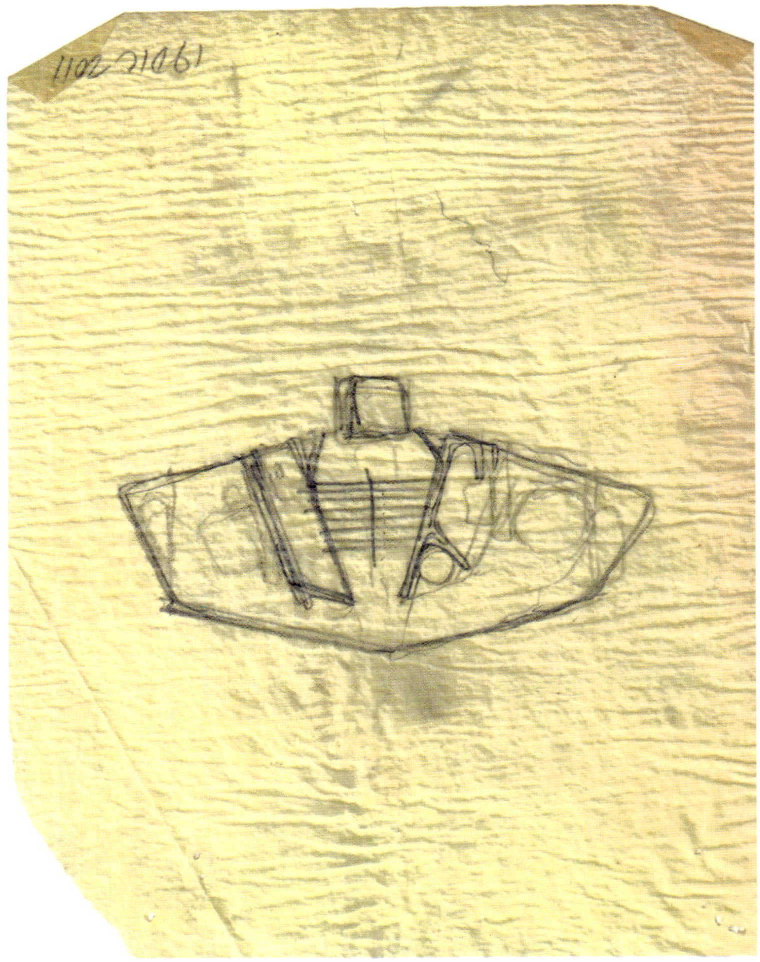

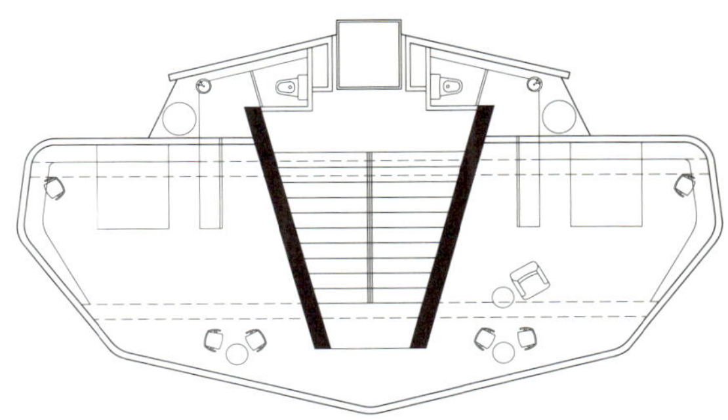

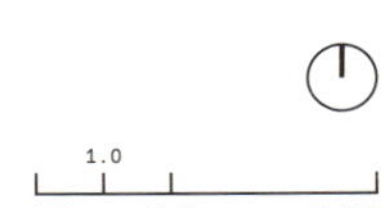

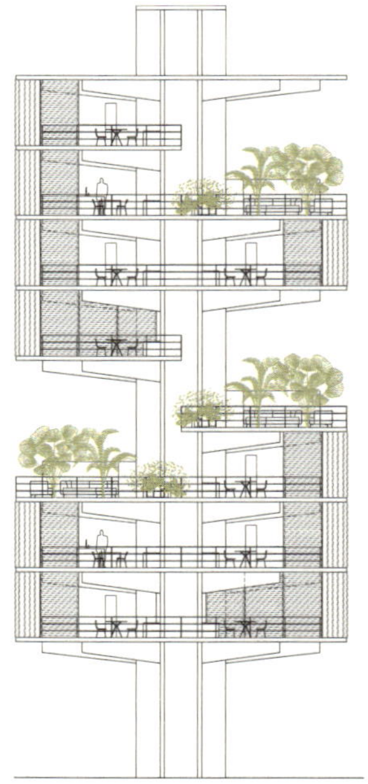

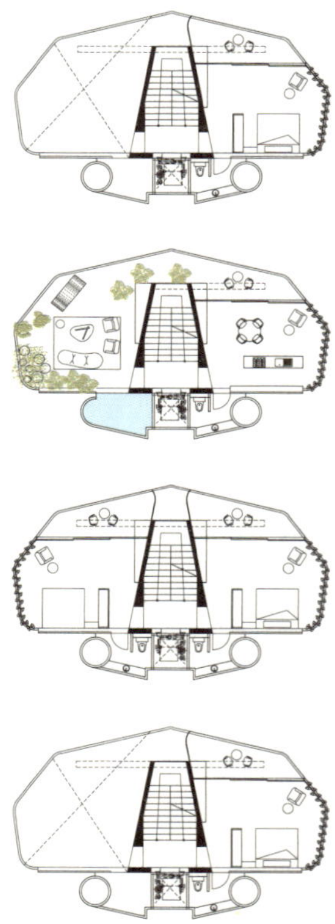

— A little tower, hidden amidst the cliffs, facing the Pacific Ocean. Vertical. Vertebral.

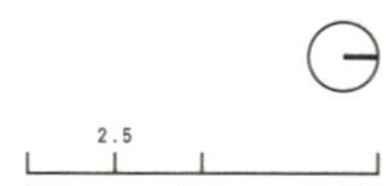

Jasmine Tower

With— Xavier González

Querétaro / 2014

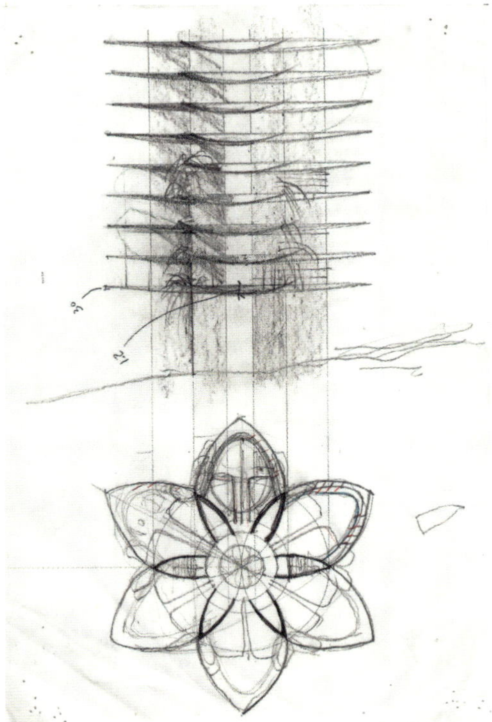

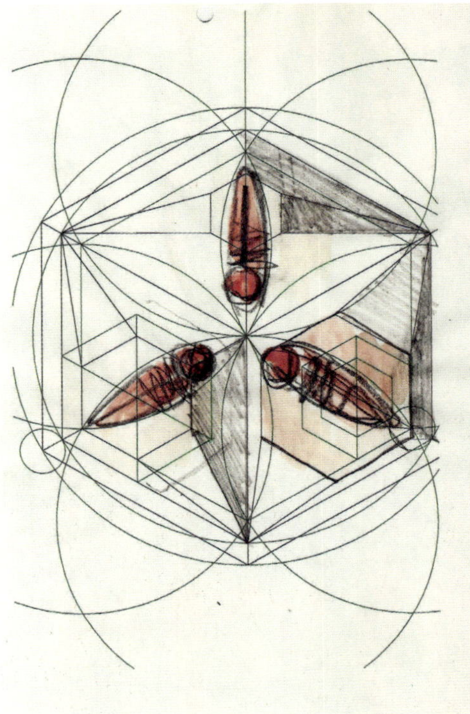

San Gimignano

Ciudad Satélite Towers

Giorgio Morandi

Towers in Groups

Faced with the alternative of concentrating the entire program in large diaphanous floor plans, Kalach favored the fragmentation of the constructed volumes in order to achieve a certain urban complexity. Towers inspired by the metaphysical still lifes of Giorgio Morandi and by the medieval towers of San Gimignano, which also influenced Luis Barragán in his conception of the Ciudad Satélite Towers. These volumetric compositions of prisms, cylinders, and cones trace new metropolitan landscapes.

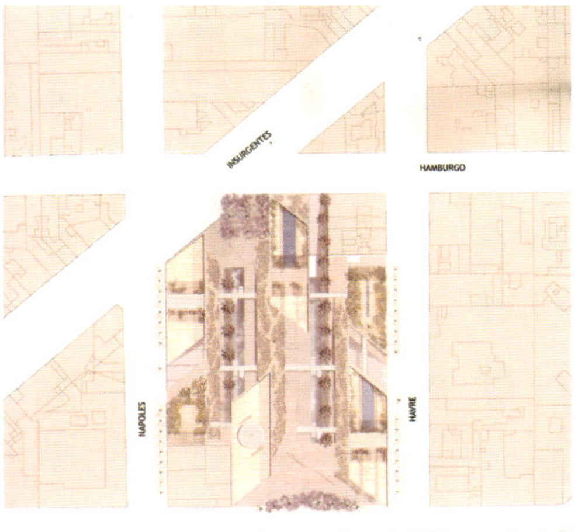

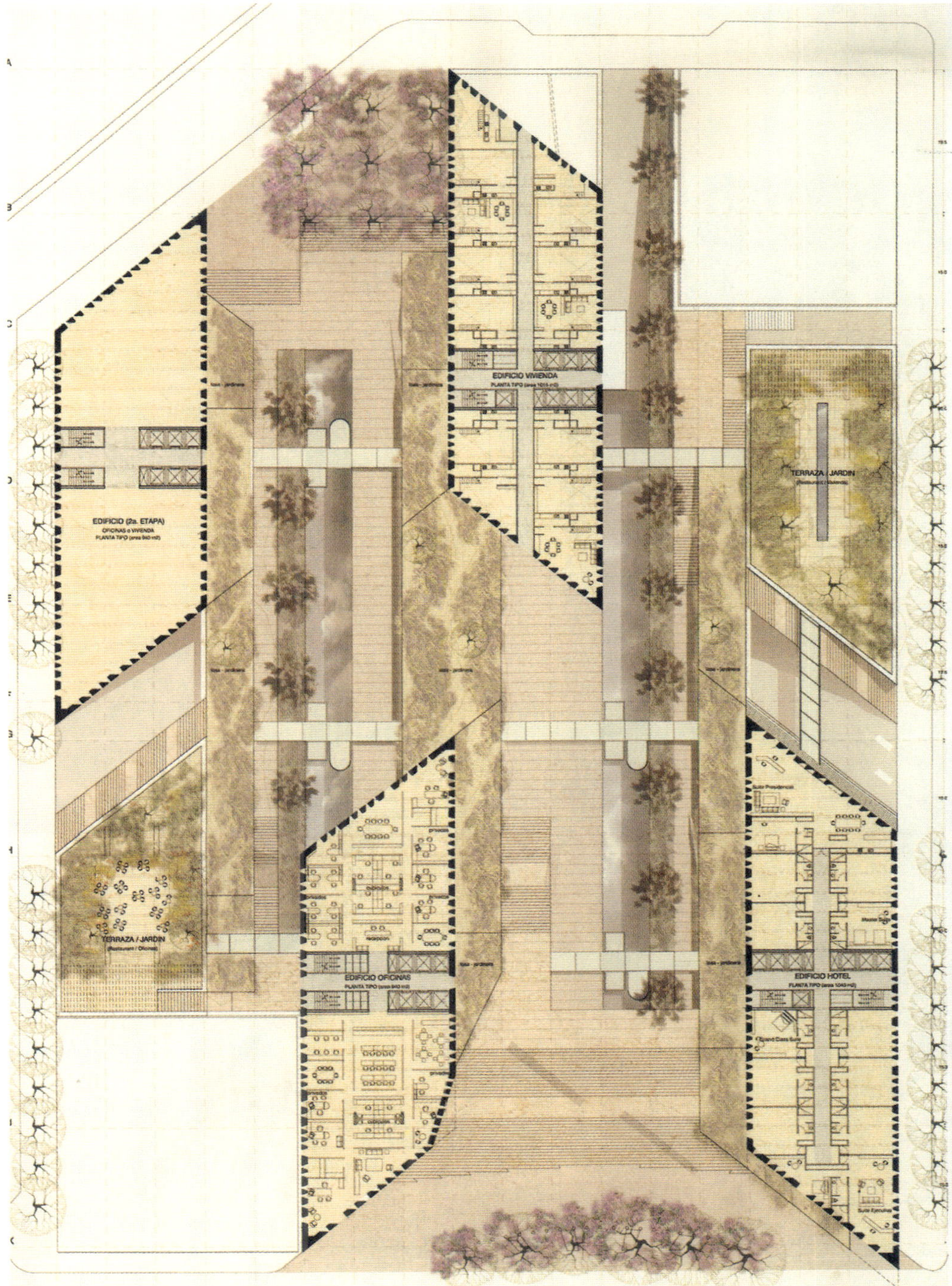

PLANTA TIPO

— This proposal, submitted to the competition for Reforma 222, was not understood by the jury. It consists of four svelte towers without bases (allowing for a green plaza) joining Reforma to Insurgentes. Most of the commercial spaces are underground, enlivened by large patios as in the Rockefeller Center.

Ritz Carlton Towers

With— Emmanuel Ramírez and Ignacio del Río

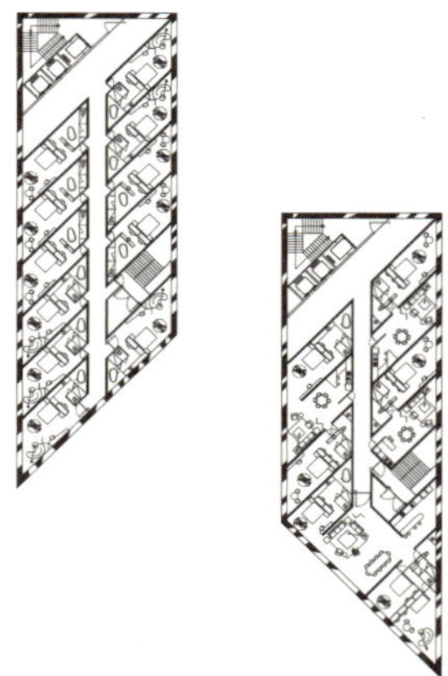

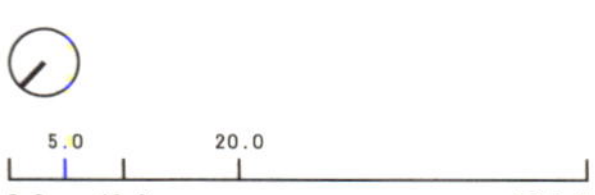

— A second attempt at the competition for the Diana Huntress roundabout. This one consists of a pair of buildings, with hotel and apartments, both different and alike, as if they were siblings, rising from the plaza with no base, allowing for a fluid ground-level public space. Like the Seagram Building in New York City, or the Lever House, and so many others.

Towers on Marina

With— Iván Ramírez and Luis Reyes

Mexico City / 2007

— Two pairs of towers embrace each other along Avenida Marina Nacional. They are efficient in their structures, which are also the façades. Distinguishing features can be observed in each one of these characters.

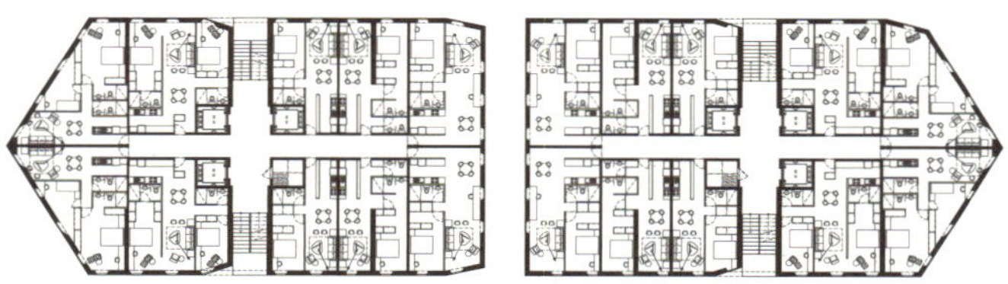

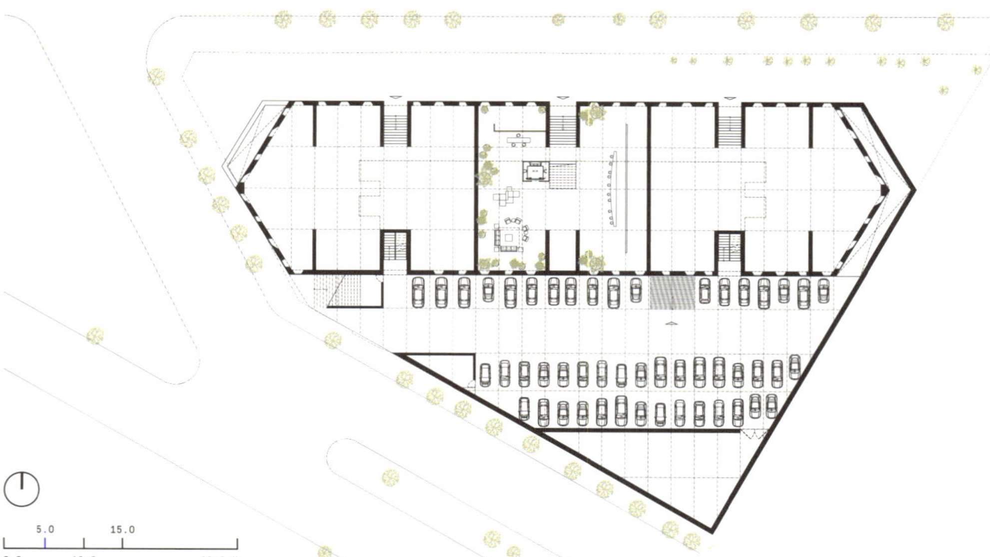

Towers on Iglesia

With— Héctor Mcdica and Iván Ramírez

Mexico City / 2007

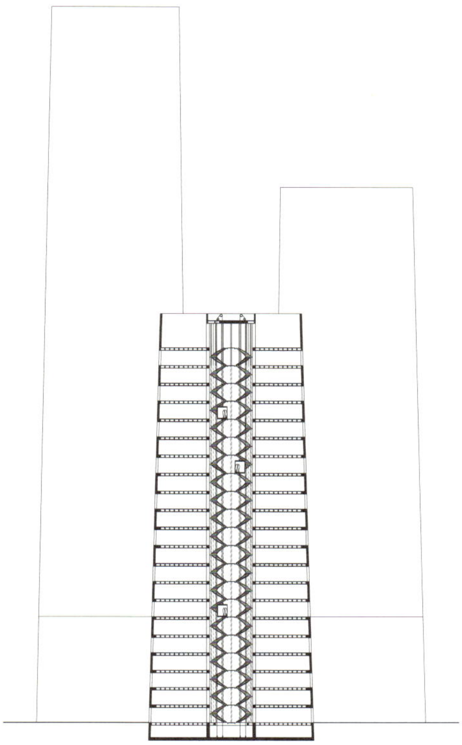

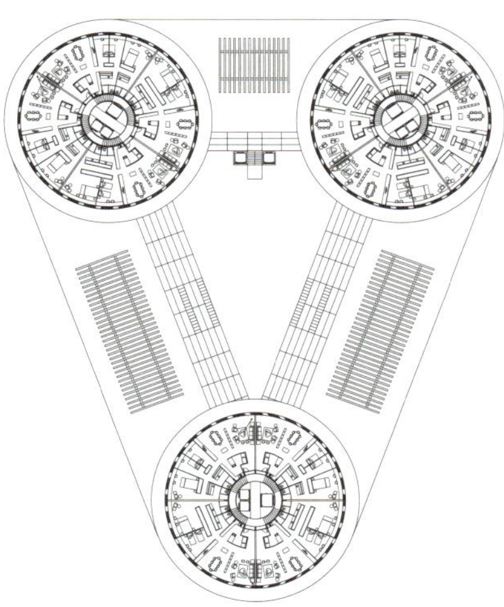

— Another grouping at the dynamic intersection of Río Magdalena sets off this urban node in a singular way. By their position and form, the towers seek out the ideal exposure to sunlight and distant vistas. A light, climbing base interweaves parking areas, towers with commercial spaces, and hanging gardens.

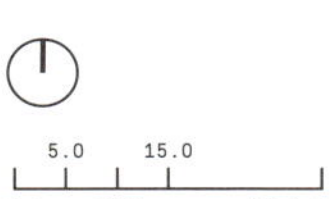

Periférico Towers

With— Iván Ramírez

Mexico City / 2013

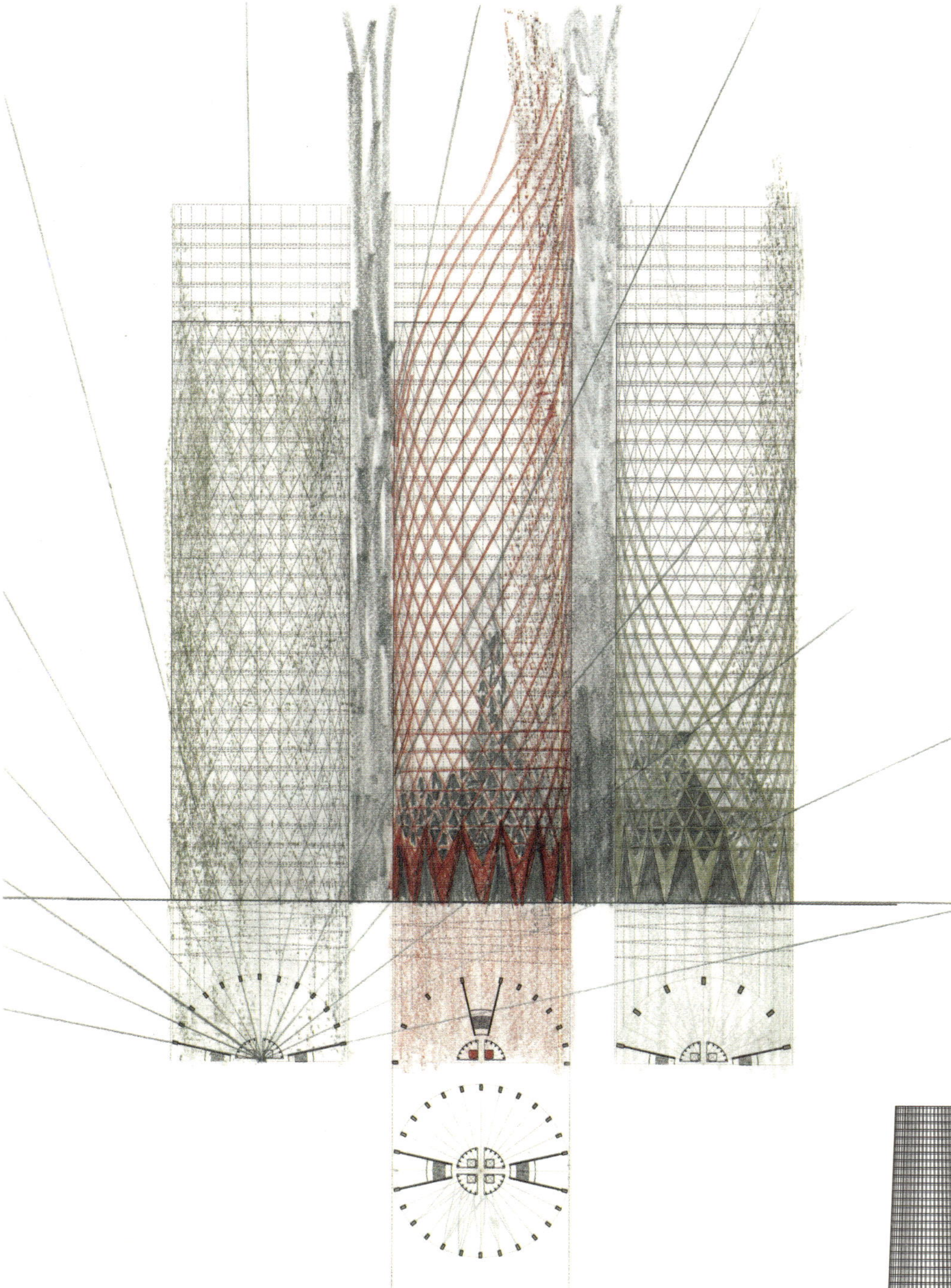

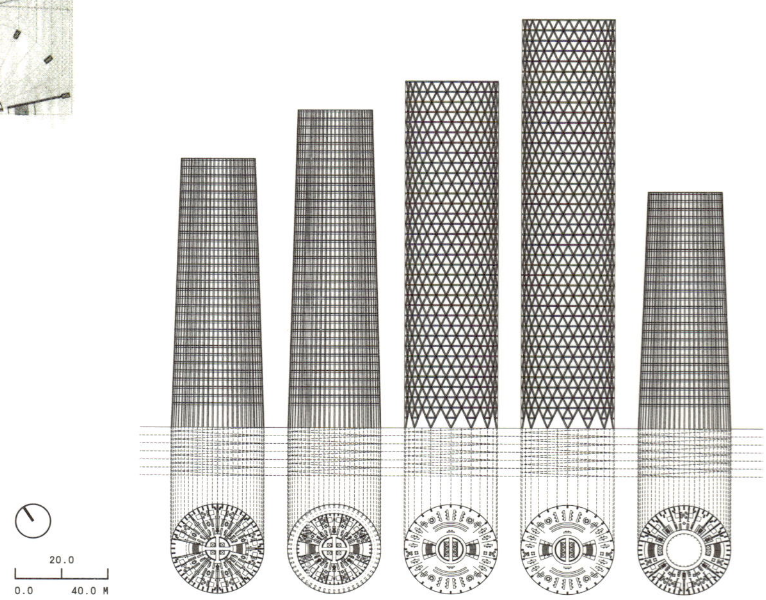

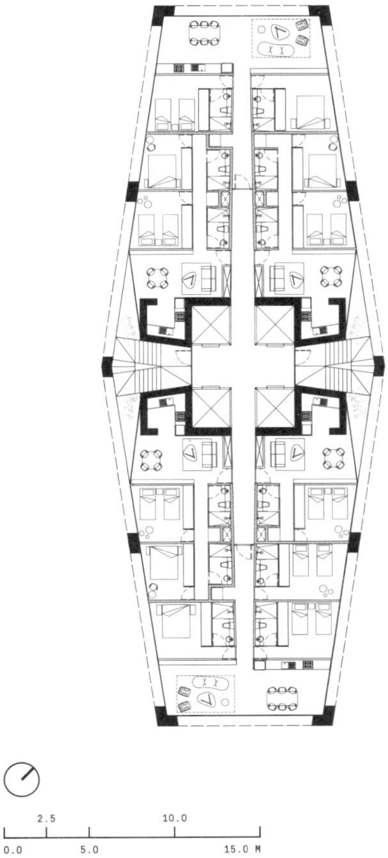

2.5
10.0
0.0
5.0
15.0 M

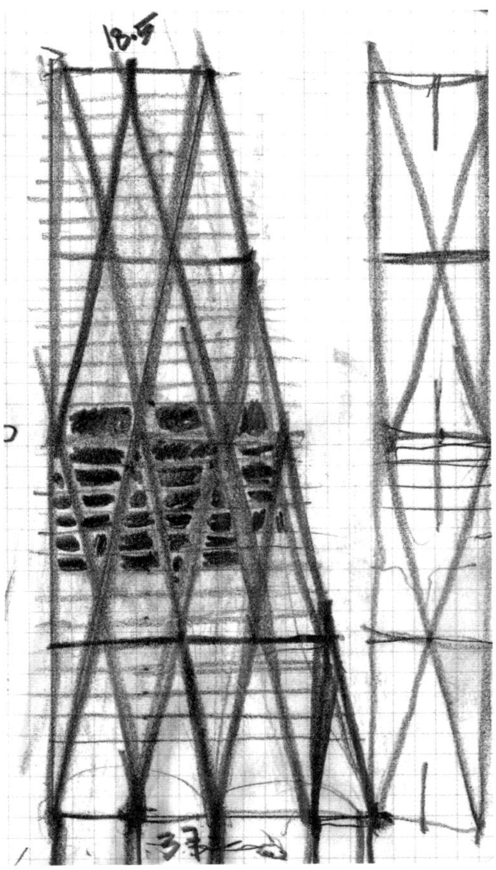

Towers on Constituyentes

Across from the Park

After occupying a large shed on Avenida Constituyentes for his offices for many years, Kalach speculated with the extraordinary potential of some residual lots located across from Chapultepec Park. He drew sequences of prisms that marked off the border of the park, creating a series of designs to occupy almost "leftover" spaces of the city: small triangles on the edges of the urban fabric –disdained by many– would be transformed into places with stunning views of the park.

43
41
39
37
13
11
ARGÁEZ

Argáez

With— Xavier González, Mariana Manjarrez, and María Kalach

The architect describes this project as “a base volume for cars, an office level, and four apartments with cheerful terraces overlooking Chapultepec Park.” The design makes the most of its location on a small street near the intersection of two important thoroughfares, directing vistas toward the green lung of Mexico City, through the superposition of open terraces all around the perimeter. The formal and structural expressiveness of the design evokes the structural simplicity proposed by Le Corbusier in his experimental prototype for the Dom-Ino House.

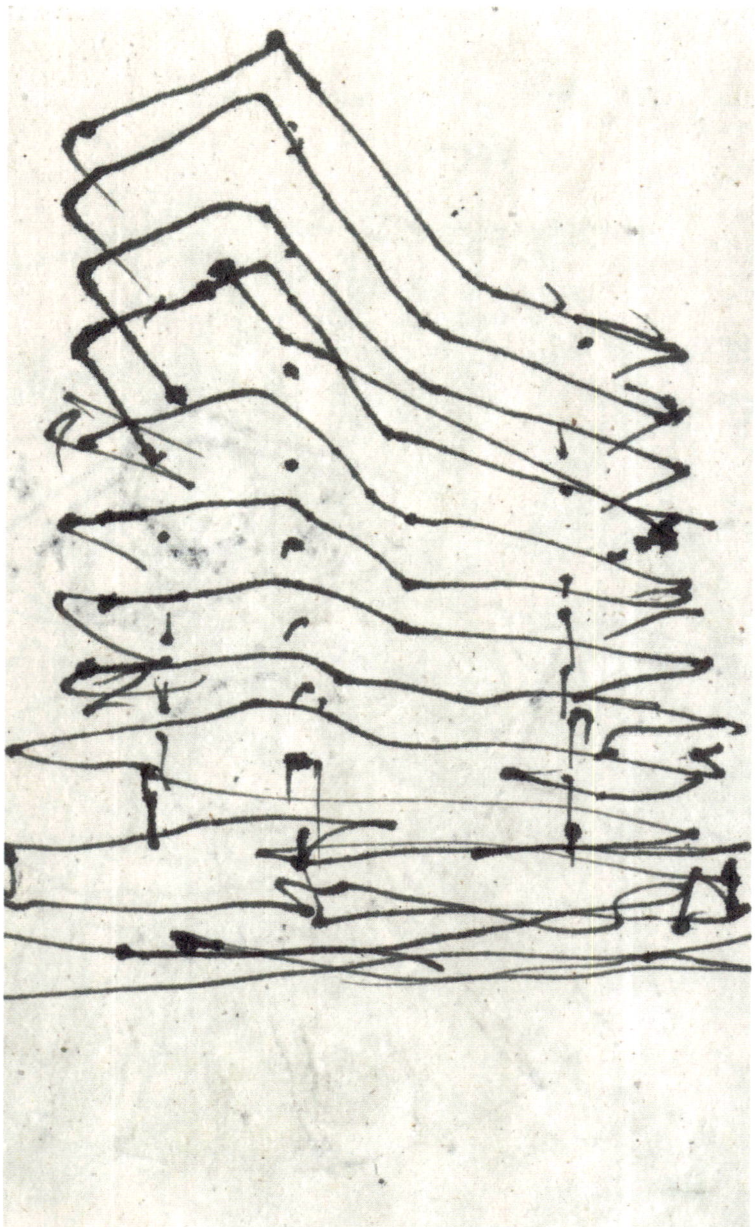

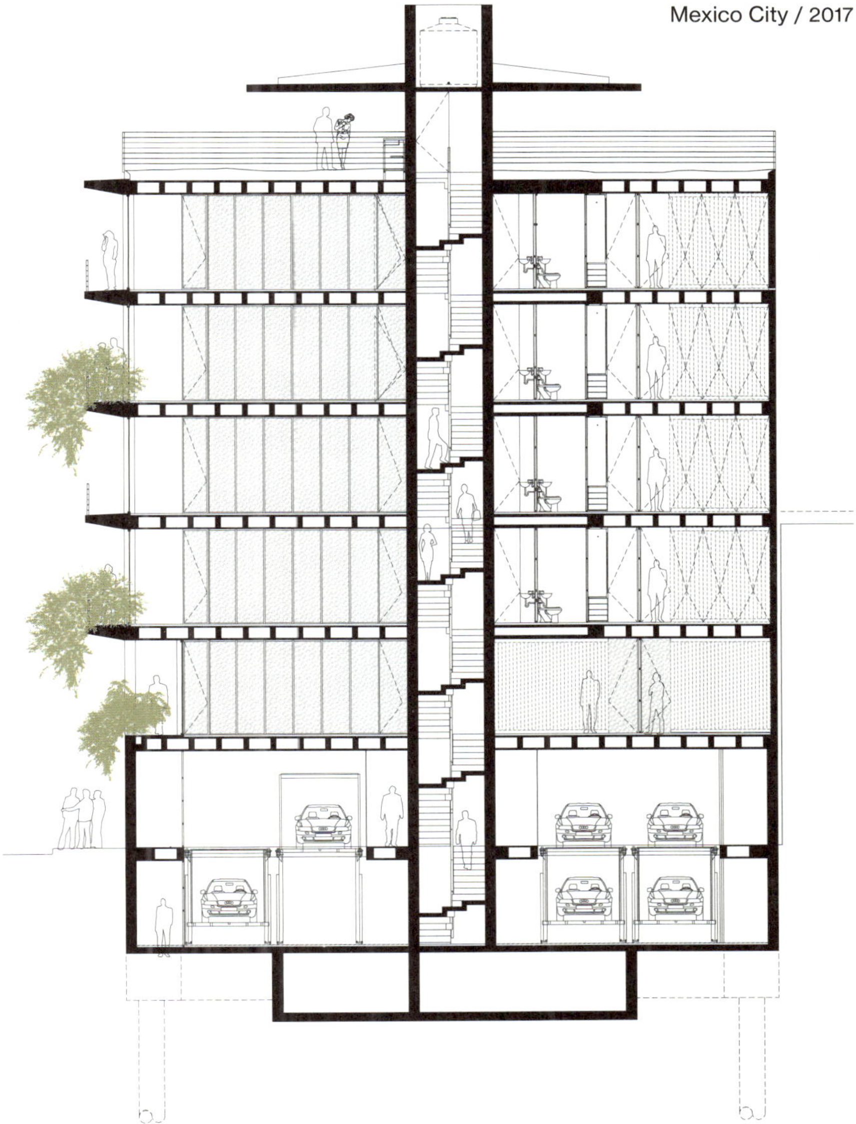

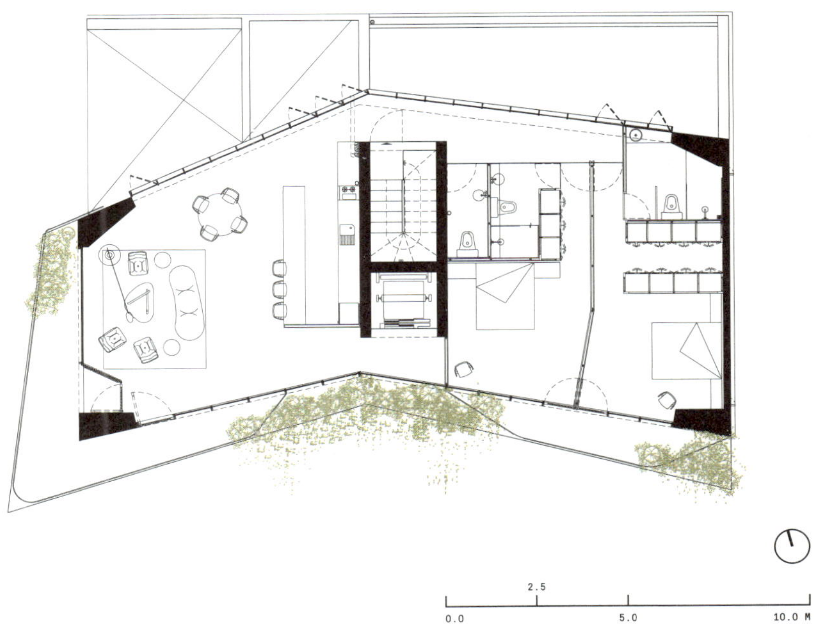
2.5
0.0
5.0
10.0 M

Constituyentes 13

With— Iván Ramírez

Mexico City / 2016

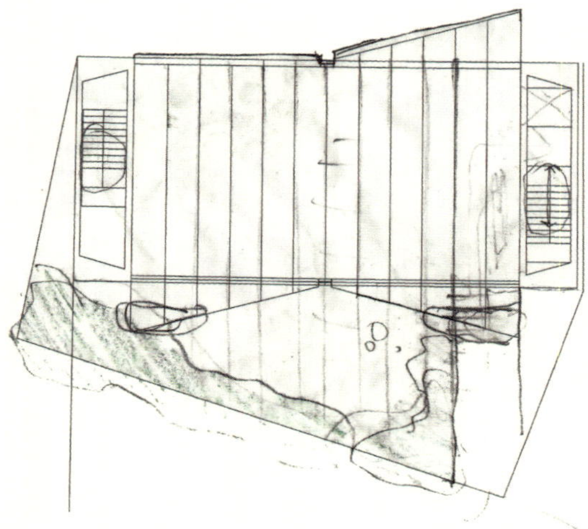

Constituyentes 11

With— Toshiyuki Kobayashi

Mexico City / 2016

Contituyentes 39

With— David Martínez

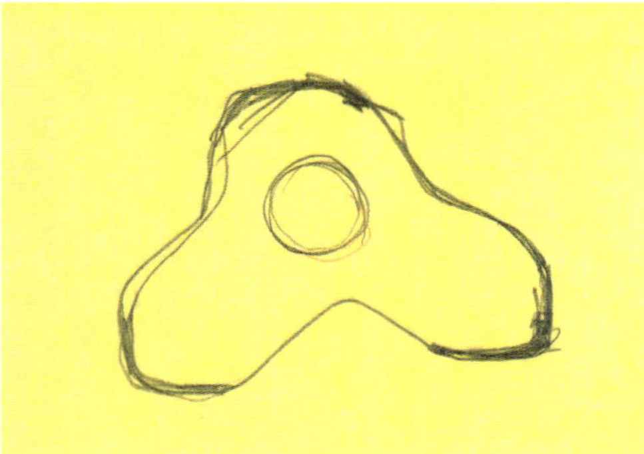

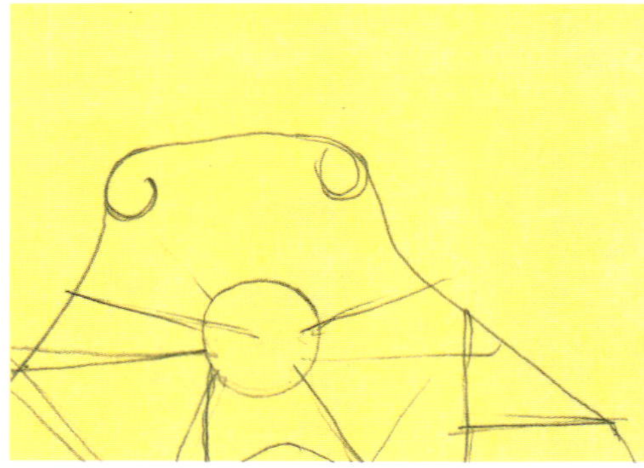

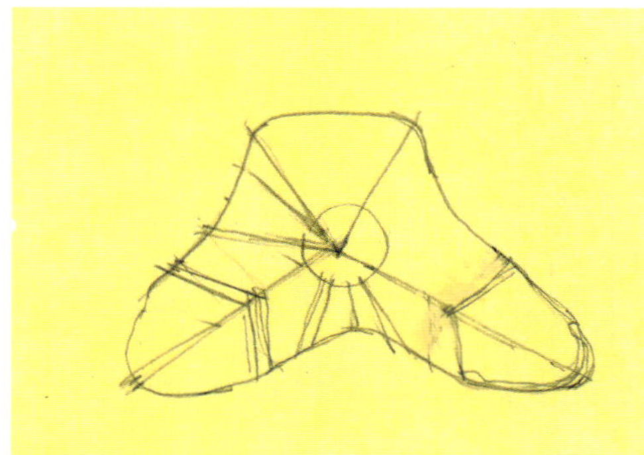

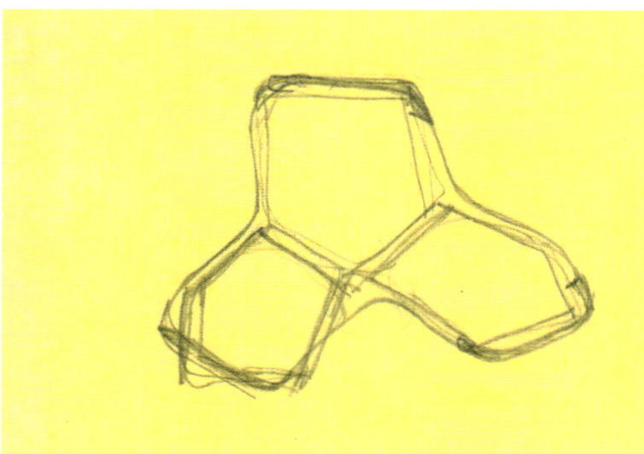

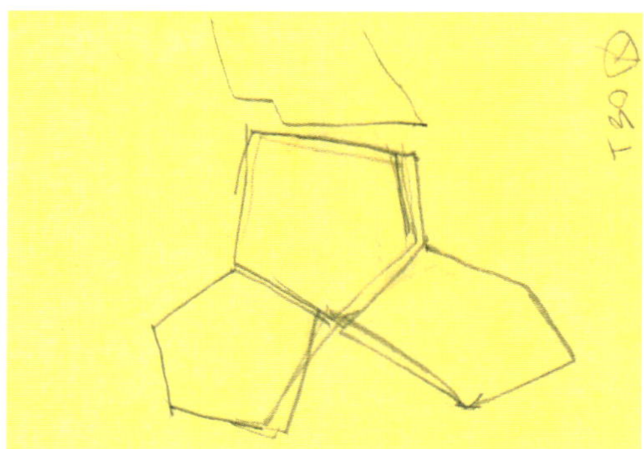

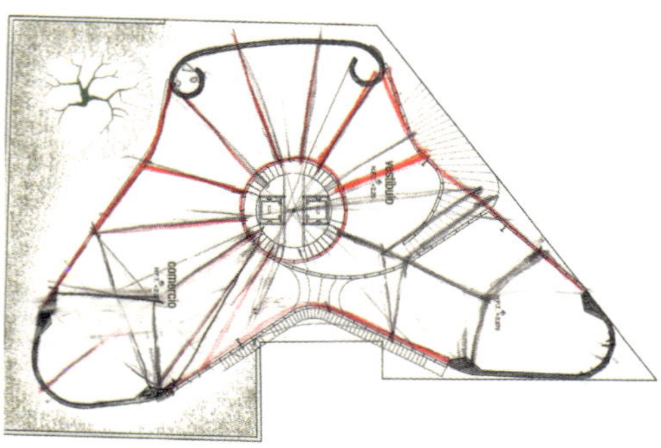

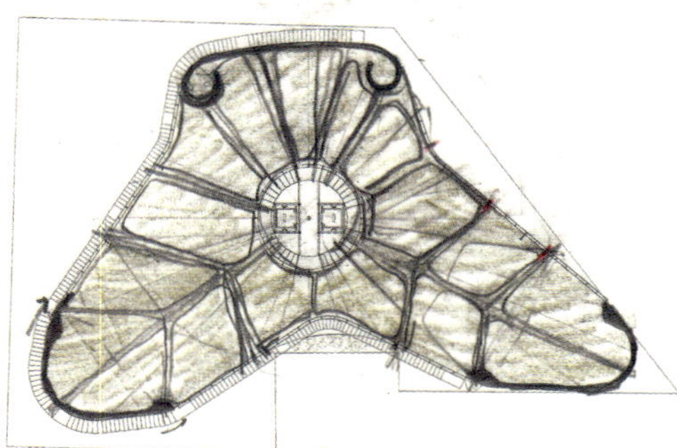

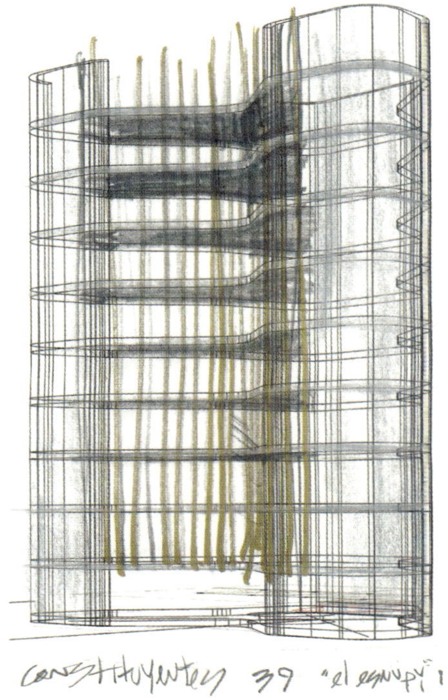

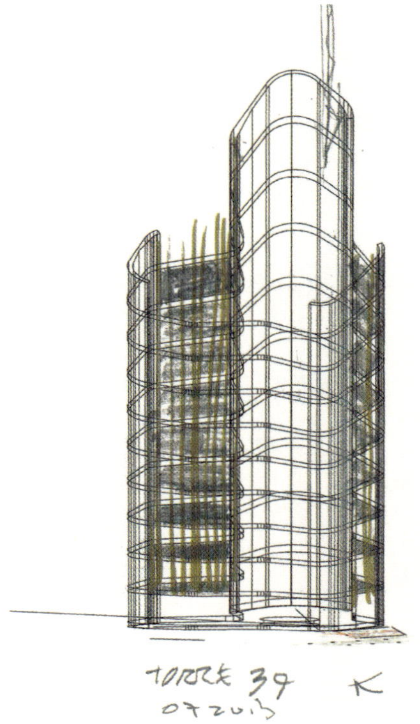
TORRE 39
07 2013

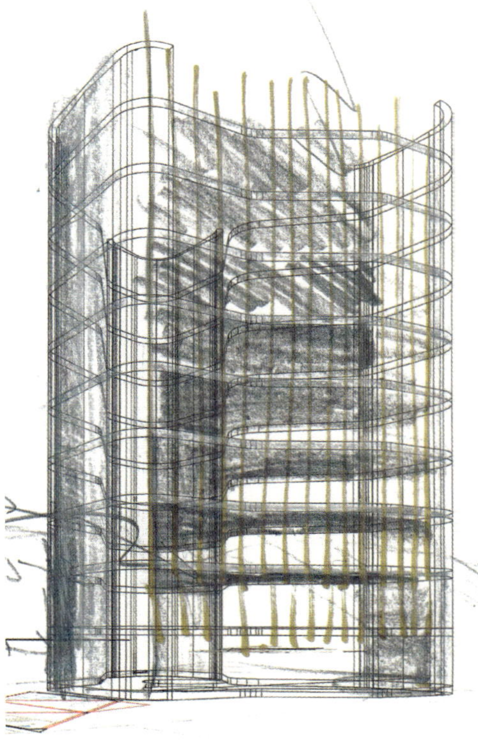

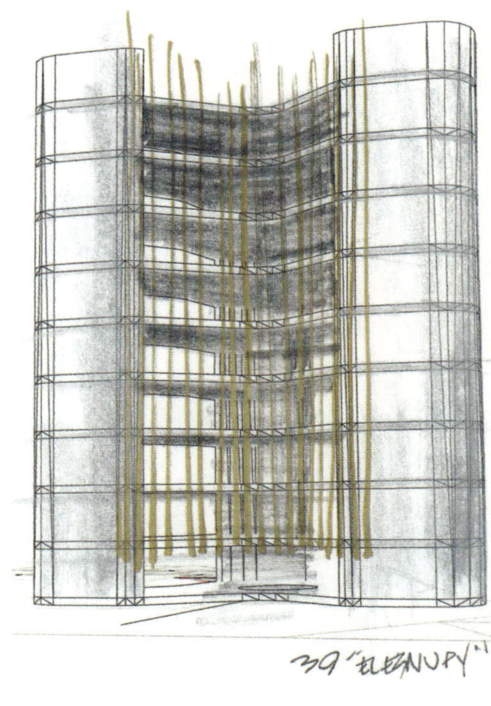
39

Constituyentes 41

With— Gabriel Mancera, Susana Pantoja, Takemune Takuma, David Martínez, Iván Ramírez and José Luis Reyes

This office building, located on a trapezoidal lot formerly occupied by the architect's own workshop, consists of two lateral concrete walls supporting steel floor slabs, reinforced by a transversal metallic structure. There are seven levels of free plans for offices, with a triple-height lobby and a rooftop garden with views over the park: the very first prism of a skyline imagined years before, to be followed by other replicas.

2.5
10.0
0.0
5.0
15.0 M

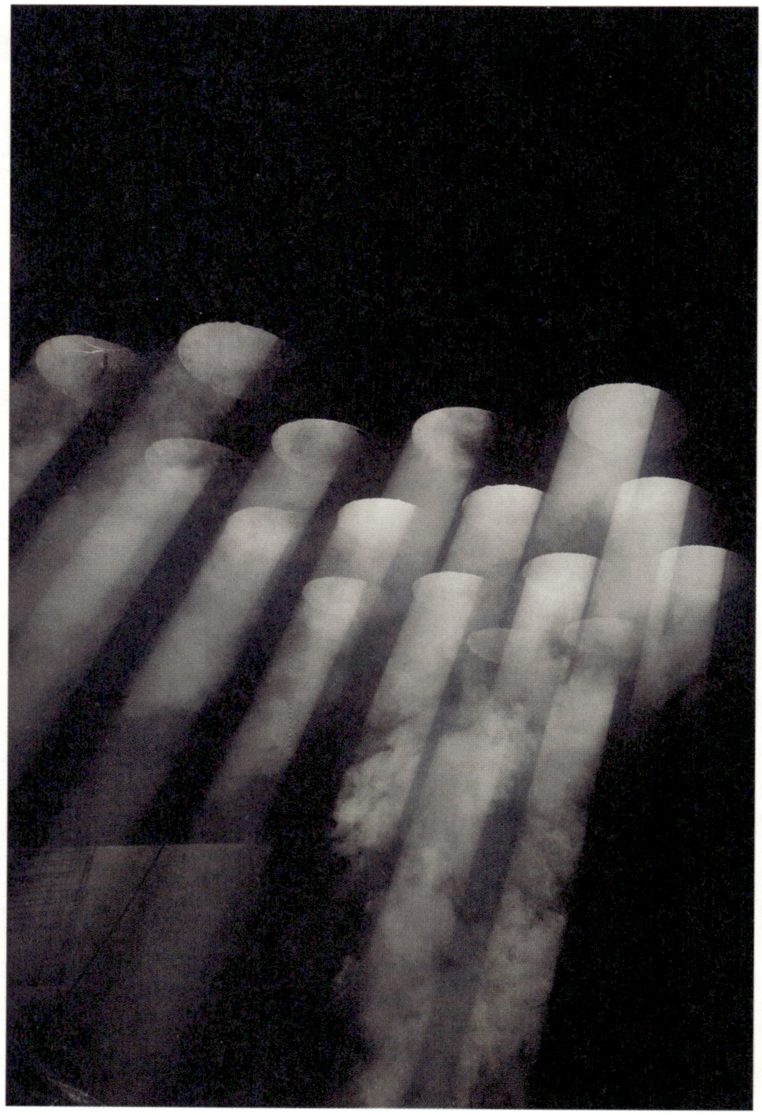

Constituyentes 86

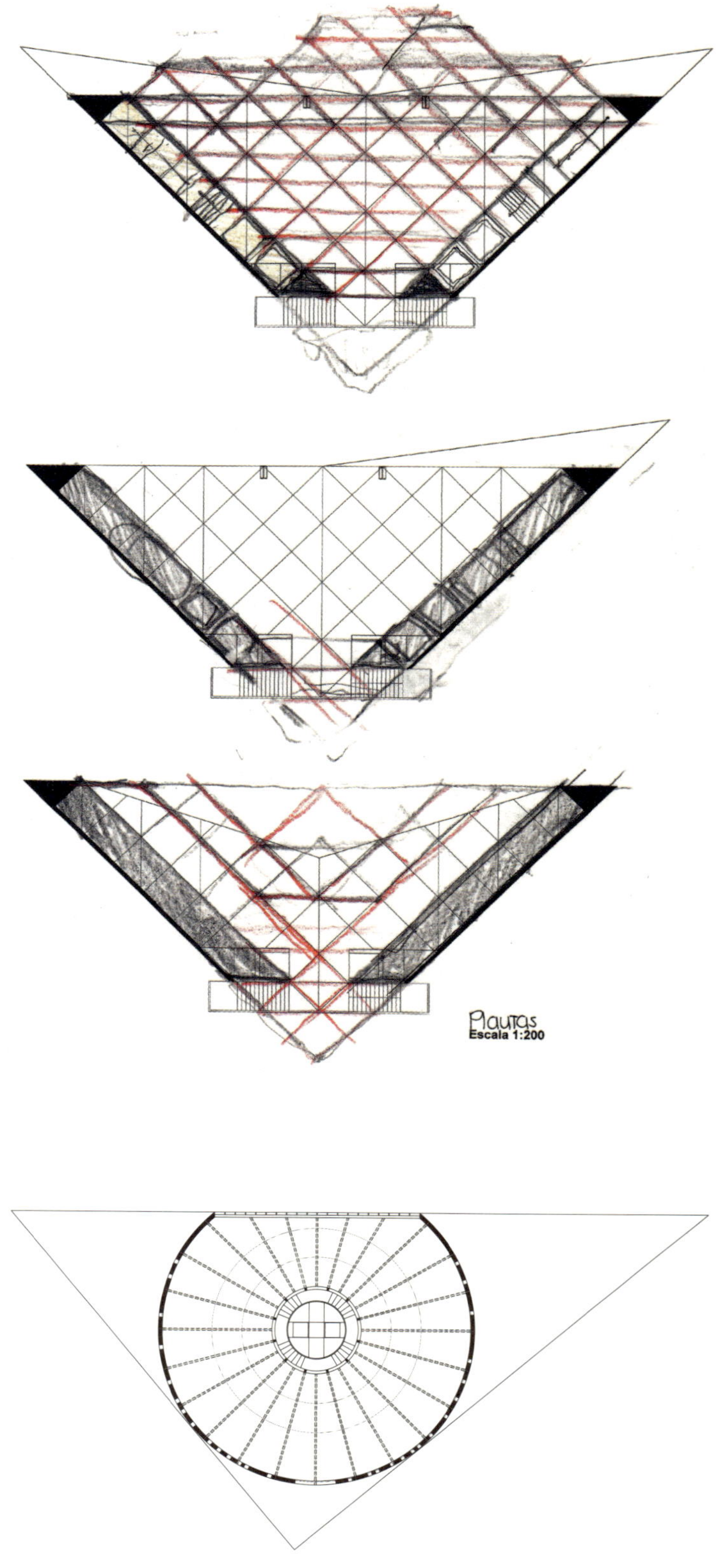

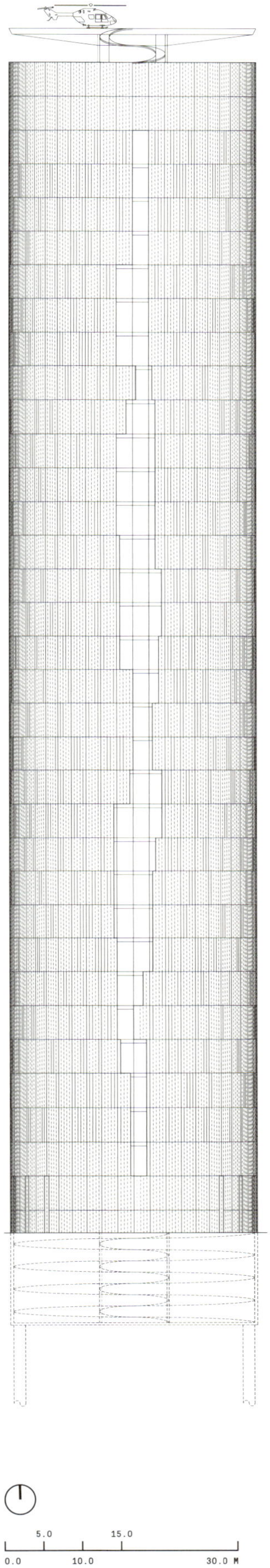
5.0
15.0
0.0
10.0
30.0 M

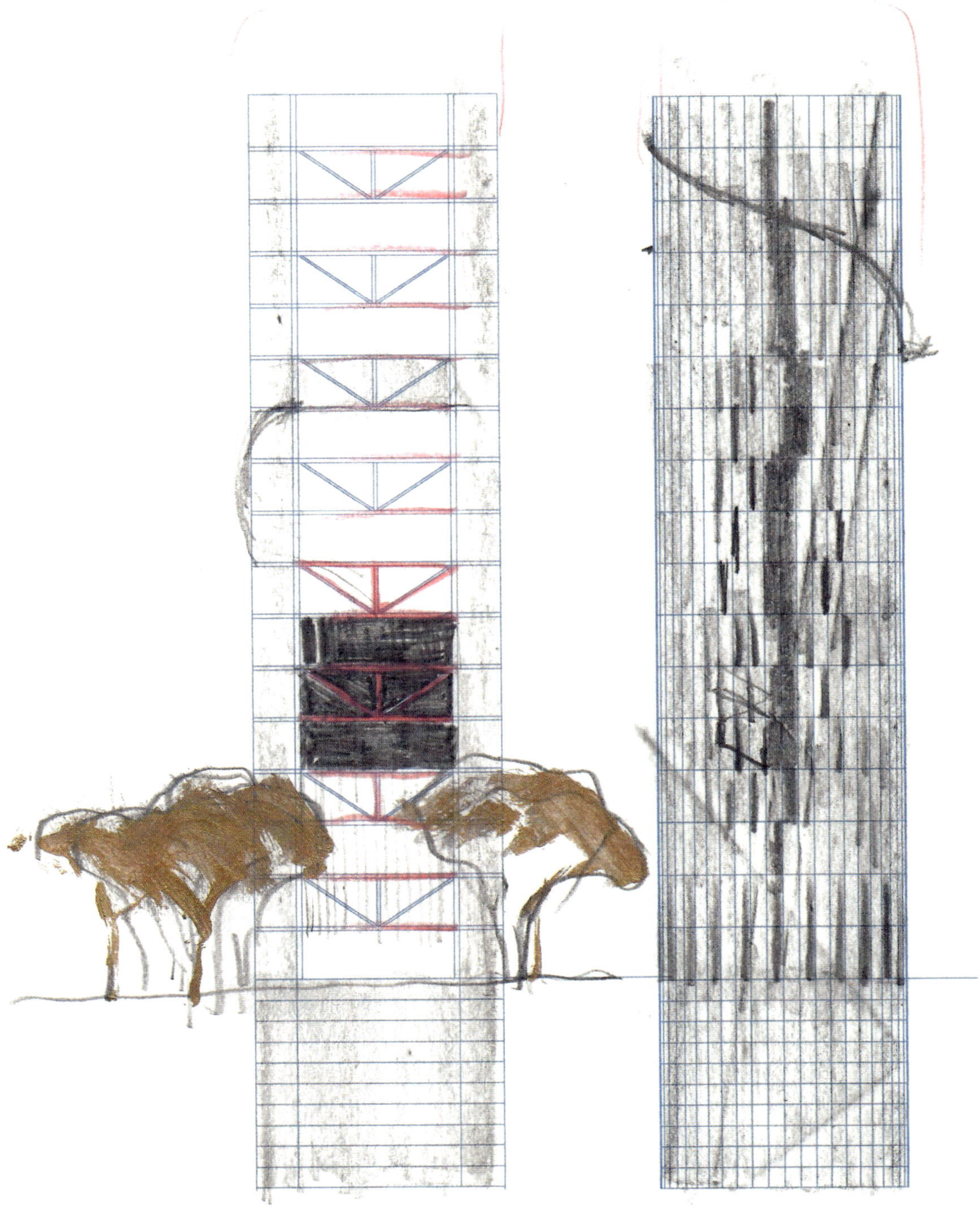

Ensembles

— I refer to ensembles as in the group of musicians painted by Picasso, conversing among themselves. Or as in a little citadel, organized by the palace, the temples, the market, the hot baths, the gardens articulated with plazas and causeways, around which all the actors congregate.

Little citadels or resting places in the landscape. The various pieces of the ensemble —buildings, musicians, actors— express themselves individually, while talking among themselves or as a group: a whole created out of individuals.

Form is a result of the complex spatial relations generated by simple shapes such as rectangles, prisms, cylinders, cubes, and cones. Ensembles put together in a plan out of a repertory of different pieces, apparently in free composition, which recall one of the principles of the baroque style: unity in multiplicity. Heterotopias, like those of Giovanni Battista Piranesi, which consisted of expressing, clearly and categorically, the contradiction between reason and the irrational.[1] The fragmentation of the program facilitates the integration of the ensemble with the landscape, and each piece responds independently to diverse needs and uses. Thus, ensembles of autonomous figures define the outlines of architectures conceived as territories.

One of the first works that brought Kalach to international prominence was the Monte Sinaí kindergarten, whose program for children is discomposed into concrete cubes. The Liceo Franco Mexicano in Guadalajara assembles the entire program within two long rectangular volumes, one of them placed at an angle in order to generate the platform mounds of the adjacent landscaping. Using this same idea, Kalach designed a series of schools (branches of the Nueva Escuela Tecnológica) and two IMSS hospitals, systematizing his solutions while finding ways to integrate them with the specific demands of each site. Thus, the Tecámac NET contains the entire program in a single rectangular volume, fragmented in the middle to mark the entrance. The Nicolás Romero NET varies the initial plan by means of curved volumes, generating greater complexity and formal richness. Finally, the design for the Papalote Museo del Niño in Iztapalapa turns to an analogous solution with even greater formal complexity, grouping the various buildings containing the museum and recreational areas around a central patio.

[1] Manfredo Tafuri. *La esfera y el laberinto* (Barcelona: Gustavo Gili, 1984), p. 58.

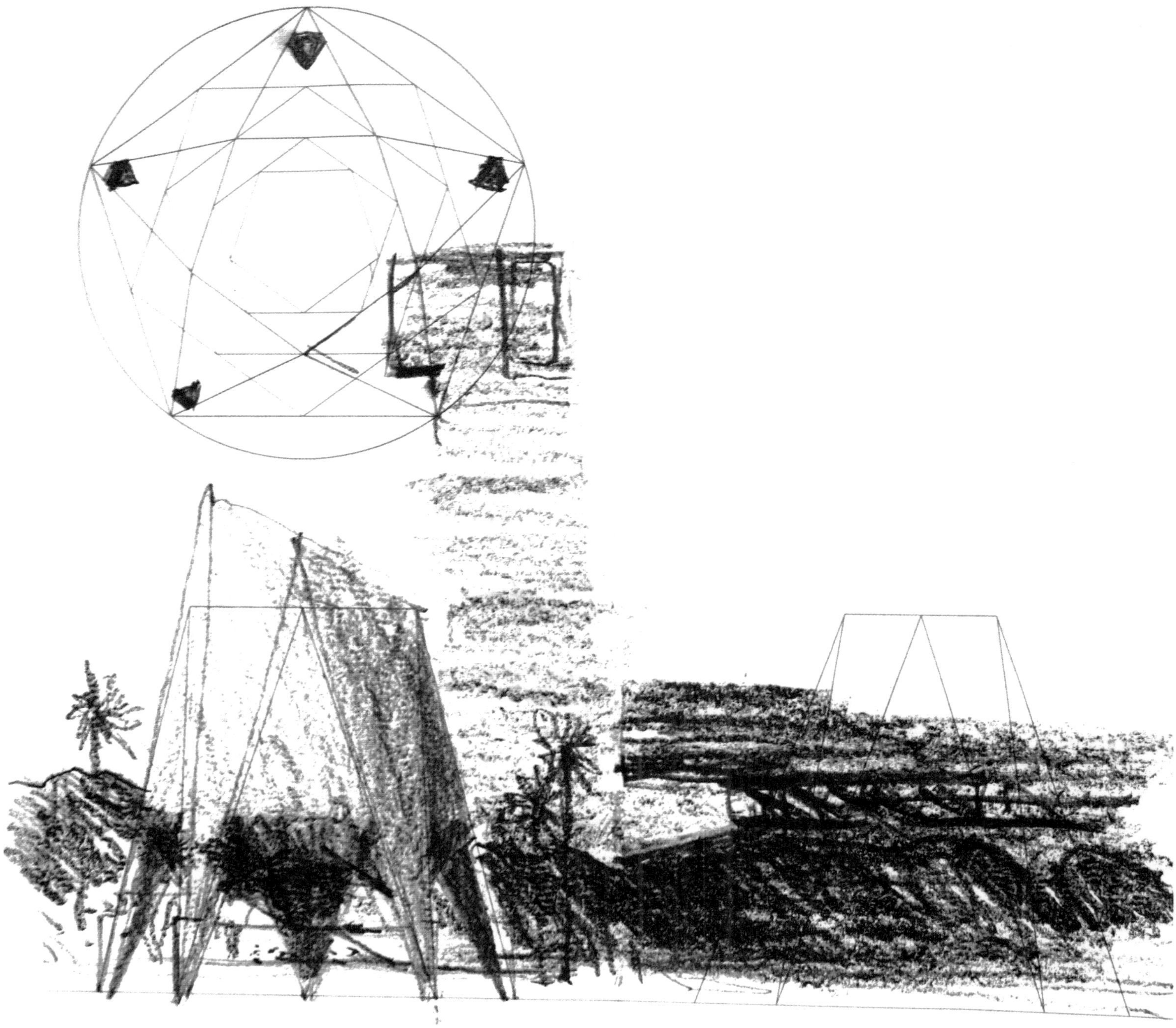

Monte Sinaí Kindergarten

With— Alberto Kably and Daniel Álvarez

Mexico City / 1990

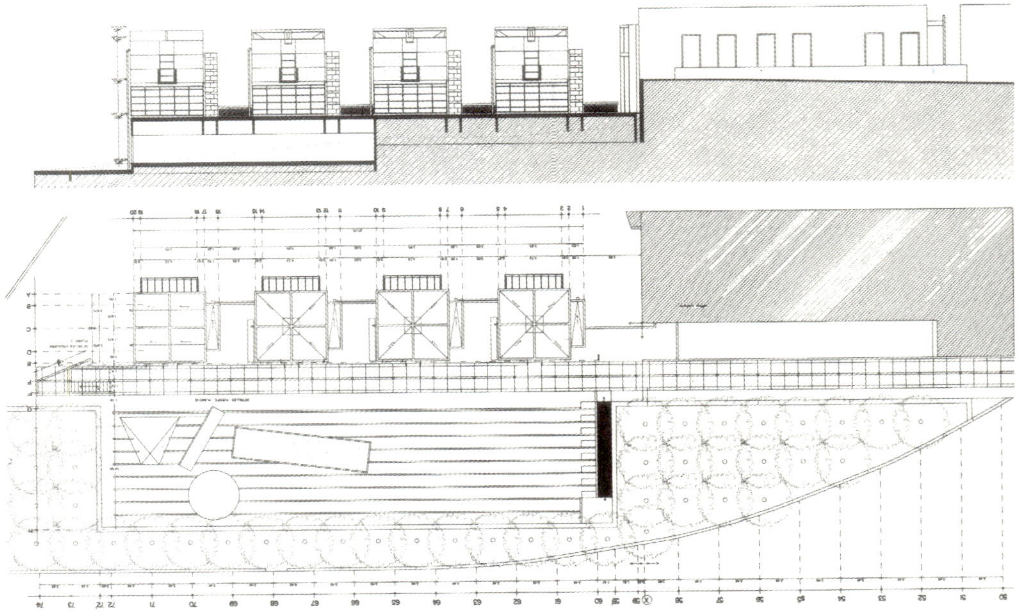

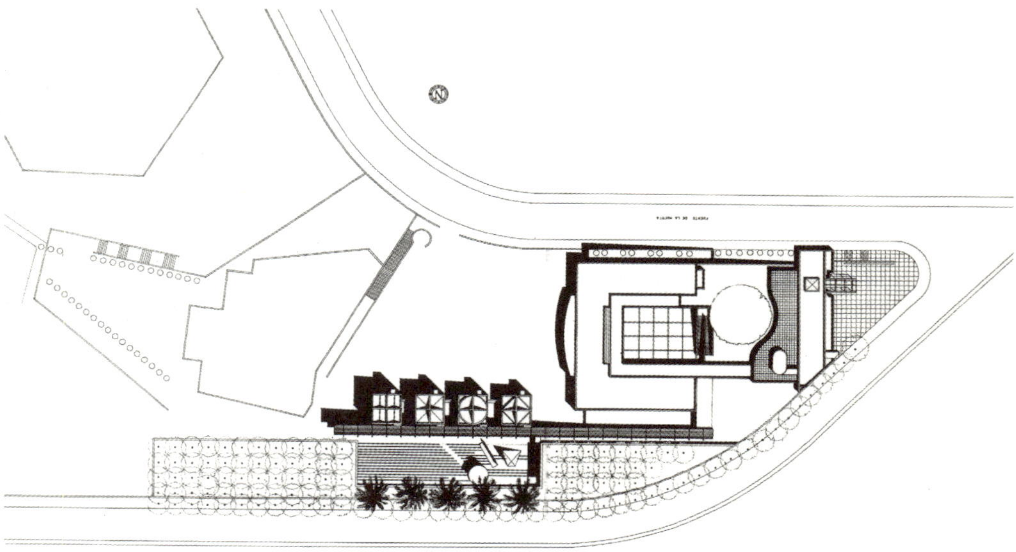

Maguen David Complex

With— Alberto Kably and Daniel Álvarez

Mexico City / 1990

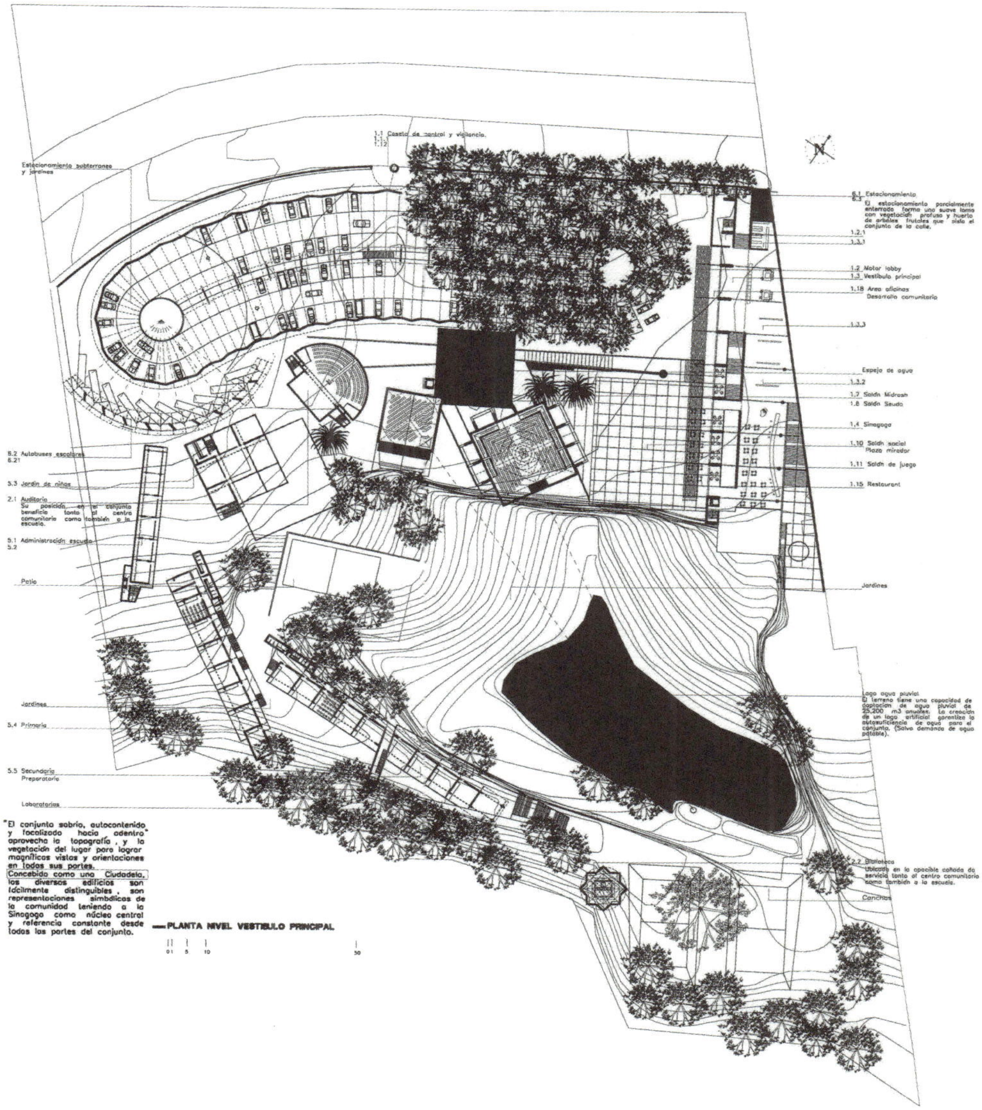

Small Inca Community

With— Gonzalo Mauleón

Peru / 2019

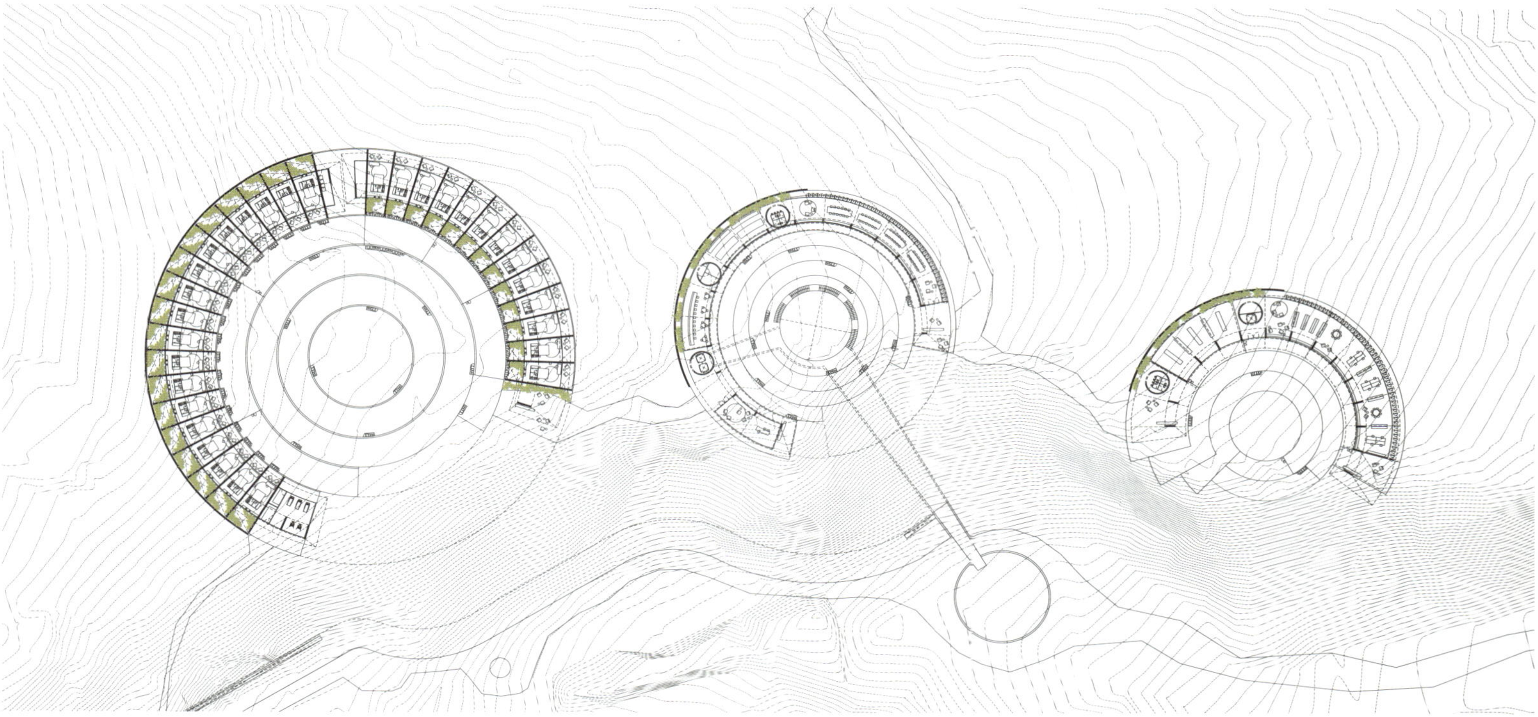

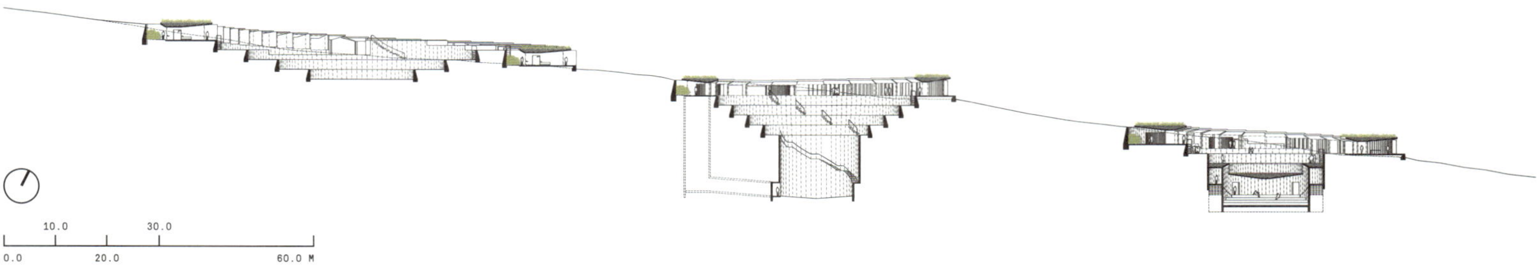
10.0
30.0
0.0
20.0
60.0 M

Sea and Desert Museum

With— Eduardo Vázquez and Héctor Módica

Bahía Magdalena / 2010

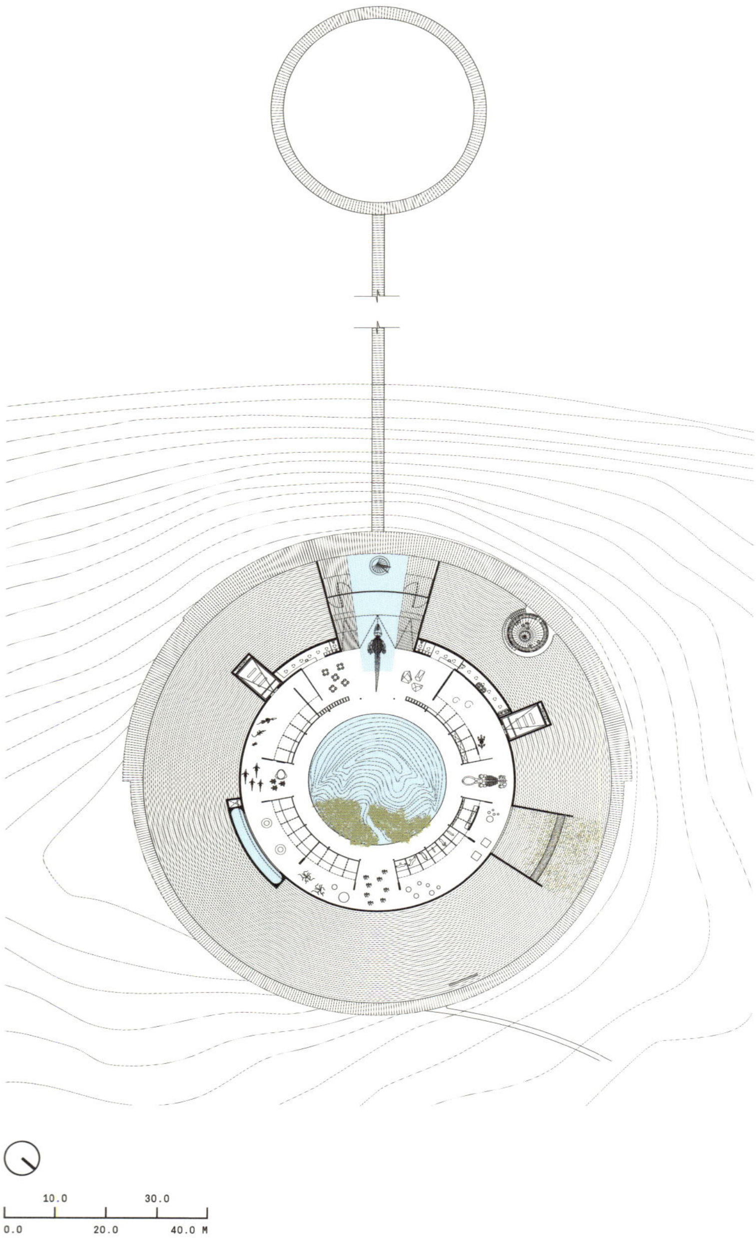

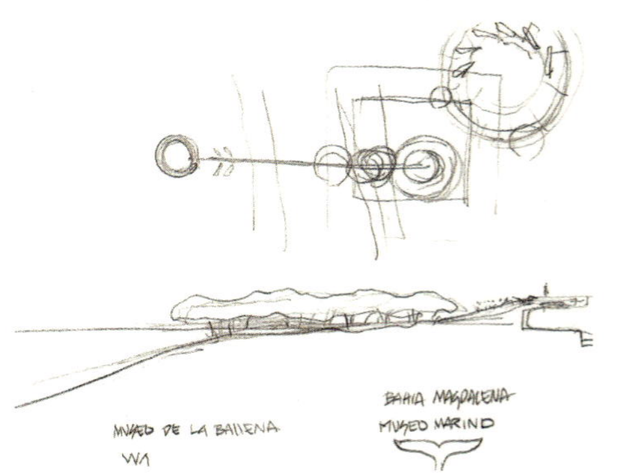

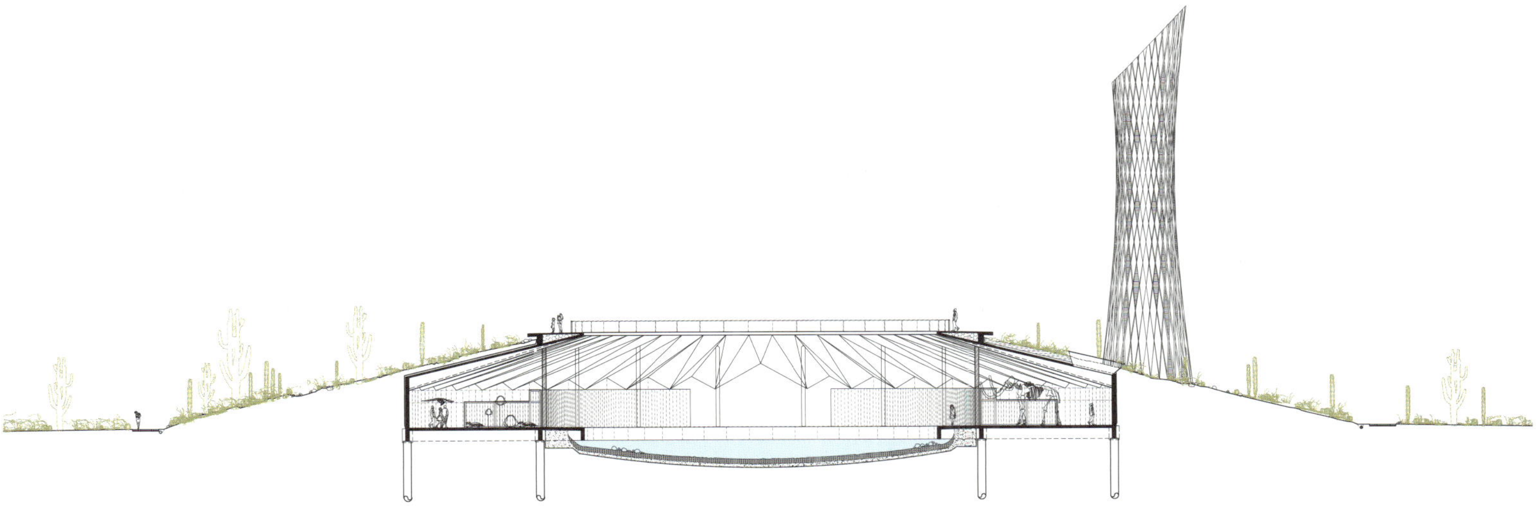

— The Sea and Desert Museum is hidden inside a large crater so that the vulnerable surrounding landscape is not affected. An observatory on the universe.

The museum itself is an open, shaded, continuous space, without glazing or air conditioning. Nestled with the geometrical crater, open chests and wooden screens display the natural treasures of the region. A long walkway stretches from the desert, across a thick mangrove swamp, to a boarding area for small launches to carry visitors out to view birds, whales, dolphins, and the extraordinary surrounding landscapes. A small research tower rises like a saguaro cactus to mark the site amidst the rugged topography.

Chimney and Oven for Casa Wabi

With— Adolfo Romero

— The chimney of the Casa Wabi is a small piece within the natural reserve of the Fundación Casa Wabi. The ecological and cultural project conceived by the artist Bosco Sodi so far includes constructions designed by Tadao Ando, Kengo Kuma, Álvaro Siza, and other artists.

The chimney, which stands out in the landscape, interacts with and complements the pottery-making pavilion designed by Álvaro Siza, with its brick, wood, and palm leaf roof. The archaic form of the chimney recalls all ages and places, going back to remotest Ur.

Augen Ópticos Laboratories

With— Felipe Buendía and Adriana León

Ensenada / 1998

A semicircular building integrates the office spaces of a preexisting industrial bay, while a cylindrical tower houses the research areas. The semicircular volume has a steel structural perimeter that selects for certain vistas and provides protection from direct sunlight. The five-story tower filters in natural light through the steel brise-soleils on the façade.

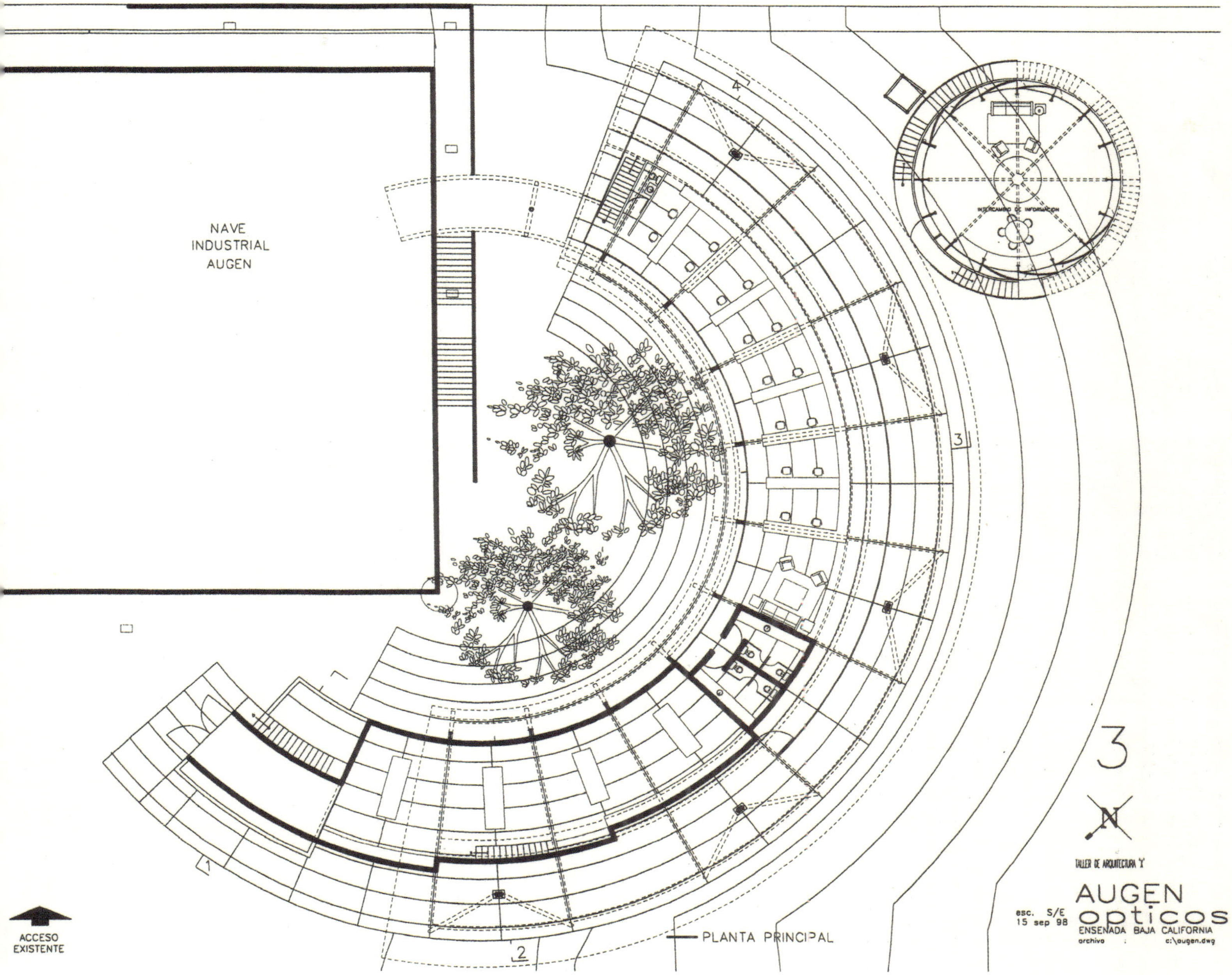
NAVE
INDUSTRIAL
AUGEN
4
3
1
2
3
ACCESO
EXISTENTE
PLANTA PRINCIPAL
TALLER DE ARQUITECTURA 'X'
esc. S/E
15 sep 98
AUGEN
opticos
ENSENADA BAJA CALIFORNIA
archivo : c:\augen.dwg

Papalote Iztapalapa

With— Juan de la Rosa, Iván Ramírez, Helena Saénz, Xavier González, and Marco Kalach

Mexico City / 2015

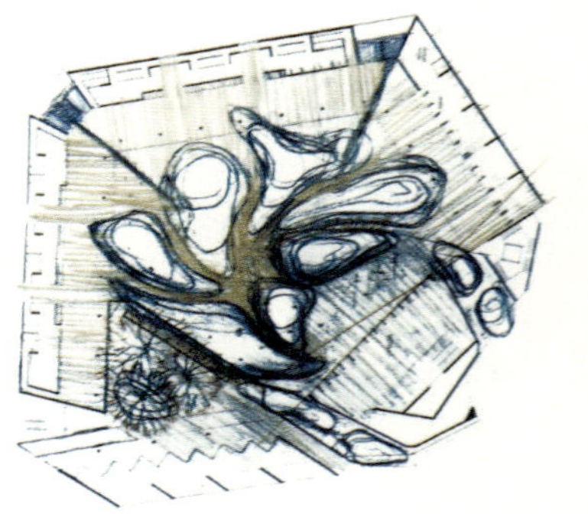

National Museum of Memory

With— Juan Ricardo Rincón, Iván Ramírez, Helena Sáenz, and Xavier González

Bogotá / 2015

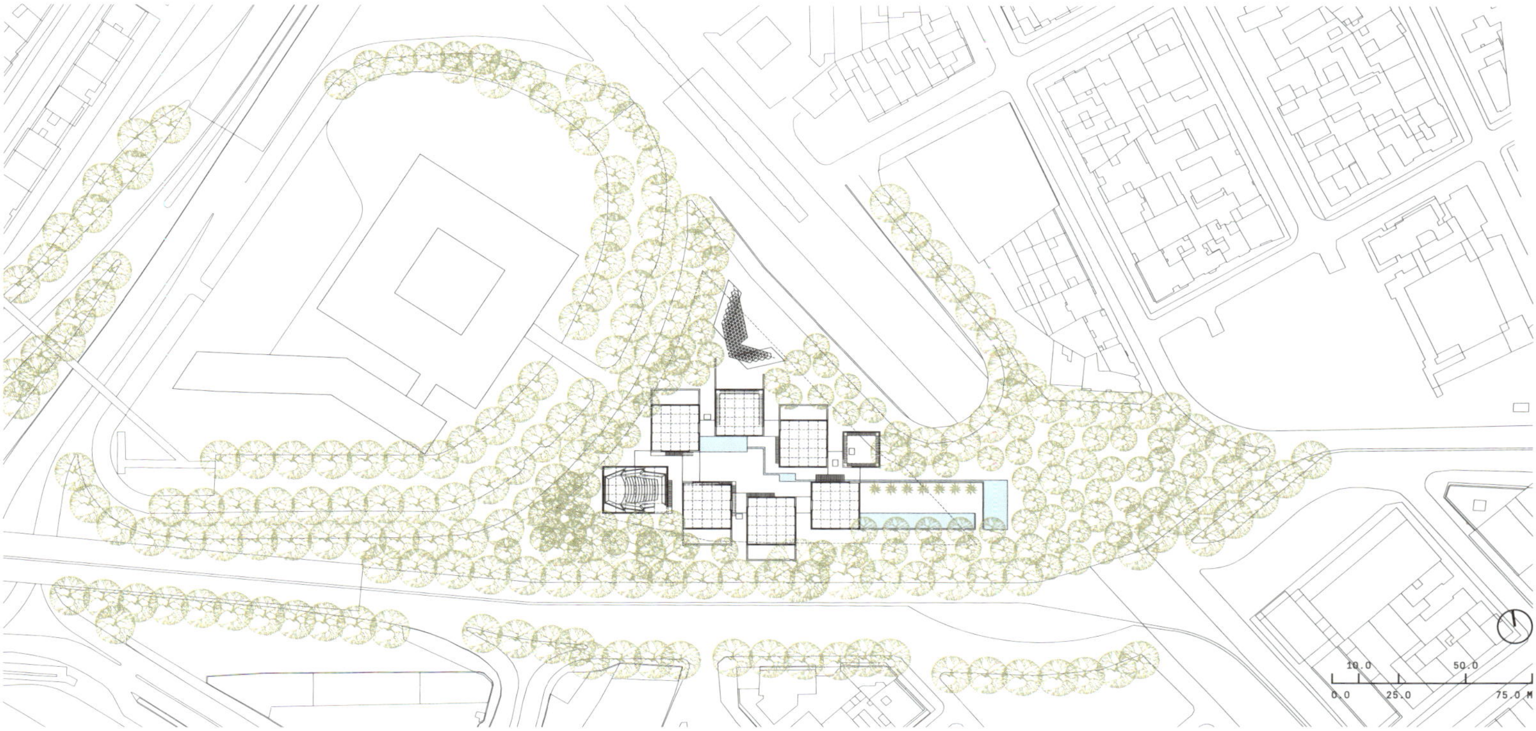

Center for the Arts Los Cabos

With— Héctor Módica

— Recalling the lost natural topography of Cabo San Lucas and the monumental granite boulders that descended from hills and ravines on their way into the sea, the pieces of this cultural center —theaters, projecting rooms, museum, library, and workshops— seek themselves to be rocks, resonating with the landscape, rather than buildings.

TEATRO EXPERIMENTAL
BIBLIOTECA
TEATRO
CINE
CINE
RESTAURANTE
PLANTA JARDIN
NIVEL +6.00

CORTE LONGITUDINAL CL_01

IMSS Saltillo

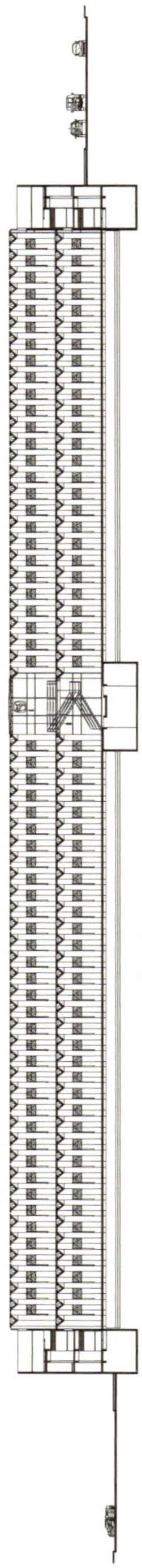

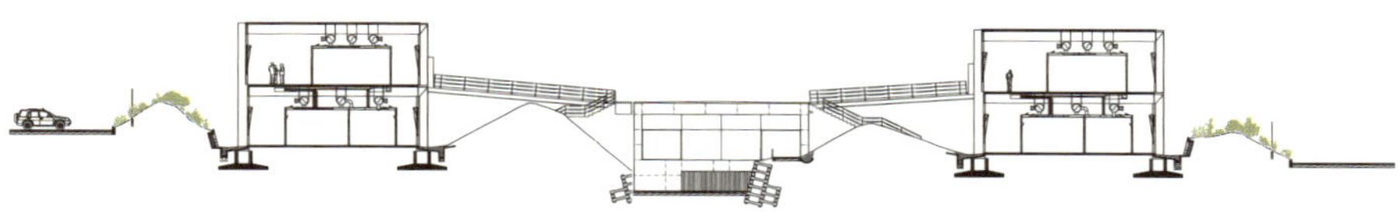

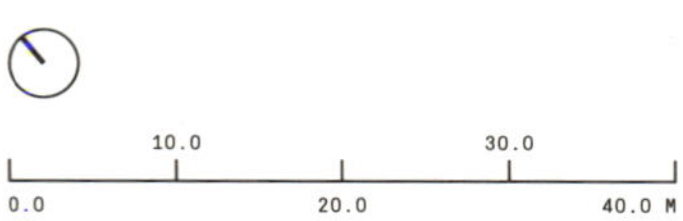

— The world's hospitals have become complicated, claustrophobic labyrinths, enclosed places without natural light or ventilation. Their design has been monopolized by groups of "specialists" who simply put together a set of blocks pre-designed with AutoCAD: operating rooms, recovery areas, emergency wards, chemotherapy units, etc., all connected one to another like a sort of Frankenstein's monster, soulless and incoherent.

These two exercises, which were not finally constructed, explore the typology of nineteenth-century sanatoria, with long pavilions stretching between gardens. I have no doubt that good architecture, laid out amidst greenery, with exposure to sun and wind, where all the spaces have some natural light and ventilation, can be of aid to patients, doctors, nurses, and visitors alike. The Saltillo clinic explores prefabricated systems that can be adapted to the different geographies of Mexico.

Hospital in Parral

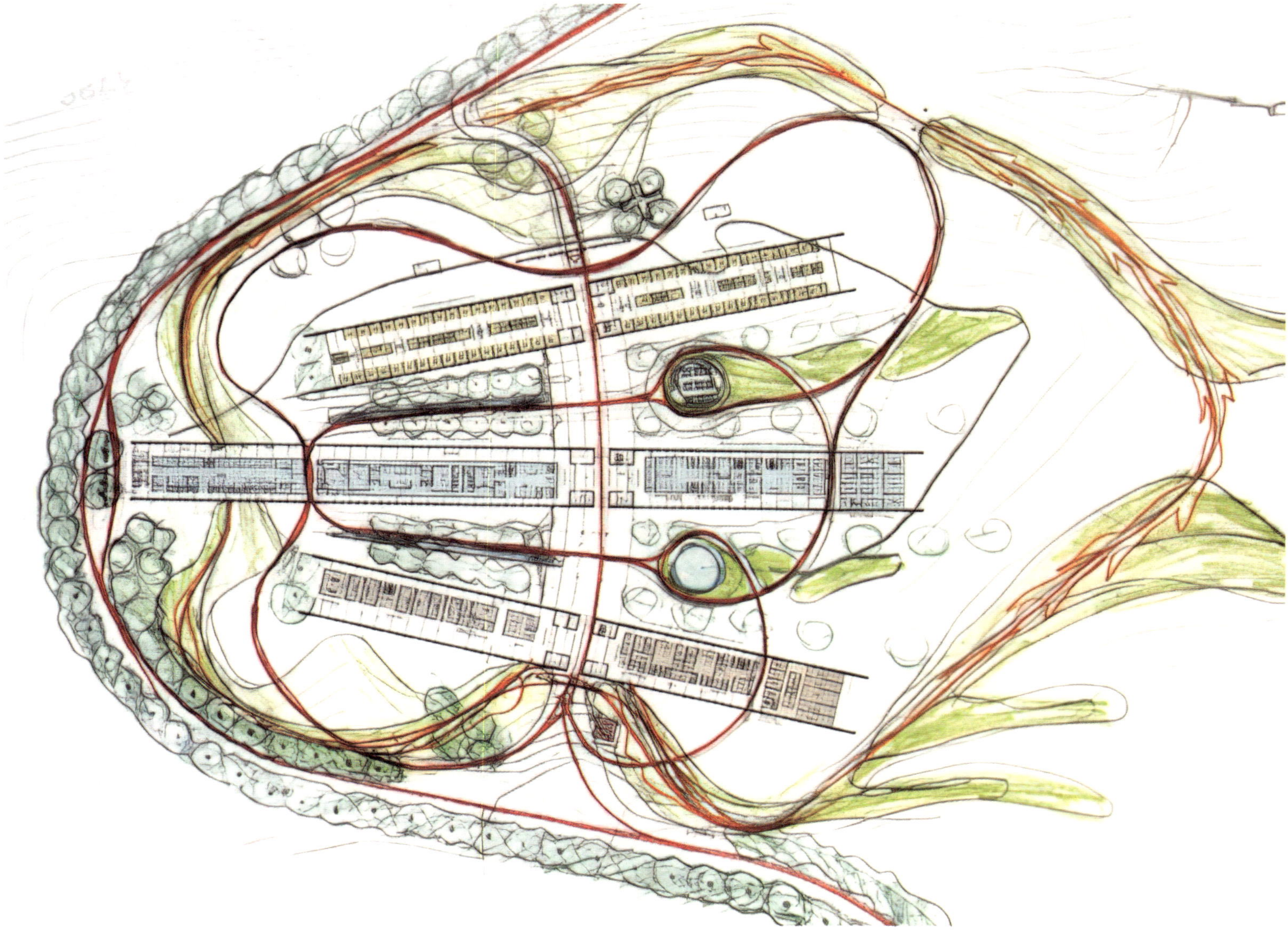

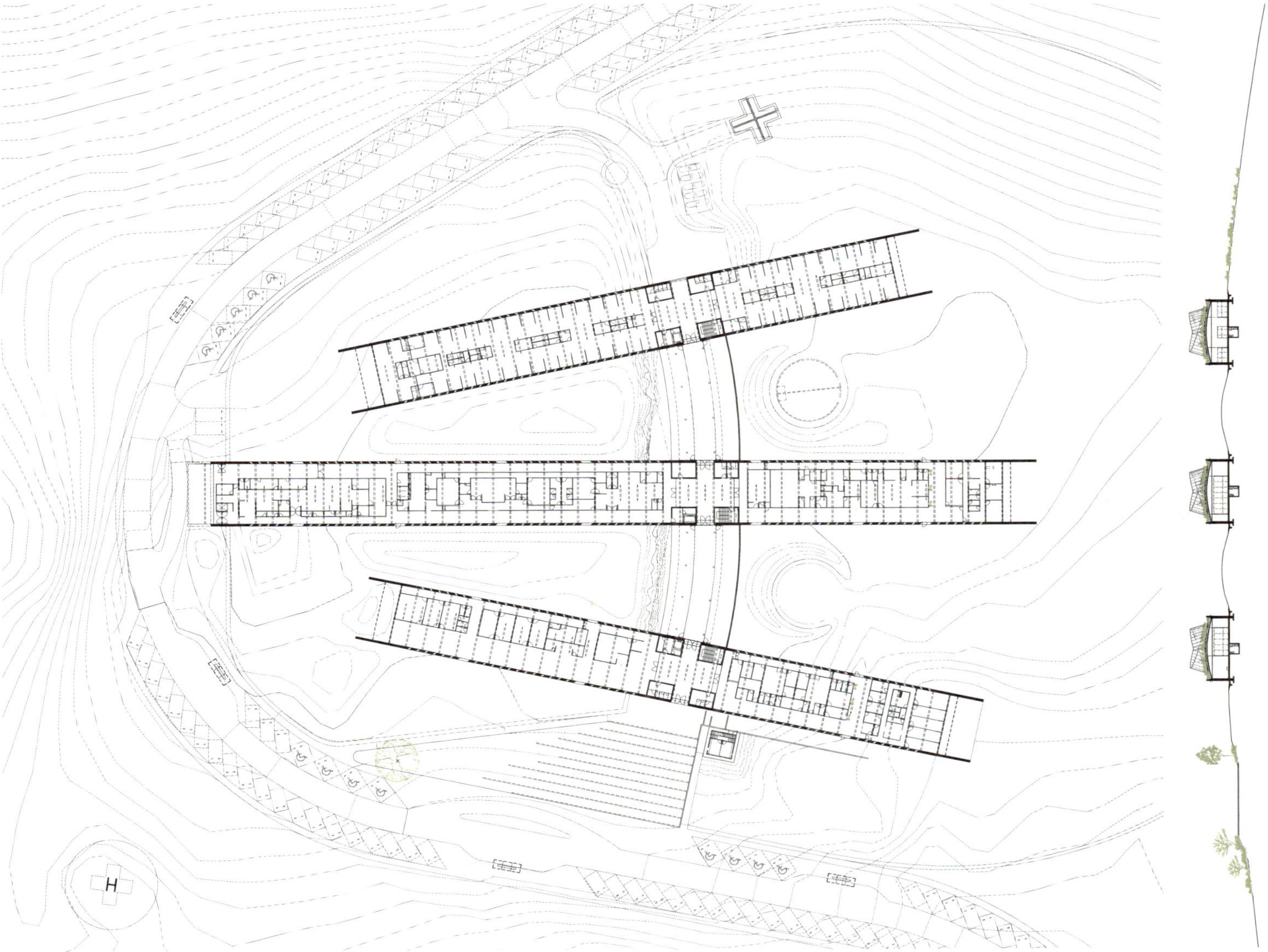

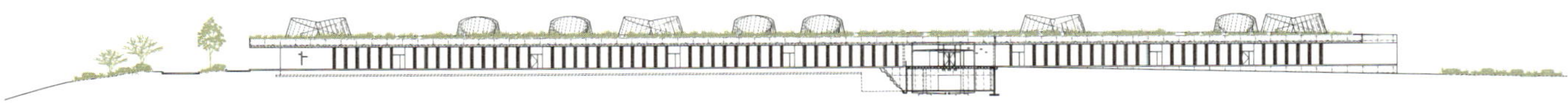

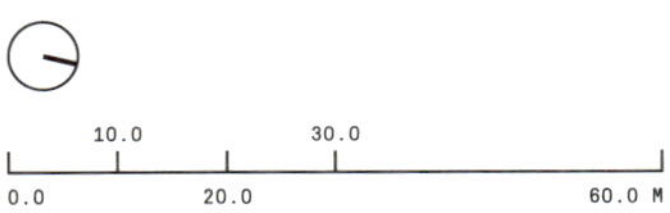

— The hospital in Parral has been built with bricks made of the local stone. Small skylights, like half-shut eyes, are let into the running concrete vaults.

Colegio Alemán
Alexander Von Humboldt

Puebla / 1987

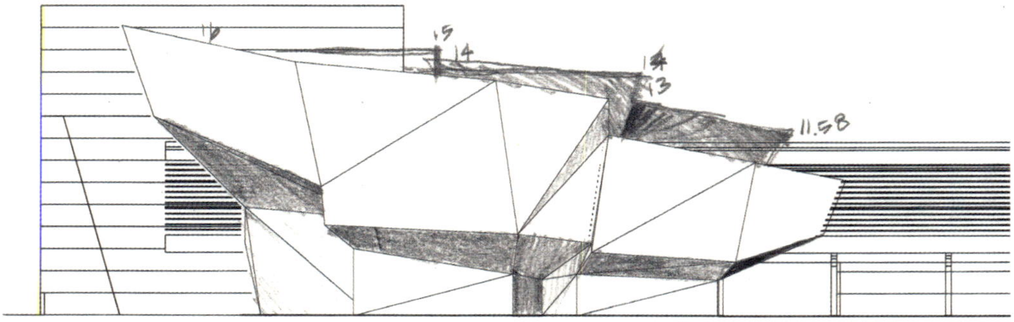

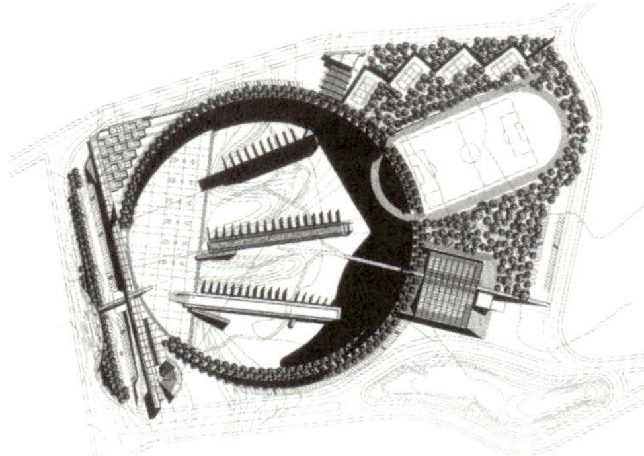

NET Ecatepec

With— Takemune Takuma

Estado de México / 2008

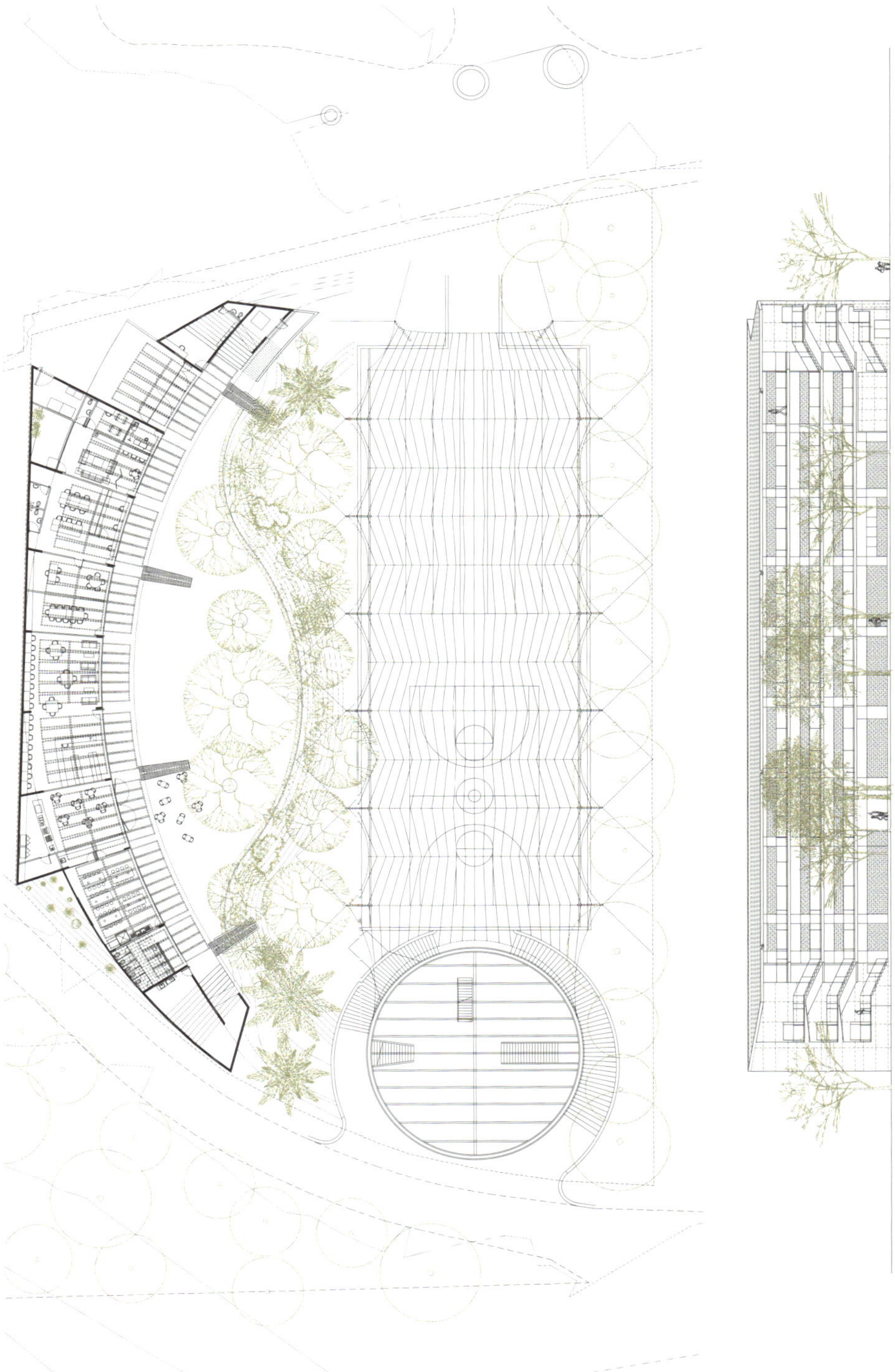

NET Nicolás Romero

With— Takemune Takuma

Estado de México / 2008

NET Tecámac

With— Takemune Takuma

Estado de México / 2007

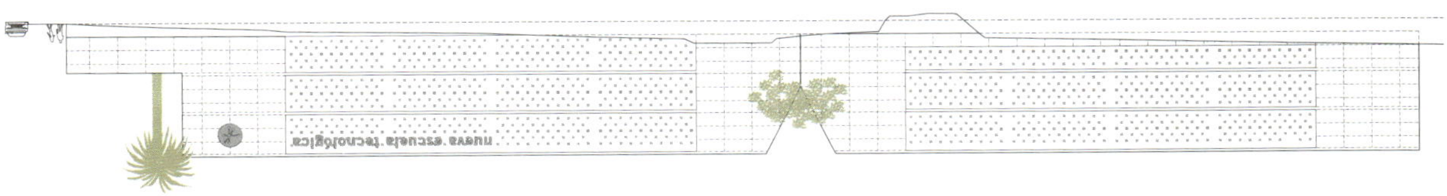

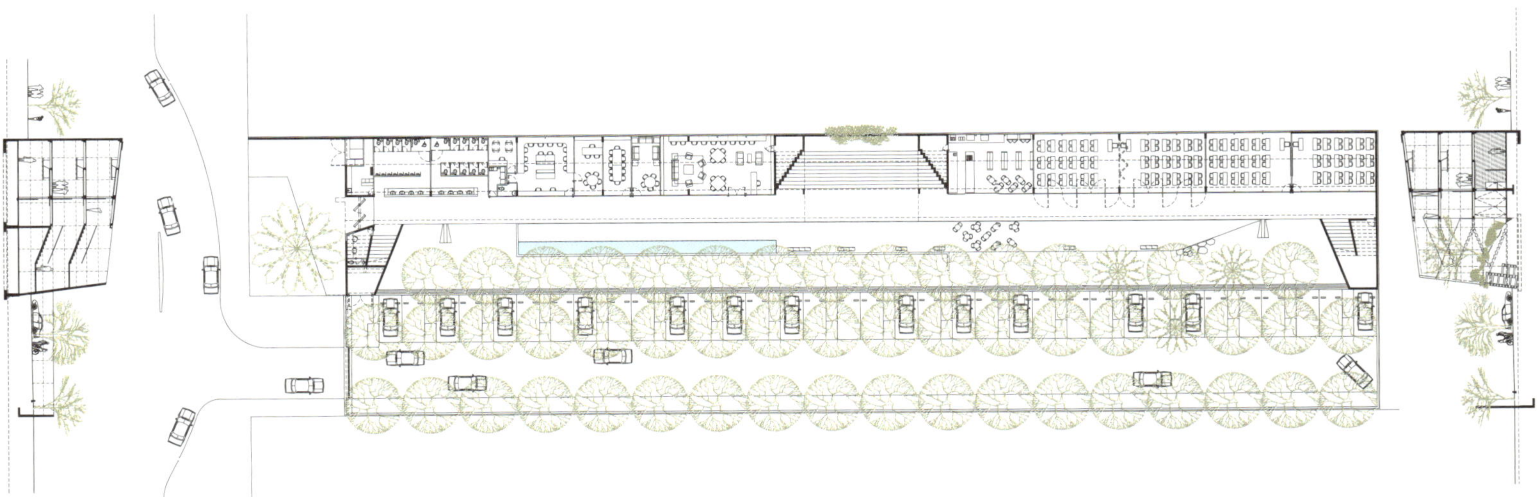

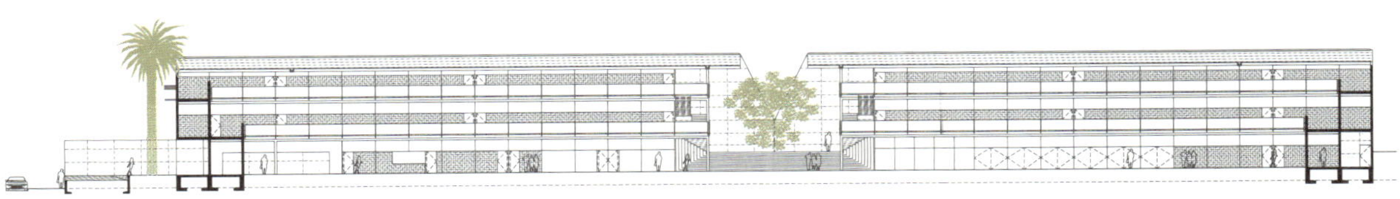

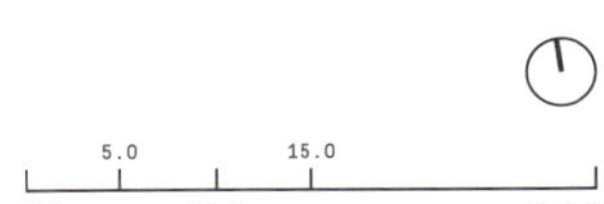

Liceo Franco Mexicano

With— Juan Palomar and Agustín Landa

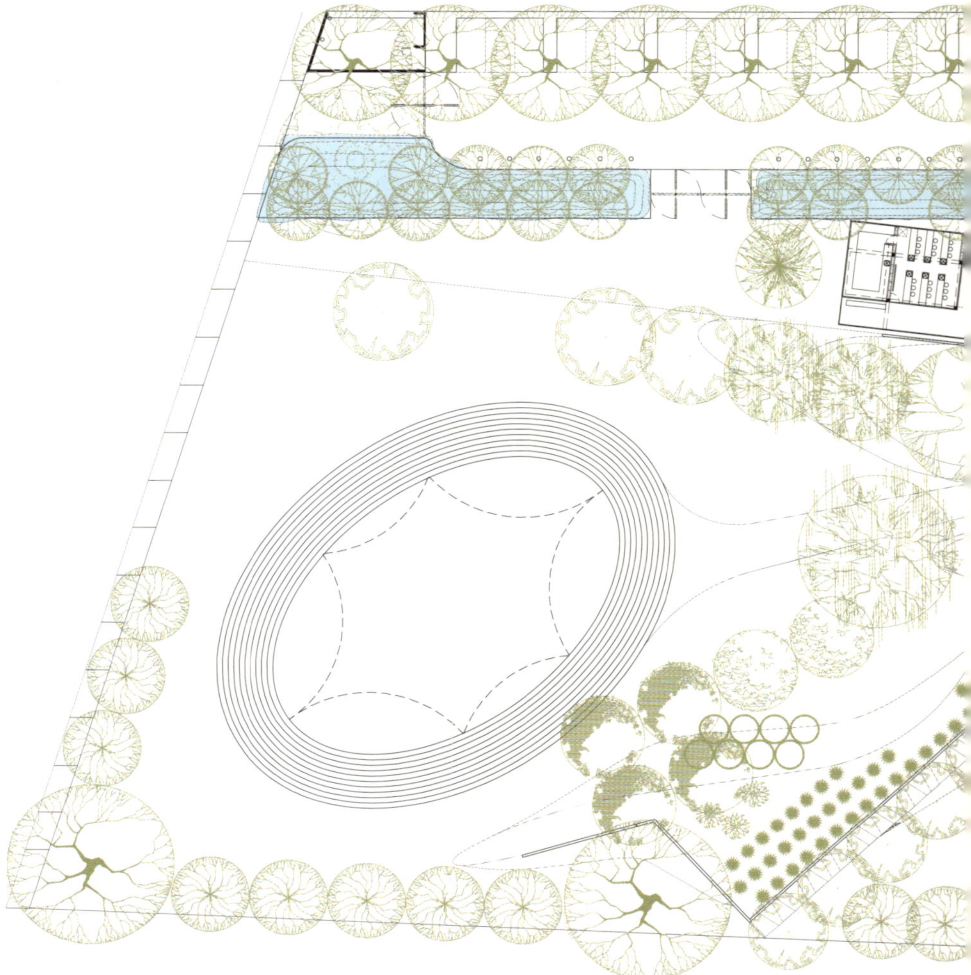

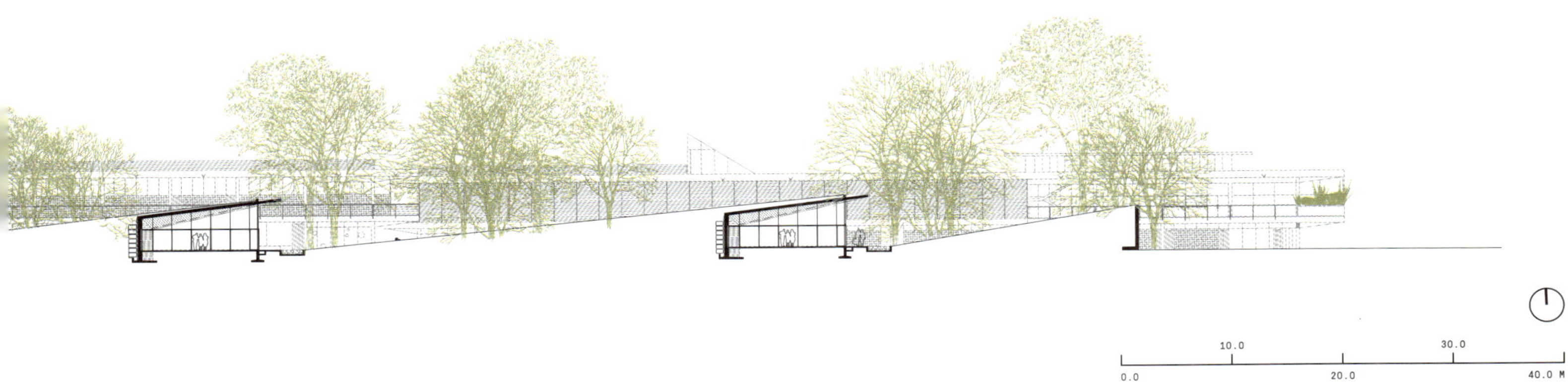
0.0
10.0
20.0
30.0
40.0 M

Museum of Natural History

With— Eduardo Vázquez

Mexico City / 2008

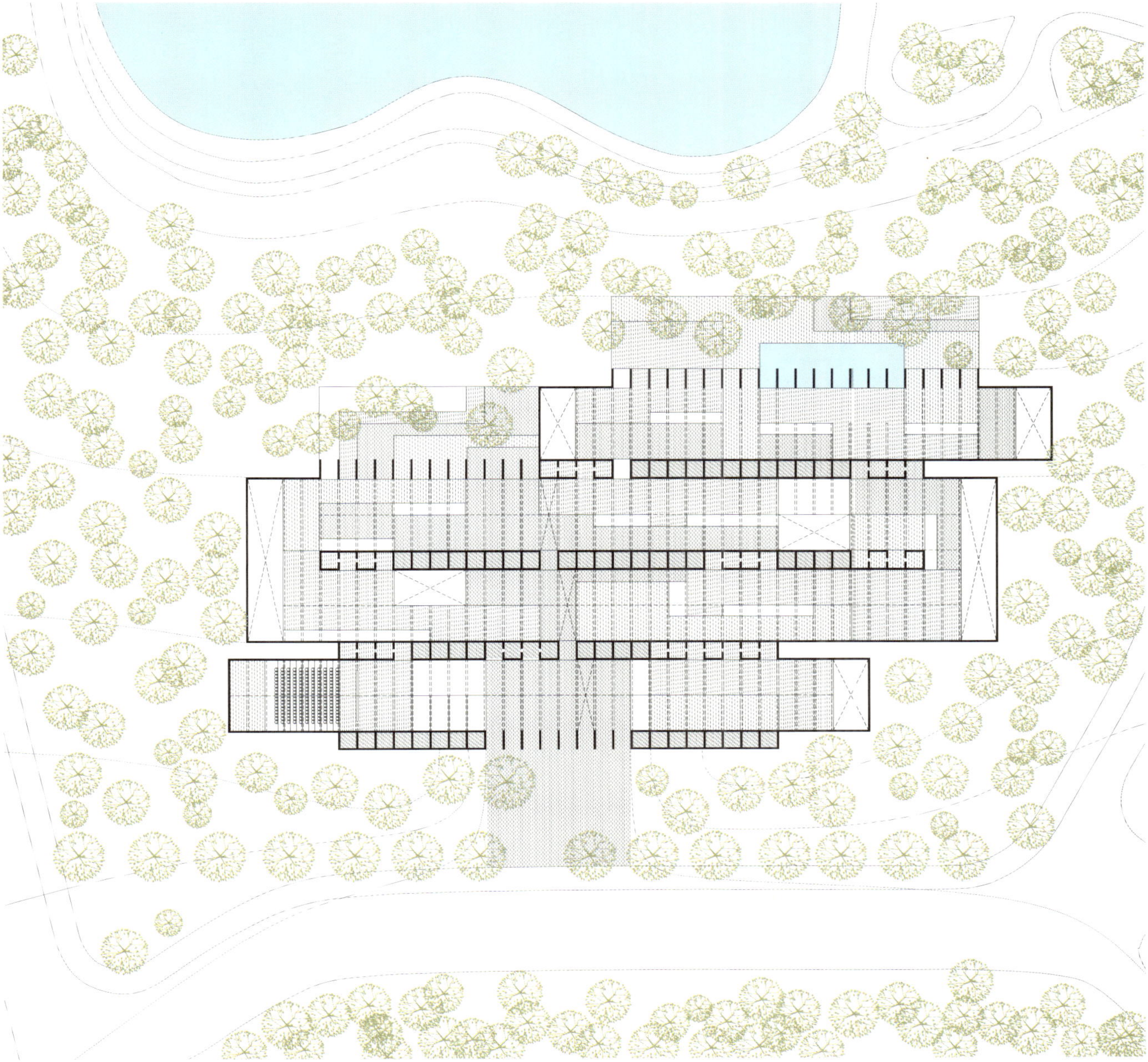

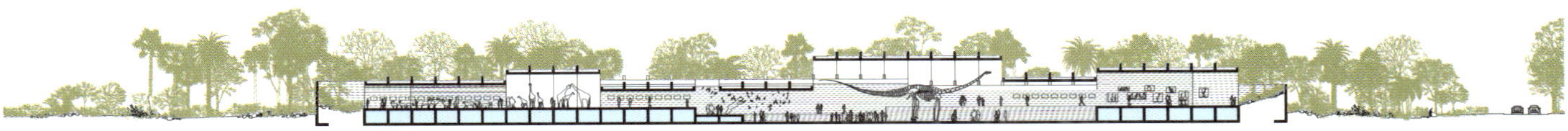

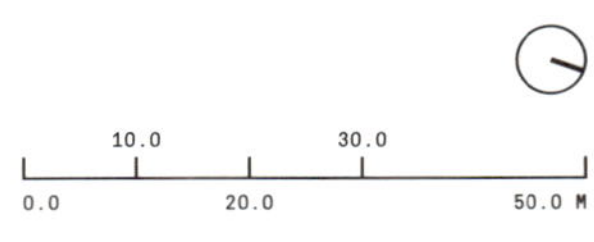
10.0
30.0
0.0
20.0
50.0 M

San Juan de Letrán Subway Station

With— Adriana León

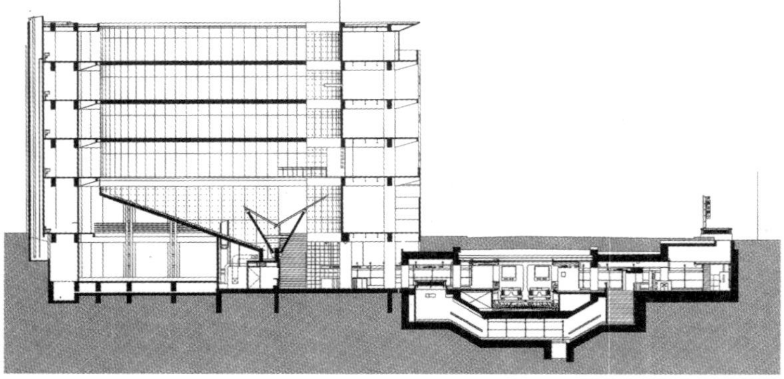

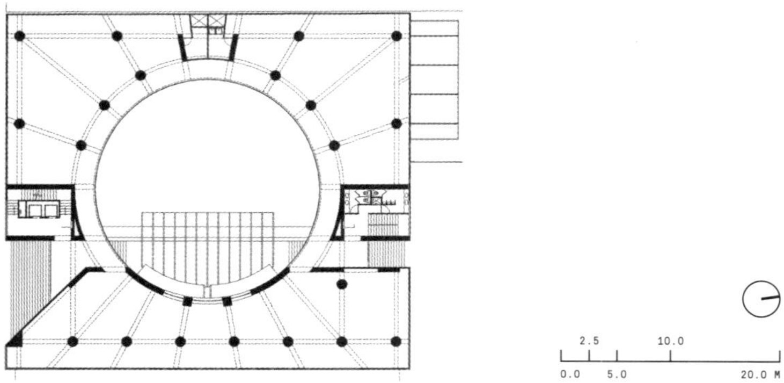

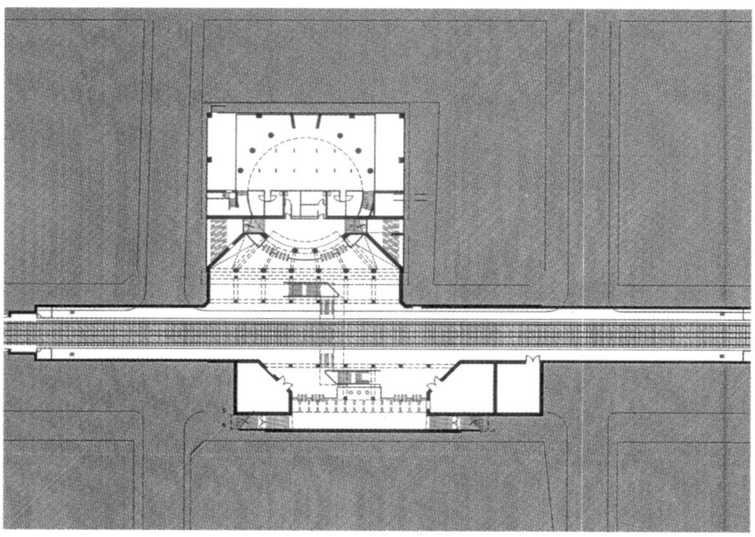

This monolithic building has a square plan and smooth concrete façades, with the subway station itself on the underground levels and five floors of offices above, providing continuity with the plane of the façade at street level. A lateral incision leads to a large circular patio, which serves as the roof of both the station and the continuous façades of the offices.

— The patio must be as ambiguous as architecture itself: a livable space open to the sky, but sheltered, protected.

NET Coacalco

Estado de México / 2007

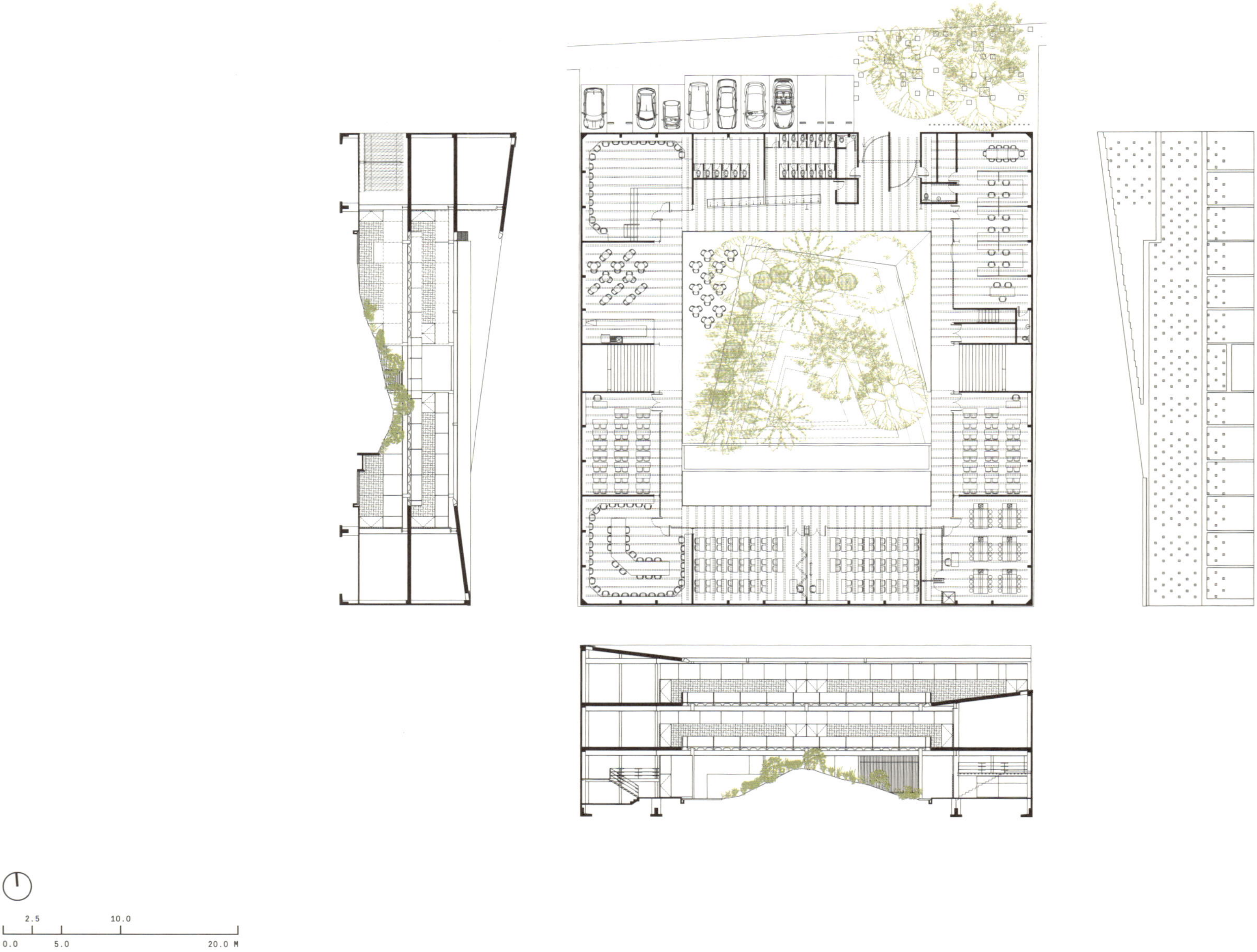

NET Izcalli

Estado de México / 2004

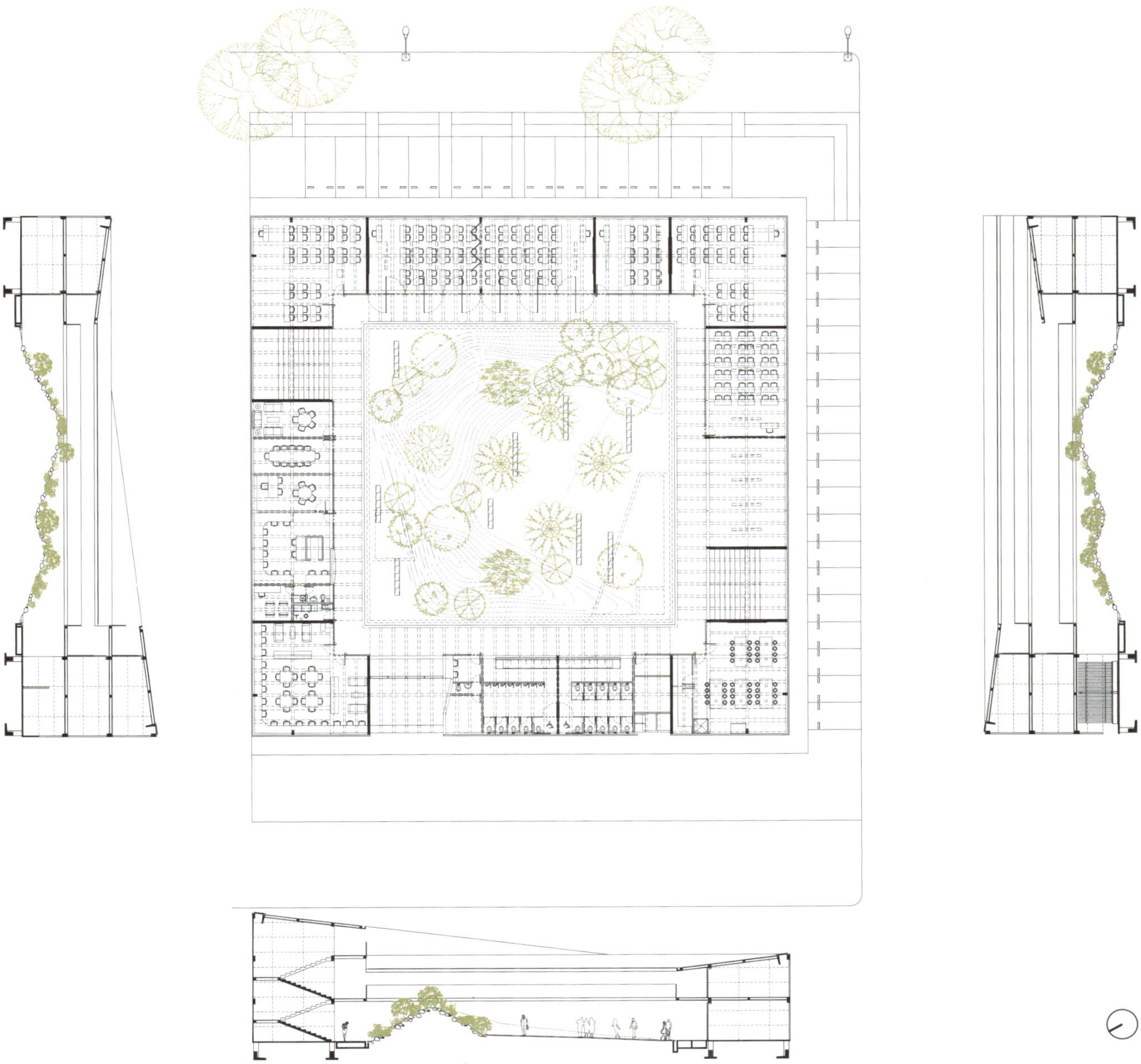

Roofs

— Roofs and roof structures go back to the very origins of civilization. Various forms of construction in different landscapes seek the most efficient and ingenious ways to resolve the problem of covering, sheltering, framing, hierarchizing, dramatizing. There are light structures that employ palm leaf or clay tiles almost like scales, like organic systems, whose small parts are to the whole as the whole to the parts. In the course of time, some structures begin to yield, to come undone in a natural process of decline, like the human skeleton. Tiles and palm leaf, however, can be rearranged organically and the roof structure can assume different positions. In many cases, the original roof may undergo particular changes, owing to exposure to sun, rain, and wind, or by the simple whim of being different.

A fascination with primitive structures, with huts and *palapas*, or palm-leaf shelters, which have demonstrated their efficiency and habitability over the ages, is reflected in certain projects undertaken by Alberto Kalach in the course of his career. Some of them are in rural zones, where the architect rethinks, in a local key, the typological and structural virtues of these kinds of constructions in order to adapt them to new needs. In some cases, the lightness of the materials, their facility in construction, their tolerance for imprecision, their low cost, and their reduced environmental impact have made such constructions a genuine option in rural contexts.

An initial experiment was El Relámpago in Valle de Bravo, followed by the house in Nanjing, which allowed him to test the malleability of the roofs and their ability to adapt subtly to different landscapes. There followed other replicas, variations, and experiments carried out by the architect in Cancún, in Oaxaca, in Cuernavaca, and in the Yucatán, at times reinterpreting regional autochthonous constructions and *palapa* roofs. At the same time, Kalach has explored the formal possibilities of bamboo structures and of tensioned canvas to cover large surface areas.

Perhap Kalach's most personal interpretation of the *palapa* is in Puerto Escondido, on the perimeter of the Casa Wabi, near other signature works by Tadao Ando, Álvaro Siza, Solano Benítez, Jorge Ambrosi & Gabriela Etchegaray, and Kengo Kuma, overlooking the Pacific Ocean. Erected perpendicular to the coastline, the *palapa* structures are repeated seemingly at random, far enough away to go unnoticed and containing a playful minimalist program that allows the natural surroundings to be fully appreciated.

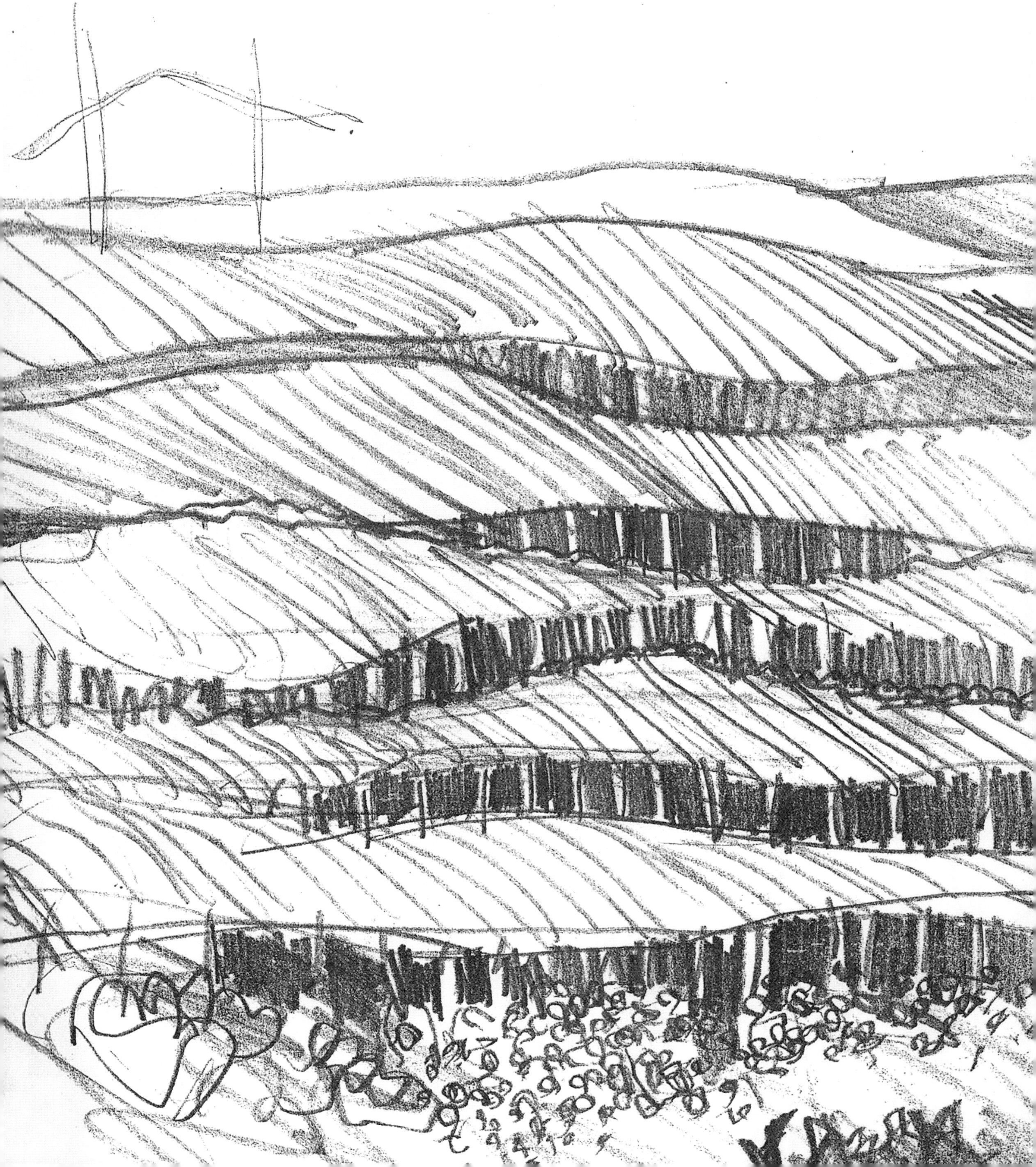

El Relámpago

Valle de Bravo / 2000

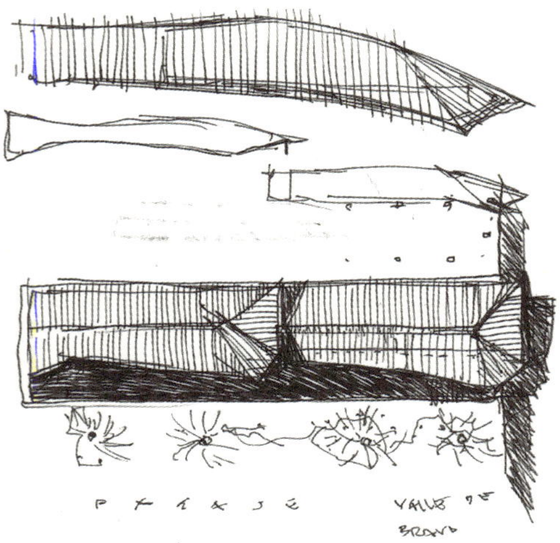

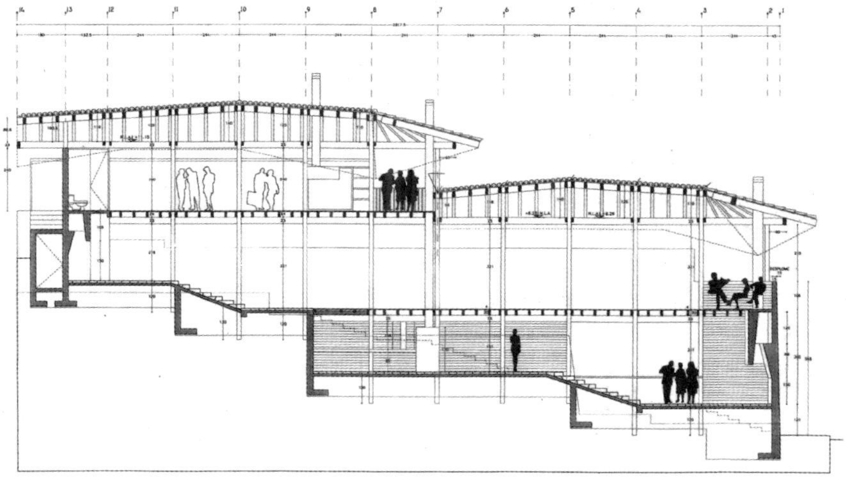

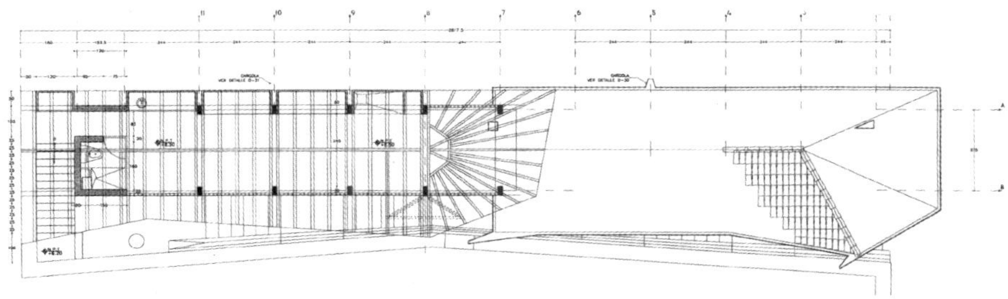

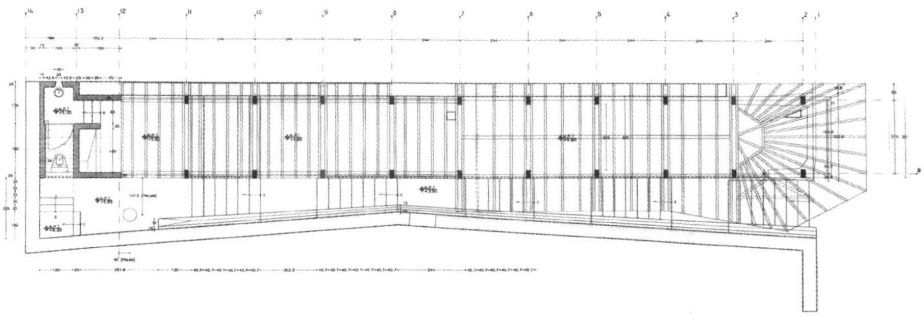

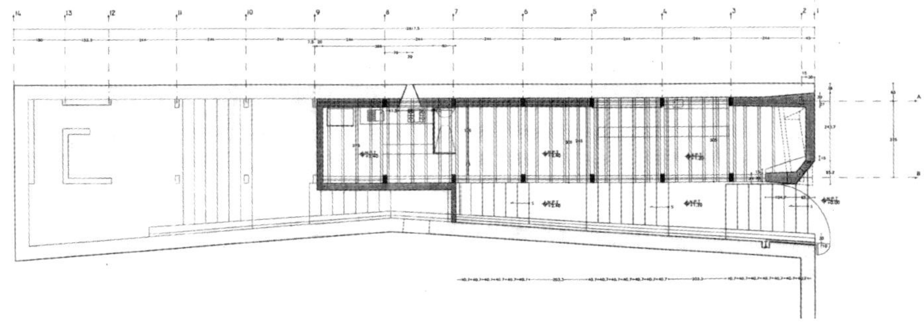

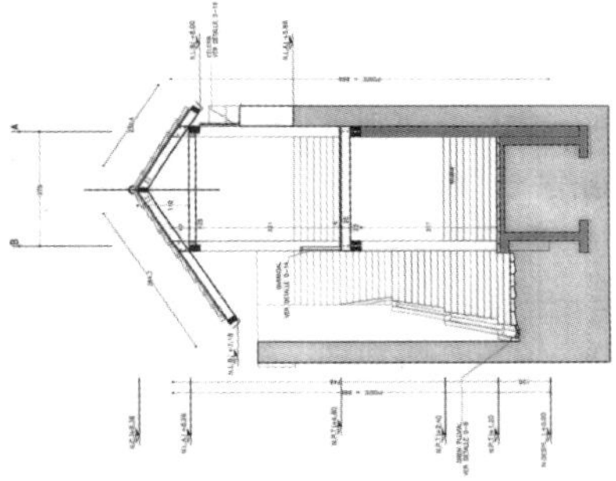

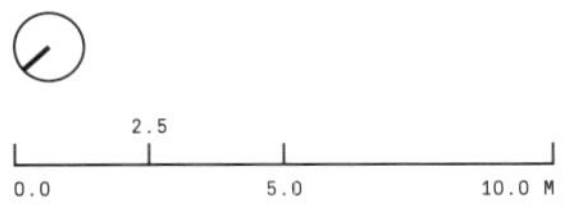

In Valle de Bravo, Kalach has constructed a wooden structure, three meters wide and thirty meters long, which forms a three-level portico and creates a new alleyway in the village. Given the narrowness of the space and the sloping topography, the wooden passageway forms a stairway running the length of the site and connecting the different levels of the building. The wooden structure is confined at either end by anti-seismic buttressing and crowned by a tiled roof with wide overhangs that protect the open spaces from sun and rain. This small building acquires a certain monumentality within the rural context, owing to its proportions and striking roof structure.

Chinese House

With— Adriana León and Félix Madrazo

— A completely wooden structure erected on piles, with a nod to the traditional Chinese roofs of straight wooden sections. The four-sided roof seems like a dragon sleeping on a lotus pool. Large overhands descend to provide privacy to the bedrooms, then turn up at the edges to open up ample vistas of the natural surroundings.

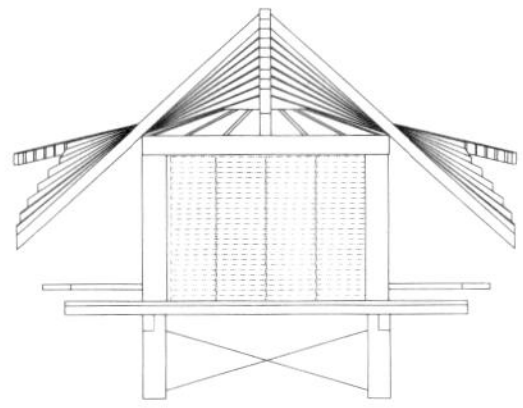

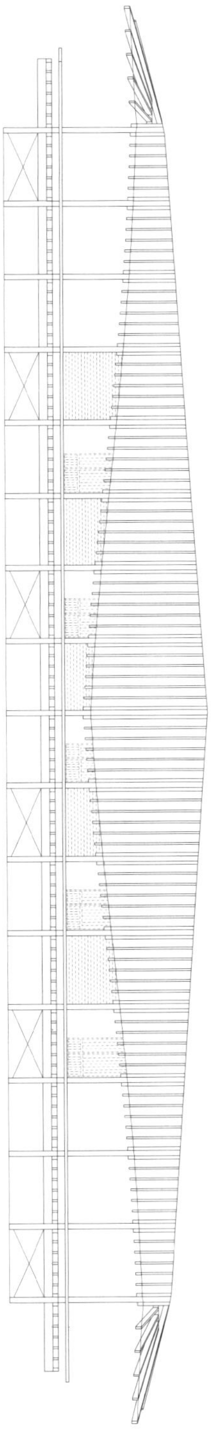

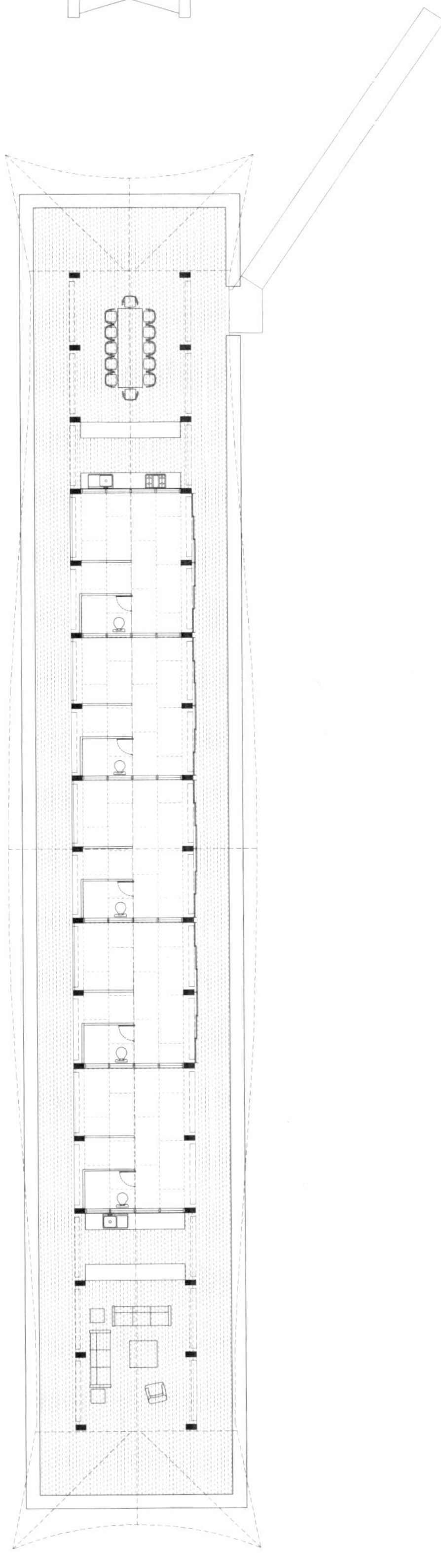

Chinese House
Nizuc palm leaf version

With— Moisés Becker

Cancún / 2005

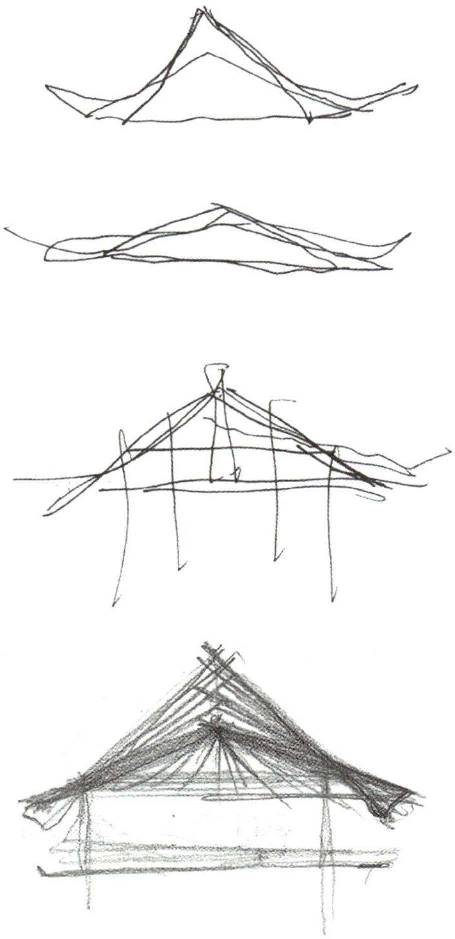

— My friend and teacher Moisés Becker and I replicated the Chinese House in Cancún, roofed here with palm leaf, for this sales office of a tourist resort. It now houses a charming restaurant with an Asian touch.

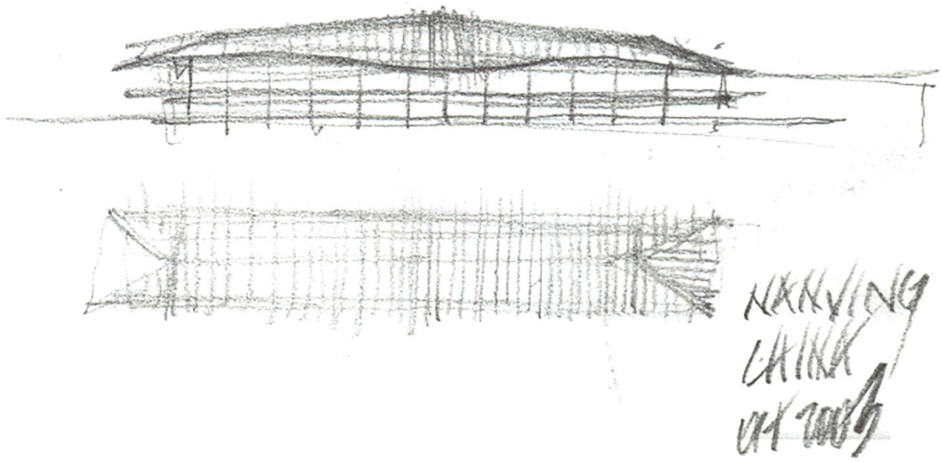

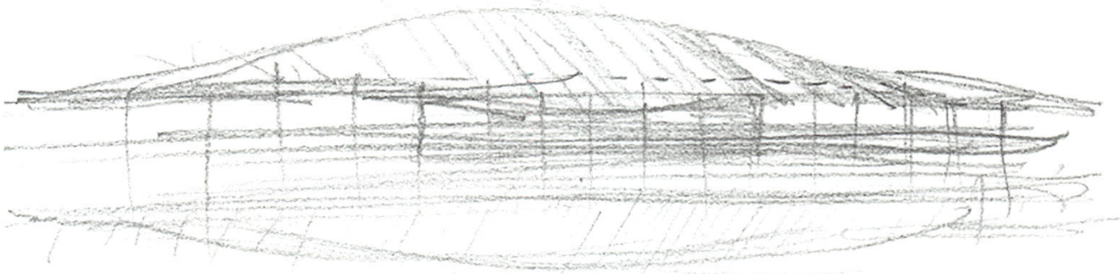

Bay in Etla

With— Iván Ramírez

Oaxaca / 2015

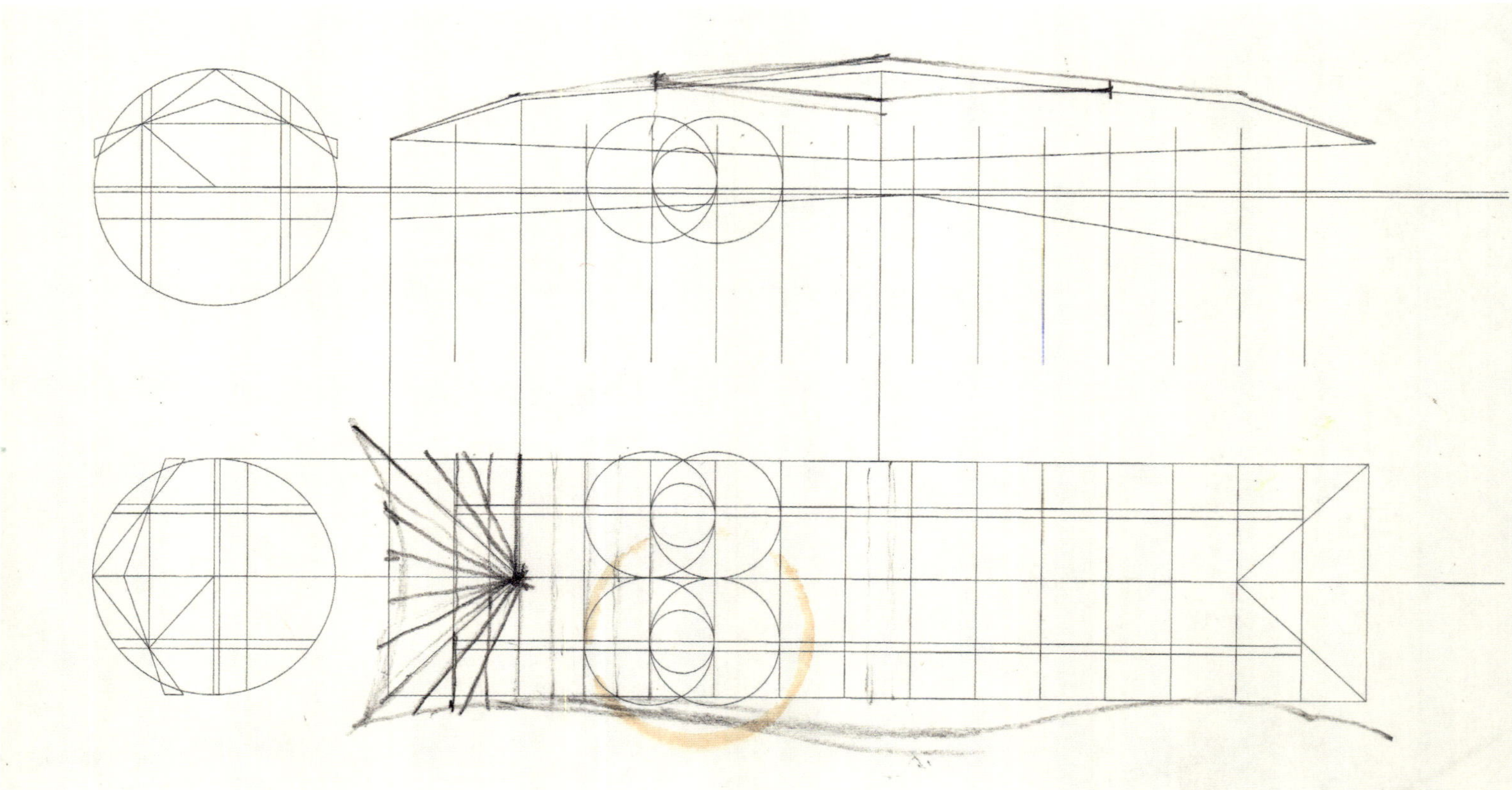

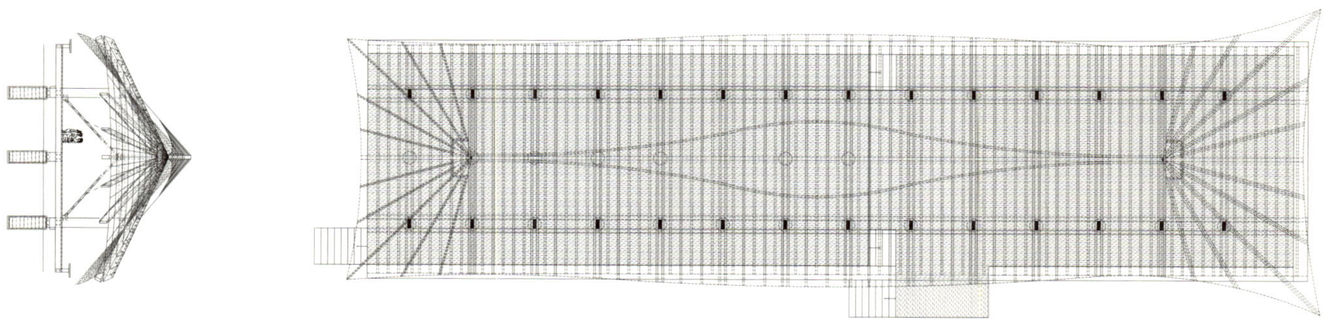

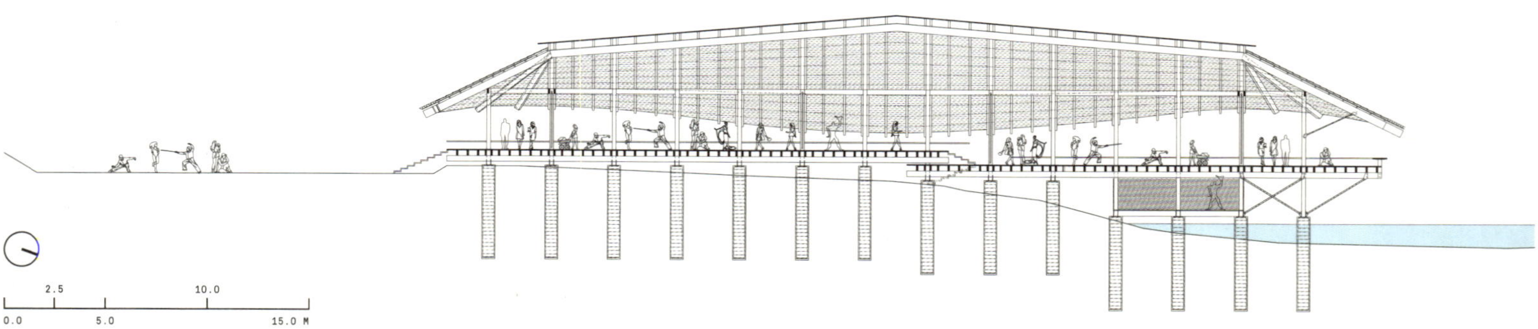

Market in Tlalixtac

With— Héctor Módica

Oaxaca / 2012

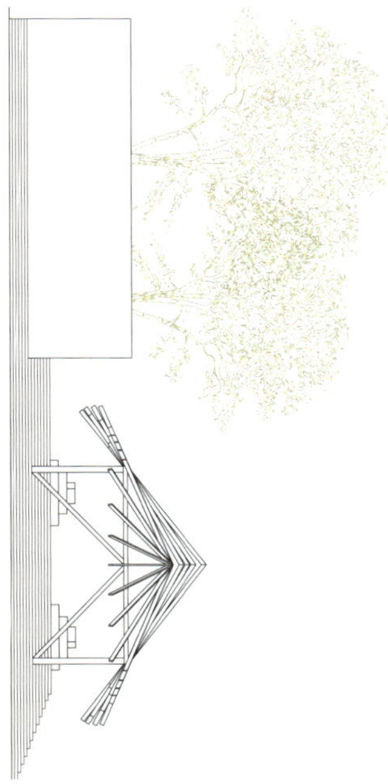

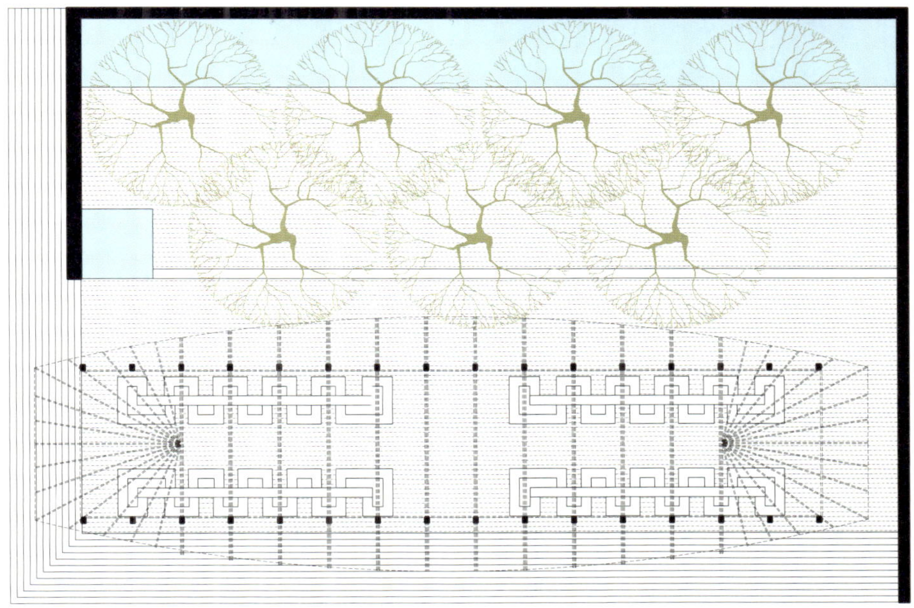

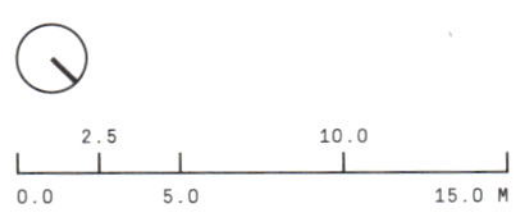

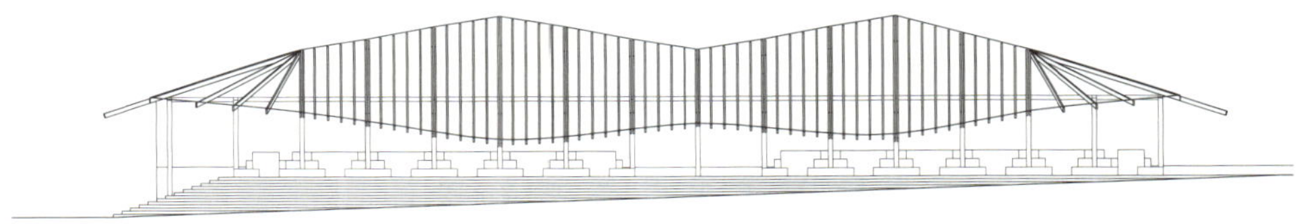

Palenque Unión

With— Iván Ramírez and Tania Lakhal

Oaxaca / 2016

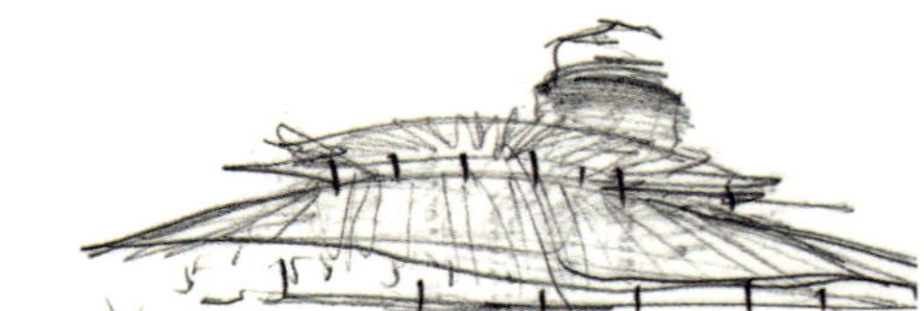

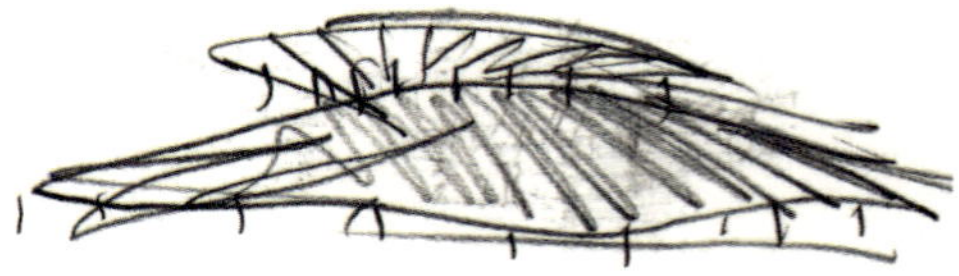

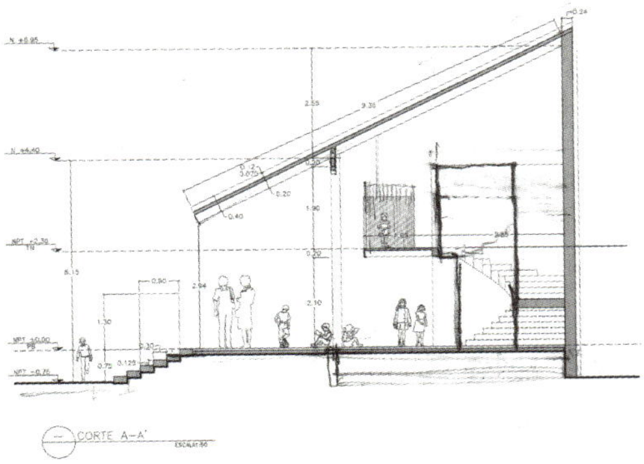

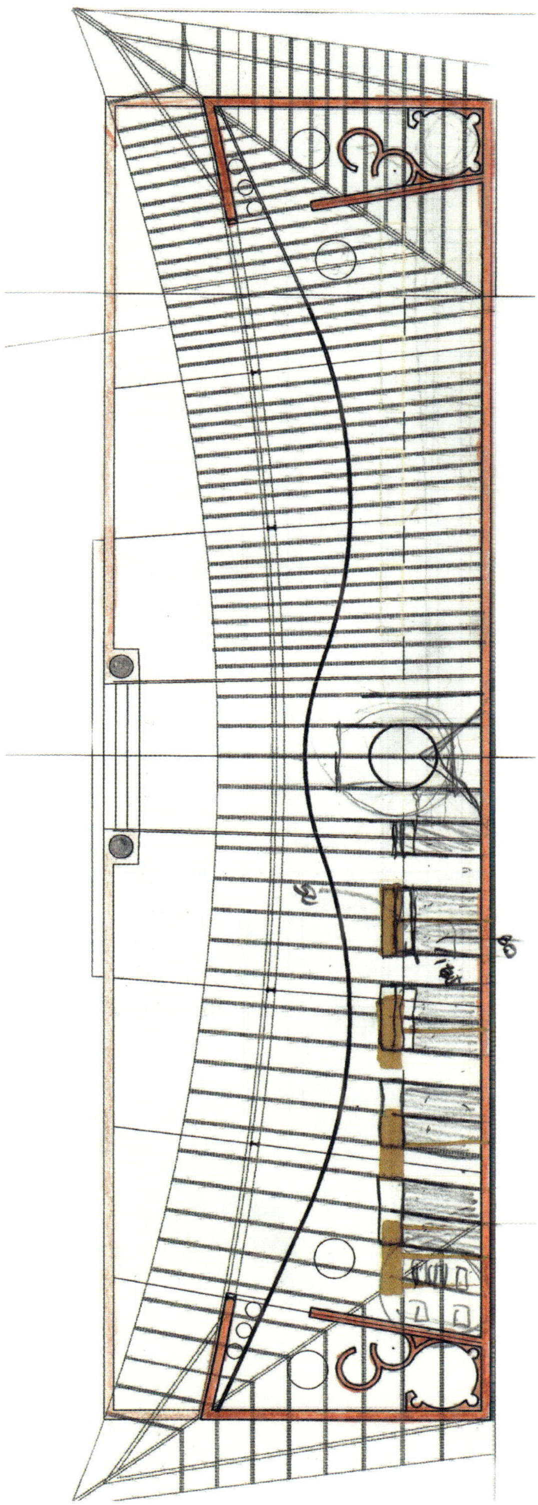

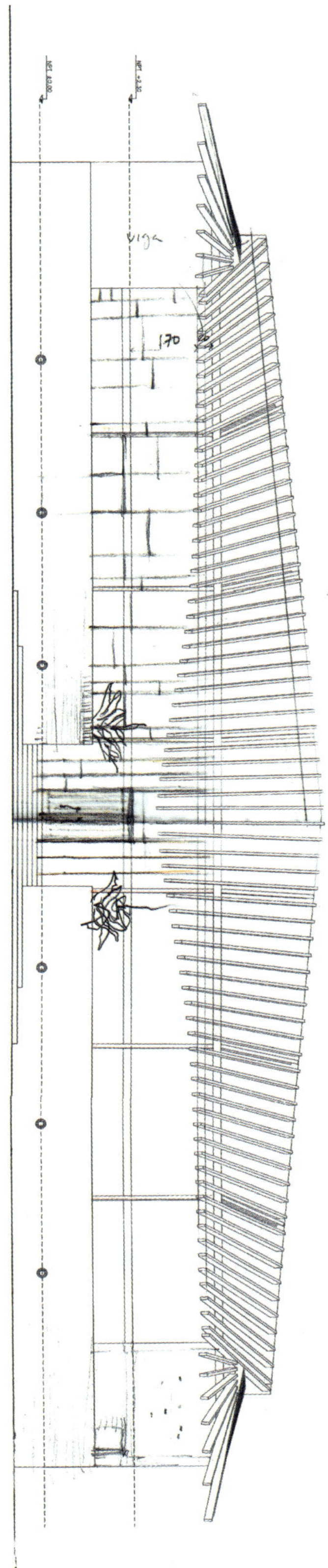

Artrópodo

Ixtapa / 2001

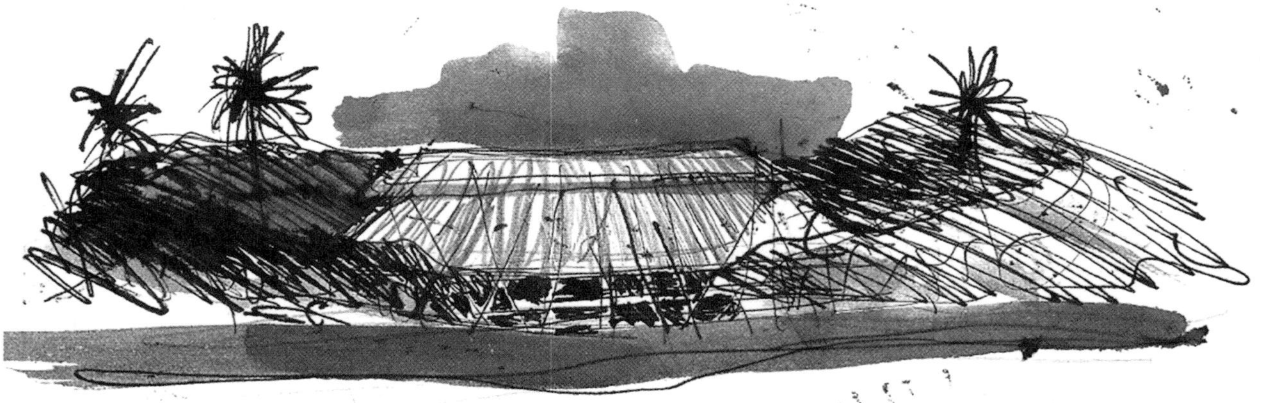

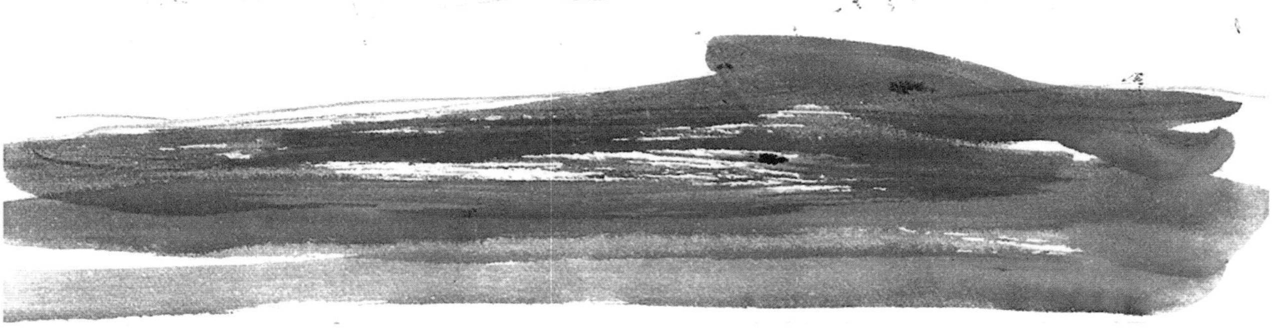

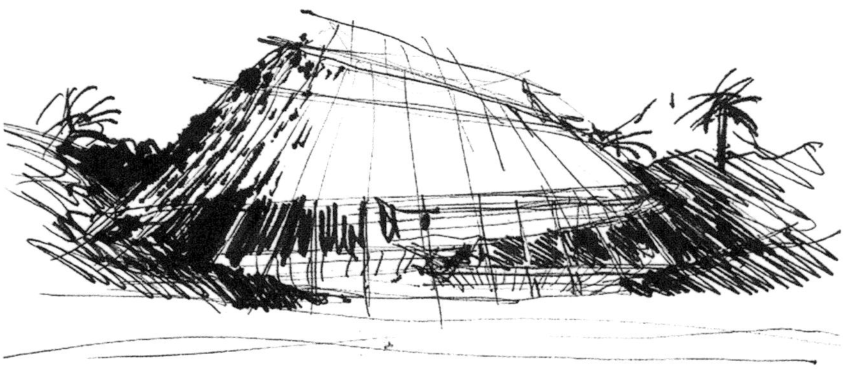

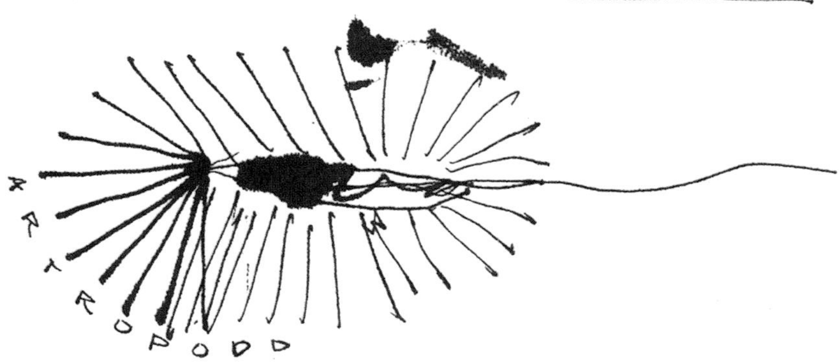

Puertecito

With— Roberto Silva

Oaxaca / 2016

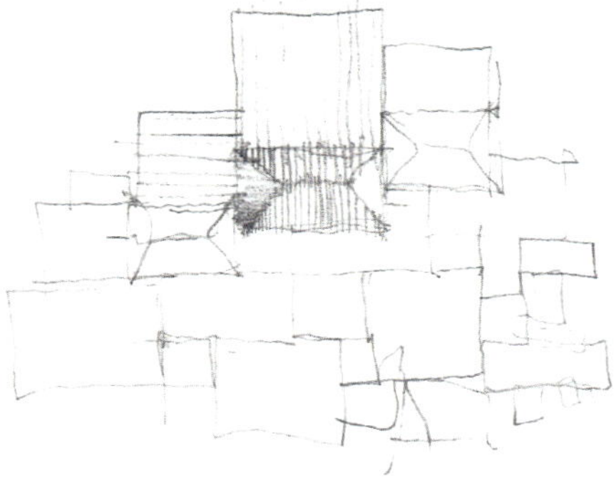

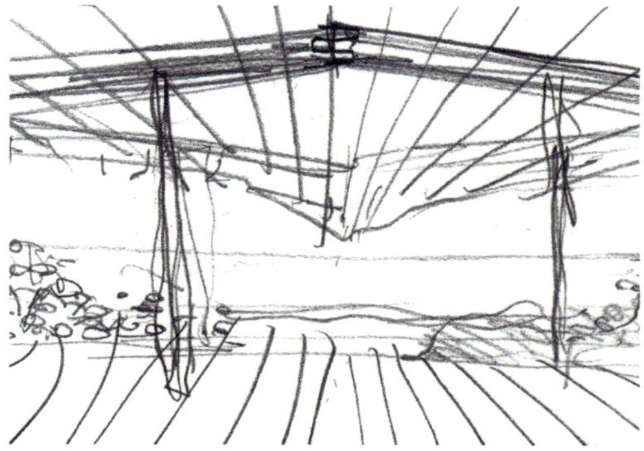

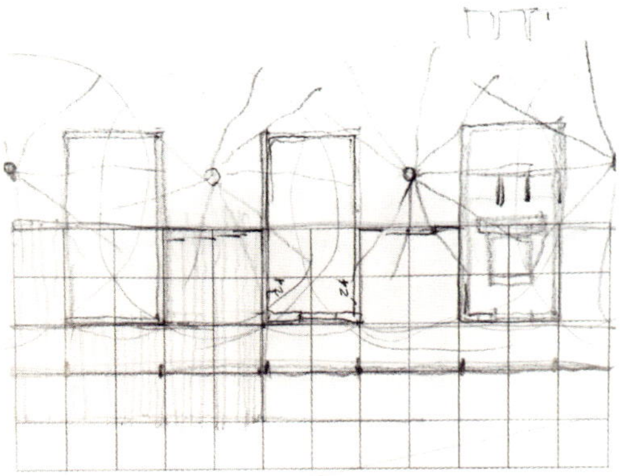

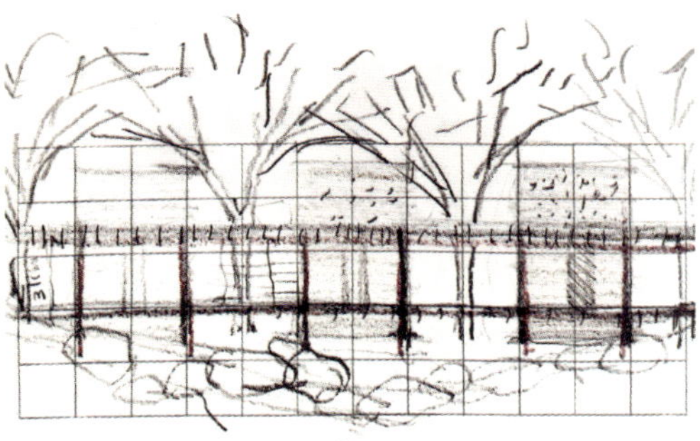

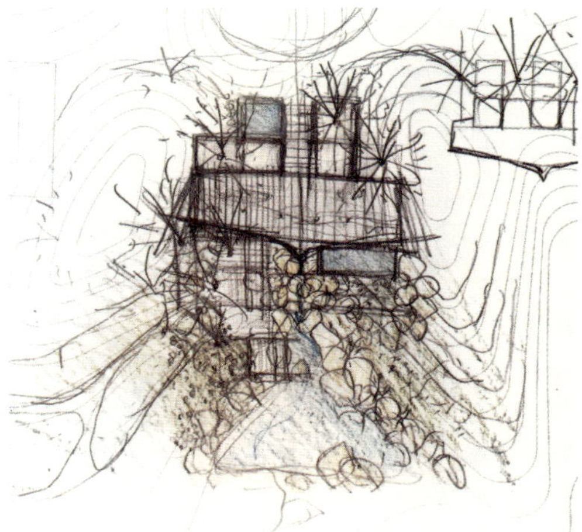

Bamboo Project

With— Toshiyuqui Kobayashi

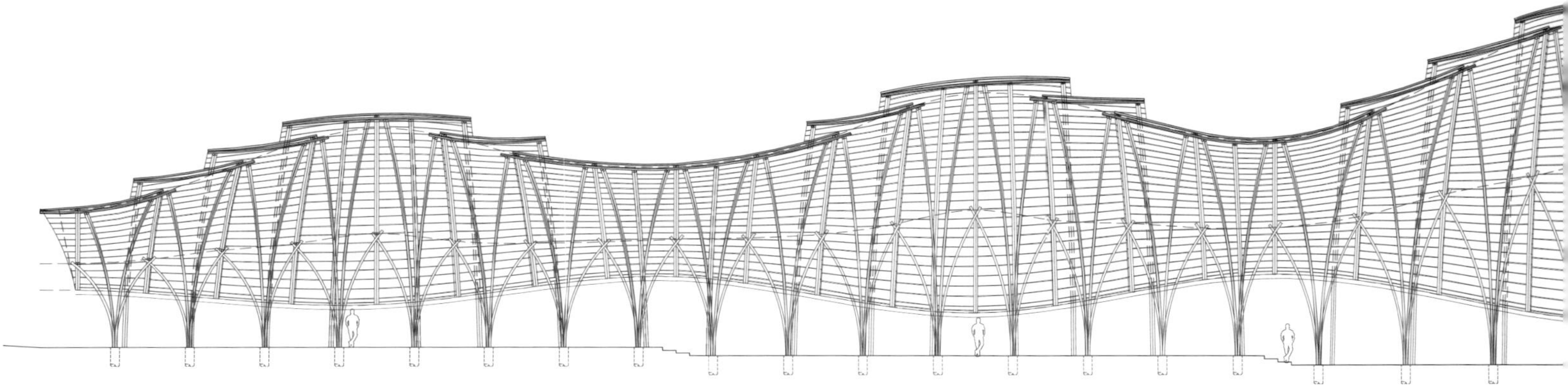

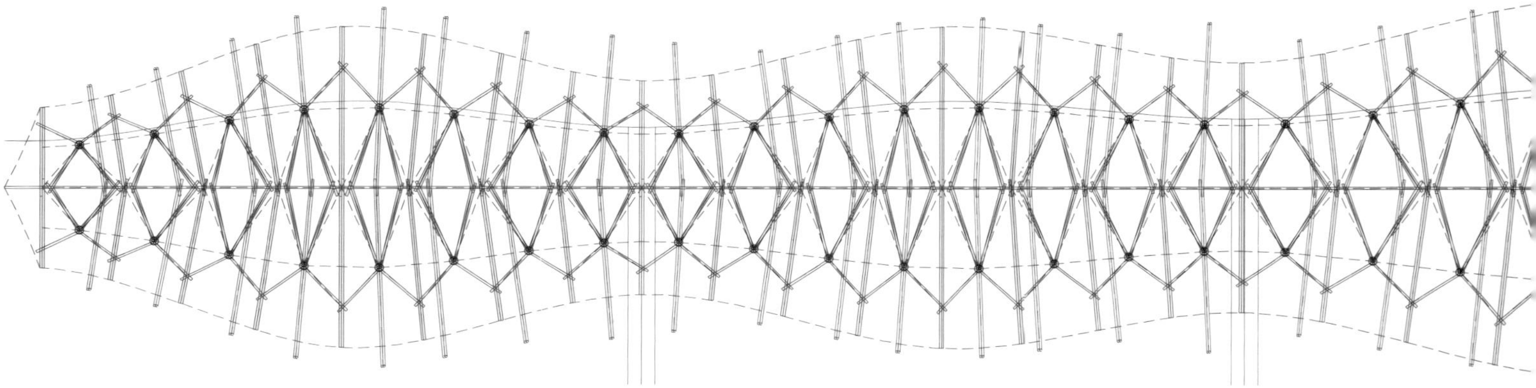

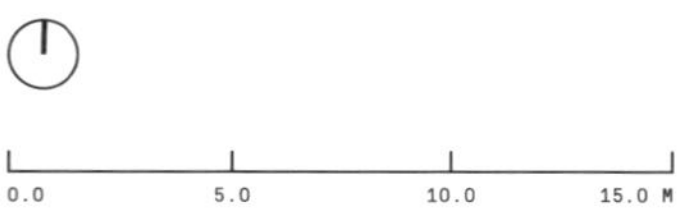

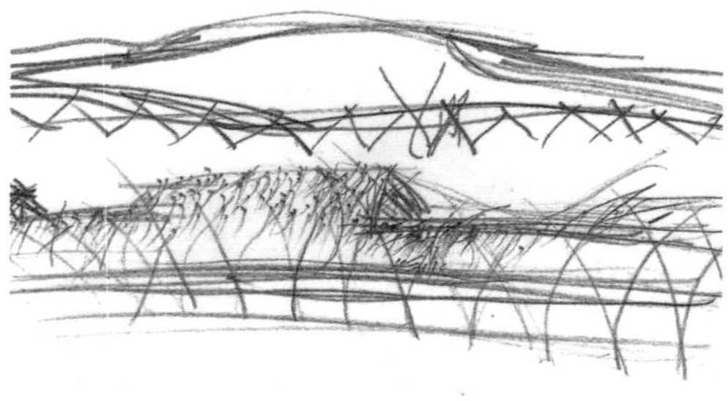

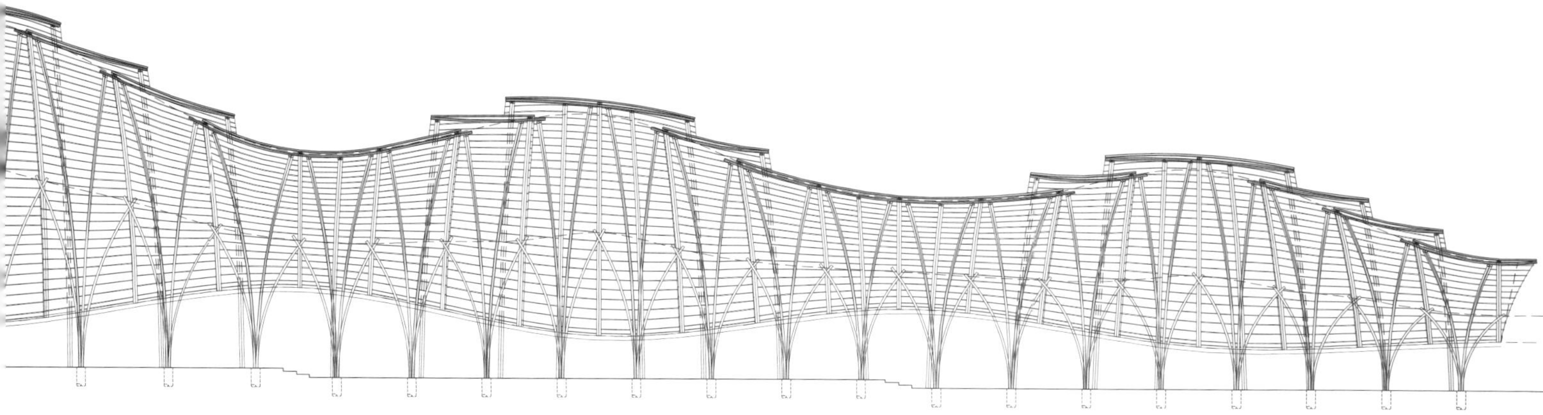

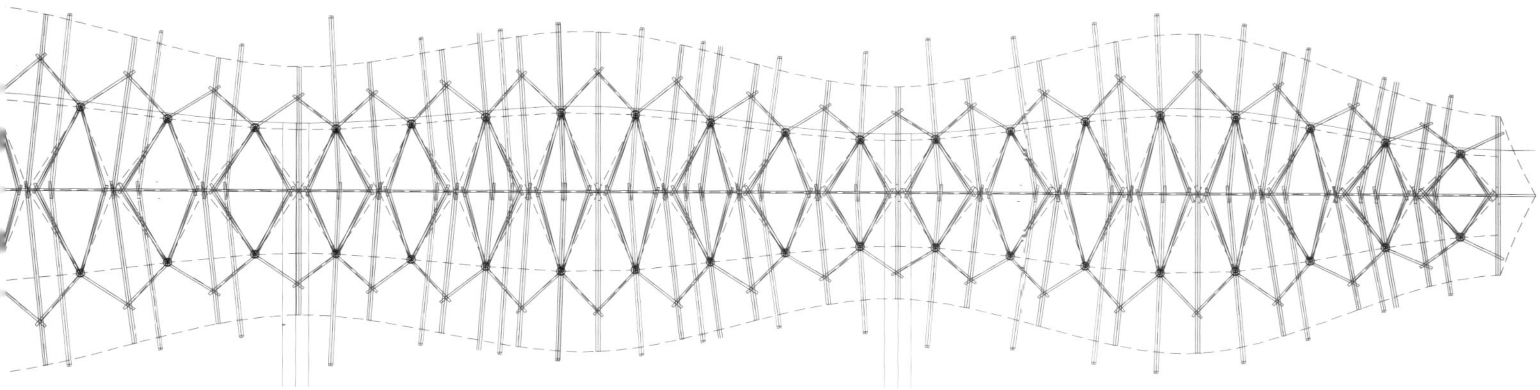

CEIBAS & PALAPA.
CULIACAN

Omakase

With— Gonzalo Mauleón, Bosco Sodi, and Luis Urrutia

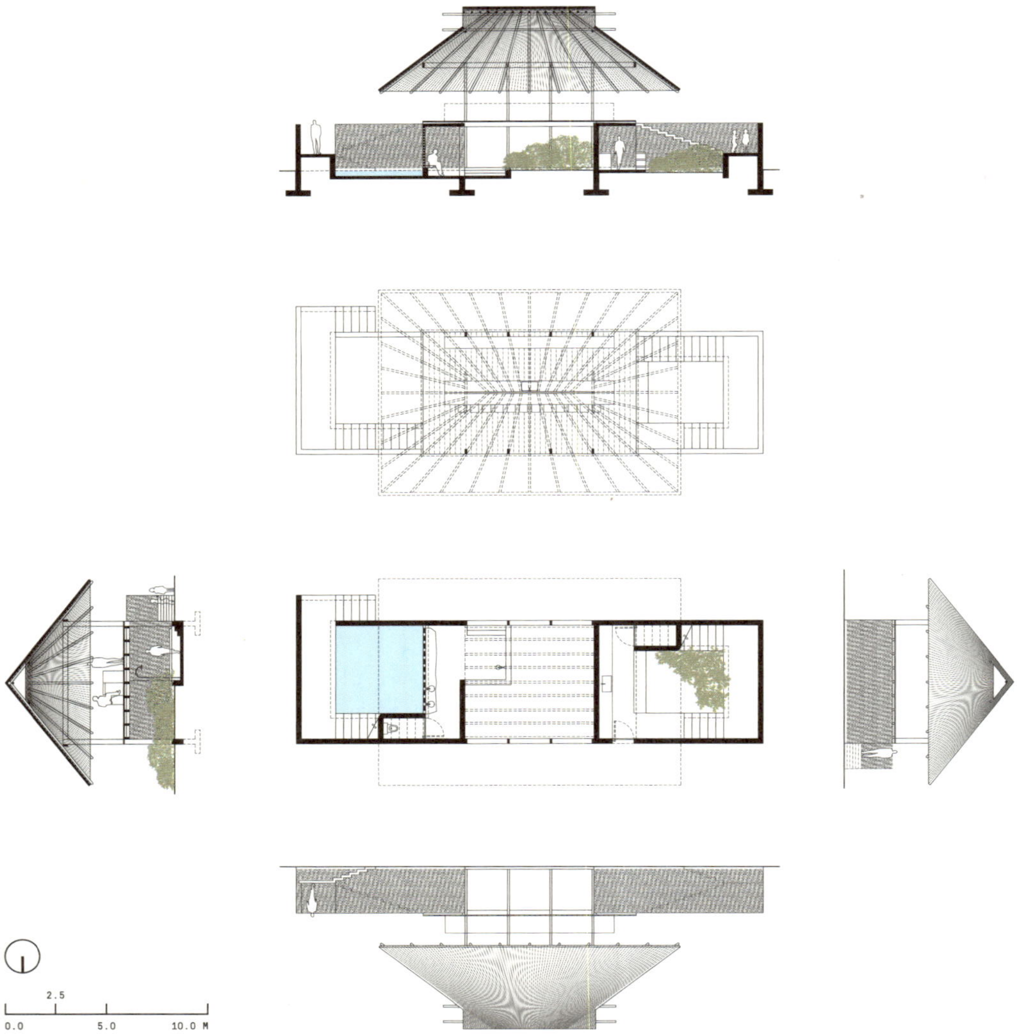

Forum in Culiacán

With— Iván Ramírez

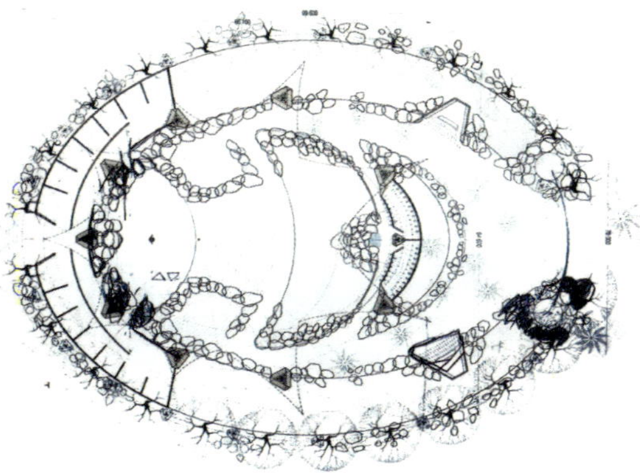

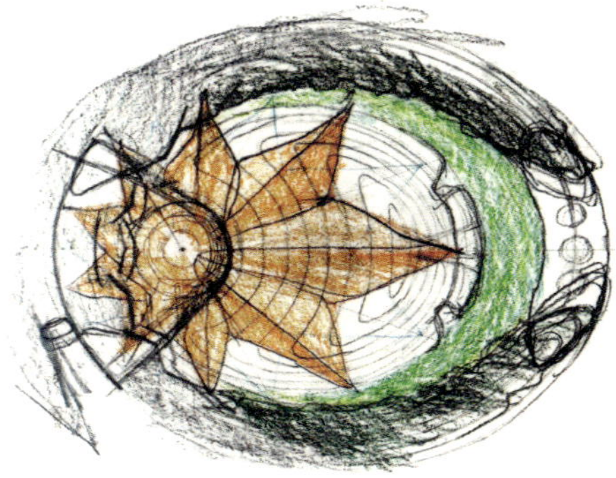

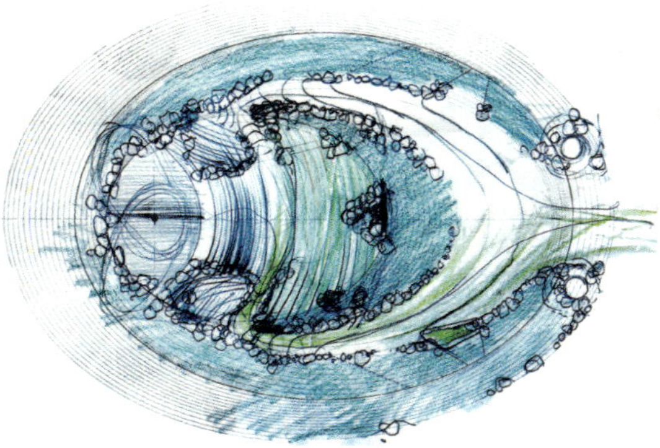

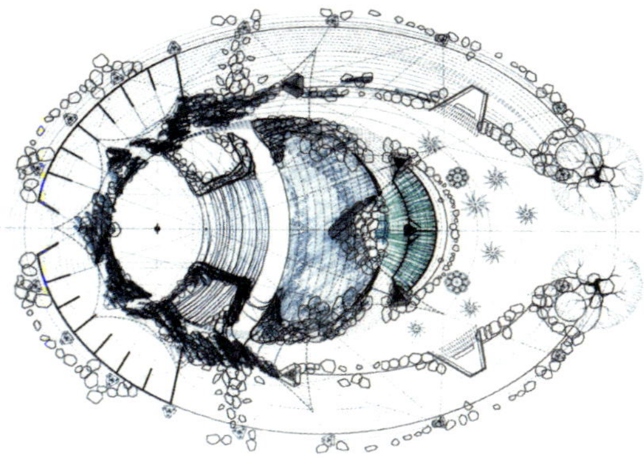

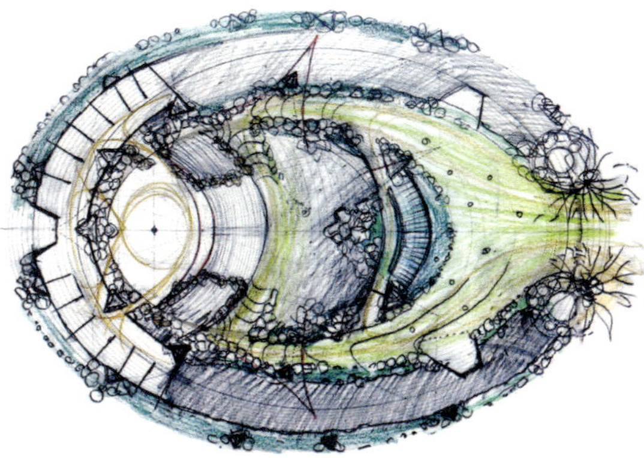

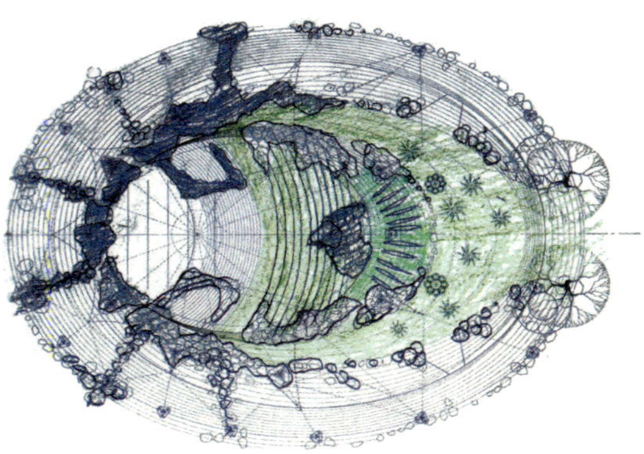

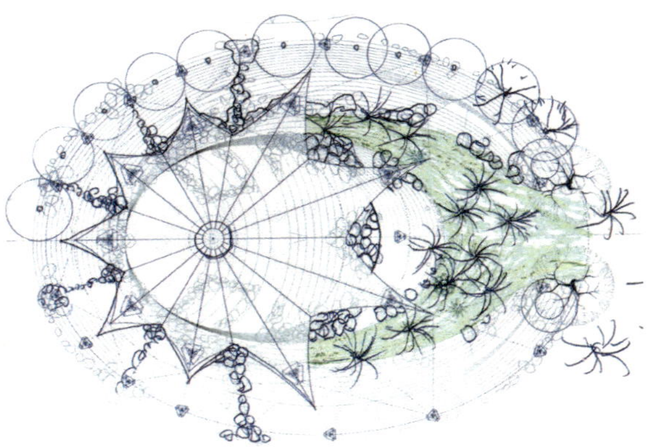

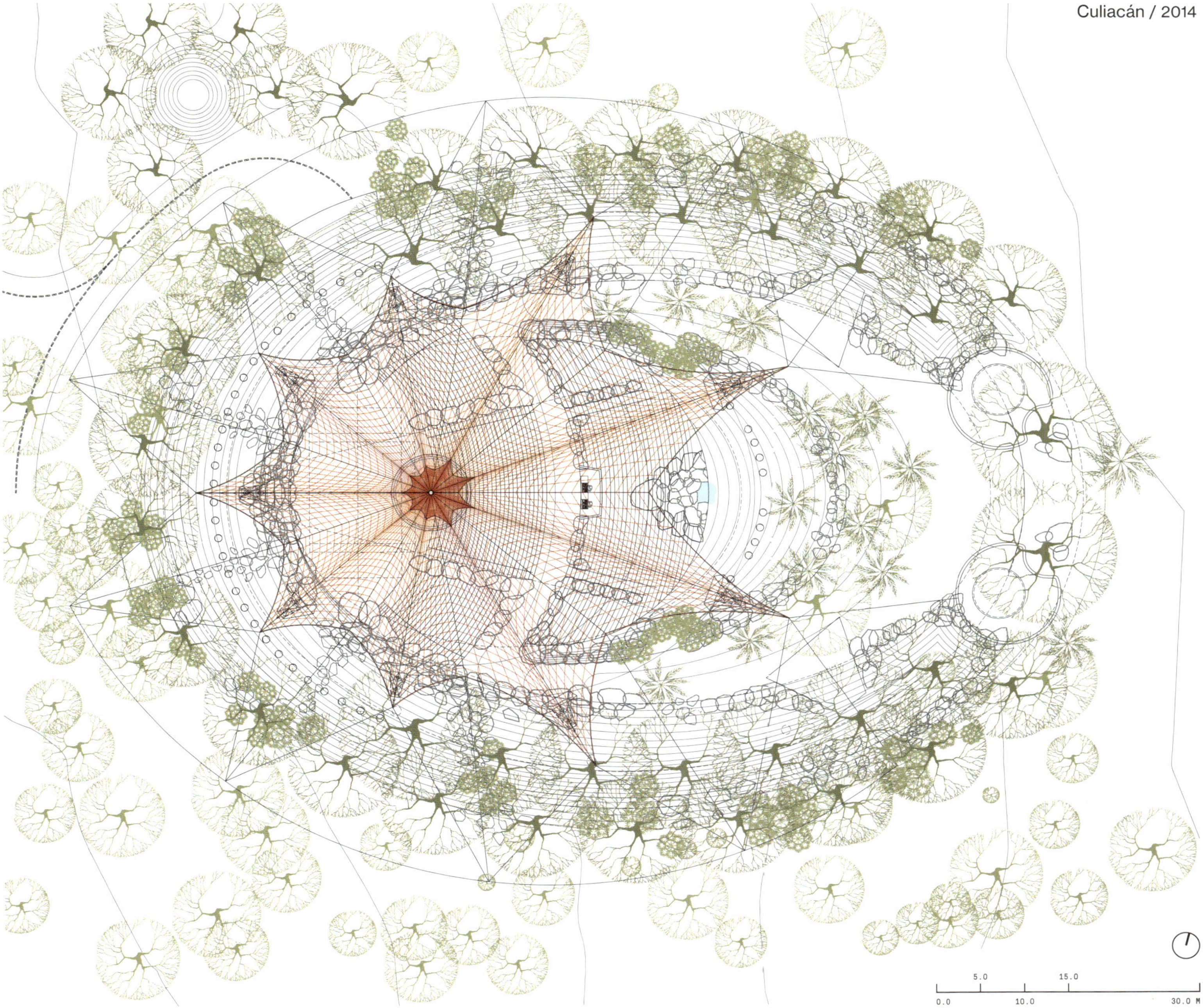
5.0
15.0
0.0
10.0
30.0 M

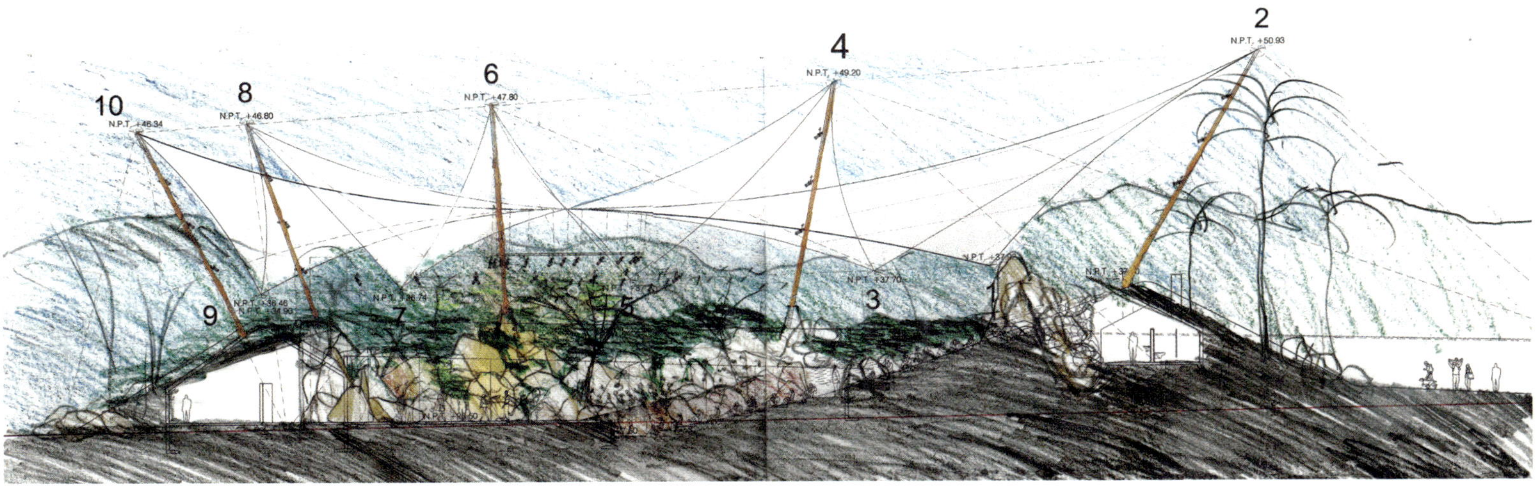
10
N.P.T. +46.34
8
N.P.T. +46.80
6
N.P.T. +47.80
4
N.P.T. +49.20
2
N.P.T. +50.93
9
7
3
1

Punta Pájaros
& Casitas by the Sea

With— Iván Ramírez, Juan Pablo de la Rosa, and Ainhoa Jiménez

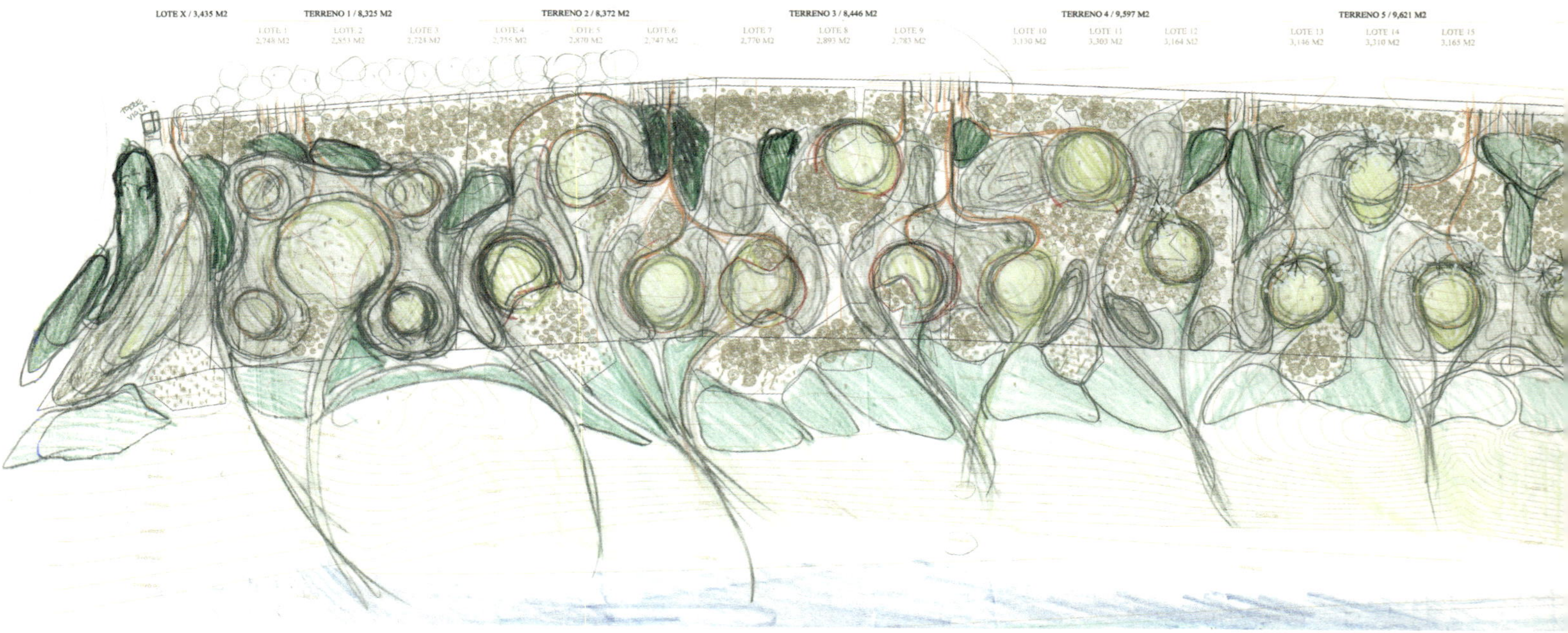

— Having observed the devastating effect of heavy constructions with broad foundations on the delicate vegetation of the coastline, we decided to build light structures on wooden piles for Punta Pájaros, like the Achaean ships drawn up on the beaches at Troy. The little houses travel in the landscape… without moving. Wide overhangs protect the houses from sun and rain. Latticework façades make the most of the breeze. A small twist in the roof structure facilitates runoff, with a wave to the clouds and surrounding hills.

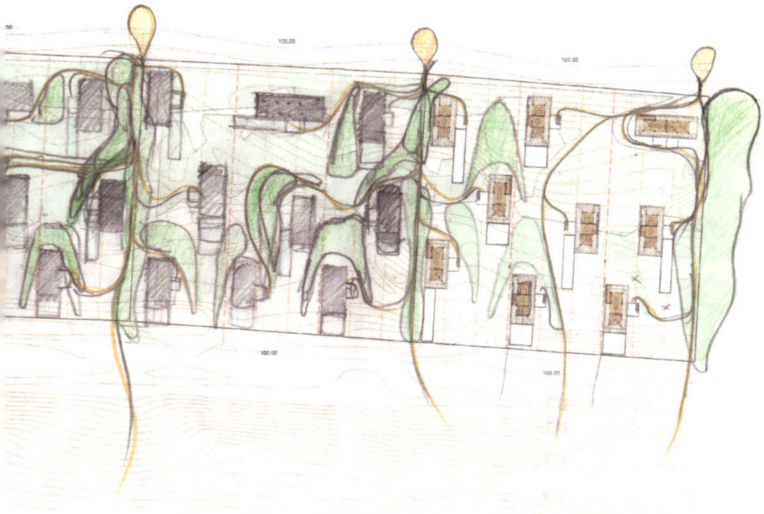

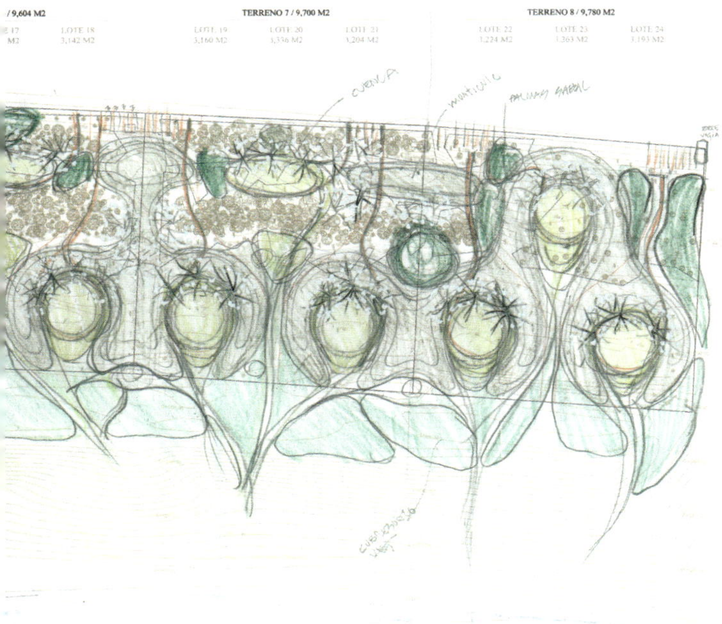

Without going outside, you may know the whole world. Without looking through the window, you may see the ways of heaven. The farther you go, the less you know.
Thus, the sage knows without traveling; he sees without looking and works without doing.
—Lao-Tse, *Tao Te King*

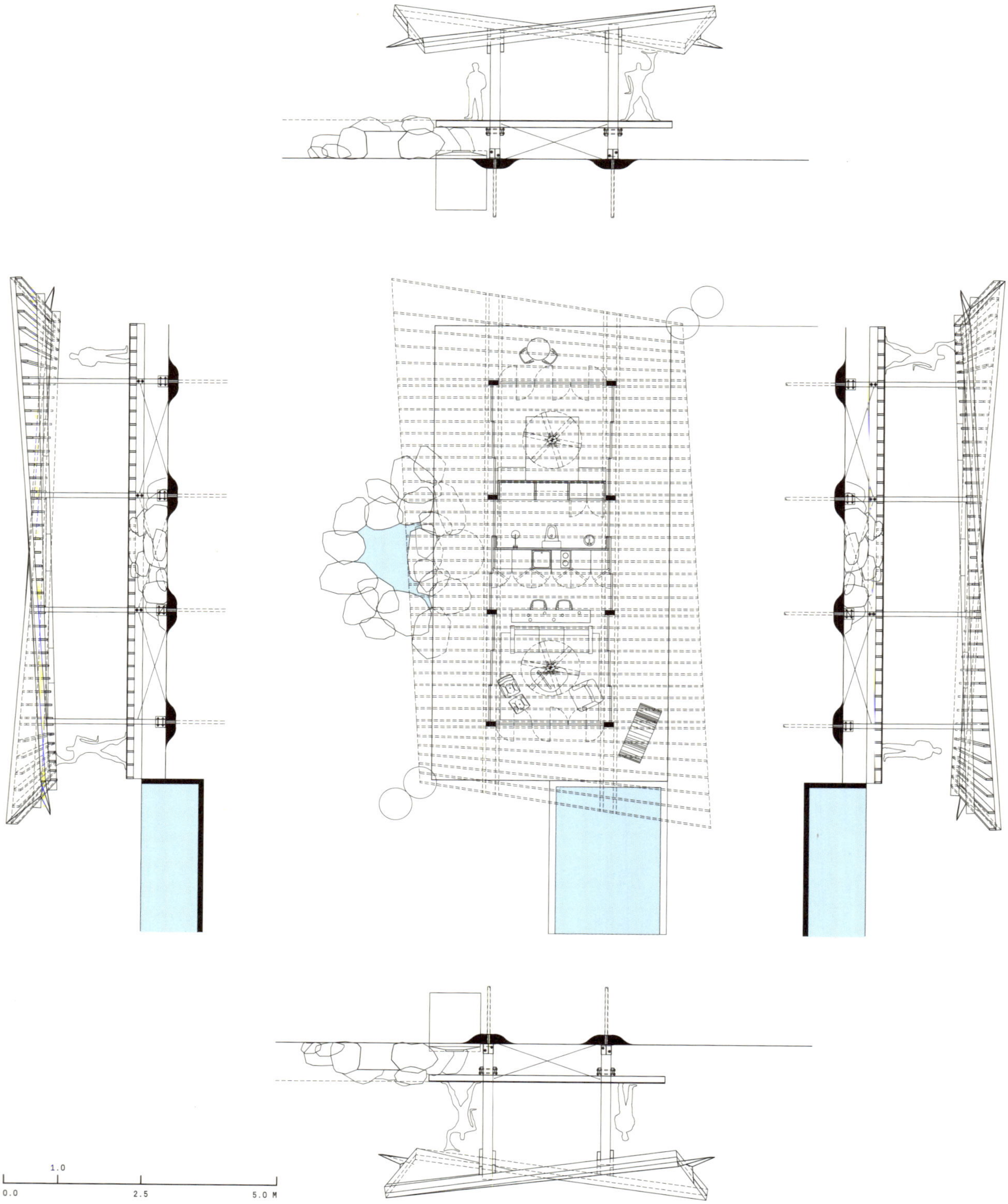
1.0
0.0
2.5
5.0 M

Restaurant in Culiacán

With— David Martínez

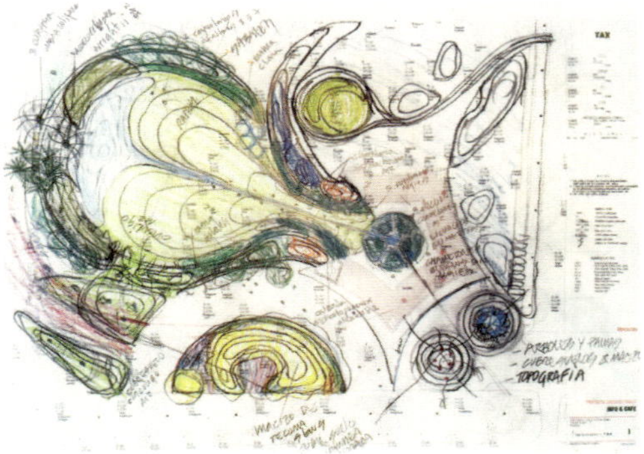

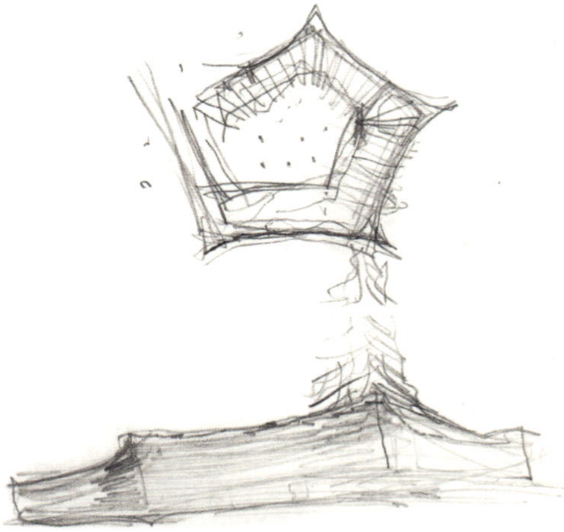

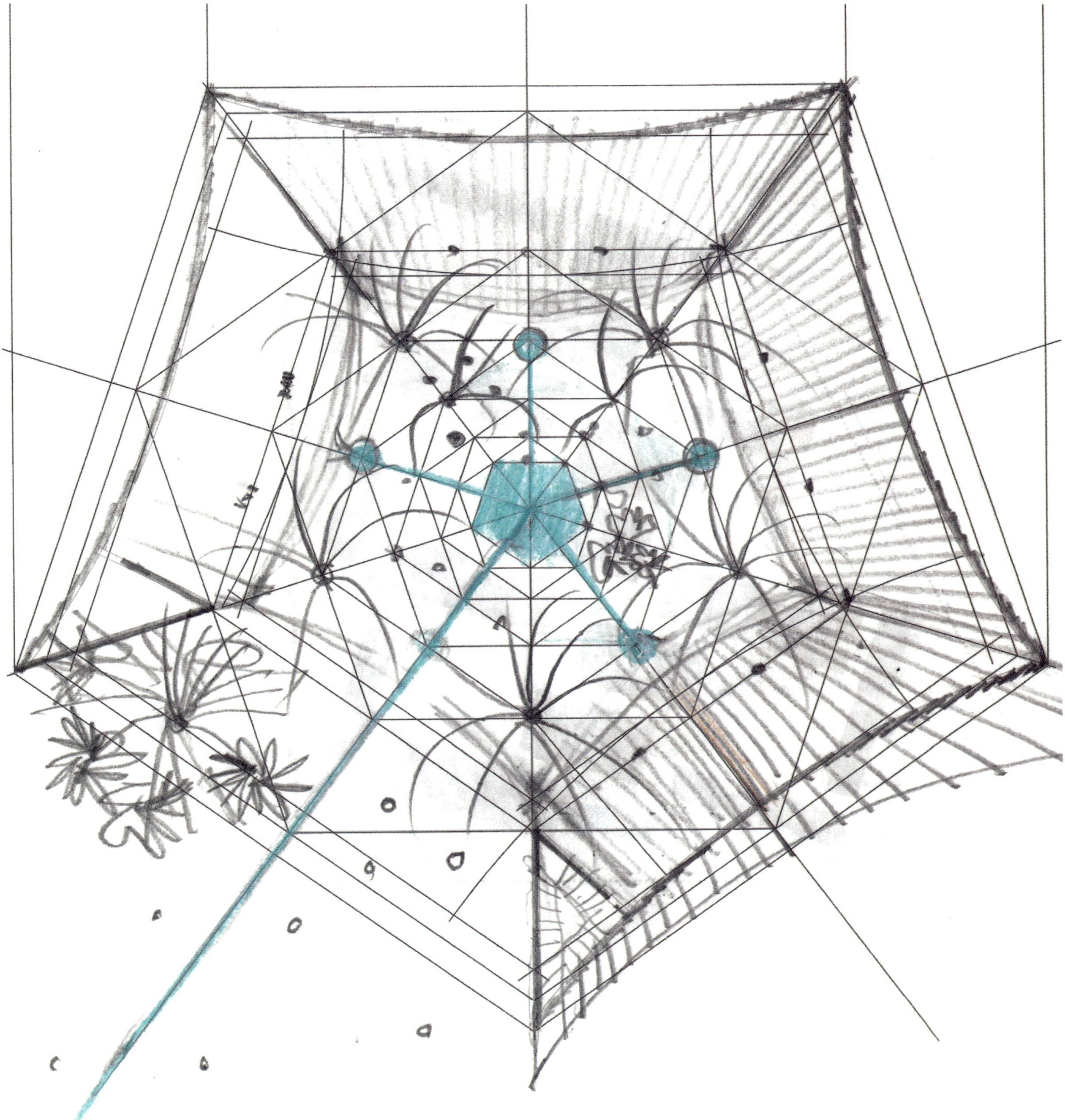

Conversations and Intermittences
— Alberto Kalach + Juan Palomar

"The time has come," the Walrus said,
"To talk of many things:
Of shoes—and ships—and sealing-wax—
Of cabbages—and kings—"
—*Lewis Carroll*

What follows is the result of long conversations between Alberto Kalach and the present writer, first transcribed and then summarized. There were different sessions, editions, additions we thought might be useful, and plenty of pruning. The principal and most wide-ranging dialogue took place on a hacienda deep in the Yucatán peninsula, for which we propose the following:

Evocation of Place

Yucatecan atmospheres. It is the dead of night, and the forest is alive with signs and premonitions. A more intense life than that of the daytime unfolds beneath the domes of the great trees, amidst the lush undergrowth, in the dark and mysterious pools. Something is being spoken in concert, now faltering, now clear, composing trees and plants, furtive or flamboyant animals. Unusual cries of unseen birds, like brief string solos, crickets of unsuspected acoustic power, with their incredible *sostenutos*, choirs of frogs making up a raucous and precise brass ensemble. The percussion is supplied by invisible insects that punctuate the evening with steady *ostinatos*. The unsettling hissing of the snakes is an ominous warning: no one can invade their domains without serious risk. The croaking of the frogs as they flop together into a pool betrays perhaps the presence of the baleful serpents. The dimly-lit arches of the corridor contemplate the spectacle, listening closely to the signals from the untamed forest: they have done so for centuries, and this is yet another evening. The tequila glows and the conversations goes deeper.

Around 1919, on the Côte d'Azur in France, near Menton, a stone's throw from the Italian border, a writer and draftsman, architect and landscaper, Ferdinand Bac, devoted a decade to creating a series of gardens, pavilions, pergolas, and pools on an estate called Les Colombières. Bac's patrons and collaborators were Émile Ladan-Bockairy and his wife Caroline. A long, slow joint effort brought order to abrupt topography, created spectacular vistas of the Mediterranean, brought out striking perspectives, and showcased a variety of flora. There is still a carob tree, hundreds of years old, on the estate today, one of the keys to the garden as a whole. In 1925, in Paris, Luis Barragán chanced upon a couple of Ferdinand Bac's books at the famous Exposition internationale des arts décoratifs et industriels modernes. One of them was entitled *Les Colombières*; the other, *Jardins enchantés*. Owing to this random succession of circumstances, the texts and illustrations of these books would become one of the cornerstones of the work of an entire generation in Guadalajara – Barragán's hometown – and, later on, a powerful influence, distilled to the last degree, on his own work, including some of the most refined and finished products of Mexican architecture. In 1931, Barragán met Ferdinand Bac in person and visited Les Colombières: a confirmation of the soundness of his efforts of those years and a sure compass for the endeavors he would undertake during the rest of his life..

It may not be unreasonable to extend this genealogy in the fields of both architecture and garden design to the Yucatán forest, near Izamal, where a few years ago a Mexican couple acquired another large property that also contained a domestic ruin and a series of open-air spaces, overrun by the freely proliferating vegetation. The intense collaboration between the owners of this property and the architect and esthete Alberto Kalach deepens the similarities. The salvaging of local species, the introduction of others, the construction of pavilions, pools, and pergolas, the adoption of a ceiba tree as a tutelary presence, and gardens of differing characters and expressions. The existence of a strong line connecting Kalach to Barragán – across generations and modes of expression – is not difficult to establish: both share (and not only in terms of formal appearances) the premise that "houses should be gardens, and gardens, houses." The practice of both is distinguished by an invariable rigor in the use of constructive elements and vegetation. Both occupied the forefront and cutting edge of architectural practice in the course of their respective careers. It could well be said – not without a certain nonchalant aplomb – that Kalach, in his generation, is the true heir and disciple of Barragán...

At the Architect's Home

JP: In the tension always existing between nature and culture, I can't help thinking of Andrea Palladio, with his villas implanted in the landscape of the Veneto. He established that hierarchical standing of the human dwelling, but then placed it among cultivated fields, woodlands, and meadows. He established the primordial garden, in which we would be as happy as we could be in this vale of tears. I believe there is a civilizing endeavor in the collaboration between architect and client.

AK: The very beginning of a project is rarely the work of the architect. You can make designs for yourself, but usually it is someone else who has the need or the vision or the dream. A project such as the one we developed in the Yucatecan jungle is part of someone else's vision. The clients had the vision and courage to go and settle in a place where there was nothing, except the remains of a small hacienda house. Finally, the architect joined the project to help them develop their vision.

JP: In this case, they are patrons, in effect: cultivated, sensitive people, with an ample vision of the world, who formulate a series of conditions in the circumstances, and have their architect, with whom they establish an esthetic and intellectual dialogue, as well as human and emotional ties. In this way, the relation between patron and architect begins to be highly creative. There is a chemistry, even a physics, between them. This interrelationship generates unexpected consequences.

AK: Vitruvius says somewhere that you have to listen to the patron and to the artisan. The artisan, the mason or builder, will tell you things about the practice of building that you didn't know, and the patron will speak to you about his way of life, with which you are also unfamiliar. You have to be open to learning from both the patron and the workman. In a good relationship, both of them will also open up to understanding your ideas, to experiment with them and to carry them out. That is what is to be expected from a human relationship: an interchange of ideas, of feelings.

JP: Returning to the houses, what do you think of this? "A house must be a shelter, a school, a workshop, a sanctuary." It's from Pope Pius XII, I believe. Díaz Morales used to repeat that definition to us. I would be interested in hearing what you have to say about the deeper part of the house, so to speak. Why a sanctuary also?

AK: Because it's a refuge. The refuge where you rest, where you relax, where your children grow up.

JP: Tell me about the fundamental houses of your life: where you have lived and what they have meant to you.

AK: A house in Acapulco that overlooked the Eastern strait, between La Caleta and the island of La Roqueta. From there you could see the cargo ships entering the port of Acapulco. The house was anchored on some gigantic rocks. Also an apartment in Polanco, which belonged to my grandparents. A fantastic building, designed by Francisco Serrano, the elder. It's a very modern building, inspired by Frank Lloyd Wright. Full of terrace balconies looking south and east. A marvelous building, very cheerful. We lived there for years.

JP: What came next?

AK: Next there was a small house in the Virreyes neighborhood, very modern. It had a cantilevered roof that slanted inward, like a V-shape. My primary school – fantastic – was designed by Mathias Goeritz, and the sports club was an elegant design by Vladimir Kaspé. Both buildings, unfortunately, have been demolished. Years later, in that apartment in La Condesa, at Iztaccíhuatl and Ámsterdam, where we were living when the neighborhood was devastated by the 1985 earthquake. It was a building very similar to where I was born, but this one was designed by Palomar and Silva, a marvelous building as well. All of these architectures have left traces and lessons. Architecture forms you, it molds you.

JP: And after that, you made your first house for yourself?

AK: After that we designed the house in Valle de Bravo. That house is a garden, an observatory concealed on the hillside, to see without being seen.

JP: In that house there is a typology I have seen you repeat with some frequency: the tower and simple shed or lean-to.

AK: I like the idea of freeing up as much space as possible for gardens and terraces, by putting the bedrooms in a little tower. The living room/dining room is also a terrace. I think maybe the idea (now that I talk to you about it) originated in the

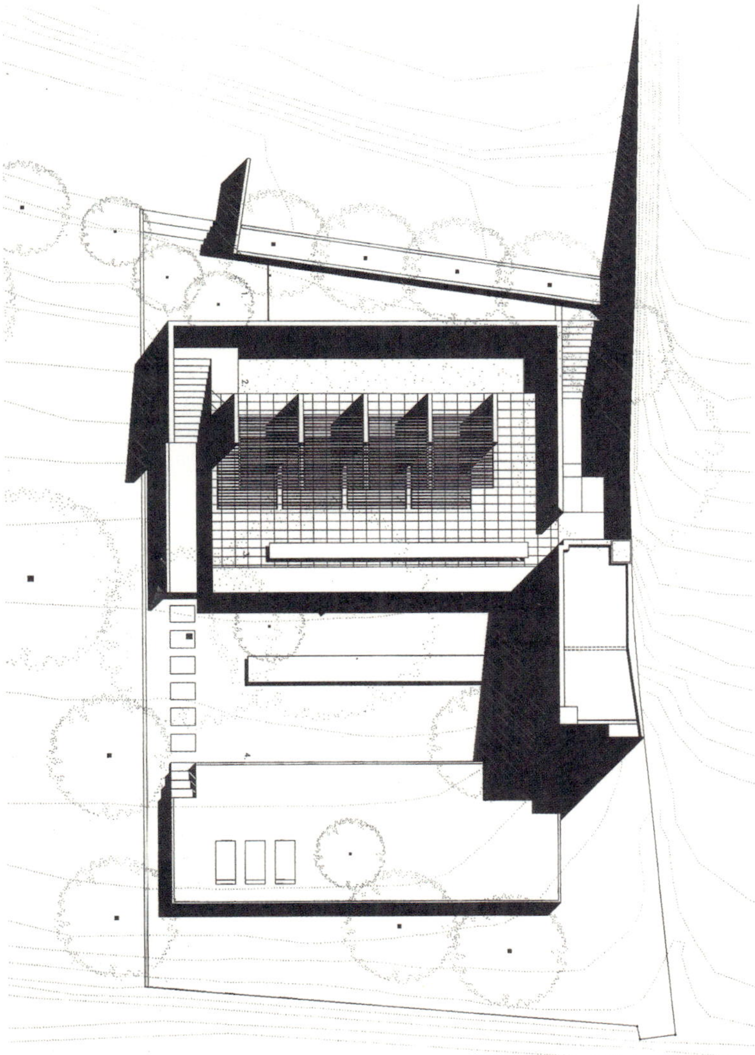

Valle House

house designed by Marco Aldaco in Guadalajara, which basically has all the bedrooms in a tower, while the rest is an interplay of living spaces, patios, and terraces.

JP: Then there is an element that seems very significant to me: the pool. I read it as a highly ceremonial space. There is a rhythm, a sequence, a sense of "now I see you, now I don't." There is something almost kinetic, like going from column to column or from wall to wall. It's like a sort of celebration of water, a celebration of sunlight...

AK: I have always loved the pool in Luis Barragán's Gilardi house, that optic fantasy between walls. Humberto Ricalde used to say it made him think of a ruin: the roof had collapsed and part of the grain storeroom had flooded. A flooded room, a pool between walls. And that's how we did it, but without cement rendering or paint, just with the bare natural materials. Now I know that was a mistake, because it doesn't get enough sun and it's freezing.

JP: I have always seen the fingerprint of Aldo Rossi on that pool...

AK: Yes, the ruin... There are those rather theatrical walls, which bear no load, but they create these very cozy spaces where you can read or get out of the sun. It's a space contained within walls, but it's a pool.

JP: From there we jump to the house you and Adriana built in Las Lomas.

AK: Yes, that was a recycling of a preexisting house, whose additions, made over the years, we removed. This is something we have done in various renovations: we find the skeleton, the spirit of the house, and we leave it bare.

JP: Subtractions.

AK: Subtractions: because over time, unnecessary rooms always end up being added on. So the first thing you have to do is to demolish everything that is ill-conceived, poorly added on. Then we devised a strategy to get rid of the cars, because that's another problem: the cars. In the house in Valle de Bravo we didn't have a parking area: the cars remained on the street, because it seems to me a sin to stick a car in your sanctuary.

JP: In that house there is something else. I don't remember whether you had ever tried it out before: the invention of an endless garden, with those grass mounds above the cars, directing your attention to the nearby woods and to the sky, effacing the street itself, the passersby. That gesture of dealing with the mounds has a certain affinity with your current house, with the little garden mirroring and dialoguing with the park across the way. You modified it in a way not so different from how people on the fringe of the city fix up their shelters. A pair of *jacalitos*[1] and a garden. And you made your home there. I see that as a desire for reduction.

AK: Yes, the house as hermitage. I have always like the idea of the old hermit. I loved the novel by Bashevis Singer, *The Magician of Lublin*. A marvelous heretical magician, who ends up confined to a hermitage he builds from the inside out, without a door, shut in forever. We are doing the same thing now by the sea. In a way, it's just a hut. But it's a hut made with order and precision.

[1] *Jacal:* a modest adobe dwelling with a thatched roof.

Contribution, Tradition, Vitruvius

JP: What do consider your contribution to society, to people?

AK: It's not really a contribution but a reminder: architecture has a language, with some invariable elements. Because there are things that have never changed: the force of gravity, earth cycles, climate. Many materials have not varied: bricks have been used for eight thousand years, wood for much longer, concrete for barely two thousand. Glass, though not used extensively, was already known to the Romans. Techniques were known long ago that have continued to be used and developed. Nevertheless, important things have been lost, such as paying attention to the orientation of rooms, or seeking harmonious relations and proportions. Which is to say, there are rules for construction and there are also rules for organizing spaces and for orienting them. Vitruvius said that a bedroom has to face – to have windows facing – the southeast. I still think that way. I still think these things are the basis of architecture.

JP: There is a pedagogical effort in what you do, perhaps. There is an effort to say that things need to be ordered and to show there is a way there in which they could be ordered.

AK: There is a way. There are very ancient treatises. We have mentioned Vitruvius. I am surprised every time I reread him, because the whole essence of architecture is there. When Vitruvius talks about the construction of the Roman Forum, which is associated with the Basilica and the Senate, he says it has to be dimensioned on the scale of the city. If it is in a port, it must be linked to the port. If there is no port, it must be at the center of the urban development. He establishes how the porticoes around the Forum should be and how to ensure that on the second porticoed level there be offices for rent to help finance the public works. This idea, which seems very novel now, these public-private investments, were already being practiced by the Romans. Much of what Vitruvius writes is of incredible relevance for today, all based on common sense and logic. We have to put Vitruvius back on the table.

JP: How do you conceive the role of architecture in the social context? What matters and what doesn't matter to you? How would our discipline be, in a best-case scenario?

AK: Architecture has the ability to change your mood. A little while ago I visited the museum of the architecture school at the UNAM. Its interior is an explosion of natural light... It's a sensation that hits you suddenly, and it raises your spirits, cheers you up. Yes, architecture has the ability to change your mood. José María Buendía used to say that beauty begets beauty. A beautiful city is going to provoke a sense of well-being in its inhabitants and its habitants are going to perform beautiful actions.

More Vitruvius

JP: Recapitulating: Vitruvius, as chosen guide and reference, seems to have covered the entire terrain twenty centuries ago.

[2] Vitruvius, *The Ten Books of Architecture* (New York: Dover Publications, 1960).

AK: So it seems: what he says is absolutely relevant today. His *Ten Books of Architecture*[2] are more than an historical document. They cover many subjects, ranging from philosophical questions to constructive matters, from materials to proportions, and including the ways of life of the Greeks and Romans. In the first book Vitruvius mentions that the architect must master many disciplines, if only in a general sense: have some knowledge of philosophy (he often cites Plato), know other philosophers, know about astronomy, about different kinds of soil and materials, about numbers (Pythagoras), about the making of clocks and fortifications.

JP: He places great emphasis on the choice of a site for any work of architecture.

AK: It think that is one of his first treatises: about the choice of the site on which to found a city. He reflects in the same way about establishing a city as about establishing a house. The place, the trajectory of the sun, the inclines, the winds. I am always surprised that he emphasizes very basic things, and architecture is indeed about all that. It is a questions of resolving basic things, with a certain grace, with a certain aim...

Tradition

JP: Let's talk now about architecture and tradition. I would like us to define your position vis-à-vis the architectural background, ancient and modern.

AK: Well, architecture is tradition. And tradition is a continuum, a way of doing and thinking that has been gradually refined over thousands of years: prior experiences. I don't see tradition as nostalgia, but rather as knowledge. We don't turn to tradition out of nostalgia, but because there is a wisdom in it. In the case of architecture, this is very clear, since some buildings have been around for thousands of years, and they are still there.

JP: There is a Freudian notion, which is perhaps worth mentioning, which maintains that, in order to come of age and take your place in the world, you have to symbolically kill your father. At the same time, as Octavio Paz used to say, there is tradition and there is rupture. He saw in the reconciliation of these two terms the possibility of being truly modern, of belonging to a tradition, but at the same time doing something different and new.

AK: Yes, I agree: reflection and invention.

JP: As for the filiations one always has, where do you place yourself, with your affinities? For example, I know that Louis Kahn is a touchstone for you in many respects...

AK: Louis Kahn is a modern architect inspired by the classical, Roman tradition. Luis Barragán is a modern architect inspired by regional architecture. Frank Lloyd Wright is a modern architect who started out from the Chicago School, working with Louis Sullivan. So you can see that even the most revolutionary architects belong to a tradition.

JP: Do you think there can be an active role aimed at founding a tradition we would consider worthy, such as responsibility to the environment, which is something that seems urgent?

AK: Yes, I do. There is reflection and intense debate about the issue. Everyone talks about it, from political leaders to children. We should think about the environment and act accordingly in architecture.

Teachers

JP: It would be interesting if you could talk about your teachers. Teachers in the widest sense, not only in architecture, but in literature, in life, in so many experiences. I think we all agree we are the children of certain teachers whom in some way we seek out. Some of them come to us by chance or for biological reasons – parents, grandparents – but the roster of chosen teachers can range from an eighteenth-century painter to a twentieth-century architect to a rock band. The list would be instructive, because everyone has his own pantheon of heroes, of models, who interest, stimulate, and encourage him to do his own thing.

AK: Yes, of course, everyone has them. There are your parents, generally. Your first teachers, who teach you ethics and morality, the foundations of everything else. In high school I had some very singular teachers. It was a very liberal high school, with an ironbound ethical code. Many of the teachers were Spanish republican exiles. There was a good mix of people. I didn't realize until many years later that an interesting seed had been planted there. Later on, at architecture school, the great "Chema" Buendía and my own classmates: Guillermo Eguiarte, Rafael Fierro, Chaco Hernández, Salvador Ferreiro, Alejandro Elizondo, Daniel Álvarez, Héctor Velázquez, and Adriana León, an intelligent group, passionate about architecture.

JP: You are suggesting that your own classmates had something to teach you.

AK: Of course, because many of them had already had experience in the discipline: they had parents or other relatives who were architects. They were very enthusiastic, very diligent and hard-working: a great motivation. Yes, your classmates are teachers.

JP: Apart from Buendía, in the course of your career, could you mention anyone who left a mark? Ricalde, of course...

AK: Yes, of course. Then there was a group of young people who began to give classes: Agustín Landa, Isaac Broid, Enrique Albin, and Enrique Norten. Chema Buendía made contact with Guadalajara through Díaz Morales and you appeared on the scene, with your band of Carlos Petersen and company. Teachers point things out, signal directions, give clues, share passions. Ricalde appeared later, breaking glasses and challenging our intellects and our moral traumas. Biting, shrewd, a great teacher and a wonderful friend. He served two disciplines: partying and work. With all these friends and teachers we shared books about architecture in which we discovered many other great teachers. The list is long: the entire history of architecture.

JP: And of all of them, with whom do you have an affinity? I was reminded of the GGG house, in which there seems to be a lot of Carlo Scarpa.

AK: The fact is there are so many fascinating architects. When you discover one you love, you want to learn from him, and you imitate him, you copy him.

JP: I think that is valid. At least to a certain point.

AK: It is insofar as you can make him yours, digest him and transform him.

JP: What you are saying is very interesting. Because you might say we possess certain tutelary presences, in our minds, in our souls, in our hearts. When you face a decision or a new problem in a work, or the blank page, the way you begin to make headway is by evoking certain things, certain teachings. Barragán, when facing a difficult problem in architecture, would ask himself: "And how would a rancher do it?" Well, in the simplest, least expensive, most orderly, most beautiful way... He would achieve, in his own way, the rancher's solution, which was always different, because everyone interprets the rancher, or Mies, or Scarpa, in a different way. But while we're on the subject, I would put it to you that one of your great teachers was Luis Barragán.

AK: Yes, I like his work, there's no doubt about that.

JP: I think it's more than just a "like." I think there is a similar understanding of and approach to making a garden, designing a room, planning an avenue. There is lively debate about who the true followers are, who are actually carrying forward Barragán's legacy. We can agree that those building "Barragán-style" walls and using "Barragán-style" colors are not the ones. But in what you do, in the spirit of your endeavors, I recognize certain lines, certain distillations of what Barragán proposed. Wholly in your own spirit, as could not be otherwise.

AK: I really got to know Barragán's work through Buendía, and then through you. Of course I was very familiar with that book with photos by Armando Salas Portugal, edited by Ambasz and published by the MoMA. But the frequent visits to "the giant's house" with you were a revelation. The sequence of spaces, the contrasts of light, the composition, the proportions... Everything in perfect harmony. When I was a student, I would try to understand the plan of the house and it seemed very difficult to read. I couldn't find in it what I understood as a clear architectural parti, a conceptual scheme. They just seemed like simple rooms, rectangles of different sizes and proportions communicated by little doors. When I visited the house itself I discovered the miracle. An order based on the variations of the parallelepipeds, on their sizes and proportions, on the spiral sequence they follow, and on the marvelous light that makes each one of the spaces a surprising experience of complete well-being. An extremely complex composition which I was unable to read off of the plans. A plan by Mies van der Rohe is easy to read: you read it quickly and you can imagine the space. If you see the plan of the Parthenon in Athens or the Pantheon in Rome, you understand what the building is all about, but that's not the way it is with the Barragán's house.

JP: Returning to another teacher, to Humberto Ricalde.

AK: Ricalde was a great teacher who has trained many of my younger colleagues. He was master of a vast architectural discipline: he knew about details, he drafted with complete precision, he knew the entire history of architecture, in plan view, section, and elevation. And he was able to transmit both his knowledge and his interest in knowing more.

JP: Moreover, I believe Ricalde transmitted unique vitality and *joie de vivre*. There was nothing like seeing how he amused himself and communicated his joy, how he would make an evening unforgettable. He was a master.

AK: A great master. When he died, Emmanuel Ramírez said that someone like that exists on this planet once every thousand years. Pia Sarpaneva, a close friend of Humberto's when he worked in Finland, wrote that the world had become smaller.

JP: And more distant teachers? Le Corbusier?

AK: For sure! The first architecture book I ever bought was about Le Corbusier. A little edition published by GG[3] that went everywhere with me. I really wore it out. I never stopped studying every plan, every section, until I had found the exact angle from which the photographs were taken. It was a very good collection. I later bought other volumes: the ones on Kenzo Tange, on Louis Kahn, on Alvar Aalto, and on Frank Lloyd Wright.

[3] Willy Boesiger, *Le Corbusier* (Barcelona: Gustavo Gili, 1991).

JP: The last-named is another of your great teachers.

AK: Yes, Frank is great.

JP: Connecting with what we saying before, about the communications among the arts, it is likely there were teachers in other disciplines from whom you learned as well. A piece of music can teach you something or help you to be consistent with certain principles.

AK: I have made designs listening obsessively to the same piece of music. I remember the house of "El Negro" González: I would listen tirelessly to Henryk Górecki's Third Symphony.

JP: Perhaps these mysterious communicating vessels are specific to one thing, or they may manifest themselves over a long period. They are not as obvious as the influence of a Le Corbusier, but they can be very significant in other, less cerebral, ways. I am thinking, for example, of your fondness for flamenco music.

AK: Yes, I share that with some of my friends, but my love of flamenco goes way back, to when my grandfather and father used to listen to Arabic music, which for me has a strong connection with flamenco.

The Discipline, the Workshop

JP: Let's talk about your studio, as pedagogy and as practice. The way you conceive of a perfectly disciplined architecture studio, the way you manage it.

AK: As far as the studio is concerned, there are almost never more than eleven players on our team at any given time, but hundreds of friends and comrades have spent time on it. Our work is to make drawings and models so that others can build them. We work on the premise that "drawing is thinking," as Humberto Ricalde never tired of repeating to his students, always mentioning Bruno Zevi. Drawing is a much more ancient form of communication even than writing. Cave paintings, pictograms, hieroglyphs... So we draw and think: we discuss ideas, comparing them, contrasting them. We open up the spectrum of possibilities, in order later to close it over one of them alone, the one that seems most fitting. It is a discontinuous process: we come and go around the ideas, letting them rest now and then in order to gain perspective.

JP: It is a very generous studio, which tries out different ways of doing things, looks for other paths, draws the same design over and over again. In general, there is a sort of reverence for work, a series of norms that lend it an "industriousness" that is worth highlighting. Time, money, and effort are invested in speculating: "How would this project have been if we had thought about it better?" This continual exercise, which you have been carrying out for many years now, seems to me a defining characteristic of your approach to architecture, of your way of handling things... You would never say it, because you keep up a certain front of cynicism, but there is a joy and affection for what you do, a love for your discipline!

AK: I really don't know. All the better that we enjoy our work! Work is accumulated energy. If an idea fails to make its way now, maybe it will do so later on.

Discipline, Expression

JP: There is a constructive and an expressive grammar in what you do. There is an emphasis on the skeleton and on understanding, in almost pedagogical terms, the way a building holds itself up. I believe this is a defining feature of what you do, of your *poesis*.

AK: I like ruins. What remains is the sturdiest part, the skeleton. Architecture is construction. And construction should hold up, defy gravity to create a space, and hopefully that space will be an inspiring space.

JP: Moreover, as we have mentioned more than once, everything ends up in ruins.

AK: So our master Aldo Rossi appears again, with that splendid book *The Architecture of the City*,[4] in which, in contradiction to that phrase about "form following function," he takes the example of the Roman Colosseum, which has changed its function many times in the course of history.

[4] Aldo Rossi, *The Architecture of the City*, trans. Diana Ghirardo and Joan Ockman (Cambridge, MA: The MIT Press, 1984).

JP: Yes, I remember that passage. Now architecture is in some way a conversation with the soul, the spirit of an age of uncertainty. But I believe your architecture seeks to be just the opposite. An architecture of certainties, of resistance.

AK: Yes, when Teodoro González de León carried out that monumental project in Bosques de las Lomas, he said that, in the face of the urban chaos, he felt the need, the responsibility, to create strong, orderly spaces. In order to create a strong, orderly space you have to be very sparing, very rational, very repetitive.

JP: I see that in everything you attempt to do, in everything you have done: that condensation of the spirit of being here and now, *hic et nunc.*

AK: Eternity is made of ephemeral things.

JP: Now, in your experience, drawings and models play a fundamental role.

AK: Drawings first.

JP: There is an urgency about making quick, inexpensive drawings to say certain things.

AK: Well, yes. In principle, the drawings are to explain things to myself, to help me understand. But later they serve to transmit an idea. The models as well. There are initial models. Quick models. Not a nice model but a quick, effective one, to be studied, torn up, changed... Then we also make another kind of model as a conclusion, as a trophy, as a consolation prize or souvenir of something that never took shape... Because a large percentage of designs are never built. I think, as a sort of consolation, that my work is not to make buildings but rather models and drawings which, perhaps, someone will construct. We haven't left anything undone, because there are the drawings and models. I even started to make models of designs that had not worked out. That were never going to be constructed.

JP: Your position vis-à-vis the city, and vis-à-vis the discipline in general, is one of combat, of a militancy that seeks to work in favor of certain things, and so against others. For example, it seems to me that this book starts from its immediate usefulness, like a tool, conceived for whoever wants to get an idea of what an architect has done in the thirty-five or forty years of his career. A tool that might help him to understand his own development. But in addition to that concrete usefulness, of showing or transmitting ideas and experiences, there is the aim of issuing a manifesto in support of an architecture that proposes certain things and is opposed to others. What do you think about that?

AK: In an intuitive and emotional way, you lean toward certain architectures and not toward others. What is appropriate? In order to know what is appropriate you have to try out ideas, draw them, make models and see how they work. I work on designs that no one has commissioned to test things I have imagined. I don't believe in testing forms per se, but rather in ways of inhabiting, ways of building, ways of relating to nature.

JP: It seems to me that, when we really had to confront the city, the reality constructed around us, we saw that it was a disaster, that there was a lot to fix. What is missing in the actual circumstances in which we live is what I have attempted to designate by the term *architecturation*. There is a need to establish order.

AK: Of course there is a very strong need to order. There are places in the world where things are much better ordered. Switzerland, Holland, or Japan are good examples of places where order permeates every activity, where everything is well arranged. In other places in the world, like Mexico or India, order or organization within large concentrations of people is something precarious. There's a lot of work to be done.

JP: I have noticed that you have a combative spirit in the face of that task, a spirit of rebellion, of saying "Let's look for something else." And I don't think your work can be understood, in detail or as a whole, without taking that confrontational stance into account. When I look at your work, I find in it some starting points to wonder: "Why not do it this way?" "Why not do it some other way?"

AK: Yes, to do it some other way, but by certain strict rules. With an architectural vocabulary established by constructive logic, by a physical and social context. Following the same grammatical rules, you can arrange words in different ways, say different things, or the same things in a different way, but in the end the phrase has to say something, has to make sense, the sense you want it to make, has to express what you want to say. Do you want to create a serene, ample, and efficient space, an optimal warehouse in which there is room for everything or a factory that is going to house machinery that functions in a given way? There are certain needs first and then there are rules for building, because there are more logical, safer, and more efficient ways of constructing.

Nature, Garden

AK: In recent years I have seen a greater appreciation for nature, for gardens, especially among the young. I'm delighted to see new trees, well planted, on certain streets. You yourself have done this successfully on certain streets in Guadalajara. And there are other instances: the botanical gardens in Culiacán, the second section of Chapultepec Park, the Alameda. There's a small awakening, some progress.

JP: In the course of your career you have been called upon to do architecture in some very different landscapes: in Baja California, in Yucatán, in the Mexican highlands, on the coast. We have been taught since Vitruvius that it is necessary to have a style adapted to the place you are working in. How do you approach these adjustments?

AK: Vitruvius says that the style of constructions will have to respond to the geography in which they are located. A house in Cairo will be different from a house in Rome or in Madrid. The house will have to respond in a different way to the specific climate of each place. If you bear this in mind, the discipline becomes a lot of fun. You are required to understand each place and to respond to it. Each place poses new questions: orientation, the trajectory of the sun, the winds. Also the vistas, the topography, water and rainfall, temperatures. Then vegetation, which changes radically from place to place. Forests, jungles, deserts. The variety of species is very extensive. The desert is very different, but follows similar patterns. The vegetal palette is very rich and it's impossible to know everything, but at least we can familiarize ourselves with some of the species and arrange them as we see fit.

JP: There is a wisdom in every well-made garden which, according to certain Eastern classics, is very consoling in the face of the fate we all confront as mortals. Gardens are masters at that: at knowing how to move at a certain rhythm, then to fade and die, and allow other vegetal generations to take their place. That might be the teaching of the garden, in a deeper, more profound way. I don't know if it is something you have formulated consciously, but I read something like that in each one of your gardens.

AK: A garden inevitably grows and is transformed. With a certain fate, like any life project, like any living being. But it is striking that some gardens have transcended the centuries. Italian gardens, for example, with their restricted palette, have certain rules, and even if one gardener is replaced by another, the vegetal palette and the general arrangement of the plants remains the same. There are not more than ten species in a typical Italian Renaissance garden. The same is true of a Chinese or Japanese garden: the number of species and their logical arrangements are limited. When the vegetal palette is more extensive, it is more difficult to control, and since there is no precise registry – even if it's a botanical garden – it will undergo a natural transformation. So gardens change, and much of their beauty and success at a given moment will have to do precisely with the person managing it, because the garden is alive.

JP: Certainly. Gardens are domesticated spaces.

AK: Sure, the garden is something artificial, made with natural elements that you use in an exaggerated way. You exaggerate in order to attract attention, to create surprise and wonder through the world of plants. So with a garden, as in any work of art, you have to exaggerate. For example, you plant a bunch of *colomos* together, you don't let anything else grow, and there's an explosion of nature in an artificial setting.

JP: Artifice.

AK: In one way or another, art exaggerates. Michelangelo's *David* is exaggerated.

JP: You are saying that the art of the garden, like any great art, touches certain emotional springs. Versailles speaks of grandeur...

AK: Barragán speaks of intimacy, the Alhambra of sensuality.

JP: What would be your four or five guidelines for learning to make a garden?

AK: First, take an interest in them, visit them, get to know them, explore them. Then, consciously or not, process the experience, as with architecture. Also, you have to see what plants there are in the area, what there is in the surroundings. Then you know that those plants take well, so they are reliable elements, they are immediate allies in creating the garden. Many of these plants will be appropriate for the background of the garden, because, like an oil painting, you have to establish a background to receive the brushstrokes and more concrete, more specific forms that follow, which will define the garden itself. Perhaps that is why there are gardener-painters, like Claude Monet, and painter-gardeners, like Burle Marx. And always you will have to be very aware of the trajectory of the sun, of the winds, the creation of spaces, the creation of sequences, of interconnections, some bigger, some smaller, some for transit only, others for lingering. The rules of composition are the same as in architecture; what changes is the intention of the spaces and materials, which in this case are plants and trees.

JP: Ferdinand Bac, when he wrote his book *Jardins enchantés*,[5] put together a story in his head, of a student who goes in search of Minguilla, a girl, but in order to find her he has to pass through series of gardens, and as he advances he invents each space and gives it a certain significance.

[5] Bac, Ferdinand, *Jardins enchantés. Un Romancero. [Trente-six jardins en couleurs dessinés par l'auteur] (Paris: Louis Conard, 1925).*

AK: It is just there that I connect architecture with literature, with a story, or a novel, or a succession of intrigues and mysteries. In *The Arabian Nights*, for example, architecture is certainly fascinating. Because literature also draws on architecture. There are fantastic literary works that unfold through a description of architecture.

JP: Do you remember Washington Irving's *Tales of the Alhambra*?

AK: *Tales of the Alhambra*, *The Arabian Nights*, Jorge Luis Borges and "The Library of Babel," Victor Hugo and *The Hunchback of Notre-Dame*. Architecture narrated, as you did in a letter to a client thirty years ago, when you described in advance the house, its spaces, its atmospheres and promenades, everything in writing, without a single drawing. Yes, there is that important connection with literature, which has to do with mystery, with surprise, with the narration of the architecture, of which Barragán is the master.

JP: We want to talk about landscape, nature, natural geometries, about all those aspects which also, to my way of seeing, permeate your work.

AK: Nature exists, and we live in it. Nature and the garden appear in most ancient literature we know. The garden as domesticated nature, safeguarded behind a mysterious wall, the *hortus conclusus*. A garden is a way of enclosing a piece of nature and domesticating it. It is as old as architecture itself.

JP: According to the biblical account, God created the Garden of Eden, and He did so in order for it to house and shelter the first human couple, Adam and Eve. Others have no doubt that we all came down from the trees, that we were monkeys and lived in intense proximity to nature. In general, people nowadays are increasingly distant from nature.

AK: Yes, but contact with it is being reappraised in some way. For years there was not so much interest in nature. Now people are even making "green façades."

JP: But don't you think that is just a substitute, something still very far from an understanding of natural life?

AK: Of course, but it's a first step on the part of alienated urban societies, disconnected from the natural environment, enclosed in shopping centers, with neon everywhere, with everything shining. The only thing that can save Mexico from its architectural ugliness is good urban vegetation. Good public tree-planting is the only thing that is going to save the city from its lack of harmony. It would be impossible to demolish all the horror of the city, all those grotesque buildings, the result of avarice, of an ignorance of construction techniques, of the demographic explosion, of a lack of culture.

The City

AK: For many years, low-cost housing in Mexico has been in the wrong hands: developers who buy the cheapest possible land, no matter where, no matter if it be agricultural lands, or wetlands, or bad ground for building on. They don't care about the distances the future residents will have to cover, or the lack of services. An equally corrupt government hands over the workers' savings to the developer so that the worst possible house can be built. Between 30% and 40% of the cost goes to purchasing the land and the construction of infrastructure, with streets that are too wide and houses that are too small.

JP: We have used up hundreds of thousands of hectares of territory, which is a limited resource, and a very vulnerable one at that. The implantation of a housing development in the wrong place, either in itself or in its relation to the city, generates a whole train of very serious collateral damage. In our large cities, enormous extensions of territory are simply carpeted with constructive debris that passes for housing developments, with the neediest paying the price of it all. There is no notion of the territory as a precious, limited, fragile resource.

Drawing for the proposal of the new Mexico City airport in Texcoco.

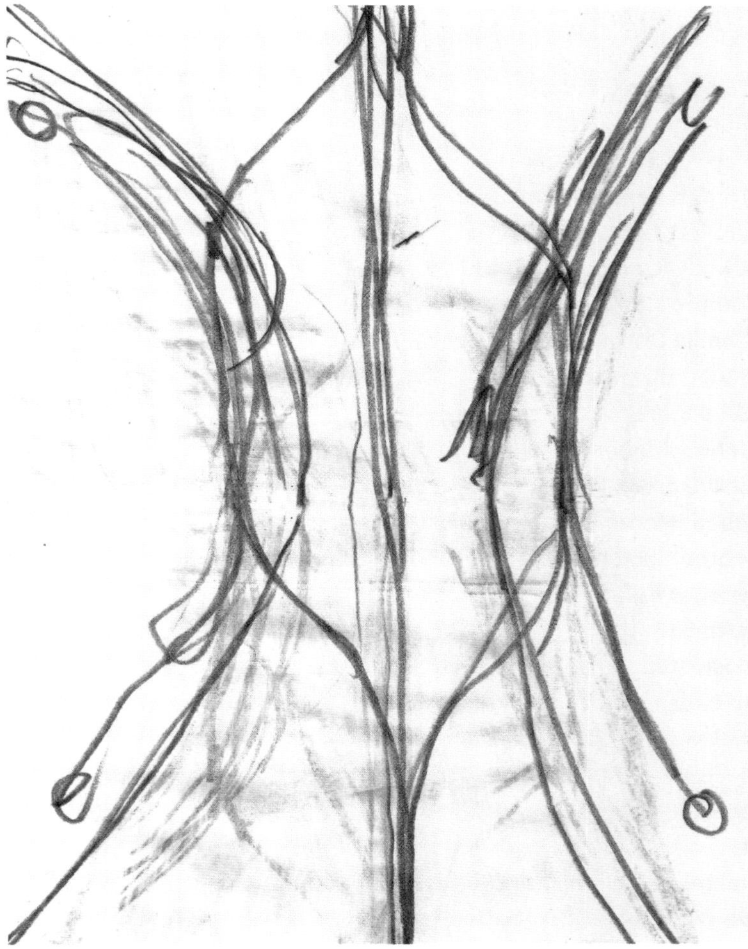

AK: No, that notion does not exist in Mexico. Recently the Secretariat of Territorial Development was established. It's just a few years old. The first years were devoted to giving away paint so that people could paint their houses! Now they construct plazas, repair sidewalks, and other minor issues. It has been forgotten that the important task is to plan the territory and constantly review urban development plans. Most towns in Mexico don't have a development plan. There are no development plans, either micro or macro.

JP: The new Mexico City airport is an issue on an eminently territorial scale. It is one of the most extensive and significant projects of your life. It is not limited simply to an airport, but to all of Lake Texcoco, the issue of water treatment, the salvaging of the riverbeds, and, in the end, the whole natural environment of the Valley of Mexico. We have a great opportunity to improve the lives of twenty million people, of performing a large-scale environmental rescue. In that gap between what should and could be done and what is actually being done by the authorities, there is a more or less tacit disdain for a territory that affects the lives of the entire population living in it. For an entire territorial system, and a human one, of course.

AK: Buendía used to say it all the time: a city is a reflection of the society that has built it. City and society are one. A cowardly society will have a city entirely consigned to its fate.

Photography credits

TAX archive, except:

Pep Ávila: p. 156 row 2
Tomás Casademunt: pp. 309 bottom-right, 310 row 2-right, 328-329, 332 top-right, 333 top-left and bottom, 370
Manuel Cervantes: p. 429
Ramiro Chaves: p. 11 left
Camila Cossío: pp. 289 right, 290 top-left
Paul Czitrom: pp. 27 left, 155, 156 rows 3 and 4, 179 right
GA Japan: p. 428
Jeff Goldeberg: p. 253 top-left, 257 right
Luis Gordoa: pp. 154, 157, 256 bottom-right, 270-top, 388, 419
Oscar Hernández: pp. 179 left, 405
Marco Kalach: pp. 120 top and bottom-left, 168
Margot Kalach: pp. 19 left, 24 right, 27 bottom-right, 38, 87, 89, 289 left, 375 (except top-left), 380
Yoshi Koitani: pp. 16 bottom, 23, 24 left, 30, 79, 80 right, 81, 82, 85, 86 top-right and bottom, 125 top and bottom-left, 126, 127 top-middle, 128 bottom-left, 130 top-right and bottom-left, 131, 133 (except row 3-right and row 4-right), 224 (except top-right and row 2-right), 234, 277-282, 284, 285, 292, 293, 309 (except bottom-right), 310 (except row 2-right), 332 bottom, 336 bottom-left, 337-338, 372-374, 375 top-left, 377, 378, 381, 409-411, 414, 415, 420-421
Jean-Luc Laloux: pp. 269 top-right, 270 bottom, 272 top-left and bottom-right
Sergio López: pp. 11 bottom-right, 45, 146, 376
Onnis Luque: pp. 22, 27 top-right, 68-69, 161, row 2-left, 290 right, 311, 332 top-left, 333 top-right, 334 left and bottom-right, 336 top, bottom-middle and right, 364, 365 top
Josué Mejía: p. 313
Jaime Navarro: pp. 33, 83 top-left and bottom, 86 left, 137, 138, 139, 142, 143, 185-187, 195, 196, 197 bottom-right, 213, 230- 233, 235-239, 296-299, 362 top, 365 bottom, 439, 446 bottom, 447-449
Studio Chirika: p. 463
Michael Toolan: pp. 244, 245
Gonzalo Torres: pp. 193, 194

Taller de Arquitectura X— Leslie Aboumrad, Paola Acevedo, Isabel Adauto, Lucila Aguilar, Juan Manuel Alemán, Andrés Altesor, Daniel Álvarez, Axel Arañó, Giulia Arienzo, Jorge Arvizu, Moisés Balas, Esmeralda Barrón, Michele Beltrán, Hernán Betanzos, Gabriela Bojalil, Brand Bosmat, Felipe Buendía, Fernando Caballero, Nino Canún, Alejandro Castañeda, José Castillo, José Luis Castro, Luz María Cervantes, Mario Cervantes, Sary Chedraui, Bernard Cherix, Carlos Clausell, Jorge Cordillo, Juan Cordero, Marcela Cortina, Rebeca Cotera, Thomas Darchy, Aura Cruz, Valentina de la Rosa, Juan Pablo de la Rosa, Ignacio del Río, Álvaro Díaz, Marisa Egea, Alejandro Elizondo, Lucas Elizondo, José Luis Elizondo, Alan Ezbán, Raquel Font, Nathalie Franquebalme, Anja Flesh, Javier Fierro, Jorge Fierro, Salvador Ferreiro, Patricia Galdós, Rubén Garnica, Bolívar Garrido, David Garza, Erandi Gastélum, Pilar Gaystardo, Rodrigo Girodengo, Pipola Gómez, Roberto Gómez, Ximena Gómez, Jorge González, Julio González, Marina González, Mariana González, Xavier González, Julio Gordillo, Jimena de Gortari, Eduardo Graf, Pamela Guerra, Sabine Haeckel, Aaron Hernández, Armando Hernández, Marcos Hernández, Hirosawa Hidemasa, Jane Hutton, Yulia Imamutdinova, Ainhoa Jiménez, Alberto Kably, Marco Kalach, María Kalach, Rossin Kalach, Yutaka Kita, Toshiyuki Kobayashi, Hilal Kobrosly, Jair Laiter, Tania Lakhal, Agustín Landa, Juan Carlos Larrea, Patricio Lavalle, Patricia Lazcano, Carlos Ledezma, Lucio Ledezma, Gabriela Lee, Roberto Limón, Walter Lingard, Miguel Ángel Lira, Sergio Lira, Gustavo Lipkau, Carlos Loperena, Rosa López, Susana López, Sébastien Lucas, Lorenza Lunas, Félix Madrazo, Gabriel Mancera, Sebastián Mancera, Mariana Manjarrez, Alfonso Magaña, Yael Margolis, Flor Marín, Sebastián Mariscal, Ana María Martínez, David Martínez, César Martínez, Pamela Martínez, Maude, Gonzalo Mauleón, Aldair Melo, Josué Mejía, Rodolfo Mejía, Elsa Mendoza, Isidro Michán, Indran Miranda, Moisés Miserachi, Eduardo Mlawer, Héctor Módica, Juvencio Núñez, Pipo Oliver, Sara Obregón, Edgar Ojeda, Fuyo Oji, Juan Palomar, Susana Pantoja, Alejandra Paredes, Catterina Pegazzi, Sean Phillips, Adrián Peña, Delia Peyón, Olaf Pingarrón, Enrique Pinzón, Alan Porter, Patricia Prieto, Emmanuel Ramírez, Josué Ramírez, Iván Ramírez, Nicolás Reitze, Rodrigo Remolina, José Luis Reyes, Ana Reyes Retana, Diego Ricalde, María Riveroll, Adolfo Rodríguez, Jesús Rodríguez, Roberto Rodríguez, Adolfo Romero, Enrique Rosas, Pablo Rosenblueth, Pedro Rosenblueth, Ana María Rossem, Patricio Antonio Rubio, Andrea Ruiz, Helena Sáenz, Cornelia Sailer, Ana Salinas de Gortari, Alejandro Sánchez, Hugo Sánchez, Mark Seligson, Roberto Silva, Santiago Silva, Cecilia Solís, Jorge Souza, Takemuna Takuma, Tami Tamashiro, Litz Tapia, Amélie Thiénot, Juan Antonio Tonda, Julio Torres, Aura Treviño, Gilda Valencia, Alberto Vargas, Mara Vázquez, Ilán Vit, Emilio Zaga, Lourdes Zúñiga, and Demetrio Zúñiga.

Alberto Kalach
Taller de Arquitectura X

First edition, 2021
ISBN 978-607-9489-44-1

© Arquine, SA de CV
Ámsterdam 163 A
Colonia Hipódromo, 06100
Mexico City
arquine.com

Texts
© Miquel Adrià
© Peter Cook
© Hernán Díaz Alonso
© Fernando Fernández
© Carlos Jiménez
© Alberto Kalach
© Juan Palomar
© Eduardo Vázquez Martín

Photography
© Authors listed on the credits page

Director
Miquel Adrià

Publishing Director and Layout
Brenda Soto Suárez

Coordination (TAX)
Valentina de la Rosa

Editorial Assistance
Valeria Fuentes

Design
Bløk Design

Translation
Gregory Dechant

Prepress
Emilio Breton

This book was produced with the support of the Sistema de Apoyos a la Creación y Proyectos Culturales (Fonca), through the Programa de Fomento a Proyectos y Coinversiones Culturales 2019. We are grateful for the special support of Aurora García de León, Guillermo González, Rodrigo and Carlos Zedillo Velasco.

Alberto Kalach was printed and bound by Asia Pacific Offset in China. It was printed on 80 gsm Enso Classic 2.0 and set in typefaces of the Neue Haas Grotesk Text Pro and Times Now families. The print run was 1,500 copies.